Riddles of the Skies

New clues have turned up in recent years on some of
the most puzzling happenings in aviation history. They
are included in this collection of dramatic air mysteries—mysteries that have stirred imaginations in the
past and today. It is a chilling and fascinating story of
classic and little-known riddles of the skies.

About the Author

Dale M. Titler learned to fly twenty-three years ago at Stultz Field, Pennsylvania, a small, grass airport named in honor of Amelia Earhart's pilot on her 1928 Atlantic flight. A flight instructor turned writer, Mr. Titler started early enough in flying to experience the final days of aviation's open cockpit era—with its Travelaires, Wacos, OX Challengers and Sunday afternoon parachute jumps at the local airport.

For ten years he taught aircraft engineering to Air Force officer pilots and aviation cadet trainees at Graham Air Base, Florida. He served in the Army Air Corps in World War II and later graduated from the Pittsburgh Institute of Aeronautics. Mr. Titler makes his home with his wife and three children in Biloxi, Mississippi.

WINGS
OF
MYSTERY

True Stories of Aviation History

Dale M. Titler

Illustrated with Maps

A TOWER BOOK

WINGS OF MYSTERY

Tower Publications, Inc.
185 Madison Avenue
New York, New York 10016

Copyright © MCMLXII, MCMLXVI by Dale M. Titler

Library of Congress Catalog Card Number 66-26666

Printed in U.S.A.

All Rights Reserved

Published by special arrangement with Dodd, Mead & Company

For a distinguished warbird and gentleman,
who gave me a glimpse into the Golden Era
of flight—*Oliver Colin LeBoutillier*

Acknowledgements

No one ever writes a book alone. Many grateful writers think there might well be a special niche in heaven for those who help them collect and investigate the material that goes into their finished manuscript. This is especially true when a book has been long in the making (this one began in the summer of 1940 when, as a boy of fourteen, I began a collection of unusual flying stories). To my collaborators go my thanks for helping this scrapbook grow into this book.

A note of special acknowledgment is due my good friend, Captain Frank McGuire of the Canadian Army Historical Section. After I had groped in vain for an appropriate title, his fertile mind came up with the perfect suggestion—and *Wings of Mystery* it was.

My thanks to Major Dennis E. McClendon, author of *Lady Be Good*, who kindly supplied the latest details on the Liberator's lost crew. We would both like to see the final chapter of this mystery written with the recovery of Sergeant Moore's remains—the only member of the crew unaccounted for.

The *Detroit News* furnished accounts of the pioneering flight of Parker Cramer and Oliver Pacquette.

I am grateful to Dr. Douglas H. Robinson, one of the world's foremost airship historians, for clarifying data on the German Zeppelin L-50.

Major Paul L. Briand, author of *Daughter of the Skies*, supplied sources of information pertaining to the last flight of Amelia Earhart and Fred Noonan.

Mr. John Toland, author of *Ships in the Sky*, provided background data on the airship era.

Mr. Richard Hall, Secretary of the National Investigating Committee for Aerial Phenomena, supplied valuable information on recent sightings.

Mr. Ted Dealy, publisher of the *Dallas Morning News*, provided information on Bill Erwin and Alvin Eichwaldt's flight from his book, *The Last Fool Flight*.

I am especially grateful to those surviving members

of the "Jinx Flight," Mr. William R. Berkeley, Colonel Thomas L. Murphy, Colonel Francis N. Thompson, Mr. Howard C. Darby, Mr. William O. Frost, Mr. Bernard L. Bennett, CMSgt Adolph R. Scolavino, and Mr. Edward M. Salley, who freely gave me their time to recount their greatest flying adventure.

Others who assisted me with information were Mr. Will D. Parker, Manager of Phillips Petroleum Company; the Lockheed Aircraft Company; Beech Aircraft Corporation; and the Imperial War Museum, London.

I also wish to thank Robert M. Furman for drawing the maps for this book.

Preface

There is a part of aviation history in our twentieth century—which is to say, most of it—that has a grand assortment of mysteries. They persist, stubbornly unresolved, as a monument to man's efforts in conquering the air ocean. This is a book about some of them; a selection of those that stirred imaginations in the past and still do today. Most of them defy solution. Those that were flights to oblivion will never be solved, for the sparse clues that have been left behind are as nebulous as the atmosphere through which these fliers and their machines once passed.

The stories are representative. "The Legion of Lost Warbirds" depicts the missing fighter pilots of all air wars; "Amelia Earhart" and the ocean fliers recalls those who failed to conquer the seas by long-distance flights. The *Hindenburg* enigma brings to mind the dirigible disasters of war and peace and, to remind us of the dead men and broken aircraft still lost on the earth's untrodden stretches, there are "The Lost Levanevsky Fliers," the *Lady Be Good,* and Captain Lancaster's *Southern Cross Minor* crumbling to dust in the Central Sahara.

The uneasy stir created by "flying saucers" persists as the most baffling and long-lived of all aerial mysteries. This elusive phenomena dates back to 331 B.C., perhaps earlier, and holds no promise of solution. Despite the official explanations, these unidentified flying objects are reported almost daily in our skies and they have caused endless controversy.

Some of the accounts will strike the reader as a bit uncommon—even for aerial mysteries. I can't explain the odd details; I haven't tried. Nor can I explain the curious supernatural twists that have somehow found a place in certain chapters. I don't believe anyone can.

Poised on the fringe of space, ready to explore our solar system and beyond, we still face a great many unanswered questions about our own world. Pilots flying alone up there get to wondering about them. I know I have. At times I've questioned my right to be there. And often, in looking down on the miles of land and water slipping under my wings, I've wondered if the long road to the stars will be as fraught with byways beyond our human knowledge and understanding.

These accounts are backed with facts and official records. But unlike most flying stories, these have few conclusions or real endings. This book will, in fact, leave you hanging.

Here's to some interesting hours of speculation, anyway....

—DALE M. TITLER

Contents

Preface

Maps

PART ONE

STORIES OF

TWO WARS

CHAPTER 1

The Legion of Lost Warbirds

How can a plane plummet into a battleground before the upturned eyes of thousands of entrenched soldiers, smash into their very midst, and disappear without a trace? The fortunes of war are strange indeed if this can happen not once, but several times. It was as though the very heavens—or earth—opened to swallow them and erase all evidence of their fall.

The mysteries of how the missing warbirds met their fates is as puzzling as the disappearances themselves. Bitter arguments still arise, and angry words, charges, and countercharges have ripped the air. In the end the question marks stand as stubbornly as before.

When a pilot fell behind hostile lines in World War I, enemy intelligence usually informed the airman's squadron of his death or capture. When possible, they reported his name, rank, and plane number, and included the details of his fall. This was generally done as promptly as channels and conditions permitted, for the enemy expected the same courtesy when one of their pilots was missing. Often the messages were flown to the home base of the victor's squadron and dropped in a cloth streamer. Thus was chivalry practiced among knights of the air.

The Fall of the Eagle of Lille

Max Immelmann flew to early fame and a bizarre death.

As a flying companion of Oswald Boelcke, this stiff-backed, proud Saxon was among the first of the German aces. But he was of a different disposition from his warm, popular comrade. Where Boelcke's manner was jovial and friendly, Immelmann was arrogant and conceited. He stood apart from his fellow officers in many ways. He neither drank nor smoked and cared little for the company of charming young ladies. He stuck to a regimen of strict exercise and diet, which excluded meat, and except for a select few, he rarely fostered friendships. Max Immelmann was considered rather odd.

The man's strange behavior neither dimmed his fame nor dulled his accomplishments. He was the Fatherland's first ace and one of the most dashing figures of World War I. Max Immelmann shot down sixteen enemy planes. He earned his victories during those early, awkward days of combat, when the shooting down of an enemy machine was a feat that automatically led to wide recognition and a decoration or two.

He flew one of the earliest Fokkers, which was equipped with a single, and highly unreliable, machine gun. Those aces who came after him, Richthofen, Voss, Lowenhardt, and Udet, had faster and more dependable planes with twin Spandau guns. Their firepower was five times more effective, and they had many more planes to shoot at.

In July 1915, Anthony Fokker, the Dutch designer who had established aircraft factories in Germany, visited Flying Section 62 to demonstrate his newest machine. It was a small monoplane with an 80-horsepower rotary engine and a single machine gun synchronized to fire through the propeller arc. Fokker predicted it would clear the skies of Allied airplanes. Immelmann and Fokker hit it off right from the start. Fokker accepted Immelmann's technical knowledge as a near match for his own. Before a week had passed, he promised the fighter pilot a job in his factory "when the war is over."

By August 1, Immelmann and Boelcke were each equipped with the deadly monoplane. On that day Immelmann shot down his first plane—the first victory of the war scored by a German pilot flying alone. Other victories followed, and when Boelcke was transferred to the Metz sector, Immelmann became the leading ace in the area of Lille. Here he gained most of his victories; here he became known as *Der Adler von Lille* (The Eagle of Lille).

In the fall of 1915, Immelmann perfected an aerial maneuver that bears his name—the Immelmann turn. He would pull his tiny monoplane up into a half loop and as the machine approached the inverted position, he would suddenly roll it upright. Thus, in a dogfight he would have the two advantages that fighter pilots need badly at close quarters—a gain in altitude and a complete change in direction. Some air historians claim Immelmann never invented the maneuver. Nevertheless, he made it deadly famous.

18

Victory followed victory; decoration followed decoration. He won the Iron Cross and the coveted *Pour le Mérite*. In June of 1916, Flying Section 62 was ordered to the Eastern Front but Immelmann was directed to remain in the west and form his own "chaser" squadron. He was excited by the honor, but he did not live to see the job completed.

On the morning of June 18, he shot down his sixteenth and final victim. Late that afternoon he took off again and flew into a fierce engagement between four Fokkers and seven British machines. It was his last taste of combat. Something happened during that air battle northeast of Douai that has been a dark mystery for over half a century. There are four versions of what happened, each distinctly different from the other, and all provide enough conflicting data to keep the controversy alive for another five decades, and more. But it is unlikely that the mystery of Immelmann's death will ever be solved. All the evidence is in.

As the famous ace made contact with the British fighters, he saw that German antiaircraft had set up a close barrage. They had found the altitude of the dogfight, for shrapnel whistled dangerously close. Possibly the German gunners had mistaken the Fokker for an Allied plane. Immelmann dropped a white signal to tell the men on the ground that they were firing on a friendly aircraft. Then he took after a British machine. A few bursts apparently disabled it, for it started down in a glide. Immelmann decided not to follow it down as was his usual custom, but instead turned back toward the whirling dogfight.

A few seconds later, observers near Annay saw Immelmann's fighter suddenly nose upward. Then it whip-stalled and fell into a diving right-hand spiral, gaining speed all the while. It began to gyrate wildly. Brace wires snapped. At 8,000 feet the slender fuselage began to whip in the slipstream and a moment later the entire tail section twisted free, leaving the control cables flapping in the rush of air.

The Fokker began to disintegrate. Now the entire rear part of the fuselage ripped free. The wings buckled and finally, with a rumble and a wrench, the rotary engine tore loose from its mounts and dropped like a stone for the remaining 5,000 feet. It buried itself in the ground, a twisted broken mass of steel. Overhead the light tail planes fluttered down in lazy curves, landing a few hundred yards from the main part of the wreckage.

Only one man knew what went wrong, but he was dead.

When Tony Fokker heard the news of Immelmann's death he was upset. The two had been close friends. It was Immelmann who sold the German High Command on several of Fokker's inventions. Fokker was not prepared to blame his friend's death on the failure of one of his airplanes, far from it. He demanded, and was granted, permission to inspect the wreckage. Two days later, to a party of representatives from the German General Staff, he and his sharp-eyed technicians pointed out certain "obvious facts." Of this investigation he later said:

Immelmann's plane suddenly fell to the ground as he was flying near the German lines. It was first given out that his Fokker fighter had failed in mid-air. This explanation naturally did not satisfy me, and I insisted on examining the remains of the wreck, and establishing the facts of his death.

What I saw convinced me that the fuselage had been shot in two by shrapnel fire. The control wires were cut as by shrapnel, severed ends bent in, not stretched as they would have been in an ordinary crash. The tail of the fuselage was found a considerable distance from the plane itself. As he was flying over the German lines there was a strong opinion in the air force that his comparatively unknown monoplane type, which somewhat resembled the Morane-Saulnier, had been mistaken for a French machine.

Tony Fokker made no bones about defending the soundness of his machines. He insisted that antiaircraft fire caused his design to break up in mid-air. But when the nation went into stunned mourning at the news of Immelmann's death, the powers decided it was far better to preserve the image of the ace's invincibility by claiming structural failure of his machine. Oswald Boelcke concurred. Not long before he was killed in an air collision over the lines, he gave this version of the fall:

"Immelmann lost his life by a silly chance. All that is written in the papers about a fight in the air and so on is rot. A bit of his propeller flew off; the jarring tore the bracing wires connecting up with the fuselage, and then broke away."

Admit that Immelmann had been killed in air-to-air combat? Never! It would have been too embarrassing for the High Command to explain to his adoring public.

Now a cloud of doubt hung over the Dutch designer's reputation and Fokker found it highly uncomfortable. He had several heated meetings with the German High Command and finally he and his airplane were exonerated, unofficially, from blame. But many years were to pass before the German people learned there were other accounts of Immelmann's death.

On the British side of the lines an entirely different story of Max Immelmann's last patrol had been forwarded through channels with an official stamp of approval. As convincingly as Fokker had argued with German officialdom that his plane was shot down by German gunners, a British combat report for the same air fight presented other evidence. The startling thing about this report is that it was published before Immelmann was known to have been killed. Significant points coincided. It stated that on the evening of June 18, Lieutenant G. R. McCubbin, a South African pilot, and Corporal J. H. Waller, observer-gunner, of Squadron Number 25, while flying an F.E.2b, shot down a Fokker monoplane over Annay. Immelmann had crashed at Annay at precisely 9:00 P.M. on this date.

For the fourth account we turn to the man who was Immelmann's flying companion, Corporal Heinemann. He had been above his leader when he saw the strange antics of the Fokker. He claimed that neither a shrapnel burst nor the F.E.'s gun were responsible for Immelmann's death dive. He, too, was curious as to what might have caused the mishap, so he inspected the wreckage, at a different time than had Fokker and his men. His findings definitely did not agree with those of the aircraft's designer. He found two things: (1) the metal tubing of the fuselage had been flattened and pulled before it separated, pointing to tension stress (pulling apart) rather than shrapnel damage, and (2) one blade of the wooden propeller had been cut through by bullets. Halves of bullet holes were found along the line of breakage, which was exactly in the line of fire of the plane's fixed machine gun. To

Heinemann, the cause of his commander's death was crystal clear. The mechanical interrupter gear (the synchronizing device that enabled the machine gun to fire only when the propeller blade was out of the way) had temporarily failed. It had happened on other machines before, and now it had happened to Max Immelmann who, according to Heinemann, had been shot down by his own gun.

Who was right? Fokker and his engineers? Boelcke? The German High Command? The Royal Flying Corps? Corporal Heinemann? All gave vastly different accounts for vastly different reasons.

Choose your own answer; the real one will never be known.

The Mysterious Death of Albert Ball

When it comes to sheer mystery amid a dark and foreboding background, the strange death of Captain Albert Ball on May 7, 1917, is difficult to match. This British ace who was barely twenty, sent forty-four German planes to earth. He was a popular hero whose death came riding in darkness and mist—a death that set the combatant nations searching for the details. He simply disappeared into a shadowy cloud bank of towering proportions, after one of the most bitter and drawn-out air battles of the war.

Albert Ball was the son of Sir Albert Ball, once mayor and alderman of Nottingham. He was a patriotic and deeply religious youth. He paid for his own flying lessons, then joined the Royal Flying Corps in 1916. His early flying skill left much to be desired, but he learned fast and developed into a topnotch fighter pilot. Into his brief lifetime he jam-packed enough flying experiences to suit a dozen combat pilots. Curiously, he didn't record many of his victories; at least eighteen were left unconfirmed.

Normally, the British gave little publicity to even their greatest air fighters, but, early in 1916, morale on the home front hit an all-time low. Something had to be done to bolster the sagging spirits. The zeppelins and Gothas were raiding London with deadly regularity, and confidence in the Royal Flying Corps was shaken. Then headquarters came up with the answer: a popular hero. Albert Ball, young, clean-cut, typically British, was their choice. His frequent victories were already in the dispatches.

Here, readymade, was the very man who could keep his senses under a torrent of public adulation.

In October of 1916 he was taken from the front and made an instructor in England. He hated it and tried to pull every string, military, political and otherwise, to get back to France. But it was not until April of 1917 that he saw action again.

At 5:30 on the afternoon of May 7, Captain Ball led one of three flights of S.E.5s over the lines. Following him were Flight Leaders Meintjes and Crowe with their flights. Orders were to patrol until nightfall and to ferret out and destroy any German aircraft in the sector.

The weather was foul; a depressing, gloomy day. Rain drizzled intermittently from the cloud layers. Spirits were low and the men were near exhaustion from an unending blur of hectic combat. Ball led "A" Flight, which consisted of himself and two other pilots, along the lines at 7,000 feet. The other planes of "B" and "C" Flights, seven in all, climbed to 9,000 feet. The visibility was so poor that within a few minutes all the flights lost contact with one another.

Suddenly the swirling cloud wall vanished and the three flights found themselves in open sky. They also found themselves smack in the middle of Richthofen's Circus.

The S.E.5s tangled with the enemy Albatroses at a fast clip. Manfred von Richthofen, the circus master, was on leave, but his *Jagdstaffel* was ably commanded that evening by his younger brother, Lothar. In seconds the sky was suddenly crisscrossed with tracer threads, gaudy painted machines, roaring, belching engines, and clattering machine guns. Here and there a widening plume of black smoke fell from the melee to mark another pilot who had come out second best.

The fight reached fever pitch as the thirty machines rolled and twisted in the gathering gloom of nightfall. Most air engagements were brief, but this one showed no sign of letup. It was bitter duel to the death. The planes spread out and covered a widespread area of the rain-drenched sky. Pilots could barely recognize friend from enemy. Spads of Number 19 Squadron and Sopwith triplanes from Number 8 Naval Squadron piled onto the heap to assist the outnumbered S.E.5s.

Lothar von Richthofen, flying an all-red Albatros with yellow ailerons, signaled his pilots to re-form for another assault. The British fighters broke away to regroup over Arras, and as they separated for a renewed attack they exchanged parting bursts.

Ball was somewhere in that scrap. As Captain Crowe tried to assemble his scattered remnants over Fresnoy, he looked down and sighted his commander at 4,000 feet, heading farther into enemy territory. The light was now very poor, and several pilots who found themselves alone, turned for home. Crowe, too, decided the show was over for the day. His goggles had been shot away by a machine-gun bullet, and at that moment five German pursuits appeared above him. He broke off combat.

Crowe glanced down again, this time to see Ball fire two Very flares—the "tallyho" signal. Ball was chasing a lone Albatros. He fired a burst into it and curved away. Crowe dived on the same machine without result, then he too curved away. Ball reappeared, and he and the German went around and around, trading fire in dizzying circles. Crowe turned to make a second pass at the enemy plane, but before he could come within range, both machines were swallowed up by a dark, ominous cloud bank. This was the last ever seen of Albert Ball by a British combatant. Crowe circled about for several minutes, waiting for Ball to emerge, but he never did. Then, with his gasoline running low, Crowe headed for base.

On May 8, in a German hospital near Lens, a German officer visited a certain Captain Hunter who was an English prisoner recovering from battle wounds. He told Hunter that Ball had been killed. Hunter refused to believe it. The next day the officer returned with Ball's identity disc as proof. He also stated that Ball had been brought down by antiaircraft fire, and his machine was badly smashed.

Three weeks passed before the Germans dropped a note telling of the ace's death. It was delivered to Number 56 Squadron.

> R.F.C. Captain Ball was brought down in a
> fight in the air on May 7th, by a pilot
> who was of the same order as himself. He
> was buried at Annoeullen.

The mysteries? There were many.

The credit for downing Ball was given to Lothar von Richthofen when the victory went unclaimed. But Lothar had claimed a Sopwith triplane, not an S.E.5 biplane. Quite a difference. Lothar might well have been the pilot Ball was last seen sparring with, and his confusion with the "triplane" could have been the result of an earlier fight. The German ace was wounded during this air battle, suffered a fainting spell at the sight of his blood, but managed to land safely. In the final analysis, he wasn't able to give a coherent account of what has actually happened.

In the clouds, Ball apparently spiraled on down to a low altitude. When he broke out of the mist in the vicinity of Lens, he was widely separated from his adversary. A German machine-gun crew stationed in a nearby church steeple was one claimant of the Englishman. He had veered close; they had fired, and the machine fell.

The strangest thing of all occurred when French civilians lifted Albert Ball's broken body from the wreckage. They found no bullet wounds on his body. His badly smashed plane verified that it must have fallen from a great height, but although it struck with great force, it did not burn.

Did Captain Ball become disoriented in the cloud while trying to fly blind? Did he stall, fall into a spin, lose control, and plummet to his death, without being hit by gunfire in the air or from the ground? An ironic possibility for a man with the superb coolness to take on any odds.

The restrictions of wartime may be responsible for the incomplete reports. Perhaps none of the accounts tell what really happened. A great Perhaps.

The ace was awarded the Victoria Cross posthumously and his body was buried with military honors in the German war cemetery at Annoeullin. The white marble cross erected after the war by his father can still be seen there.

Borne by Angels

His comrades waited in vain for a message of hope. At twenty-two, he was France's leading ace with fifty-four German machines to his credit.

His name was Georges Guynemer.

Twice rejected by the French Army, his gaunt frame wracked with tuberculosis, this pale little figure with the burning eyes threw himself again and again into the bloodiest part of the fighting. He was shot to earth eight times, but after each crash the steel-nerved Champion of France emerged unscathed from the splintered wreckage to mount the skies again in search of the hated Hun.

The phenomenal luck of "Guynemer the Miraculous" ran out on September 11, 1917. The man who had risen to command the famed *Stork Escadrille* took off that day to fly in company with Lieutenant Bozon-Verduraz and Captain Deullin. Over the lines northwest of Ypres, Guynemer sighted a German two-seater Aviatik, and with a quick signal to tell his companions to remain behind as cover and lookout, the ace banked *Vieux Charles*, his favorite Spad, into a dive.

Deullin apparently became detached from the other two at this point. Bozon-Verduraz later said that he last saw his commander plummeting toward the enemy, then found his own hands full as eight German fighters appeared. He lured the attackers away from Guynemer, hoping they would not spot him until the ace could finish his work. After a short encounter, Bozon-Verduraz slipped away from the Germans and returned to the place where he had last seen Guynemer.

The sky was empty and silent.

Bozon-Verduraz searched the front and scanned the sky overhead until his dwindling fuel supply forced him to return to base. Guynemer never returned.

The Storks kept a faithful vigil. Field telephones were busy all along the front, seeking some news of the missing flier. There was no news. The Germans released no victory dispatches for several suspense-filled days, as they assuredly would, had one of their pilots brought the famous *capitaine* down.

More days passed, and reluctantly the French were forced to release the dispatch that told of Guynemer's apparent loss. Then the Allies heard a rumor that a German aviator named Wisseman had killed the Frenchman. The French asked the Germans for confirmation, and finally an official German communiqué listed the ace's death. But it was given as 8 A.M. on September 10, not 8:35 A.M. on the eleventh. The Red Cross followed this with a statement that Guynemer had been given a military funeral at Poelcapelle, Flanders.

From this point, the mystery deepens.

Almost a month later, on October 4, Allied infantry took the town but were unable to find Guynemer's grave. Now, the Germans volunteered yet another answer. Guynemer, they claimed, had been brought down south of Poelcapelle Cemetery, but they omitted the details as to how he had been brought down. A surgeon from an infantry battalion, they said, had seen the body and examined it closely. He found that the ace had been shot through the forehead and that the forefinger of his left hand had been shot away. He had suffered a broken arm and a broken leg. As the area was then under heavy Allied artillery fire, the surgeon and his medics were forced to leave the body beside the plane. They, too, the report concluded, were now dead, and the entire area had been churned up by artillery shells. The impression was given that all trace of Guynemer and *Vieux Charles* had been obliterated, scattered and pounded into the Belgian ground by the heavy barrage. The only word that could be reasonably accepted was the hastily scribbled field memo of a methodical German surgeon who was under fire as he wrote it, and who was himself only a few minutes from death.

There is no explanation, however, why the Germans were reluctant to give an early report of the ace's death. And if Guynemer was given a military funeral at Poelcapelle as the Red Cross claimed, whose body had the surgeon examined and left beside an unidentified airplane in a rain of artillery shells? Whose body was buried at Poelcapelle Cemetery in a grave that was never found? And what of Wisseman, the pilot who was credited with the victory? What were his comments? No one knows, because four days after Guynemer's disappearance, the man who became France's greatest ace, Réné Fonck, killed Wisseman in an air duel.

Did Guynemer meet a fate the Germans thought best to hide? Did he die in prison? The wall of silence has never been breached. To this day, the children of France believe their hero never really died, but that he was borne by angels and "flew so high that he could never come down ..."

What Became of the L-50?

Nothing during World War I struck more terror into the English populace than the zeppelin raiders. On one such raid, nature had to do what the island's air defense could not do—bring down the lumbering gray ghosts.

These first air raids by the throbbing cigar-shaped monsters had great psychological impact. In this new type of warfare, they could glide smoothly overhead, out of reach of the highest-flying fighter planes and above effective anti-aircraft reach, hover motionless at night and select their targets with deadly precision.

By the fall of 1917, Germany had developed mass formations of zeppelin raiders. One of the largest raids, set for October 19, proved to be the most devastating attack of the war, but it was also the one in which the zeppelins suffered their heaviest losses. It was known as the Silent Raid.

Shortly after noon, eleven Navy zeppelins left their masts at Tondern and nearby coastal bases to rendezvous over England. All afternoon they droned toward the south shore and by 6:30 in the evening, the first raider crossed the coast at 13,500 feet. Antiaircraft batteries and specially designed rocket volleys reached up for the huge bomber, and when the other airships arrived, the commanders gave orders to rise to safety. The fleet finally leveled off at 16,500 feet.

Darkness fell, a moonless night with black clouds. The airships were well hidden from the probing searchlights that tried to find them in the clouds. In the next few hours the fleet spread out over Hull, Sheffield, and Grimsby and, guided by lights and glowing chimney pots, they dumped their lethal loads and slipped away. The damage was heavy and widespread, and because of poor visibility and dense cloud cover, the zeppelins completely escaped ground fire and pursuit planes. To all appearances, the most successful raid of the war had been accomplished without loss.

But nature has a way of robbing men of ill-gained glory. By midnight, the returning airships discovered that the brisk tailwinds, which had been boosting them homeward, were suddenly growing troublesome. Unknown to the zeppelin commanders, the winds aloft had shifted rapidly in velocity and direction. Up to 10,000 feet, they were still light, but between 10,000 and 20,000 feet (the zeppelin's cruising altitude), the winds rose to forty miles per hour, and at higher altitudes, over 20,000 feet, they fast approached gale force.

As the flying machines struggled in the mounting windstorm, their lacy structures creaked and groaned against the turbulence. In the distance, in Flanders Fields, the steady flash of artillery could be seen by the crewman. At 3:00 A.M. the airship navigators were forced to admit that their return flight was not proceeding as planned. They were still over the water when a British destroyer and several land batteries opened up on the armada. The uncomfortably close barrage of antiaircraft fire and rockets caused the zeppelin commanders to jettison ballast and force a quick rise to the rough winds at 20,000 feet. Now the sputtering diesels gasped for breath in the thin air; the crews suffered from the icy-cold blasts and lack of oxygen. They were no better off there, for the varying winds began to scatter the airships over a wide area.

Six of the airships made it safely back to base, but at daybreak the other five found themselves adrift and helpless over France. One Allied fighter plane spied the L-55 and harassed it up to 25,300 feet before it abandoned the chase. The zeppelin's crew stood up bravely against the sudden rise to new heights; a few became unconscious from trying to work in the rarefied atmosphere, several suffered broken eardrums and blood spurted from their nostrils.

Despite the alcohol in the engines' radiator systems, the coolant mixture froze. So did the water in the ballast tanks. Lieutenant-Commander Hans Fleming became desperate and finally valved gas and jettisoned fuel to land at Tienfort, Germany, safe and sound.

Fleming's companions didn't fare so well. Within minutes of the L-55's landing, the L-44 was shot down by antiaircraft fire as it tried to cross the lines at Luneville. The three remaining zeppelins, the L-45, L-49, and L-50, were still aloft over France until, at 11:25 on the morning of October 20, with only an hour's fuel remaining, Captain Koelle of the L-45 ordered a landing in the Durance Valley. As soon as the airship touched lightly on a sandbank in the middle of a small river near Sisterton in the South of France, Koelle set his men to work. In a few minutes they had smashed the engines and punctured the gas bags. Then Koelle ordered his helmsman to fire a signal pistol into the leaking hydrogen. The man obeyed, and within seconds the zeppelin went up in a ball of red-orange fire.

Meanwhile, at Bourbonne-les-Baines, the L-49 was slowly coming down. When it landed, the crewmen stumbled dizzily about, too groggy from the effects of oxygen starvation to get organized. Before the Germans could recover their senses and destroy the airship, French soldiers were on them and the zeppelin was captured intact.

Only the L-50 remained aloft. With his fuel running low, Captain Schwonder turned east, hoping to fly over the French Alps and reach asylum in nearby Switzerland. Although his crewmen wore crude oxygen masks, most of the supply of the life-giving gas had been exhausted by the time the mountains came into sight. Schwonder knew that in the thin air at high altitude, his engine mechanics in their exposed gondolas were falling unconscious. He had ordered the oxygen strictly rationed in the control gondola, and now his officers were becoming drowsy and slow in responding to orders and instructions.

With its six unattended 240-horsepower engines bursting full out, the L-50 headed for the peaks near Dommartin. It almost cleared the first peak, but the helmsman was too weak to move the rudder wheel. Captain Schwonder tried to help him; then, sensing that he too was about to pass out, he grabbed for the power signal and rang STOP ENGINES. Nothing happened. Those mechanics in the engine gondolas who had heard the order were slumped on the engine catwalks, too groggy to move. Schwonder later reported that at this point he tried to ram the airship head-on into the ridge.

Clumsily, the L-50 collided with the peak, but Schwonder succeeded only in wiping off the control gondola and one aft engine car. Somehow the men in both capsules survived the impact, as did those who regained their senses in time to jump from their gondolas. They crawled painfully from the broken wreckage, stumbled to their feet, and watched the airship strike another mountain. The lightened airship shot upward to 23,000 feet and slowly faded into the fog and mist.

Schwonder and several crewmen survived, spared the unknown fate of the four who drifted away, unconscious, in the pilotless L-50. Later that day the derelict hull floated over the captured crew of the L-45 at Sisterton. As it continued on out to sea, it was chased by French fighter planes that failed to alter its course with Destiny. At last report it was far out over the Mediterranean, where it was finally lost to sight.

No trace of the L-50 or its remaining crew were ever found. It had vanished as completely as the *Mary Celeste*. Perhaps it settled into the blue waters of the Mediterranean; perhaps, in the early morning hours of October 21, it slipped unnoticed across North Africa's coast and drifted into the Dark Continent. Perhaps it came to rest somewhere in the vast stretches of the Great Sahara. No one knows.

The Ace Who Was No Sportsman

Among the British subjects interned in Turkey when it aligned itself with Germany in World War I, was a tall, spare Scottish telephone mechanic. In April of 1915 the Turks released him along with other prisoners they considered too unfit to be of military value to the enemy. The man was over thirty, frail, and in poor health. He had suffered from birth with a badly deformed and almost sightless left eye. The Turks would not have felt so confident had they had any way of knowing that this man was to become Britain's greatest air fighter—Edward Corringham Mannock.

One of the puzzles of Mannock's enlistment is how he managed to pass the physical examination when he volunteered for the Royal Flying Corps in August of 1916. But pass he did, and started his flight training within a few days. To compensate for his handicapped vision, he had to apply himself to the flying lessons with great diligence. Landings were a nightmare. He spent extra hours in the gun pits, trying to improve his aim. From the moment of his arrival at the front during "Bloody April" of 1917—the month the British suffered their highest air losses—until his death fifteen months later, his victory score never slowed its upward climb.

Major Mannock was a strange, driven man. Old for a fighter pilot (he was in his mid-thirties by then), he became the leading British ace. Only Baron von Richthofen (eighty victories) and Réné Fonck (seventy-five victories) bettered his score of seventy-three victories. His unorthodox cold-blooded behavior toward the German fighting man was the only thing that prevented him from becoming an idol to his men. Although he was a staunch patriot, the British never learned to admire him as they did Bishop, McCudden, Barker, and Ball. But Mannock didn't seem to care. Weird quirks showed themselves in his character. He seemed obsessed, emotionally disturbed. The strain of day-in, day-out combat flying began to show itself after a few months, and Mannock made no secret of his pathological hatred for the Huns. He spoke with genuine pleasure of such things as a doomed rear gunner in a German plane who had "tried frantically to beat out the flames with his bare hands." When he returned from patrols he would sometimes say, "Sizzle, sizzle, sizzle, wonk, woof!", which was his way of describing a German plane he'd sent down burning. He collected with relish grisly souvenirs from his kills.

Mannock's fame was greatly dimmed by his treatment of prisoners. His own men swore they saw him swoop down and machine-gun the helpless crews of enemy planes forced down on Allied ground. When ordered to account for his inhuman act, he replied angrily: "Those swine are better off dead—no prisoners for me!" Small wonder he was scorned by fellow officers.

He gave scant attention to what others said or thought about him. To Edward Mannock war meant killing, with no holds barred. Then the pressure took him almost to the breaking point. In May of 1917 he suffered a serious nervous upset. He fought to bring it under control and to all outward appearances he succeeded. Then he began to suffer lapses of memory. His combat reports were frequently vague and incomplete.

In June, nervous tension dealt him another setback. After one landing, his arms and hands shook so badly that he had difficulty controlling them. He was the picture of absolute fatigue. During his last leave in England, he voiced a premonition of death. "I'm coming to the end," he said, "but I don't know whether it will be in the air or not. I don't know . . ." and his voice would trail off.

Back in France, Mannock commanded Number 85 Squadron. On the night of July 25, 1918, he was drinking brandy in the mess. His score now equalled Billy Bishop's —seventy-two planes—and he was well ahead of other British aces. He was unaware that Bishop would never fly operationally again, for the Canadian ace had been appointed to the Air Ministry in London. Mannock could have spent the remainder of the war getting the one victory needed to break the tie, but he actually cared little about being top man. Killing Germans was his only interest.

Although Mannock had no qualms about sending Germans down in flames, he lived in violent dread of going down burning himself. It was his only fear. The idea haunted him. Before he took off on his last flight, he checked the revolver he always carried in his cockpit and remarked casually to Lieutenant Donald Inglis, who was to accompany him, "I'm not going to burn if they get me. I'll blow my brains out first!"

At 5:30, Mannock and Inglis were airborne in their S.E.5 scouts. Inglis had been instructed to follow closely and do exactly as his leader. In a few short minutes they were whizzing over the German trenches near Merville, thirty feet up and zigzagging furiously to give the ground troops a poor target. Inglis stuck close to the major's tail and hung on for dear life. Suddenly he saw the plane in front wheel and climb. Then Mannock dived on a low-flying two-seater. He opened up with his guns but his speed was too great and he overshot his mark. Inglis followed and shot up the German's fuel tank. The enemy plane staggered, nosed down, and began to burn.

Mannock swept in and crowded the burning machine closely, with Inglis trailing. They were circling dangerously low, an inviting target for ground fire. Mannock continued to ascend around the flaming victim, even as it crashed and burned. Then, after several quick circles over the wreckage, he leveled off and streaked for home.

Without warning, something went wrong.

A flame burst out of the side of Mannock's S.E.5 and trailed an ugly black streak through the air. A second later the entire plane was enveloped in flames. It spun crazily to earth and exploded near its victim. No one will ever know whether the ace had time to make good his boast and use the revolver. Inglis risked a quick circle at twenty feet to try to get a glimpse of his commanding officer, but the plane was burning too fiercely. British antiaircraft gunners at Hazebrouck watched the entire action through binoculars, and confirmed Inglis' report.

There was much speculation as to the cause of Mannock's death. Did he jump, unseen by Inglis, when the flames first burst around him? The most persistent rumor had it that infantry fire struck his fuel tank, but unless the foot soldiers were firing bullets of the tracer or incendiary type (highly unlikely), this possibility is farfetched. Another theory suggested that a final lucky round from the German rear gunner, who *was* firing incendiaries, found its mark in the S.E.5's fuel tank. Finally, it was presumed that as Mannock closely circled the falling wreckage, a fragment from the flaming victim may have lodged in the S.E.5 and set it afire.

We shall never know beyond doubt. Mannock's death remains as much of an enigma as the man himself. A German officer removed his valuables and personal effects, noted Mannock's brother's address from his wallet, and sent them home through the Red Cross. German troops buried the major nearby and notified the Central Prisoners of War Committee, but the grave could not be found after the war.

The most puzzling thing of all was this: Although it was alleged that Mannock's body was trapped in the blazing aircraft, none of his personal effects showed traces of exposure to fire.

So rests Britain's "Ace of Aces"—somewhere near Merville. Perhaps he found at last the peace his troubled life could not give him. His final patrol was one to remember, for he went out as he had lived—violently.

Mannock was a curious war bird driven by hatred, a man not easily forgotten when old soldiers talk of the Great War. But in the hearts of his countrymen he never earned the adoration given comrades of lesser fame. In his home town of Canterbury his name is listed without special note on the war monument with others who served their nation.

Mannock's fame, or lack of it, caused many fighter pilots to reflect that humanity is expected of one, even in wartime.

They're still arguing about the fates of Guynemer, Immelmann, Mannock, and Ball, and the disappearance of the L-50. Somewhere, these magnificent skyfighters are having a grand time talking it over.

They're in good company.

CHAPTER 2

The Plane That Almost Bombed New York

When the European conflict entered its third year, the United States was poised to intervene. It was then the German High Command put its stamp of approval to a military plan so fantastic that even today it defies the imagination of the most devoted reader of Jules Verne and H. G. Wells.

When the die was cast, less than a dozen men in Berlin and Potsdam knew the purpose of the venture. Priority war materials, sorely needed for the stepped-up production of German fighter planes, were quietly sidetracked and routed to selected factories throughout the Fatherland. Simultaneously, extreme security measures were put into effect by German Intelligence. They did their job so well, obscured and cloaked the activity of this master project so thoroughly, that the details needed to complete the story are still missing.

If all went well, within a few short months the Allied effort would reel under the most daring assault in the short history of aerial warfare. Unlike the pounding of London with mass flights of heavy bombers, this blow would be struck by a single, but very unusual, aircraft.

In the gathering dusk of a heavily guarded aerodrome near Poll on the Rhine, a huge bomber, a *Reisenflugzeug*, was scheduled to be rolled from the depths of its hangar. Antlike figures—the mechanics—would scurry under its huge span. In the belly of the ponderous monster would rest four tons of bombs and enough fuel to feed its ten engines for eighty hours. Its crew, three experienced bomber pilots and two master navigators, would enter the giant and prepare for takeoff.

At navigators' stations along the forward flight deck were certain instruments never before used in aerial navigation. They were sextants and great-circle charts. Bunks, an innovation for an airplane, were provided along the wide aisle. The navigators had been crosstrained to direct the bomber to its target and then to double as bombardiers. No gunners were carried. Gunnery turrets were, in fact, conspicuously absent. Since the target was totally defenseless and incapable of offering ground or aerial defense, they were unnecessary.

When the plane's rumbling engines warmed, fire pots along the length of the runway would be ignited, and this rumbling, roaring colossus, the mightiest plane ever built, would lumber into the air. To avoid the western battle-front it would head northwest over Holland, then into the darkened North Atlantic, where it would set a course for a city 3,300 miles away. Thirty hours later, the bomber would sweep over the unsuspecting metropolis, its bombs tumbling into the crowded streets. The stunned and panic-stricken populace of a city, which considered itself a safe distance from Europe's battlefields, would realize that, without warning, New York City was being bombed by a German plane.

Was this a mad, suicidal, one-way dash by the most daring of Herman Goering's *Luftwaffe* during World War II?

No. This mission was scheduled to occur in the late fall of 1918. Had not the tide of war suddenly turned, this amazing machine could have flown its deadly mission as planned.

The Poll Giant was no idle dream of a crackpot engineer. It was very near the flying stage when the fortunes of war brought its construction to a halt.

The Teutonic militarist is no slouch when it comes to the effective use of psychological warfare. History is dotted with his use of fear weapons. He didn't talk about them, he made them and he put them to use. His use of the V1 and V2 weapons against England during World War II was the first mass employment of a morale-shattering media. The conflagration that followed crippled Britain's war production. Twenty-five years earlier he engineered the devastating zeppelin and Gotha raids over southern England and developed the first use of psychological air warfare.

Americans are prone to smile when told that their cities were slated as German aerial targets in 1918. "America bombed in 1918! Impossible! Why, Hitler couldn't even do it in 1943!"

But Hitler's *Luftwaffe* would have had to penetrate a 3,500-mile radar net, naval patrols, and flying boats to reach America. Kaiser Wilhelm's *Lufstreitkrafte* would not. His High Command might well have adapted the proved zeppelin, but for some unexplained reason they didn't. Their airship fleet was more than adequate at the time; it consisted of several formidable Navy zeppelins of the L-70 type. One was the L-71, rumored to have been especially designed to bomb New York City. It was later proved that no zeppelin was ever designed for this reason, though airshipmen never questioned the L-71's ability to fly such a mission. This super airship was completed at Friedrichshafen, in the early summer of 1918, as a high-altitude, high-speed bomber. It was 693 feet long, 300 feet longer than its predecessors that bombed London. Its seven engines totaled 2,030 horsepower. Although most zeppelins droned along at fifty-five to sixty-five miles an hour, the L-71 cruised steadily at 100 miles an hour and carried fuel for 12,000 miles nonstop.

Fortunately, neither the L-71 nor its sister ships made bombing runs on the United States. Instead, the L-71 stayed close to its mooring mast for the duration of the war. In 1919, it was entered as a contender for the £10,000 prize for the first nonstop Atlantic flight. On the eve of its departure, Captain Lehmann (later of *Hindenburg* fame) was informed it had been removed from the competition by jittery German officials who thought Americans might not be happy to see a wartime zeppelin hovering over New York City. In due course, and in compliance with the Peace Treaty of World War I, the L-71 was delivered to the British as a war prize.

The terrifying London raids were checked in May of 1917, but only after considerable cost to the Germans. Seventy-seven of their airships were lost as the mounting effectiveness of the Home Defense Squadrons was felt. Antiaircraft guns, night fighters, and the English weather took their toll of the mighty zeppelins. In that same month, Germany, looking for another weapon that could break the Lion's spirit, found it in the Gothas and Giants —large multiengine bombers capable of carrying more than 1,000 pounds of explosives at 12,000 feet and higher. Unlike the clumsy, unwieldy zeppelins, they were faster, more maneuverable, and deadlier.

The huge flying machines were based at Ghent, 170 miles from London. With clocklike regularity, formations of from fourteen to twenty-two planes began to appear day and night over the uneasy English capital. They ranged so high that fighters and antiaircraft barrages were unable to reach them. Now, even larger numbers of combat-ready planes and pilots were restricted to the island empire, and the Royal Flying Corps in France was feeling the effect. The Flanders battleground could have put the machines to use. Improved antiaircraft weapons and some help from the elements finally forced the German Flying Service to limit their raids to night missions. In late 1917 and early 1918, the German bombers were forced higher. Their bombing accuracy suffered accordingly, but the huge machines created far more havoc than had the earlier zeppelins, and their losses by comparison were slight.

What, precisely, did Germany hope to gain in the bombing of England? Destruction of her war plants? Neutralization of the naval emplacements and training centers? Hardly. Pinpoint bombing of primary military targets was never intended; it was twenty-one years in the future. Although the raids upset war production and cut munitions output by 20 per cent, the over-all objective was to cripple home morale and divert much needed fighting machines from the front. To this end the raids were justified before stiffened aerial resistance spelled *finis* for the great war birds once thought capable of leveling London.

But when Germany withdrew its London raiders, it had not abandoned the concept of the heavy bomber. The limited success of the London raids, as well as the expected intervention of a productive America, stirred the Central Powers into thinking in parallel terms of psychological warfare. A giant ocean-spanning bomber, a *Reisenflugzeug*, over New York City would shock the Americans into looking to their own defense. This would hold back men and equipment from Europe's battlefields, at least until the great German offensive could smash on to victory.

The story of this great machine and its assigned mission against New York City did not come to light until ten months after the Armistice. And strangely, it wasn't revealed by the defeated Germans. The monstrous, semifinished aircraft was discovered by a group from the International Aeronautical Commission of Control sent to Germany to prepare an inventory of remaining German aircraft. During September of 1919, the group centered its work around Poll on the Rhine. There, in a darkened hangar of an abandoned aerodrome, they uncovered the components of an incredible flying machine. Its design was unlike anything seen before; its proportions were so gargantuan for its day that it defied credibility. The results of the investigation are contained in a little-known report entitled: *Ex-German Aerodromes and Materials in Back and Occupied Areas.*

In Chapter Three of the report, under the heading "Machines of Interest," is a nine-page report subtitled: "The Poll or Forsmann Giant." Nowhere in this illustrated document is it claimed the assembled components were manufactured at Poll. This suggests the huge, heavily guarded airfield was merely the assembly point and that the subassemblies were manufactured elsewhere under strict security and were shipped secretly to the Rhine aerodrome. The parts contained no manufacturers' marks, nor could the workmanship, praised as "good" by the commission, be traced to any aircraft builder. Several parts—landing gear, control surfaces, bomb releases—were never found.

After a careful analysis of the parts, the commission decided the machine was under construction as a "heavy-bombing, long-distance machine, alleged to have been intended to bomb New York."

The word "alleged" invites controversy as to the plane's purpose. Allied chiefs would have considered the planned raid suicidal as well as highly improbable, but more than once they had underestimated the ingenuity of German aircraft design and performance and had paid the price over the Western Front. If anyone has since found another purpose for the big bomber, he has failed to bring it forward. The plane was definitely not a research and development project. Germany could not afford the luxury of diverting skilled craftsmen, critical materials, and valuable time on an off-track military venture that expensive. It was not intended to bomb London or industrial France; the Gothas and Giants were adequate for this. To what possible use could this machine have been put, designed with a nonstop 6,000-mile range, other than to raid New York City?

The commission estimated the Forsmann Giant would have carried fuel for eighty hours of flight at a cruising speed of 120 miles an hour. Sketches attached to the report show an amazing clarity in the plane's design. The skilled investigators who reported these findings were fully aware their words and figures would be carefully read by their supervisors in government and military positions; their accuracy could easily be checked. But the report was never questioned. The sober analysis of the contents of Poll aerodrome hangar was accepted as fact. The Poll Bomber did exist.

It was a triplane, with its upper and lower wings spanning 102 feet. Its center plane measured 165 feet. On this wing thirty-three-foot ailerons, which were never found, would have been fitted. The wings had a standard chord (width) of twenty-two feet, with a well-cambered (curved) airfoil to compromise between load carrying and speed. At its thickest part the airfoil measured one foot. There were several equally spaced compression struts that extended five inches below the lower wing surfaces. All the wings had two main spars of sturdy box construction and each one extended the length of its wing. The front spar was unusually close to the wing's leading edge, so for maximum strength, all main lifting surfaces were covered with three-ply veneer, over which a thin sheet of muslin had been glued with varnish. Each wing was separated by eighteen feet. Once assembled, the aircraft's top wing would have been forty-five feet above the ground.

There appeared to be some similarity in design between an earlier bomber, the Schutte-Lanze R1 of 1918, which was designed to be powered with six Basse u. Selve or Maybach engines of 300 horsepower each. But the Forsmann Giant would take ten of these engines arranged back to back. They would have been supported in an unusual pyramid-type strut arrangement to hold the engine bearers on steel-plate fittings and tubing.

Almost as novel as the aircraft's size was its fuselage construction. It measured nine feet and three inches at maximum width, and the square structure was, like the wings, entirely of wood covered with three-ply veneer. It tapered smoothly to a flat wedge at the rear and converged bluntly at the nose. The main members were four longerons and a number of cable-braced members.

No cables, however, crossed the fuselage interior. This was an unobstructed passage for almost all of its 150 feet. There was an unusual raised walking platform running the length of the fuselage, under the forward part of which, it was believed, the bombs would have been carried internally. Eight square windows lined each side of the fuselage. Unlike most crude bombers of the early helmet-and-goggles days, there were no open cockpits; all occupants were enclosed.

The stabilizing tail plane, only one side of which was found, was nine inches thick and twenty-eight feet long, plywood covered. The pitch control of the cumbersome machine was of a highly stable design but would probably have created a problem in flight, since both the leading and trailing edges of this normally rigid part were movable. When operated simultaneously with the elevators, only a slight control pressure would have been needed to put the plane in a climb or dive. The vertical fin and rudder were never found.

As far as we know today, the only remaining part of this machine is one of the wooden wheels taken from Poll and placed among the aeronautical exhibits of the Imperial War Museum in London. The huge disc measures ninety-nine inches across its center. The laminated beech rim is ten inches wide. There is some doubt that the wheel is complete; officials of the War Museum suspect that even with three other similar wheels, it probably could not have supported the heavy aircraft. This hardly disproves its intended use, for the plane was not meant to withstand continuous abuse on rough fields. After its test flight, there would be only one takeoff and, eighty hours later, one landing. This is all that would have been required of the wooden monster. It is likely the gear would have been dropped after takeoff to reduce drag. Once back at Poll, the plane could have been bellied in, or it could have been deliberately ditched at a predetermined spot in the Atlantic where a waiting U-boat would pick up the crew.

Forsmann, the intrepid Swede believed to have designed the plane, was employed by the Siemens-Schukert Werke in Berlin at the outbreak of the war. He designed a number of large aircraft, among them the S.S.W. Giant, a biplane of seventy-two-foot wingspan and a gross weight of five tons. Production models of the Giant bombed London with the Gothas, and one of Forsmann's similar designs carried sixty passengers, a feat in those days.

There was nothing to show that work on the project was interrupted before the Armistice. A small, one-page item that appeared seven months earlier in *The New York Times* (April 23, 1918) gives a clue to indicate the Poll bomber was under construction then. It also points out a minor, though distorted, break in German security that leaked through neutral Holland and into the United States. The title of the news item may have been substantially correct, and perhaps only the details were garbled.

New York Times, April 23, 1918
TALKING OF POSSIBLE AIR RAID ON NEW YORK
Special Submarines to Bring Planes Within Reach Being Built, says German paper . . .
Special Cable to *The New York Times.*
THE HAGUE, April 22nd—The *Vossische Zeitung* alleges that it learned indirectly from Paris that the American coast is patrolled by water-planes.

The paper says that Major Havers declares that an air raid on New York is not only possible, but probable, and that special submarines are being built in Germany to carry airplanes which can be dismantled. Each airplane would then drop 100 kilos (2,200 pounds) of explosives on the roofs of New York and would even penetrate 450 kilometres inland.

Americans gave the news item scant notice. A few were amused by the idea. New York bombed? Preposterous!

True, Kaiser Bill's special plane-carrying submarines did not materialize, but this did not preclude another type of construction going on at a secret base in Germany. This was not at the navy pens of Kiel or the humming inland factories, but in the tranquil, picturesque valley of the Rhine. Here, where the world's finest wines are made, was found the hopes of the German High Command—a death-dealing war bird in the making. A flying machine of unbelievable proportions, designed to perform an impossible task—the bombing of New York City. Without a doubt this was Germany's secret weapon of World War I.

When Germany lost the war, work at Poll stopped. Riggers and fitters, carpenters and fabric workers scattered to their homes. The airfield was abandoned and the hangar doors were sealed until the team from IACC opened them ten months later. By then, information was hard to get and the trail was growing cold.

We may never know how close Germany came to getting this B-19 of its day airborne on its mission. All we can surmise is that given a few more weeks, perhaps a month at the most, World War I's most daring long-range bombing raid might well have come to America's shores, on schedule, on target.

CHAPTER 3

Derelicts and Ghost Planes

During World War I, two Australians flew their riddled aircraft on a mission over the German lines. They were dead, but they brought their aircraft home. In 1941, from the great battleground over England, fighter pilots reported a ghost plane that sent German raiders flaming to earth. And more than one squadron of RAF pilots watched a specter escort hover nearby during the height of the London blitz.

Tales of strange apparitions of the skies, phantom planes, their mysterious appearances and even stranger disappearances, have been received with skepticism. But despite the contention that "supernatural" sightings are to be expected under severe wartime stress, those who saw—believe.

Boelcke's Derelict

One of the most grisly occurrences of the first air war was Boelcke's Derelict. It was named for the German ace who discovered it.

On a crisp September morning in 1916, Captain Oswald Boelcke, who was then the Kaiser's top ace, led five of his ablest warbirds homeward after a successful dawn patrol. Among his pilots that morning was Baron Manfred von Richthofen, the man destined to become the highest scoring airman of the war. Over Armentieres, as a tight formation swung close to a towering cloud bank, a British reconnaissance plane abruptly burst from the vapor. It headed under full power directly for the German formation. The squadron scattered, narrowly escaping collision. Boelcke was quick to recover his senses and signal for the attack. One by one his squadron mates darted toward the two-seater and poured round after round of machine-gun fire into it.

Strangely, the British crewmen held their fire. They took no evasive action but continued to drone monotonously onward in a wide circle to the left.

Perplexed by the strange behavior of the plane and the failure of his finest pilots to down it, Boelcke signaled his men aside, centered the enemy machine squarely in his gunsight, swooped, and poured a long burst of lead into the cockpits.

Unwavering, the two-seater flew on.

Boelcke stared in disbelief. His withering attack apparently had had no effect on the machine. He saw his flaming tracers penetrate the plane; saw the gunner crouched over his weapon. Cautiously, the ace inched his speedy Albatros pursuit closer, ready for an English trick. When only a few yards separated them, he banked his machine and peered into the open cockpits.

The ghastly sight across those few yards of space chilled the marrow of even this hardened air fighter, for there, strapped bolt upright in the wind, were the death-stiffened bodies of the pilot and observer. Their riddled corpses were smeared with blood, their sightless eyes glazed, staring into nothingness.

They were riding a hearse of the sky.

Boelcke escorted the derelict for several minutes, then, with a dip of his wings he touched his forehead in a final salute and rejoined his waiting pilots. They returned home, leaving the plane to continue its journey to an unknown destination. Boelcke recorded the incident in his combat report but refused credit for the kill. He suspected that the men were already dead when their plane darted from the cloud bank. He was correct, although he never learned of the events that preceded their meeting over the Western Front. A month later Boelcke was dead.

At dawn that day, two Australian airmen of Number 3 Squadron, Australian Flying Corps, Lieutenant J. L. Sandy and Sergeant F. L. Hughes, pilot and wireless operator, had taken off in their R.E.8 for no man's land. Their mission was to direct a ground mortar battery to knock out a German rear position. No sooner had they begun their work in directing artillery fire than they were jumped by a squadron of German pursuits. A mile distant, two other Australian airmen in another recon plane saw their plight and flew to their rescue. One of the Germans was downed before the battle ended. As the rescuers turned away, they waved to the artillery plane which, to all appearances, was back at work. Their gesture, however, was not returned.

A few minutes later Boelcke met the plane when it popped from the cloud bank. After a vicious attack he left it to seek its own end.

The battered aircraft lumbered on until, forty minutes later, over St. Pol, its engine sputtered from lack of fuel and became silent. As though by ghostly hands, the derelict glided smoothly to a safe landing in an open field. French soldiers rushed to the plane. They found the bodies of Sandy and Hughes, and transported them to a nearby hospital where an immediate autopsy was made. The findings: both men had been killed instantly by a single bullet, an armor-piercing projectile that had sliced through Hughes's left lung and lodged in the base of Sandy's brain. They had been dead more than an hour when the plane landed.

The most inexplicable part of the incident was this: of the hundreds of bullet holes in the plane, made by more than a dozen pursuits in the two air engagements, not one bullet had struck a vital part of the propeller or engine, the gas tanks had not been pierced, nor was any part of the plane's control mechanism damaged.

The aircraft had penetrated deep into enemy-held ground, but the wind, blowing from the northeast that morning, drifted the plane back over home ground.

This derelict of the sky had sped onward with its lifeless crew to the last drop of gasoline and the final kick of its engine. It was a flying hearse with Death at the controls, a warplane that stubbornly refused to be downed by the best of the Kaiser's fliers.

Phantom Fighters of the Blitz

It is difficult for the average person to accept a phantasm of the dead, how would one go about asking him to believe an apparition of a house or a sailing vessel—or an airplane? Ghosts, it appears, are not limited to the deceased, they may be "things" as well. Machines guided by the personalities of men who persist in hovering near. Of such is the next story.

During the early struggle for European air supremacy

45

in World War II, tales of ghost planes that haunted the battle skies were whispered about in the squadron ready rooms and flight-line dugouts. The White Angel of Warsaw was one of these. It preceded German bombers minutes before they arrived over the Polish capital. It streaked silently from the west, shimmering with an eerie luminescence even in bright daylight. The specter plane would circle the city once, then disappear. After Warsaw fell to the advancing German armies, it was never sighted again.

There are still a few ex-RAF pilots who remember the legend of "Old Willie" and some who swear they saw him. He was supposed to have been the ghost of a World War I pilot named Henshaw, a Canadian. This Canuck had an insatiable desire to shoot down a German plane, but in his eagerness he grew careless. On his very first encounter with an enemy machine, he was wounded, lost control of his plane, and crashed between the lines. For two days, without food, he was forced to lie in a water-filled shell hole and nurse his wound as best he could while a heavy battle raged. He was finally able to inch his way back to friendly lines. His wound meant the end of the war for him and he was furloughed home. But until the day he died in 1929, shooting down a Boche remained a driving obsession.

A youthful RAF pilot who claimed to have seen Old Willie, recalled the following:

When the Blitz began, we really had our hands full. During one night patrol our squadron got quite a surprise. We were preparing to attack a large formation of Heinkels when we noticed another plane in our formation. It was British all right. Our squadron leader saw the cockade insignia, but it wasn't the latest-type machine by any means. We tried to signal, but there was no response. Then our leader recognized it as an old Canadian bi-plane that was somehow managing to keep up with our fast pursuits.

Suddenly it peeled off our formation and screamed straight for the two lead Heinkels. They saw it coming, too, and they swerved in their right formation, collided, and went down in flames. The Canuck pilot veered over toward us, waved a snappy "thumbs up" and simply disappeared into the mist. He's been seen at night many times by other RAF pilots. They say he always uses the same trick—diving straight for the enemy planes until they collide, or unnerving their pilots until they get careless and become an easy mark for our lads.

While Old Willie was the self-appointed protector for the Fighter Command, its counterpart, the "Hot One," looked after the boys of the Bomber Command. This specter ship, a Handley-Page bomber, was guided by invisible hands over enemy territory, on the long-range-bombing runs to Berlin. It too had a specialty of its own. According to the pilot of a Whitley bomber who was flying over "Hellfire Corner" one night:

This huge Handley-Page swooped down on us from above, traveling at a terrific rate of speed. It was brightly lighted and I could see there was no one at the controls.

It dived past and quickly outdistanced us. Suddenly the Huns let loose with a great barrage of flak from hidden antiaircraft batteries on the ground. The bomber was caught squarely in the middle of bursting shrapnel. I saw it in time and turned away.

The bomber must have been hit in a thousand places, but it pulled away ahead of us, climbed steeply into the clouds, and disappeared. If it hadn't attracted the fire from those concealed batteries, the German gunners would have caught us in a trap.

Other pilots have sworn that the timely appearance of the Hot One has saved their mission as they carried their bombloads to enemy targets. So, to the venerable and respected ghosts of England's historic castles and manors, has been added a touch of modern warfare—planes of vengeance.

The Phantom Fokker

One of the strangest flying stories of World War II came to light twenty-three years ago.

During the height of the London blitz, when Hermann Goering's *Luftwaffe* droned almost endlessly over the English Channel carrying death and destruction to Britain, a young fighter pilot named Grayson flew his first night patrol near Dover. The weather was alternately clear and hazy, with low-scattered clouds and blustery winds over the choppy waters below. Grayson was alone, or so he thought, piloting his lone fighter plane on a course along the shores of southern England.

Then, out of the gloom and directly ahead, he saw the vague outline of a strange aircraft. He realized the machine must be one of the enemy so he opened his throttle to overtake it. The other plane veered away and headed across the English Channel toward Germany. Despite Grayson's efforts to overtake the fleeing aircraft, the elusive outline managed to keep the same distance from its pursuer.

For an instant, the "enemy" machine emerged into the clear where the moonlight revealed its color to be dull blood-red. Grayson congratulated himself. Yes, it was a German plane all right; the wings and fuselage were clearly marked with small black crosses, but the airplane's design was strange, certainly not of the type now used by the *Luftwaffe*. If so, his instructors had failed to mention this strangelooking contraption with three wings and a round tail.

In a flash it dawned upon Grayson that he was chasing a plane of the type used during World War I! But this was 1940, and his fighter plane was designed to fly three times faster than the relic leading him.

A cloud loomed up; rain and mist spattered his windshield. When the squall passed a few seconds later, the lead plane had vanished.

Puzzled and confused, Grayson tried in vain to catch another glimpse of the mysterious aircraft. Probably, he reasoned after a while, a large insect had flattened itself against the windshield after he had taken off, and later the rain squall had washed it away. Then, too, in the excitement of his first night patrol, he probably only imagined he had seen German markings. Strange things were to be expected under the stress of war. Amused at the trick his mind had played, he turned back toward England and finished his patrol without further incident.

Later that night, Grayson relaxed over a drink with his squadron mates. As the conversation lagged, he sheepishly related his experience of chasing an "insect" half way to Germany. Instead of the expected outburst of laughter, a hush fell over the room. Grayson stared at the small group of silent men along the bar, each with their eyes fixed on him.

"What's wrong?" he asked. "What did I say?"

Several seconds passed before a veteran patrol pilot murmured, "So you've finally met the Red Knight."

"The Red Knight!" Grayson cried. "Who's he?"

"The ghost of Baron von Richthofen," his friend replied. "He was the Kaiser's deadliest ace until he was killed in 'eighteen." He went on to explain that the baron's death, like those of Guynemer, Mannock, and Ball, was shrouded in controversy and mystery. Other pilots nodded. They, too, had been escorted by the baron. The fathers of some had flown against Richthofen's Circus twenty-two years earlier.

With much relief those highly respected shades of Merrie Olde England stopped biting their nails and gnashing their teeth when the shooting war was over. The sprightly later-day ghosts who stole their thunder during the blitz by performing tricks ghosts of old never dreamed of, appear to be in retirement.

Riddle of the Berserk Blimp

America's involvement in the war with the Axis brought about this bizarre air event—a sky derelict of a different sort.

In the tense months that followed Pearl Harbor, the West Coast of the United States bristled in anticipation of a second sneak Japanese attack. The main concern of the U.S. Navy was that an enemy submarine would slip into San Francisco Bay to further cripple the Pacific fleet. Navy patrol planes and surface vessels were spread thin and had to be assisted by scouting blimps, nonrigid helium-filled bags powered with aircraft engines. They were slow and ponderous, but with a load of deadly depth charges they could hover over a submerged undersea boat and blast it with pinpoint accuracy.

On a certain morning in 1942, at a few minutes past 6:00, Blimp L-8 lifted from its mooring on Treasure Island and headed out to sea. The weather was good, and two experienced airshipmen aboard, Lieutenant Cody and Ensign Adams, expected their mission to be another routine sweep of the approaches to the bay.

The L-8 droned on as the officers scanned the Pacific for signs of unusual activity. They made routine radio contacts and checked on several fishing boats. Then, at 7:50, Lieutenant Cody radioed Treasure Island that they had found a large oil slick below.

"Looks like there might be a Jap sub waiting around the channel," he reported. "I'm taking the ship down to three hundred feet for a closer look."

When the captains of two nearby fishing trawlers saw the blimp circling lower, they knew it was on the track of a sub. They gave brisk orders to drag in their nets and retire to a safe distance, where their hulls would not be damaged by the concussion of an exploding depth bomb. Two armed patrol boats, alerted by radio, also paused at a distance to wait the result of Lieutenant Cody's investigation.

The airship turned slowly and droned over the oil slick, but instead of releasing a depth charge, it hovered momentarily, then ballooned upward to disappear in a scattered cloud layer.

About ten o'clock, several fishermen casting nets along the beach near the Coast Artillery Patrol Station looked up to see the L-8 drifting toward them. When the gondola touched the beach, they rushed forward and grasped the draglines to hold down the semibuoyant airship. Their efforts were futile; the blimp dragged them roughly along the shoreline for a hundred yards. Before it finally shook them loose, they looked through the open door of the gondola and saw there was no one aboard. The L-8 was a derelict of the air.

As the huge gas bag raked itself awkwardly along a cliff that bordered the beach, one of its 300-pound depth charges jolted free and plunged into the earth beside a highway. The sudden release of weight gave the blimp new buoyancy. Again it shot upward and away. Thirty minutes later it settled clumsily into the streets of Daly City on the outskirts of San Francisco.

The Navy immediately ordered a salvage crew to the scene and the now-limp gas envelope was emptied, disassembled from the gondola, and transported back to the base for a thorough examination.

What caused the strange and unexpected antics of the L-8? Where were Cody and Adams? Why did the airship ascend suddenly into the cloud layer?

A careful inspection showed all equipment in the control gondola to be in place. Nothing had been damaged.

The parachutes were neatly stowed in their racks; the rubber life raft was in its proper location. One investigator noted that the airship's two yellow life jackets were missing, but this was normal. All crewmen were required to wear them on flights over the water.

Then came a surprising discovery. Evidently the blimp had not touched down in the ocean at any time after it departed from Treasure Island. No water was found in the space beneath the deck of the gondola. Did Cody and Adams fall into the ocean as they circled the oil slick at low altitude? Was it the sudden loss of weight that caused the blimp to balloon upward? Apparently not. There was no one member of the four boat crews on the area who had seen bodies fall into the water, and the brilliant-yellow life jackets as well as the splash on impact would have been too obvious to be overlooked. A sea and air search conducted that afternoon and in the days that followed failed to turn up either life jackets or bodies, and the strange case of the berserk blimp and its missing officers is still no nearer to a solution than it was in 1942.

Dead men at the controls. Phantom pilots on phantom wings. Spectral escorts of the night, haunting the skies where once they fought and died. In air wars of the future, will they return?

CHAPTER 4

Jinx Flight

From a vantage point in 1966, the former members of a certain B-24 crew can look back on a hoodooed bomber sortie of World War II and agree on one thing—there were no preflight forebodings to that mission.

"We were too young to have premonitions, I guess," reflected Colonel Thomas L. Murphy, who had copiloted the jinxed bomber as a second lieutenant twenty-four years earlier. "From all the things that happened to me over there, I think I must have been the jinx. I graduated from flying school on Friday the thirteenth!"

Scattered now from Europe to the Pacific, eight of the original nine-man crew are hale and hearty today. And each retains a vivid recollection of four suspense-packed hours shared over the Bay of Bengal as one flight system after another failed on their homeward-limping Liberator. Sergeant Ed Cunningham, a reporter for the wartime *Yank*, said of their fantastic survival: "They played tag with borrowed time so often, the law of averages is in grave danger of being repealed." But when the war ended, five of the men remained with the Air Force and three are still on active duty. All were highly decorated; some were awarded the Distinguished Flying Cross and the Air Medal.

The enlisted members of the crew began training as a team at Salinas, Kansas, early in 1942. They were M/Sgt Howard C. Darby, bombardier; T/Sgt William O. Frost, engineer; S/Sgt John E. Craigie, radio operator; S/Sgt Bernard L. Bennett, tail gunner; S/Sgt Adolph R. Scolavino, belly gunner; and Sergeant Edward M. Salley, waist gunner. By September, the group was in east-central India where they quickly shaped into a seasoned combat team of the Tenth Air Force based at Allahabad. Of their quarters in the ancient holy city, Salley said, "We lived in the McPherson Barracks, once the home of the famed Bengal Lancers. The buildings were of stone, two-story, and very large. We slept on wood beds with rope stretched across them to support straw mattresses. The field was fairly modern, with concrete runways."

Their B-24D carried a picture of a green shamrock on its blunt nose. It belonged to Flight 1 of the 436th Heavy Bombardment Squadron.

Three days before a raid was scheduled to come off on Rangoon's railroad marshaling yards and shipping docks, a briefing was held for the crews that would take part. Six aircraft were assigned the mission, with its flights directed to have a five-minute separation. Cruising at 22,000 feet with an airspeed of 220 miles per hour, they were timed to strike the target at dusk or shortly thereafter. In Flight 1, the shamrock-embellished bomber would lead with First Lieutenant William R. Berkeley as pilot, Second Lieutenant Thomas L. Murphy as copilot, and First Lieutenant Francis N. Thompson as navigator. Each B-24 would carry its capacity load—12,000 pounds of demolition bombs. The alternate target was the Japanese airfield north of the city.

William Berkeley, who retired as a lieutenant colonel in

1960, recalls that at about 2:00 P.M. on the afternoon of October 29, he lifted the heavily-loaded bomber from the strip at Allahabad and headed southeast on the 1,000-mile run to South Burma. In the right-hand seat was the man who is now a colonel in the Strategic Air Command, and the Director of Safety at Barksdale Air Force Base, Thomas L. Murphy. Murphy flew thirty World War II missions in B-24s and B-25s.

"The mission was to involve five hours of daylight flying and four hours at night," Murphy recalls. "It was led by a 'pink elephant'—a B-24 recently transferred from the African desert theater. I don't remember the command colonel's name, but he was supposed to show us how to lead a bombing raid. As it turned out, monsoon weather and his unfamiliarity with weather-penetration procedures for our formations broke up the flight before we reached the target."

Despite the gauntlet of monsoon thunderstorms and the disturbing fact that Berkeley was forced to pull near maximum power to keep up with the other flight, Lieutenant Thompson zeroed the bombers over the target as the sky was darkening into nightfall. It was then that the plague of unexplained electrical and mechanical failures began—failures that ultimately forced nine men to spill into the pitch-black sky, a mile and a half over Bengal Province.

M/Sgt Darby was lead bombardier of his flight. Today he is a ranger with the United States Forest Service in California.

"We were told the weather would be good over the target," Darby said, in looking back to that memorable raid, "and the forecast proved to be generally accurate. I was preparing for the bomb run when I smelled something burning. It was my chute. Thompson, who was nearby, pulled it away from a heater, just before I dropped the load of thousand pounders. He put the fire out with an extinguisher."

At takeoff, Darby's parachute was inadvertently laid over the heater that was used to defrost and warm the Plexiglas nose section. The scorched pack meant one man would be short if the crew had to abandon the plane, and a familiar joke then making the rounds among the fliers suddenly became a deadly serious matter. It went something like this:

A bomber crew was bringing their plane home after a mission when they were hit by enemy *ack-ack*. The engines began to smoke and misfire as the plane lost altitude rapidly.

"Anyone know how to pray?" the pilot asked over the intercom.

"I do, sir," replied the bombardier.

"Fine," came the pilot's reply. "You pray. Everyone else get ready to jump—we're one parachute short!"

"The shortage could have been serious," Darby admits, "but there just happened to be an extra chute on board. Sometimes on day flights we carried a photographer in the lead ship. He must have left his chute in the gunner's well, where it got covered up and was overlooked by the ground crew during their inspection. I believe it was Bennett who found it."

The smouldering fire flooded the bomber with smoke— an alarming in-flight situation. Then, as the men settled their nerves in anticipation of the bomb release and turn toward home base, without warning all four engines cut out!

T/Sgt Frost, the engineer, was occupied in the top gun turret when the silence exploded around him. In the dim half-light of the late evening, he saw the four whirling propellers slow. Like everyone else on board, he froze momentarily as the bomber began to settle.

In the cockpit, the first stunned instant of shock passed as Berkeley and Murphy feverishly worked through the emergency procedures. Propeller pitch . . . mixture control . . . throttles . . . turbo-boost selector . . and the four 1,200 horsepower engines caught—and resumed their comforting drone. To a man, the crew went limp. A few even grinned. Then the engines cut out again.

"It got awfully quiet for a moment or two each time."

During all the confusion, Darby was bent over the bombsight in the nose. He was holding the release button and waiting for the cross hairs to come on target. "In this type of business, these things are to be expected," he reflected. "I was busy and didn't give it much thought, but I wasn't exactly pleased with the situation, either. Despite the smoke, haze, and commotion, it was bombs away. The strike was 100 per cent effective."

Sergeant Salley, gunner in the waist position, remembers those moments well. Today, a member of Delta Air Lines Flight Control in Atlanta, he recalls: "I could only see the target now and then as there was considerable cloud cover. We were advised to expect heavy *ack-ack*, and possibly fighters. Rangoon was considered the roughest target in Burma but none of the Japanese antiaircraft bursts were close until our engines cut out, then we dropped directly into it."

As the B-24 slipped into the midst of the exploding shell bursts, it was rocked and buffeted by the shock waves. A few crewmen were certain whining shrapnel sliced through parts of the wings and fuselage. Because of the two power failures, the plane lost altitude it could never regain and it lagged still farther behind, unable to rejoin the planes as they disappeared homeward over the Bay of Bengal. Again Berkeley and Murphy got the engines operating. As the minutes ticked by, the crew's frayed nerves slowly returned to normal. With an inflight fire and two complete power failures behind them, they gained confidence with the thought that they had left their troubles behind, at least for this mission.

They were dead wrong; their headaches were just beginning.

William Frost, today Pan American Airway's Senior Maintenance Supervisor at Stuttgart, Germany, tells what happened next:

Why all four generators failed is a mystery. We learned later that other B-24s had similar difficulty when their generator mountings broke, but it didn't seem possible that this could happen to all four of our generators. Shortly after we left the target, the first one went out, then a second one failed and nothing I could do would keep them on the circuit. We were still about an hour and a half from our base when the remaining two failed suddenly. I went to the APU [auxiliary power unit; an engine-driven generator used for emergency power] and started it, but it only ran a few minutes before it blew the cylinder head. This left the storage batteries, which for some inexplicable reason, probably a short somewhere, drained dead in short order.

The propellers on a B-24 were controlled throughout their constant-speed ranges with an electrical step-head motor that was designed to hold the propellers at the rpm at which they were set if a complete electrical failure occurred. But they didn't hold; the blades kept creeping to a lower pitch little by little because of the air pressure against them. The engine rpms gradually got higher and higher, moving toward overspeed.

In the gathering gloom of the cockpit, Berkeley and Murphy were sweating out the instrument readings. As one generator after another failed, Murphy watched the tachometer needles inch toward the red danger line:

The engines were trying to overspeed all along. The hours crept by and although the propeller pitch was supposed to be fixed, it slipped up a little at a time. Our propeller governors needed electrical power to reposition the control valves that held a constant engine speed, but now the slightest change in altitude caused our rpm to increase or decrease. We flew over four hours at night, trying to hold the same altitude. Once a propeller changed pitch, we had no means of bringing it back. When our troubles couldn't be corrected, we realized we were in deep trouble—night and over water—with more than four hours to go. I imagine each man did a little reviewing plus a prayer or two. I know I did.

As the battery energy drained to a trickle, the instrument lights in the cockpit grew dimmer until finally the interior of the throbbing bomber was in total darkness. The pilots peered out their respective cockpit windows at the faint outlines of the propeller arcs and watched the engine cowlings carefully. The first signs of overspeed showed themselves as the engines began to vibrate, slowly at first, then with a steadily increasing tempo. Every electrically operated instrument was dead now, and all communications were out. Even the intercom was useless. They had no lights for signaling, no way to send radio identification to friendly aircraft, or a distress call to search and rescue units.

Then Murphy remembered a personal item—his flashlight. He brought it out and trained it on the instrument panel. Aside from the engine gauges, only the vacuum instruments, the flight indicator and gyro compass, were working. As long as the flashlight held out, they could navigate homeward. Of those apprehensive moments, Murphy said, "We dreaded to think of those batteries going dead, too. I took the flashlight with me when I abandoned the plane."

All the while, T/Sgt Frost and S/Sgt Scolavino, the assistant flight engineer, worked frantically to regain electrical power or even part of it. But their blind fumblings in the darkness of the bomber's belly were futile. The electrical system would never work again.

Now the blacked-out B-24 was moving over the coastal lowlands near Calcutta, still over 200 miles from Allahabad. With engine operations touch and go all the way from the target back to India, Berkeley and Murphy were anxious to set their bundle of trouble down as quickly as possible—*if* possible. They banked the plane into a wide, cautious swing over blacked-out Calcutta and looked for an airfield. Dum-Dum Field was down there somewhere . . .

That's when they discovered they were not alone in the sky.

Because their intercom was dead, no one know who first spotted the new threat. It was probably Salley, who says of his frightening discovery: "I had been in the waist position for most of the mission, near my single fifty-caliber machine gun. It was just a little before 9:00. I was standing at the open left waist window and saw a plane make a pass from behind and above on my side of the ship. He made two passes that I saw, and each time I was frozen with the fear that he would open fire on us."

In the tail, S/Sgt Bennett also saw the plane zoom past, uncomfortably close. "We spotted another aircraft with a single exhaust, indicating it was a fighter type, presumably a British Hurricane and later verified as such. Besides an impending strafing, our engines were on the verge of disintegration."

As the British fighter plane whizzed over the Liberator and flashed past the cockpit windows, Berkeley and Murphy, with enough trouble on their hands to last them for the remainder of the war, were not heartened when they caught sight of the exhaust glow. Murphy recalls: "When the Hurricane made a pass at us in the darkness, we got ready to jump because we had absolutely no way to signal him—no running lights—nothing. The Japs had visited

Calcutta before, and as we were heading directly toward it, he had every right to start shooting. But since we took no evasive action he let us go."

The big twin tail of the B-24! That's what the Hurricane pilot must have recognized on his last pass. After the second look, the fighter vanished into the night sky. Once more the crew breathed a sigh of relief. They had a little more time.

Their reprieve was short-lived, for now the serious condition of Number Three engine captured their attention. It was rapidly approaching the critical danger point. Frost knew what would happen when the overspeeding power plant reached its limit of endurance. "The rpms were gradually become excessive, and with no hope for electrical power, it was impossible to feather any of the propellers. I saw sparks and flames belch from Number Three. When it became very rough, Lieutenant Berkeley ordered me to notify the crew to prepare for bail out. I assembled the men, part on the bomb-bay catwalk and part in the cockpit."

Darby, in the nose, was unaware of the dangerous state of Number Three engine. "I had come out of the nose and was in the rear-gunner's compartment. Frost signalled me with a flashlight. I walked through the bomb bay to the engineer's station, and he told me the crew was preparing to bail out."

The decision to abandon the hopelessly failing bomber came none too soon. Murphy was nearest to the backfiring, and now wildly vibrating, engine and the danger was growing that flying parts would hurl from it at any moment and slice, shrapnel-like, through the cockpit. It had happened before.

"I was on the right side and watching the engine closely," the copilot reports, "so I had advance warning before it started to break up. As the propeller rpm moved close to 3,000, we knew it wouldn't last long even with the throttle cut back. With everyone in the bomb bay, we told them that when the doors opened (they were hydraulically operated), just go—don't ask questions. The propeller broke up first, then the engine wrenched itself completely out of the wing. We went then."

Craigie, Bennett, Darby, Frost, and Salley were the first to leave. Bennett remembers: "Frost told us to go as soon as the door opened. Fortunately for Darby, the extra chute allowed him to join us on our trip down. He can talk about luck. Craigie left the ship seconds before I did."

With a .45 strapped around his waist, Darby regarded the black pit only fleetingly before he dropped through the right side of the forward bomb bay. "After I opened my chute I reached in my coverall pockets to see if I'd lost my cigarettes. I hadn't, and since I had nothing else to do, I lit up. It seemed the natural thing."

Frost took time to consider protection for himself and the crew once they had assembled on the ground. He was well armed, at least when he jumped. "We bailed out about 9:10," he narrated, "and I went out the bottom with a Thompson submachine gun, 125 rounds of ammo and my musette bag. I counted to ten and jerked the rip-cord. As the chute popped open, the loosely adjusted chest strap snapped into my face, cut my mouth and smashed my nose. Nothing serious, but when I came to my senses I was floating at 5,000 feet with nothing left but my flight cap in my hand—and it was on my head when I bailed out. A few moments later I saw our plane explode and burn below us."

Edward Salley remembers his big step into dark space this way. "About ten minutes after the Hurricane scare, I got the word by way of mouth (shouted from the catwalk above the engine noise) that we were to abandon the plane. When the doors opened, I dived out head first, clutching the ripcord in my right hand. I almost opened my chute too soon, because when it popped I saw the tail of the bomber right above me.

"The chest buckle hit me in the mouth and forced my teeth through my bottom lip. I was only out momentarily and came to in time to see the plane hit."

For Adolph Scolavino, the last minute of the plane's flight under the pilot's control was jammed with urgency and suspense. "I was the sixth man out . . . left the plane at 7,800 feet. Then came Lieutenants Thompson, Murphy, and Berkeley. When I left the plane, Berkeley was still holding it from diving so we could bail out. I dropped through the rear bomb bay and counted to ten as I'd been trained. (It may have been a fast count though.) After my parachute opened and I got oriented, I saw the plane disappear into the night, its right wing low and losing altitude rapidly. I didn't see it hit, but when the sky was suddenly lit up by the explosion and intense light, I mistakenly thought it was a Jap searchlight trying to pick us up as we floated down."

Satisfied that the enlisted crew had cleared the bomb bay, the plane's officers prepared to exit. Murphy recalls; "Berkeley's order when the time came to bail out was a simple one—'Go!'

"I went out the bomb bay. Thompson preceded me, rather reluctantly as I recall. He said: 'Don't rush me . . . I'm going!' I was in a hurry as was Berkeley who was the last one out. No moonlight—pitch dark."

The night stillness was broken only by the wind whistling through the riser lines to flap against the nine parachute canopies floating over the Indian jungle. Although each man bailed out only seconds apart, they had opened their chutes at different altitudes. This, and the wind, drifted them apart. In the moonless descent not one crewman saw another. Craigie suffered the most severe injury from the loose parachute chest buckles and he was bleeding profusely from a broken nose cartilage when he splashed into a lake. For nine hours, half swimming and half wading in rice paddies and jungle swamps, he fumbled about in the darkness.

Bennett landed uneventfully on dry land an immediately shed his parachute harness.

I called to Craigie, thinking he'd be close by, but I couldn't get him to answer. When I tried to walk around, I found I was practically surrounded by water, so there was nothing to do but try to settle down for the night. The seat cushion of my parachute made a good pillow and I lay down and stared up at the stars—until I became sharply aware of the weird noises coming from the rice paddies and swamps. My imagination had a field day. I'll never forget that night at the edge of the jungle, surrounded by a host of invisible enemies.

Finally, I fell asleep from sheer exhaustion and when I awakened it was daylight. I saw a native coming through the swamp in a dugout and called to him in broken Hindustani. I motioned for him to come closer, but it was of no use. After what seemed like hours, another native approached and I used every means of persuasion to convince him I was an American in need of directions and transportation.

The way that finally worked was by waving money in the air.

The native took me to a small village where I quickly improved relations by feeding the small children chocolates from my survival kit. A boy of about fourteen told me—in broken English—there was a British airfield about twenty-five miles away. There was no transportation available, so we hunted around for something. The only thing that looked promising was an old bicycle with both tires flat. There was no pump to be had anywhere. Then I remembered the CO_2 cylinder (for inflating our Mae West jackets) and I used it to inflate the tires. They held, and away we went, double-deck.

After a few miles my "faithful native guide" pointed out a railroad track and we followed it to a small telegraph house. The telegraph operator graciously served us tea and crumpets and stopped the next train to Calcutta. When I boarded it, I was surprised to find Salley and Craigie, much disheveled, but none the worse from the experience. We all started talking at once, excitedly asking about the other crew members. We had a few laughs, such as: Why did Craigie, our radio operator entrusted with carrying secret-code data, tear it into little pieces and let it float away on the water?

Salley and Craigie had met earlier near the crash site and boarded the train one station ahead of Bennett. Salley told of his frustrating inability to see the ground during his descent, and recalled:

When my feet hit a small tree limb, I knew I was near the ground. The limb broke under my weight and I landed rather gently. I recall that I sat for some time, shaken and scared, before I removed the parachute harness. I left it where it lay and began to look for the other crew members. I called out several times but no one answered.

I lay down in a plowed field with my Mae West for a pillow and went to sleep. Just before I dozed off, I remembered I'd left all my survival equipment in the chute back where I'd landed. My lip, though swollen and tender, didn't prevent me from sleeping —restless though I was.

Shortly after dawn I found a village. I was greeted with much suspicion until I made the natives understand I'd bailed out of an airplane. They communicated to me that some people from the village had already found my chute and brought it there. When I found someone who spoke English, I explained my plight more fully and as soon as he translated to the villagers they couldn't do enough for me. They produced the chute and I unzippered the back of the pack and took out chocolates, a machette, and the other survival items stowed there. I cut the pilot chute off (I still have it) and gave the main canopy to the natives. My sore lip prevented my eating anything solid, but I managed to take some of the chocolate and drink some coconut milk.

After a short rest, my English-speaking friend and I walked about five miles to another village on the river bank, where I met Craigie walking into the village followed by an Indian boatman carrying his chute. He was still dripping wet, tired from sloshing through rice paddies and swamps, and weak from loss of blood. His nose was very swollen and he had difficulty talking. Ironically, he was the only one of our crew who had heard the shouts of the others. He distinctly heard Bennett soon after he landed, but couldn't call back because of his injury.

Natives guided us to a railroad five miles upriver. The station was little more than a shack and very near our crashed plane. We walked over to it. It was scattered over a wide area and had burned on impact. We found a rather puzzling thing at the site: the bulletproof glass from the turret lay off to one side with hardly a scratch, while the turret itself was a twisted and crumpled mass of metal. We boarded the Calcutta-bound train and at the next stop Bennett joined us.

Darby, during his descent, scarcely had time to enjoy a few drags on his cigarette before he found himself on the ground.

I landed in a rice paddy on the edge of a jungle, and walked around until I reached a small village. I spent a couple of hours on the porch of a native hut until dawn. As I was preparing to move out, a native constable told me there was another American nearby. He pointed out the direction and we struck out with another native trailing behind with my chute. They took me to a British outpost on a river—and here I met Frost.

Frost often wonders who found his Thompson submachine gun (or if it was ever found), the 125 rounds of ammunition, and his musette bag. Without protection in the night, he wisely decided to play safe.

I had no injuries on landing, and decided not to attract attention by calling to the others. I didn't know where I was or who might be around me, so I spread my parachute on the ground, pulled it over my head for protection against mosquitoes—and spent a very restless night.

Just after daybreak some Indian villagers came by, but they were so frightened when they saw me they wouldn't talk. About mid-morning I met Darby along the bank of a canal and we got on one of the barges that took us to the outskirts of Calcutta.

Scolavino landed knee-deep in water in a rice paddy with a cut lip and thigh.

I crawled out and found a dry spot of land (it was pitch black), curled up in my chute, and fell asleep. About 3:00 A.M., I sensed someone nearby and opened my eyes. There, looking down on me was a native dressed in white cloth. I sat up quickly and reached for my knife, having decided not to wait to find out if he was friend or foe. When he saw the machette he ran.

I got up immediately and began to grope about; finally got to a river about daybreak. Two hours later I spotted a boat coming downstream paddled by two natives. I called to them and when they rowed near, I took my book on Hindustani from my jungle kit and managed to make known who I was. They rowed me to a village where the headman gave me water and took me to a railroad station. I boarded the next train for Calcutta and the conductor showed me to a compartment where I found Lieutenant Thompson.

For Lieutenant Tom Murphy, a pattern of close calls was becoming evident in his wartime flying. On an earlier strafing mission over Akab, Burma, his B-25 was severely shot up by Japanese ground fire. The left vertical stabilizer was completely blasted away; one man was killed in the nose and two others were wounded. Then both engines of the crippled bomber quit twenty-five miles at sea. He and his pilot managed to ditch the struggling Mitchell safely and survive five days afloat in the Bay of Bengal by lashing together their five-man and two-man rubber life rafts. They had water but no food. About midnight of the fifth night, rough seas tossed them out of the rafts and two hours later they were washed ashore—back in Burma. They ran into a band of Ghurkas led by a British lieutenant. A radio message relayed through to Dum Dum Field brought a C-47 to their rescue. Later in the day it landed on the beach and picked them up—six miles above the Japanese lines.

So Murphy was an experienced hand at survival when he tumbled from the bottom of the condemned B-24. Like others of the crew, his chute chest strap slipped upward when the canopy billowed, and aside from a cut chin and lip, he suffered a large knot on his forehead. He kept his D ring as a souvenir.

Except for a few strap burns and some other bruises, these were the extent of my injuries. On the way down I tried to stop the chute from swinging by pulling on the risers. But being a rank amateur, I dumped out all the air and fell—I don't know how far—before the canopy filled again. Needless to say I quit that.

I made a soft landing in a rice paddy and didn't even fall down. Then I walked exactly fifty feet out of the paddy onto an earthen dam. I got plenty scared when Indian dike watchers found me, and a whole gang of them gathered nearby. Just a week earlier a British Blenheim crew was murdered by villagers twenty-five miles west of Calcutta when they made a crash landing. All I had to defend myself with was the machette from my parachute emergency pack. I stayed awake all night long, watching them, but even so they managed to steal my pocketbook.

In the morning I made my way to a village on a river bank where, to my amazement, along came Berkeley in a dugout canoe. We located the nearest railroad and boarded the first train for the city. Except for Frost and Darby, who joined us later, we had a gala reunion that night to celebrate our good luck. At the Grand Eastern Hotel, where we stayed for eight days, we had the chef cut the biggest steaks in Calcutta and fix them Western style.

Salley told of the crew's arrival in the city:

We were met by Mr. Harold Marshall, Chief Inspector of the Calcutta Police, who escorted our disheveled troop to a hospital. Merrill's Marauders had just come out of the Burma jungle and had taken up every inch of space. We got a cursory examination, some minor patching, and were dismissed.

There wasn't any reimbursement for any part of the expenses we incurred. In fact, we had to buy clothes to wear while we were awaiting transportation back to base. They were semi-British uniforms bought in the hotel's shop. One night, in the dining room, a British officer tried to throw us out. It seems the place was off limits to British enlisted men. We thought we'd have some fun, so we led him on until the situation got pretty heated. Our officers heard the ruckus and came over in time to straighten him out.

Darby and Frost were reunited with the remainder of the crew two days later when Harold Marshall brought them to a Calcutta theater during intermission. On November 6 a plane was available to take the men back to the 436th, but there weren't enough chutes on board. They arrived in Allahabad by train, and a few days were reoutfitted and back on combat status.

Lieutenants Berkeley, Murphy, and Thompson were given another crew; Frost, after forty-one missions, was assigned to supervise aircraft maintenance. The remaining five of the original crew joined the team of the *Rangoon*

Rambler, another B-24 whose record fortunately failed to produce another episode as singular as that of the jinx flight.

Scolavino returned to the States after fifty-six missions. He ended the war instructing B-24 engineer-gunners in Wyoming. A chief master sergeant with an F-102 Fighter Interceptor Squadron in Germany, he is nearing thirty-year retirement with the Air Force. "I guess we were just plain lucky or it wasn't our turn," he reminisces. "Some people break a leg roller skating, and here nine men parachute at night over a country wild with rivers, jungles, and cobras—and end up with slight cuts. Sounds too good to be true, but it is."

Salley flew forty-nine missions with the Tenth Air Force and was discharged in 1945. Darby ended the war with thirty-seven missions. He reenlisted, was commissioned, and retired as a first lieutenant in 1959. His philosophy remains as cool today as then, when he peered through his bombsight on that black, shrapnel-filled night over Rangoon. "I think we survived because we were all previous servicemen," he said. "All well trained in our fields, with many years of experience among us—the type of men who don't get 'shook' easily, if at all. We knew our jobs and trusted one another in theirs."

Bennett came back with over fifty missions under his belt. Today he is an electrician at the Charleston Naval Shipyard.

The only member of the original crew who is not living is John Craigie, who died after the war.

All three of the bomber's officers remained in the Air Force. Francis Thompson is now a full colonel. Following his return from the Far East, he remained in the service and attended pilot's school. His present address lists a San Francisco APO number. William Berkeley retired as a lieutenant-colonel in 1960 and is an information officer for MATS at Scott Air Force Base.

The one member of the crew who is still an active aircraft commander is Colonel Murphy, whose oversize frame snugly fills the cockpit of a B-52 or a B-58. He has flown Mach 2.1 in the Hustler. After thousands of hours in military aircraft ranging from the B-25 to the B-58, his comment twenty-four years after his narrow escape from death should make the heart of any patriot beat proudly.

"In the majority, it takes young men to fight wars along

with some mature leadership. I have no overpowering philosophy about these things. Luck? Yes—but the greatest gambit is the will to survive and go on again.

"Americans keep that with them always."

CHAPTER 5

Ghost in the Desert

No one willingly travels the Sahara's Desert of Thirst. No one, that is, except scientists who sound the barren wastes for traces of oil.

In November of 1958, two flying geologists of the D'Arcy Exploration Company, operating out of Cufra Oasis in Libya, sighted a ghost of World War II. It was an abandoned Liberator bomber, a B-24. The huge four-engine plane had bellied onto the desert floor twenty-five miles southeast of a gaunt, solitary limestone pillar named Blockhouse Rock.

Wrecked planes are still common near the North African coast, where smashed trucks, burned-out tanks, planes, and scuttled or torpedoed ships lie offshore as reminders of the struggle fought little more than a generation ago. But here, 426 miles southeast of Benghazi, it was odd indeed. The bomber's faded pink color, blending at times with the surrounding terrain, told the geologist fliers it had once been assigned to a desert region.

They dropped to a low altitude and circled. There was no sign of life. After marking the location on their map, they returned to Cufra and told the other members of the oil exploration party of their find.

It was not until the following March that the party's convoy of desert vehicles reached the sun-baked plateau, an uncharted land that simmered under a cloudless sky. Here in the dry dust where daytime temperatures reached 130 degrees and plunged to near-freezing at night, not a blade of grass could survive. Day by day, as the oil men pushed their survey operations farther into the area marked on the map, they kept a sharper lookout. Then they saw it. Glistening in the heat waves that shimmered off the desert floor lay the long lost derelict.

The bomber's fuselage had broken behind the wing

when the plane skidded to its stop. The right outboard engine had twisted off on impact. Apparently its propeller was still turning when the plane had pancaked into the sand years earlier. On the bomber's nose was clearly discernible "64." The geologists jotted down other identification numbers and on making a closer examination of the wreckage, marveled at how well the arid desert had preserved it. Water flasks and jugs of coffee were still full and platable. Log books and instruments were unaffected. Gun belts were full; flight clothing hung on hooks. Cigarettes, chewing gum, and emergency rations were neatly stored away and in the shadow of the plane's wings they found dried, mummified bodies of birds that had sought relief from the sun. The men fanned out to look for clues. They knew that unless the crew had been rescued soon after they abandoned the plane, they had perished.

One of the men suggested that wandering nomads may have captured the crewmen and sold them into slavery deep in the Sahara. Perhaps, somewhere, they were still in custody. A Libyan guide shook his head no. This region, he said, was so uninhabitable that even desert tribesmen refused to enter it. "They say it has been cursed by God. It is called The Desert of Thirst."

When the men reached civilization in April, they notified Wheelus Air Base at Tripoli. A full-scale investigation sparked by the 17th Air Force and headed by Major General Spicer, got under way. Responsibility was given the Army, however, because during World War II the Air Force was part of the Army. From the retired records section at St. Louis came the first clue: 124301 had been missing since April 4, 1943, exactly sixteen years, with its nine American crewmen. It required two years of research and sixty pounds of records accumulated from four locations in the United States to tell the complete story.

The following month a two-man team from the Army Mortuary Service Headquarters in Frankfurt, Germany, flew over the bomber. By now, the records began to produce more information. The crew, as well as their mission, was positively identified; for the third time the Army Adjutant General's Office contacted the next of kin listed on the records. The first time had been shortly after the crew's disappearance, when they were declared missing in action, then, a year later, another report was made when the men became legally dead under the Missing Persons Act.

The bomber was the *Lady Be Good*. It was once assigned to the North African Ninth Bomber Command, which was composed of the 98th and 376th Groups. They were known as the Liberandos. Their mission: to bomb Sicily and Italy, cut supply routes, knock down enemy air strength. They were based at Soluch, one of the airstrips in the Benghazi area, on a base that was little more than a gritty, red-brown scar, scraped level through hard desert sand, and blown by the Libyan *ghiblis*, fierce desert sandstorms. It was a hellhole for the civilized soldiers who endured rationed water, dysentery, yellow jaundice, diarrhea, and eye infections. They ate their gritty rations standing up at mess.

The crew were old men by World War II standards. At the time when most crews consisted of nineteen- and twenty-year-old youths, the *Lady Be Good* didn't have one man under twenty-one.

First Lieutenant William J. Hatton was the pilot. He was twenty-six and he had left a bride when he departed overseas.

The other officers were Second Lieutenants Robert F. Toner, the copilot, who was twenty-seven; Dp Hays, the navigator, twenty-three; and John S. Woravka, bombardier, twenty-six.

Technical Sergeant Harold S. Ripslinger, the flight engineer, was twenty-two. The remaining enlisted men were staff sergeants; Robert E. LaMotte, twenty-two, was the radio-operator gunner. Vernon L. Moore, twenty-one; Guy E. Shelley, twenty-six; and Samuel E. Adams were gunners. All had met late in 1942 at Topeka, Kansas, for crew training and check-out in a B-24D.

Once assigned a bomber, they flew the South Atlantic ferry chain, and on March 27, 1943, they became part of the 514th Squadron at Soluch, Libya.

It was a dark beginning for Hatton and his crew, for now began a series of seemingly jinxed occurrences, bad luck, misfortune—call it what you will—that ended seventeen days later, 400 miles in the desert.

As news developed about the finding of the missing bomber, rumors began to fly. One was that in 1943 a nomad camel caravan had seen an Italian armored convoy in the vicinity of the crash site. They had captured eight or nine Americans. Five perished and were buried by the Italians. But investigation ruled this out. Montgomery's Eighth Army had swept the desert clear of Italian and German forces by January of 1943—three months before the *Lady Be Good* crashed.

So, with no trace of the missing crew, the ghost bomber took on a mantle of suspense and mystery.

At Wheelus, plans were laid for a detailed air and ground search. A light Army L-19 preceded an Air Force C-47 to the scene. The party included the two mortuary men, Captain Fuller and Wesley Neep, and Captain J.M. Paule, an Air Force flight surgeon and expert on desert survival. Seven months had elapsed since the oil company pilots had found the bomber. Everything was as their later ground party described it. It had remained in an unbelievably good state of preservation.

The military men probed into the bomber's fuselage and noted two important items missing: life preservers and the hand-cranked Gibson Girl emergency radio. The plane's controls, they also noted, were not on autopilot.

The search party made camp and stayed two days. They took pictures, made sketches, and inspected the area for clues. During this time, the long-range radio in their C-47 failed. They discovered that the bomber had the same model. Curious, they removed it and installed it in the cargo plane. It worked. Radio failure on the *Lady Be Good* was not the reason it had strayed. The plane's two magnetic compasses and the radio-compass automatic direction finder also operated perfectly.

The missing parachutes clearly showed that the crewmen had bailed out. But where? Twenty miles away? Thirty? A hundred?

The bomber's nose pointed east. Were they flying in this direction when they abandoned it? Or were they flying south? Low flights in all directions around the plane revealed nothing. When they returned to Wheelus, the search party brought back enough questions to keep the world guessing as to the fate of the missing crew.

The mortuary men decided the only way to get the answers was to organize a full-scale ground sweep. C-47s airlifted supplies and men, Libyan natives were enlisted, and special ground vehicles were assembled for the largest search ever attempted in the Sahara. The Army furnished light aircraft, and the expedition, under Captain Fuller, pushed off in July. Working on the assumption the men had bailed out north of the site, the searchers fanned out on a wide front and moved in that direction. At eight miles they found heavy tracks of Italian military vehicles heading north-northwest. They reasoned the tracks must have been there when the plane crashed. Had the *Lady's* men found them, too? Two miles farther along the trail they had the answer.

"Over here!" one of the searchers called. They found a pair of aircrew high-altitude boots weighed down with stones. The toes pointed northward in a V. Their elation faded as they wondered how many of the crew this lone pair of boots represented. They still had no way of knowing whether or not the crew assembled after it bailed out.

They pressed on. The scorching afternoon sun grew hotter. The temperature climbed to 130 degrees. Here, a man's skin dries hard, sand dust penetrates the hair, clothing, and eyes. Surely the men of the *Lady Be Good* could not have survived long with their limited water supply.

The following morning they found the first of eight parachute markers—strips of cloth arranged in another V pointing along the trail. Someone had remembered their survival training. A few more miles along the trail six faded Mae West life preservers were discovered. All had their CO_2 inflation cartridges punctured. This told the searchers the crew had bailed out at night and that they had thought they were over water. Now parachute markers were found at regular intervals. Captain Paule was certain they would discover the bodies soon. He remarked, "without water, they couldn't survive more than a day. With all the water they could carry, two days would be the absolute limit. They weren't riding either, they were walking." The trek was a veritable walk in hell all right, and no one in the party cared to dispute the captain's opinion. But the officer's estimate of the missing crew's endurance later proved to be in error.

Twenty-eight miles up the trail the motorized convoy found British tracks crossing the Italian ones. They came from the north-northeast and were identified as part of a huge British force that had joined the Free French forces in 1942 to destroy the Italian garrison at El Gezira, 140 miles southwest. Now the search party was faced with deciding which trail the crewmen had taken. They pitched camp for the night and as they did, one of the men found another parachute marker a quarter of a mile up the Italian trail. Their question was answered for the moment at least.

The next day, the fifth, sixth, and seventh parachute markers were found. Then nothing. This had to be it, the searchers reasoned. The land vehicles spread out in a circular search pattern. One truck followed the Italian trail for another twenty miles until it disappeared in the dreaded Sand Sea of Calanscio, a region of shifting sand dunes that rise as high as 700 feet.

Captain Fuller decided to move the base camp forty-five miles due north of the *Lady Be Good,* between the Italian and British trails. He intended to search the entire northern part of the plateau. Then, one of the drivers found an eighth marker beside the British trail, pointing north-northeast. To the searchers, this could only mean the crew had split up after all, and would be found in two places.

The desert vehicles were equipped with sun compasses mounted on their hoods. This is the only reliable way to remain oriented in a land devoid of landmarks. As one truck held a straight course, another would follow at a faster speed, zigzagging across its path. Over 1,000 square miles were covered and not one other scrap of evidence was found. Doubt began to creep into the men's tired minds. They began to suspect the bodies would never be found in the northern part of the plateau.

Thus far, all the search efforts resulted only in uncovering a preview of what must have been the fate of the missing men. An Arab nomad and his five camels were found where they had perished years earlier. The bodies were mummified, skin stretched taut over their skeletons. When they fell, the moisture in their bodies evaporated quickly, and with bacteria unable to survive in the arid, sterile desert, the remains petrified. The one-man caravan lay as it fell, undisturbed by the desert winds. Equipment found nearby indicated the man and his beasts died before 1900.

At this state of the operation, General Spicer took a hand in the search. He flew to the base camp in late July and was briefed on the progress. He inspected the markers, checked maps, and conferred in detail with Fuller and Alexander Karadzic, the desert expert and its contractor of the vehicles. General Spicer decided to push for an all-out effort. Headquarters sent a C-130 to airlift Army helicopters to the site. It arrived with its cargo in mid-August. The whirlybirds penetrated twenty miles into the Sand Sea but found nothing. Next, RB-66s, jet reconnaissance planes, took strip photographs of the plateau and fringes of the Sand Sea. Nothing new was discovered.

Tired and disappointed, Fuller and Karadzic finally called off the search. The desert refused to give up the men after a demanding and expensive three-month search that covered over 5,500 square miles. In approving the decision, General Spicer said, "Too many factors remain unknown—now perhaps forever—to make a definite conclusion." It was certain that the missing crew lay somewhere in the great Sand Sea and that only by an improbable coincidence would they ever be found. Before the search party withdrew, they returned to the *Lady Be Good* and painted markings on her to brand the plane as a derelict of the desert—a desert that had added a few more bodies to the thousands it already claimed.

Silence settled once again over one of the most puzzling air mysteries of World War II since attention had become focused on the *Lady Be Good's* last flight and how it overshot its home base by 426 miles.

In March 1943, Lieutenant Hatton and his crew had ferried a brand-new B-24D to Libya, but when they landed at Soluch, the 514th was short of planes. Their bomber was turned over to combat veterans and for nine days they were a spare crew without a ship. On April 4, things changed. The crew of another B-24, the *Lady Be Good*, was in Malta with engine trouble on a spare plane they had been forced to fly temporarily. They left their plane behind for the ground crews to check over; now, with inspections completed, the *Lady Be Good* was ready to go. It was assigned on a temporary basis to Hatton's crew for a twenty-five plane unescorted high-altitude mission that afternoon. The target was to be the marshaling yard and harbor at Naples. Two sections were to hit the target at sunset, scatter, and return home singly to elude enemy fighters. A hundred and six B-17s from Algeria were scheduled to strike the port city earlier in the afternoon.

The bombers were divided into two sections. Section A had twelve planes; Section B, which included the *Lady Be Good*, had thirteen. When Section A took off, they

73

blew so much sand and dust behind them that the waiting planes of Section B took some of it into their air filters and intakes. The result was felt en route as Section B lost plane after plane due to engine failure, until finally, at 7:45, just five minutes out of Naples, only four planes remained in formation. The *Lady Be Good* moved up to lead position and following it were Lieutenants Worley, Swarner, and Gluck. Because of their delayed takeoff, these four trailed late all the way, and now, still several miles from Naples, the sun set. Section A had already blasted the target, but Hatton, knowing they would not be able to see the target in the darkness, canceled out. He led the remaining planes south, where they scattered according to instructions, dropped their bombs, and headed back for Soluch.

Then, except for three seemingly unrelated and insignificant reports, the *Lady Be Good* flew into history and was not seen again for sixteen years.

The next morning the *Lady Be Good* was the only one of the twenty-five planes unaccounted for. Lieutenant Worley remarked that Hatton's "64" had been with them until they turned back over Sorrento at sunset. The other pilots of Section B agreed. No doubt the plane had ditched in the Mediterranean, out of fuel. Then, one pilot, Lieutenant Ralph Grace, mentioned that he heard a B-24 pass directly over Soluch, headed southeast, sometime *before* midnight and *after* all the planes had returned from the raid. No one paid much attention to his comment.

They should have, for another pilot recalled that Hatton broke radio silence to get an emergency bearing from nearby Benina RDF Station. Had they checked the time of the call, simple logic would have told them where to send the search planes that needlessly combed the Mediterranean for the missing bomber.

The tragic fact was this: Hatton had called for an *inbound* bearing *after*—not before Lieutenant Grace had heard the B-24 pass over the airfield. It was at 12:12, to be exact. The Benina operator, assuming that the bomber must be somewhere north and heading toward them, turned his loop accordingly. He got an aural null as Hatton counted over the radio and replied to the pilot: "Your bearing three-three-zero magnetic from the station. Repeat. Bearing three-three-zero. Over and out." Actually, the *Lady Be Good* had already passed the station and was

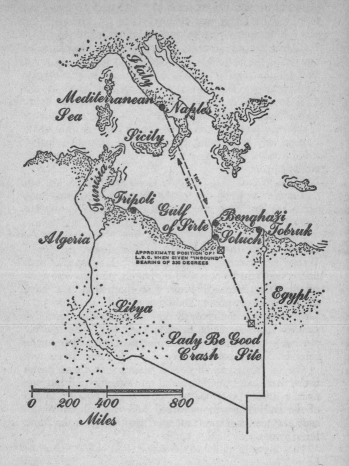

Italy

Mediterranean
Sea

Naples

Sicily

Tripoli

Gulf
of Sirte

Benghazi

Soluch

Tobruk

Algeria

Tunisia

APPROXIMATE POSITION OF
L.B.G. WHEN GIVEN "INBOUND"
BEARING OF 330 DEGREES

Egypt

Libya

Lady Be Good
Crash Site

0   200   400   800
Miles

The Lady Be Good *mistakenly received an "inbound" bearing after it passed over its home base at Soluch.*

reading on the *back* side of the Benina loop. South. Its bearing was actually reading in the opposite direction, 150 degrees, and by now the plane was well into the desert. If Sergeant LaMotte had simply tuned in their Automatic Directional Finder on Benina, the ambiguity error would have immediately become apparent and left no doubt of the *Lady Be Good*'s position with respect to the station. But he did not, and with the entire North African coast blacked out, the only way for the crew to spot the coastline on that moonless night was by the thin, light line of breakers against the beach. Somehow they all missed it. With no way of knowing the wind direction and velocity, and no sign of land beneath them, they had no choice but to hold course.

By one o'clock the *Lady Be Good* was 225 miles into the Libyan Desert. A few of the crewmen grew suspicious that something was wrong. Hatton dropped lower. He knew they had had a tail wind up to Naples and would probably have a head wind back, but it was taking too long to reach the coast. He peered downward for a glimpse of something recognizable, but there was nothing. Benina had said he was 330 outbound, and he was making good the reciprocal bearing so they would not have anything to worry about. They droned on.

The fuel ran dangerously low after another forty-five minutes. LaMotte made an emergency call to Benina. No reply. A few minutes later the nine men stepped from the plane into the inky night sky. Two of them, Toner and Ripslinger, carried small pocket diaries. For almost seven minutes the Liberator lumbered onward, then all but one of its engines sputtered into silence. The bomber glided drunkenly downward, pancaked into the Libyan wasteland, careened sideways, snapped its fuselage in half and slid to a stop.

Not a living thing heard the sound.

On February 11, 1960, six months after the Army-Air Force team called off its search, a desert-supply pilot flew provisions to a campsite of the British Petroleum Company Limited, successor to the 1959 D'Arcy Exploration Company. He landed at Failing Cap, seventy-five miles north-northwest of the desert derelict. Before he took off for the return flight to Tripoli, the man in charge asked him to relay a message to Wheelus Air Force Base. His men had found five bodies of the bomber crew in the same area searched by the military team the previous summer and fall. A C-47 arrived the next day and the oil men led the party, which included a chaplain, to the final encampment of Hayes, Hatton, LaMotte, Adams, and Toner. They were lying close together amid their useless equipment; parachute cloth, jackets, shoes, canteens, and flashlights. The silk "escape maps" were found, which had they included another 120 miles south, might have shown the men to Blockhouse Rock and the nearest oasis at El Gezira. A sunglasses case with "Dp Hayes" imprinted on it left no doubt as to one man's identity. They had walked sixty-five miles in eight scorching days with little food and almost no water, to die.

The Air Force men reverently covered each body with an American flag, and the small group stood bareheaded in the sun as the chaplain offered a prayer for the spirits of the long-dead fliers and for their yet-to-be-discovered comrades.

Toner's diary, found nearby, attested to the unbelievable week in the desert Hades and told of other members of the party who had pushed ahead. His brief entry for Friday, April 9, reads:

Shelley, Rip, Moore separate and try to go for help, rest of us all very weak, eyes bad. Not any travel, all want to die, still very little water, nites are about 35 degrees, good N wind, no shelter, 1 parachute left.

Huddled with the other four, Toner lived to make three more entries while the others struggled on, through the sand dunes, slipping and falling, knee-deep in the soft dust, inching their way painfully forward, hoping that just over the next dune would be water. The half canteen they bailed out with was empty. Each man was rationed to a capful a day.

Again, a massive air-ground search got under way. The helicopters, C-130s and RB-66s were recalled for "Operation Climax" but failed to turn up anything. Meanwhile the British Petroleum Company men worked doggedly on. As the military searchers were again about to call off operations, the geologists found Ripslinger and Shelley, an

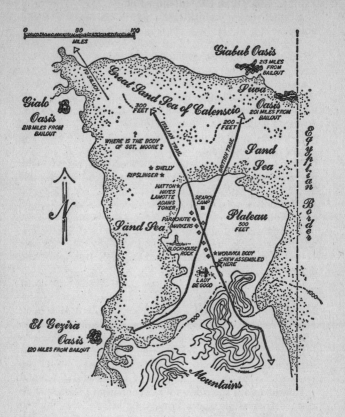

The crash site of the Lady Be Good, *showing the positions of the bodies of the crew and the distances of the oases from the wrecked plane.*

unbelievable twenty-one and twenty-seven miles from where they found the first five. Shelley had walked ninety agonizing miles from the bail-out point.

The final entry in Ripslinger's diary was marked Palm Sunday.

Palm Sun. Still struggling to get out of the dunes and find water.

The stamina of the men was, without a doubt, far beyond the expectations of survival experts. Somehow they must have drawn upon some source of power to keep going as long as they did. Their endurance gave survival schools much to ponder.

Army and Air Force personnel now surmised that the mystery marker on the British trail must have been placed there by John Woravka. They were certain his body, as well as Moore's, would be found in the great Sand Sea.

After seventeen-and-a-half years, the seven American airmen went home with military escort for a long-delayed military funeral. When the last flier was laid to rest, the file was closed again on the last flight of the *Lady Be Good*.

Stubbornly, the file refused to remain closed. In August 1959, the desert gave up another part of the puzzle. Another group of the British Petroleum Company, working near the bomber, solved one mystery and created another. They found Woravka's body twelve miles north-northeast, in full view, where it had lain those many years. It was dressed in flying suit, Mae West life jacket, and parachute harness. The parachute canopy appeared to have only partially opened. John Woravka died quickly and mercifully. His parachute either fouled, or he had delayed too long in pulling the D ring and death spared him the ordeal of his fellow crewmen. A canteen three quarters full of water was found with him. It was still potable and free from bacteria.

A mile south of the body, Air Force men found a stack of parachute harnesses and burned-out signal flares. Here the *Lady's* men assembled and tried to contact Woravka. It was now clear that the Liberator's bombardier was not the man who made the lone marker on the British trail.

Who then, did? Sergeant Moore? Hardly. He would have had to backtrack the twenty-six miles he came; yet, as the only member of the crew not found, his fate is still an enigma. Perhaps the oil hunters, whose wanderings repeatedly uncovered what the combined and organized efforts of two military services could not, will discover his body, too.

If there was ever cause to brand a plane as jinxed, the *Lady Be Good* was it. It left a heartbreaking and costly trail. Things were going well for the 376th before the bomber joined up. When the *Lady Be Good* came along, it aborted its first mission and ended up with an escort of only three of the thirteen planes it started with. Eight days later its crew was dead on the Sahara; eighteen days after that Lieutenant Swarner was killed and two months later Lieutenant Worley and his crew were missing in action. They were never found. The sole surviving plane commander among the four who turned south over Sorrento is Lieutenant Gluck.

Later, in August of 1943, the 376th led 175 planes in the Ploesti oil-field raid, the most disastrous single American air strike of World War II. The lead plane plunged into the Mediterranean after takeoff, killing the crew. Twelve more aborted for various mechanical reasons before they reached the target. Forty-one B-24s were lost over the target, thirteen more on the way home, and 440 airmen were killed or listed as missing.

The jinx of the *Lady Be Good* was far-reaching. Its radio was installed in the first C-47 to land at the desert crash site. Less than a month later, this plane was caught in the grip of a fierce *ghibli* and forced to ditch in the Mediterranean. One propeller sheared off on impact with the water, whirled into the cockpit, and killed the pilot.

A single-engine Army Otter followed the ill luck of the Air Force cargo plane. While at the crash site of the B-24 earlier, its crewmen salvaged the *Lady Be Good*'s armrests and installed them in their plane. Eight months later this plane, with ten aboard, flew into another *ghibli* and disappeared. No survivors were ever found, but later, scraps of wreckage drifted onto the Mediterranean shore. Among the debris was the *Lady*'s armrests.

Some mysteries persist, of course. What happened to the *Lady*'s emergency transmitter? Who placed the eighth marker—the one pointing north-northeast—on the British trail? Where is Sergeant Moore?

Perhaps, in the final analysis, petroleum-company scientists will provide the answer. The odds against improbable coincidence furnishing the answers diminishes every day. Oil men will continue to crisscross the desert wastes and if Sergeant Moore perished as did the others, eventually his body will be found.

PART TWO

TRAILBLAZERS

AND ADVENTURERS

CHAPTER 6

Where Is Salomon Andrée?

This happened years before there were such things as aeroplanes. Years before the Wrights made their first run, skip, and jump from the slopes of Kitty Hawk in their flimsy gliders. Nevertheless, it was a perplexing air mystery—aviation's first. It's the story of three daring balloonists who vanished into the Arctic night. The greater part of the mystery, from its beginning in July of 1897, lasted for thirty-three years and left behind some questions.

Salomon Auguste Andrée was a Swedish engineer and scientific aeronaut. At forty-three, he dedicated his life to two things: the unexplored polar regions and ballooning. With ten years of Arctic experience he was certain he knew its winds and ways. He staunchly believed that from Dansk Gatt in northwest Spitsbergen he could pilot a balloon expedition across the North Pole to a mainland on the other side. Such a fantastic proposal in the late 1800s prompted the newspapers of the day to picture the tall, distinguished man as a daredevil, but polar explorers and fellow scientists knew Andrée better. He was simply a determined man with a strong personality and a stable temperament.

In 1876, twenty years before his departure into the barren ice fields, Andrée came to America with three dollars to his name and a limited knowledge of English. The young man wanted to meet the world's foremost aeronaut, John Wise, whose writings he knew by heart. He wangled a porter's job at the Philadelphia World Exposition where the sixty-eight-year-old Wise was to make a tethered ascent. Shouldering through the crowd, Andrée managed to lend a hand in running the ropes out and hauling them in for the landing. When the exhibition was over, he introduced himself and begged Wise to give him balloon lessons. Wise looked the young engineer over carefully and was impressed with Andrée's sincerity. Wise nodded. Yes, he would help; he offered his knowledge and the hospitality of his home as a study.

The old man and the young man worked together for

many weeks. Wise taught Andrée how to select balloon cloth, how to design an aerostat, apply varnish, and make a gas generator. He suspected Andrée had some great project, some burning ambition in mind, and he finally asked the Swede point-blank one day: "Why are you really so interested in balloon flying, Salomon? What do you plan to do with your knowledge?"

Andrée replied without hesitation, "I'm going to reach the North Pole in a balloon!"

Wise could scarcely believe his ears. Andrée continued. "Ships have failed, sleds have failed. The best of men—Nansen and Abruzzi—have failed. How else but by balloon can man reach there?"

"But the weather! The winds!" Wise protested. "No one knows them!"

"*I* will know them," Andrée replied confidently. "I'll study them. And when I come back, I'll tell the world what's up there—whether there's land, or people, or just a great frozen sea."

Back in Sweden, Andrée kept working toward his goal. In 1882, the First International Polar Year, he joined Dr. Nils Ekholm in setting up bases on polar tracts. He collected weather data, made exhaustive notes on wind directions and velocities, and tried to learn as much as possible about the mysterious polar regions. But when he tried to raise money for aeronautical research (which meant flying balloons in Arctic weather), the response was as cold as a polar midnight. Finally, the Lais Hierto Scientific Foundation gave him funds to build a small balloon. Within a year, Andrée crammed as much flying experience under his belt as most aeronauts gained in ten. Twice he was marooned in the Baltic Sea after being wafted over wasteland and open sea at the wind's will. Each time he was rescued by a passing fishing boat.

In 1895, Salomon Andrée spoke before the Swedish Academy of Science to present his proposal on reaching the North Pole by balloon. With confident authority he reeled off, one by one, precise facts of the venture. Specifically, he would need an aerostat of 6,600 pounds lift with a gas volume of 212,000 cubic feet, three men, scientific instruments, a four-months' supply of food and equipment for safety. An average south wind of only sixteen miles an hour from Spitsbergen would carry them in the vicinity of the Pole in two days. With more favorable winds, another four days would put them on land off the Bering Strait. He went on to explain how the balloon he had developed would not have to be at the mercy of the winds. He had already tested it successfully in earlier flights. Two adjustable sails running up each side of the gas bag from the basket would be used with draglines that slipped over the surface of the ice or water. Andrée discovered that the friction of the lines against the surface would cause enough relative motion between the wind and balloon to control the direction of flight as much as forty degrees.

To Andrée's complete amazement, the academy endorsed his plan. They decided it wasn't as wild an idea as they had imagined earlier. Now, Andrée worked furiously to raise money for the expedition. He lectured and wrote articles. It wasn't enough. Then, fortune smiled as Alfred Nobel contributed half of the $36,000 needed, and King Oscar II presented the remainder. Andrée was on his way. He built his balloon and stocked equipment.

Of the many volunteers for the polar flight, only the qualifications of twenty-four-year-old Nils Strindberg satisfied Andrée. A good photographer and cook, Strindberg was equally talented as an athlete. Andrée also wanted Nils Ekholm, with whom he had worked earlier, as the third member of the party, but the professor was hesitant. He was leery of balloons and flimsy-looking rigging, but finally, after two months of indecision, he said yes.

The North Pole Expedition ship *Virgo* left Sweden in June of 1896 and arrived at Danes Island three weeks later. A fresh snow had buried the building material for the balloon shed and caused a three-weeks' delay. Then a dense fog moved in. It wasn't until the end of July that the gas generator could be set up for discharge, and the balloon, named the *Eagle*, finally stood, inflated and ready, in its crude wooden shed. Sometime before August 20, the Polar Expedition would have to lift off, because then the *Virgo* would have to sail for home to await the passing of winter.

Andrée supervised the loading of the balloon basket. There were three sleds, a canvas boat, guns, ammunition, camera equipment, scientific gear, and food. There was a new Primus stove, designed for cooking, lighting, and melting snow for water, three dozen messenger pigeons and thirteen wooden keg buoys to be dropped on the ice ocean with records of the expedition's progress.

Now, the trio scanned the skies impatiently. They needed the right wind. Several times a stiff south breeze picked up and the men hurried to the balloon basket. Each time the wind died and reversed itself. Ekholm became increasingly nervous with each false start. Andrée, watching him, knew the professor had serious reservations about the flight. Then, one day in early August, Ekholm told them to come with him to the balloon shed. Inside, he led them in silence to the upper scaffolding. From over the aerostat's great dome the professor pulled aside a fabric strip that covered a stitched seam. They all heard it; hydrogen gas was hissing out. A leak. Andrée returned to his quarters on shipboard to mull over the depressing state of affairs. He decided there was little hope of making repairs and getting the right wind before the 20th, so on the 13th he released eight of his pigeons with this message:

From Andrée's Polar Expedition
Danes Island
August 13, 1896
No South Wind. Returning to Sweden.

ANDREE

Andrée identified his homecoming with personal failure, but underestimated the enthusiasm he had sparked in the polar venture. The Swedish government gave him more money and the use of a gunboat to take another expedition to the jumping-off place. Alfred Nobel offered to finance a new balloon, but Andrée politely refused. This one, he said, would be airworthy with repairs.

Nils Ekholm withdrew. Andrée felt it was just as well; Ekholm was nervous and high strung. His replacement was Knut Fraenkel, a young civil engineer who was more than eager to see the unexplored Arctic from a balloon gondola.

In May of 1897, the men were back on Danes Island with their work party. By June, their aerostat had been inflated and tested. Again it was loaded. And again the false winds came and died, until, on July 11, a brisk galelike blow picked up from the south and within a half hour formed whitecaps in the bay. Andrée watched the waters churn under the wind, then he left the gunboat and went ashore to order the balloon shed demolished. As all but the south wall fell, he walked around the *Eagle* for a final inspection. Strindberg hurriedly took pictures. He handed the exposed plates to the gunboat's captain along with a hastily scribbled letter to his fiancée. The ground crew cut loose several ballast bags from the basket and the huge bag rose a foot off the ice, kept in check now by only three ground lines.

There was a moment of hushed silence. It was time. Andrée looked about him at the men who had shared the hopes and labors of his twenty-year-old dream. Then, impulsively, Andrée, Strindberg, and Fraenkel embraced the workmen. They all wept unashamedly. Andrée pulled away, hoisted himself to the basket, and called, "Strindberg! Fraenkel! Let's go!" As the two men clambered aboard, Andrée called out to the ground crew, "One, two, three, cut!" and three knives slashed down in unison to sever the restraining lines. The *Eagle* trembled for a moment, then moved heavily upward. Its fabric steering wings billowed out as it pointed northward across the bay. Shouts and cheers spurred the balloonist on, but halfway to the mountains on the other side the *Eagle* narrowly averted disaster. It faltered and dipped toward the icy water. Observers at the camp saw ballast hurriedly cut free, but still the balloon fell. It touched the water, bounced back into the air, and struggled for lift. Slowly it rose again.

Alexis Machuron, a member of the base party, stood with others watching the aerostat grow smaller. He described the last sight of the *Eagle* this way:

> The balloon travels on, maintained at the same altitude by the guide-ropes. In the neighborhood of the hills there is an upward current of air; the balloon will follow this . . .
>
> We see it clear the top of the hill, and stand out clearly for a few minutes against the blue sky, and then slowly disappear from our view behind the hill.
>
> Scattered along the shore, we stand motionless, with hearts full, and anxious eyes, gazing at the silent horizon.
>
> For one moment then, between two hills, we perceive a grey speck over the sea, very, very far away, and then it finally disappears.

The way to the Pole is clear, no more obstacles to encounter; the sea, the ice field, and the Unknown!

We look at one another for a moment, stupefied. Instinctively we draw together without saying a word. There is nothing, nothing whatever in the distance to tell us where our friends are; they are now shrouded in mystery.

When word reached Europe that Andrée's expedition was aloft at last and headed for the Pole, the news was flashed to the northernmost telegraph outposts of every country and then, more slowly, to the mining, fishing, and trading posts. Eventually, word reached the fur country, the farthest populated reaches of Arctic Siberia, Canada, Greenland, and Alaska. As the world grew hungry for news, strange things began to happen in the northern reaches. After several days, vague reports claiming to be sightings of the polar balloon drifted into news services from all over the world's northern wastelands. In a sense it was natural and expected, for Swedish authorities had made certain that whites and natives in the extreme outposts were informed of the balloon's departure and were cautioned to be on the lookout.

On July 13, the bark *Ansgar* was plowing east, two days out of North Cape, Norway, and 800 miles south of Andrée's takeoff point, when its crew sighted a "downed balloon." When the ship reached Denmark in early August, the crew said they were certain it was Andrée's balloon. They gave the details to the newspapers. It was black in color and "some of the gas had leaked out." They said it was "two fathoms above the waterline and covered with a net."

It was not Andrée's balloon; it was later proved to have been a dead whale.

On July 17, a woman in a small Swedish town, "whose truthfulness was beyond question," had gone to her window to pull the shade, when she saw what she took to be a balloon with drag ropes and a net. She said one man was in the gondola.

A dispatch from Stavanger, Norway, dated August 13, reported that the crew of the steamer *Kong Halfdan*, off Norway between Haugesund and Ryvarden, had sighted a "big balloon." It passed so close to the ship that "its drag ropes were seen."

The scientific world waited as the months slipped past, waited and wondered. Where was Salomon Andrée?

Searchers began, sparked by an item that appeared in a Swedish newspaper in May of 1898.

ANDRÉE'S BALLOON FOUND IN EAST SIBERI-AN FOREST

Andrée's balloon has been reported found in a forest in eastern Siberia. The Arctic explorer with two companions ascended near Spitsbergen in July 1897, in an attempt to reach the Pole. It was the last seen of them. The Swedish government has ordered an investigation of the report.

It was possible that the *Eagle* could have drifted into central Arctic Siberia; so, in the summer of 1898, the J. Stadling expedition journeyed overland from Stockholm to the Venisei River well north of the Arctic Circle. It contributed nothing to the solution of Andrée's whereabouts. At the same time, Walter Wellman was leading an expedition to the Franz Joseph Islands. He was convinced that Andrée could have made Cape Flora, where a store of provisions had been left by an earlier party. But Wellman found no sign of the missing men and abandoned all hope of finding them alive. In the February 1899 issue of *Century Magazine*, he wrote with an unmistakable air of finality: "Poor Andrée! Poor, brave, dead Andrée!"

A. G. Nathorst, the famed Swedish polar explorer, set to work to interest the Swedish government in a search of Northeast Greenland. In the spring of 1899 he was off, riding a wave of popular sentiment and government sympathy for the lost aeronauts. In the far-northern regions he talked with travelers who had seen "strange pigeons" flying about (Andrée's messenger pigeons?), and one man reported that natives had killed and eaten a bird unfamiliar to them, and lost a message that had been fastened to it.

Between Northeast Land in Spitsbergen and Victoria Land lies White Island, which Nathorst twice visited during this time. He landed on the north and south shores, said that Andrée's balloon had "probably drifted close to this place," and then became absorbed in studying the island's plants and moss.

In 1910, there was one last flurry of interest before Andrée's disappearance faded from the public mind. In that year a Canadian newspaper carried the account of one William Irvine, a seventy-one-year-old trapper who reputedly was told by Eskimos in the Upper Hudson Bay that years earlier, Andrée's expedition had landed there. There was a gunfight and all had been killed by the natives. Irvine concluded by saying: "They'd be hard to find now."

All the stories seemed to have this one thing in common: they could not be proved.

Well then, where was Andrée's lost expedition? Surely, explorers pondered, there must be some valid record, some trace of their fate. But, except for the finding of two message buoys and a single pigeon, the world last saw Andrée on that gray, leaden day when he faded from view over the mists of Virgo Bay. Four days after the balloon's departure, the Norwegian sealer *Alken* was a hundred miles north of the takeoff point. A pigeon alighted on the rigging, carrying a message from Andrée. It read:

From Andrée's Polar Expedition to *Aftonbladet*, Stockholm.

July 13
12:30 Midday. Latitude 82 degrees 2' Long. 15 degrees 5 E. Good speed E. All well on board. This is the third pigeon post.

ANDREE

Of the thirty-six birds carried by the balloon, this was the only one ever accounted for. Of the thirteen message buoys, only two were found. One was picked up on the north coast of Iceland in May 1899. It had been thrown out a few hours after takeoff. The other buoy was found in August of 1900, on the coast of Norway. It had been dropped before the other. Its message read:

From Andrée's Polar Expedition
July 11, 1897; 10:00 G.M.T.
   Buoy No. 4, the first thrown out.
   Our journey has hitherto gone well. We are moving on at a height of 830 feet in direction which at first was N. 10 degreees E declination. Four carrier pigeons were sent off at 5H40 P.M. Greenwich

time. They flew westerly. We are now in over the ice, which is much broken up in all directions. Weather magnificent. In the best of humors.

ANDRÉE STRINDBERG FRAENKEL

Above clouds since 7:45 G.M.T.

Thirty years passed after this message was found. Andrée's whereabouts now became part of Arctic legend. Seamen told and retold the tale in every ship's forecastle. Then, in August of 1930, the Andrée mystery was suddenly revived. It centered, strangely, on White Island, which in itself was always a rather mysterious place. Barren, windswept, and desolate, the small island in the Arctic Ocean is strewn with rocks and granite, its only vegetation nonflowering plants.

The *Bratvaag*, a Norwegian sealer captained by Pedar Eliassen, plied its way through the floating icebergs that surrounded the elliptical-shaped island thirty-five miles east of Spitsbergen. On this voyage the ship's crew was host to geologist Dr. Gunnar Horn of the Norwegian Spitsbergen Polar Sea Research Institution. When walruses were sighted on shore, the ship anchored and landed two whaling boats. One crew went to hunt animals while the other searched for fresh water. A new snow had fallen, but here and there the rocky terrain showed through the white blanket. On a slope a hundred yards from the harbor, two sailors found a small brook and followed it inland. After a short trek they paused to rest and drink. As one of the men bent over the clear water, the dull glint of a metallic object caught his eye. It was half-buried among the rocks on the other side of the stream. He pulled it loose and wiped it clean. It was an aluminum pot lid, a strange thing to find there.

The men looked around carefully and found a canvas boat under a melting mound of ice.

Dr. Horn and Captain Eliassen were on shore when the sailors returned, breathless, to tell of their find. As soon as Eliassen saw the aluminum lid he exclaimed simply. "Andréel"

Back at the canvas boat the landing party scraped the ice and snow aside. They uncovered a brass boat hook of the late 1800s and an ammunition box marked: ANDRÉE'S POLAR EXPEDITION, 1896. There was no longer any doubt that thirty-three years ago, long before many of the

Bratvaag's crew were born, Andrée, Strindberg, and Fraenkel had sought safety on White Island.

Was this merely part of their abandoned equipment? Had the explorers pushed on to the peaks of Northeast Land, which they must have seen in the distance? Captain Eliassen answered the question a short time later when he discovered the first body. It lay "leaning against the slightly sloping wall of rock" above the canvas boat. The skull and upper torso were missing, having been, presumably, carried off by bears. The skeleton's lower ribs protruded through a rotted jersey jacket, inside of which was sewn the letter A. That this was the remains of Salomon Andrée was confirmed when both a large and a small diary were taken from the inside of the jacket. Although the record books were frozen solid, with careful handling they later told in Andrée's own words the details of the party's amazing adventure.

Lying near the bones was a rifle, another box of ammunition, eating utensils, and a package of photographic plates. Twelve of these were developed successfully, having been taken by Strindberg three decades earlier. The Primus stove was found half filled with fuel oil. Dr. Horn noticed the air valve was closed. He pumped up the apparatus, opened the valve, and lighted the fine spray. It worked perfectly. Perhaps, as Dr. Horn was to surmise later, it may have worked too well.

Beside Andrée's body was a smooth place free of rocks. Here were found most of the party's supplies, another sled, a sleeping bag, matches, utensils, medicines, and Fraenkel's pocketbook. This was the site of their tent.

A hundred feet to the north, a sailor discovered another body. It was wedged between two large boulders, covered with stones arranged in a burial cairn as protection against animals. Carefully, the men separated the bones from the rubble. On the remnants of the skeleton's jacket were the faded initials *N. S.*, and a gold locket was found with the still-discernible photograph of a girl. This, then, was Nils Strindberg.

Within the hour the skies churned up a threatening storm. At this time of year the weather could change quickly, so Eliassen ordered the crew to gather their belongings and return to the ship. By the time they reached their beached boats, the swelling waves were pounding the shoreline. Soon afterward the *Bratvaag* set out for home and the news was radioed for relay around the world: "Andrée's Expedition found on White Island."

Newspapermen thronged to Skjerno, a small village on Norway's north coast, where the *Bratvaag* would make port. Foremost in their minds was the question: "What happened to Fraenkel?" Had he drowned? Was he carried off by bears? Maybe he fell from the balloon. Andrée's diaries would surely give some clue, but it would be weeks before they would be ready for deciphering. Swedish journalist Knut Stubbendorf couldn't wait. Even before the *Bratvaag* landed, he set off in the sealer *Isabjorn* for Andrée's camp, in the very face of the coming winter. Fortunately the elements smiled on him, for the snow had melted even more than when Horn and Eliassen were there and several things they'd overlooked were now laid bare in the bright sunlight. He found a third sled, a human backbone, thighbone, and pelvis. Whose was it? Certainly not Andrée's nor Strindberg's. Stubbendorf suspected that Fraenkel didn't perish before the party reached White Island. He searched around the site carefully and found Strindberg's logbooks and almanac. There was more equipment; the remains of game they had killed.

The journalist paid close attention to the cleared space where the tent had been, and nearby he found something else the *Bratvaag*'s crew overlooked in their haste—a human skull. It later proved to be Andrée's. He found fabric from the *Eagle* and, in the lee of the ledge on which Andrée's remains were first found, he discovered what appeared to be a stack of thawing reindeer hides. Slowly, one by one, he peeled them back. Underneath was the missing part of the puzzle, the remains of Knut Fraenkel, except for the backbone, thighbone, and pelvis.

By the time Stubbendorf returned to Sweden, Andrée's notebooks were being carefully analyzed and transcribed. They had survived the thirty-three winters remarkably well. Strindberg's notes were added to round out the story of their ordeal, complete except for the last few days.

On the afternoon of their takeoff from Dane's Island, they made a brief entry and recorded the loss of their draglines. They made new ones that proved to be too light and too short. So, from the beginning, the *Eagle* was without much of its steering ability. Nevertheless, the men were in high spirits that first afternoon aloft. They drank ale, watched the passing panorama below, and spliced some ropes. Strindberg took some pictures before a light fog closed in during the late afternoon. As it became thicker, Andrée dropped ballast and the balloon rose into clear sky at 2,200 feet. From this height they began to float down slowly, as tiny imperfections in the bag allowed the expanded hydrogen to seep out. They took turns sleeping, made sun observations to find their position, and dropped the second message buoy.

Early the next day Strindberg noted a cloud mass rising ahead of them. They dropped more ballast but the balloon only rose to 1,500 feet, not quite high enough to clear the cloud bank. The aerostat settled slowly into the front and, as the sun's heat was lost, the gas cooled rapidly. In an hour the *Eagle* dropped to within a hundred feet of the frozen sea. More ballast was released before the balloon checked its descent.

At breakfast all three men were scanning the ice fields. The fog broke long enough for Strindberg to take another sun reading. All were elated when he announced they had traveled an incredible 250 miles northeast from Dane's Island. "We'll reach the Pole yet!" Andrée declared confidently, but even as he spoke a fine rain began to fall. It soon froze on the great bag and began to weigh it down. The men emptied the last of their ballast bags and tossed their rope supply overboard. This checked their descent again, but that afternoon a grappling hook was thrown out when their craft started to settle once again. It continued a slow, downward drift. A few hours later, when their basket was only scant yards off the ice, Andrée discarded the polar message buoy (the largest, and the one intended to be dropped at their closest point to the Pole). It didn't help; the basket touched the ice and dragged along. Andrée dropped a heavy tarpaulin over the side and the balloon lifted twenty feet. The men cheered.

By evening, however, the situation fast became critical. Little else remained that they could afford to lose in the way of ballast. The fog continued to freeze on the dome and huge icicles hung from the balloon's perimeter. Again the gondola slapped into the ice. It scraped, bounced, and bumped along the rough frozen surface. Slowly, the great gas bag shrank to a flabby shapeless thing and settled on the frozen pack. Strindberg estimated they'd traveled 115 miles west of their last position.

By noon of the third day the sun expanded the balloon's remaining gas and melted the ice from the bag. They were soon airborne again and as they ate lunch, Andrée freed the homing pigeon that made its way to the *Alken*. About three o'clock in the afternoon, fog again shrouded them, ice reformed, and the gondola resumed its bumping along the frozen ocean. In desperation, Andrée cast a medicine chest overboard. Abruptly, and to their complete amazement, the aerostat floated up to 200 feet. Its canvas sails filled with wind and its makeshift draglines worked as they were designed. With a west wind, they now retraced their course of the day before, then a south wind pushed them northward. But if the intrepid Andrée still had hopes of reaching the Pole, he abandoned them that evening when the balloon sank again to within a few feet of the surface. The fog became thicker, the night colder. Sheet ice alternately formed, cracked, and reformed on the dome. The men dropped two of their draglines without effect. When the third line was snagged in the ice early on the 14th and had to be cut free, they all knew the balloon voyage was over. Reluctantly, Andrée selected a safe stretch of ice and opened the gas valve. The hydrogen hissed from the escape port and the *Eagle*, which had carried them 500 miles in sixty-five hours and thirty-three minutes of flight, slowly settled onto the ice. They were 540 miles short of the Pole.

They planned their next move as they ate lunch on the ice. It was too late in the season for a rescue ship to reach them; next summer would be the earliest. Meanwhile they would have to head for winter quarters at one of the depots Andrée had stocked for just such an emergency as this. The depots were on islands strung southward from Cape Flora to the Franz Joseph group back to Danes Island. The expedition was 300 miles from their departure point but the nearest land depot was only 175 miles away at Ross Island. For some reason, Andrée rejected both Ross and Danes Island and decided to strike out for Cape Flora, 300 miles southeast.

The party was fogbound for a week, during which they loaded their sleds for the long pull. Finally, eleven days after they lifted from Danes Island, they started to pull their sleds across the broken, semifrozen ocean. They soon discovered that the surface was far more treacherous than they had estimated from the air. The summer sun had melted the ice unevenly and there was slush and large open lakes of water. The pack ice, which looked solid enough, crumbled under the weight of a man and sled. Leads of water, shallow and deep, had to be crossed. The morale of the men was high, however, and their health excellent. With adequate clothes for warmth, a stout tent, and waterproof balloon cloth, each man pulled his 450 pounds cheerfully.

Before the first day had passed, they decided it was easier to travel the lakes and leads than to drag their sleds over the rough ice fields. Using ice floes as rafts, they ferried their sleds across the water. When their watches told them it was evening, they raised their tent, ate supper, and slept. As much as possible they lived by hunting bear, sea gull and walrus, to preserve their stored food. In the late evenings, which were still bright with the Arctic sun, Strindberg wrote notes to his sweetheart as Fraenkel checked and rechecked the equipment. Andrée marveled at the colors in the ice and wandered about to collect bits of frozen leaves and plants.

After the fifth day of steady, backbreaking travel, Strindberg announced they had covered only two miles to Cape Flora. While they had been struggling foot by foot southward, pulling and ferrying their cumbersome sleds over the windswept hammocks, the huge drifting ice mass on which they were traveling had drifted them almost as fast northwestward.

Andrée called a council. This situation was serious and highly discouraging. With the Arctic winter night coming on, they were in danger of not reaching a winter quarters at all. They decided to discard some more equipment to lighten the sleds for faster traveling. They cut down on their sleeping and eating time. This helped very little. The drift continued to cancel out their progress. During the first few days of August they actually lost ground on their giant treadmill.

Andrée was forced to make another decision. On the 4th, he announced they would abandon their efforts to reach Cape Flora and head instead for Ross Island. Abruptly, the drift stopped and reversed itself. Within the week they covered more ground than during the earlier two.

When the sun dipped below the horizon for a few minutes on August 31, they knew the Arctic winter was at hand. For a while there would be night and day; then, just night. It would get bitter cold, but now they were hopeful of reaching a safe haven in time.

By early September they had covered 150 miles, but the terrain and drift of the pack was causing their path to run due south, between Ross Island and Cape Flora. Again Andrée changed his plans, this time striking out for Northeast Land in the Spitsbergens, seventy-fives miles southwest.

Their extra efforts to get settled down before the Arctic night could overtake them was now hampered by sickness and an injury. Andrée wrote in his diary: "Fraenkel fell into the water today, and has diarrhea, and Strindberg has a pain in his foot, and I have diarrhea, but we covered a good distance today in any case." They discovered that seal blubber and the fat of bear meat eaten raw was effective in reducing their intestinal disorders.

Now a week-long howling wind upset their plans by pushing their ice island well away from Northeast Land. The fickle floes shifted unpredictably back and forth. They cracked and groaned; the leads became rushing torrents. Two sleds were damaged and the pain in Strindberg's foot worsened until he could barely walk. The men knew what had to be done; they would dig in where they were and pray their floe would reach land somewhere before the ice cap froze solid. They set to work building a foundation for a snow hut and on September 17 sighted a small land mass. It proved to be White Island. At first their floe moved toward it, but when it changed course their spirits sank. They drifted slowly past the island, helpless to change their direction. Fortunately, the currents came to their rescue and the next day they were drawn into the south shore of the rock-strewn haven. By now, however, their snow hut was finished. They felt so secure, so warm and comfortable, so amply stocked with game and birds, that when their chance came to go ashore for the winter, they elected to remain on the pack.

Early in the morning of October 2, fate changed their minds. The low rumblings of the ice pack grew into an ear-shattering roar. The floe trembled and broke as a huge water-filled ravine opened beneath their hut. One wall disappeared into the swirling torrent as water rushed in to soak them. Quickly they assembled their supplies and scrambled for White Island, only a few hours away.

Here Andrée's handwriting is smudged and illegible. Thirty-three years of exposure to the elements did its damage only to these final pages of narrative and left little in the way of information. What happened after the trio reached the shore isn't clear; from the clues at their final campsite we can only surmise what followed.

Even if the notes had been complete, they still would not have revealed how Andrée and Fraenkel died, though possibly how Strindberg did. We know he was buried by the other two, that his foot was injured, and that he probably perished within a week and a half of the party's arrival on the island. Did he catch pneumonia? Did his injury and recurring diarrhea so weaken him that he died? How long did Andrée and Fraenkel live after they buried their comrade under the stone cairn? A day or two at the most. Conditions showed their campsite to be only partly set up, with one sled yet to be unpacked. At this late date in the season Andrée and Fraenkel must have been busy getting settled down for the winter. Death interrupted them.

Certainly they did not freeze to death. They had more than enough clothing, plus an oversize sleeping bag. True, they were lightly clothed when found, but more clothing was within arm's reach. They must have been inside their tent.

Nor did they starve to death. They were on an island abundant with game and fish; they had guns and ammunition. The remains of a bear they shot was a few yards away and their sleds still held a good store of canned and preserved food.

Apparently, Andrée and Fraenkel died together, or at least within a few minutes of one another. They were separated by scant feet, Fraenkel in the "tent area" and Andrée on a ledge. If either had died some time before the other, he would have been buried by the survivor.

In the final analysis, we find that Andrée's favorite toy —his Primus stove—was the probable cause. Sometime after the two had laid Strindberg to rest, they were cooking inside the tent. The temperature outside was not very cold as the winter's first snow fell. The blanket of white that covered the tent also insulated it. As the interior became warmer, Andrée and Fraenkel removed their heavy coats. Probably, during supper, the air grew so warm it was almost stifling. Suddenly, Fraenkel keeled over in a dead faint. Andrée, dazed, slowly realized what was happening, fumbled for the air valve, and turned the stove off. He staggered to his feet and groped his way through the tent flap, gasping for a breath of air. But he had waited too long and he probably crumpled against the ledge to succumb, as did Fraenkel, of carbon monoxide poisoning.

But who can say for certain that this is the way it happened. Of all the theories, it seems the soundest. Death by asphyxiation had occurred to earlier polar explorers who remained in a closed place with an oil- or coal-burning device.

Sweden paid a final tribute to the explorers. Down the streets of Stockholm in solemn mourning, the remains of Andrée, Fraenkel, and Strindberg were carried to the Church of St. Nicholas. Thousands of their countrymen, in company with Gustavus V, attended the service. When the coffins were taken to their burial place, the King spoke these words:

> In the name of the Swedish nation I greet the dust of the Polar explorers who, more than three decades since, left their native land to find answers to questions of unparalleled difficulty. A country's hope to be able to honor them in their lifetime after a successful journey was disappointed. We must submit to its tragic result. All that is left us is to express our warm thanks to them for their self-sacrifices in the service of science. Peace to their memory!

CHAPTER 7

Somewhere at Sea

The early over-water flights carried neither wireless nor flotation gear, so the clues most needed to explain the loss of planes at sea—position reports and survivors—were frequently missing. In most cases the question, What happened out there? will never be answered.

Early radios were heavy, cumbersome, and undependable. Transmitters lacked range; receivers were subject to whims of the weather. Many an Atlantic air adventurer believed his chances as good without them, especially when he plotted his course off the established sea lanes, anyway.

Anyone can theorize on the causes of air losses over the North Atlantic between 1919 and 1931. Speculation is cheap, especially with the cockpit full of ghosts that haunted the early daredevils. The weather was a gloomy, ever-present threat. Forecasts were little better than guesswork. Ice could choke the engine and destroy the airflow over the wings and propeller. Snow could weigh down machines already overloaded with fuel, and there were no devices to eliminate these hazards. No plane could fly above the weather as they do today; pilots had to outwit the elements, endure them, or fall victim to them. Even in clear weather, fickle winds from unexpected quarters at unexpected velocities magnified the problems of steering with an erratic magnetic compass. Looking back, it seems miraculous that a few determined men and women survived the hazards and ran the gauntlet unscathed.

Here are the stories of some of those who did not.

The first attempt to fly the Atlantic in a heavier-than-air machine was made by Harry Hawker and Mackenzie Grieve. On May 18, 1919, they took off from Newfoundland for the $50,000 prize offered by the *London Daily Mail*. Their Sopwith biplane, powered by a 375-horsepower engine, was forced down in mid-Atlantic, and when it failed to arrive in England, the worst was assumed. Then, seven days later, the Danish cargo boat *Mary* docked in England and lashed aboard it was the missing plane. The two fliers were safe, fished from the water as they clung to their floating aircraft.

The White Bird

May 8, 1927. Le Bourget field, outside Paris. In the pale dawn, mechanics pushed a ghostly white biplane from a darkened hangar. Thousands of spectators, many of whom had been waiting for this moment since midnight, broke into cheers. Today the rash Nungesser and his one-eyed navigator, Francois Coli, were going to fly to America.

The pair stood to gain fame in one of two ways if they

102

were successful. A new transatlantic record, or if they landed at New York, the $25,000 Raymond Orteig Prize. News of their stepped-up departure date traveled fast. When Nungesser learned that a little-known airmail pilot by the name of Charles Lindbergh was ready for a New York takeoff at any moment, he moved his departure date ahead two weeks.

To the average Frenchman, Nungesser was surrounded with an aura of supernatural invincibility. They called him Nungesser the Indestructible. And well they might. He had emerged victorious from forty-five air-to-air combats over the Western Front; he survived seventeen crashes that broke almost every bone in his body. His entire lower left jaw, palate, and shattered left leg were reinforced with platinum plates. Time and again his poorly mended bones had to be reset. Certainly he was the most daring of the French aviators and the most determined. When Réné Fonck, with whom he had competed for France's top war victories, failed in his attempt to fly from New York to Paris, Nungesser convinced himself that he would succeed.

After the war, Nungesser operated a flying school, then barnstormed the United States. Late in 1926 he announced his plans to cross the Atlantic by air, not west to east to take advantage of the prevailing winds, but east to west—the hard way. As he boarded the boat that was to carry him back to France, he bid his brother goodbye. "Farewell, Robert. I'm going home the slow way, but I'll be coming back the *fast* way—by aeroplane!"

The air hero set to work. He wanted a large monoplane with an enclosed cabin. Fonck's plane was like this, but when news came that he had crashed on takeoff and two crew members had perished, Nungesser changed his mind. Next he considered a small, light airplane to carry one man and much fuel, a flying gas tank. The government refused to subsidize him so he went to the manufacturers. Their assortment of planes was anything but encouraging. Finally he decided upon the great Levasseur P.L.8 biplane, then under manufacture for the French Navy as a carrier-borne three-seater patrol bomber. Nungesser had it modified to suit his needs. A 450-horsepower Lorraine engine was installed and extra gas tanks were fitted. In fact, the entire forward part of the fuselage was one great fuel cell. The fuselage was reworked into two open cockpits (Nungesser decided to carry a navigator) and the landing gear was designed to be dropped after takeoff to lighten the machine, give it less drag, and prevent it from flipping over when it landed in New York Harbor. The boatlike fuselage contained watertight compartments to keep the plane afloat in case of a forced landing at sea. To aid in immediate recognition should such an emergency occur, the entire plane was painted a chalky white.

Each side of the fuselage bore the macabre insignia Nungesser painted on all his planes—a large black heart inside of which was a skull and cross bones. Over the skull was a coffin. He considered this his good luck charm as well as his trademark.

When Nungesser and Coli appeared, riding toward the waiting plane in an open car, the cheers turned to a thunderous roar. The car stopped. A young girl stood on tiptoe and threw Nungesser a rose. He caught it in mid-air, touched it to his lips, and blew the girl a kiss. Then, erect, but with a slow limp, he walked to the plane, Coli trailing. The mechanics topped the tanks as the two fliers watched, and 880 gallons of gasoline was ready to be lifted into the air by the clumsy-looking biplane.

Captain Coli, accustomed to the precise workings of ocean navigation, was less devil-may-care about the venture. Nungesser had not taken time to test the Levasseur with its full load of fuel, so neither knew for certain if it would get off in the half mile of runway. The ace refused to worry about it. "We'll either make it or we won't," he said lightly, and dismissed the question.

Coli was still uneasy. His calculations could only be based on the *assumed* wind conditions over the Atlantic, and they expected to buck head winds all the way. The normal cruising speed of the patrol bomber was about 120 miles per hour. It could stay aloft for forty-two hours, but its ground speed might vary from 80 to 120 miles per hour, depending on the wind direction and velocity. At the very best, Coli could afford only a 200-mile leeway. This was cutting it close, but the nonchalant Nungesser accepted it cheerfully. The navigator shook his head. Everything, he knew, would depend on Nungesser's flying ability and his own navigating skill. And the weather . . .

The plane carried no radio, it had been removed a few days earlier. There were no life jackets or rubber dinghies, no survival equipment. Coli, long experienced in the fickle ways of the sea, protested, but Nungesser replied coolly, "The idea, Captain, is not to swim to America, but to *fly* there. If we have to land on the water, the fuselage will keep us afloat until we're picked up."

But Coli knew the sea. Especially did he know the North Atlantic. If the waters were rough, l'Oiseau Blanc would sink with its crew in a matter of minutes.

By any standard it seemed almost unbelievable that an experienced pilot and navigator would attempt to span the Atlantic under these uncertain conditions. The only encouraging word was the weather office's last-minute report that, miracle of miracles, they could expect a tail wind for the first third of their journey. Nungesser was elated; Coli felt better.

The two men, dressed in yellow flying coveralls, climbed into the cockpits, where their carefully weighed provisions—canned fish, bananas, sugar, chocolate, coffee, and brandy—had been stored. Nungesser looked over the crowd. There was Maurice Chevalier, Georges Carpentier, and incomparable Mistinguett, France's darling. On the fringe of the crowd stood General Girod, his wartime commander. Nungesser was pleased; all France was there to see him off; the workers, the *artistes*, the military.

The engine roared to life. At 5:17, *The White Bird* lumbered reluctantly forward. It seemed impossible that the five tons of airplane and gasoline could become airborne in Le Bourget's 2,500 feet of runway. The tail lifted sluggishly, then slowly settled back down. A cry of dismay swept the crowd. "*Mon Dieu!*" cried Girod. "He'll never get off the ground!"

The tail lifted again as the white, straining machine rolled faster. Nungesser swept past the halfway mark of the runway; his main wheels still had not broken ground. Then they lifted slightly and settled back. Less than 500 feet remained and the overloaded plane made every effort to fly. In the cockpit, Nungesser saw the end of the runway looming up fast. It was too late to stop now and he knew another backward pull on the control stick to try to force the lumbering plane to fly would be disastrous. His bird would stall and crash as had Fonck's a few weeks earlier.

As the final yard of runway slipped under the wheels, the huge biplane staggered into the air and held. Its engine labored full out as the wide wings reached out for enough air to begin to climb. The crowd went wild. Nungesser was holding fast; his uncanny luck was still with him.

Lifting itself by inches, the plane headed toward the sea. It was escorted by other planes as far as Cape Etretat, north Le Havre, which it passed at 6:48 A.M. Nungesser and Coli were last seen, officially, heading over the open water, pointed toward the southern coast of England.

The next day a false report of their successful landing in New York Harbor stirred France to a brief celebration. But when the truth became known, the celebration turned to a riot. In Paris, indignant Frenchmen burned stacks of newspapers that carried the unconfirmed report. Editorial offices were in danger of being sacked and pillaged. Windows were smashed.

Hours passed and no word came from any quarter, ship or land, of a sighting. It was obvious the daring pair had come down somewhere in the North Atlantic. On May 10, they were officially reported missing.

Despite the many theories as to where Nungesser and Coli went down, it was never disproved that they might well have crashed only minutes from the shores of France. There was, however, a fairly accurate report that a plane resembling *The White Bird* was sighted off the Irish coast, well out to sea at 10:05 hours on the morning of May 8. Considering the plane's cruising speed and the elapsed time from Le Bourget, officials decided "this could have been *l'Oiseau Blanc.*"

Beginning at midday of May 9, conflicting reports appeared. News agencies claimed Nungesser and Coli were indeed sighted over Cape Race, Newfoundland, and over Newbury and Boston. New York papers were unable to get confirmation. Had a plane actually passed over these points? Yes, one had, but it was not *The White Bird.* From New York to Halifax, observers scanned the skies, and despite mist and fog, a squadron of U.S. military planes set out from Boston to meet the Frenchmen. They returned without making rendezvous.

On May 24, a trawler that had been in the Atlantic at the time of the flight, reported seeing a smaller vessel towing a white hydroplane. Nungesser and Coli? The British Admiralty promptly cleared up the matter; one of their planes had been forced down at sea. In the wake of this, two other ships, the *Bellaline* and the *Dana*, each reported having sighted the missing plane not far from the American shore. An investigation showed they had indeed been on the route plotted by the fliers, but at the time the sightings allegedly occurred, the biplane had long since exhausted its fuel.

Did *The White Bird* come down on land or sea? What about Labrador? Did the pair crash somewhere on its frozen wastes? Then came a report from that very place. Trappers saw rockets in the sky one evening about the time of the flight. The lights had been some distance from their camp and on searching the area the following morning, they found nothing. From Newfoundland came other reports of an airplane engine heard overhead when it was certain no other plane was flying in that region.

Canada? What of its sprawling forests and snow plains? A Canadian trapper claimed he found a written SOS message signed "Nungesser." In fact, he produced it. It said Nungesser and Coli had come down in the Far North. In Paris, Nungesser's mother examined the handwriting and thought it like her son's. But because of the poorly worded text of the message she said, "It seems unlikely that Charles could have written it."

There are Frenchmen who believe today that Nungesser and Coli still live. Like their faith in the invincibility of Guynemer, to them these fliers will never die. Frenchmen may admit their heroes crashed, but only after they reached America. They came down in the Canadian North where they live on today as captives of a remote Indian tribe. Others believe they died of starvation; or that faulty American weather reports caused them to crash within sight of land. These beliefs were nurtured by messages found later in floating bottles. One turned up on the Dutch coast in 1929. Another was found in 1933, and the last one was picked up in 1934. All were cruel hoaxes played on a sympathetic public by mentally deranged persons.

Perhaps Nungesser and Coli almost made it to America. Early in 1961, off the southwest coast of Maine, a Casco Bay lobster fisherman pulled up one of his pots. Caught on the side of it was a jagged piece of metal wreckage. It appeared to be a riveted scrap of aircraft aluminum. The man scraped away the slime accumulated during its many years on the ocean bottom and found it had once been painted white. A remnant of *l'Oiseau Blanc?* Who can say?

Two weeks after Nungesser and Coli disappeared, Charles Lindbergh made the first nonstop solo flight from New York to Paris. Somewhere along the way he may have passed near the place where the brave Frenchmen faltered and fell. As other successful transatlantic flights followed, the Nungesser-Coli tragedy gradually faded from the public mind.

How final were the words of Captain Venson, one of the pilots who escorted the intrepid airmen to the cliffs of Etretat, when he described his last view of *The White Bird*.

"She gradually vanished ahead of us in the opaque milky haze tinged with red . . . as day rose."

The Saint Raphael

A feverish, almost compulsive spirit caught hold of airmen when they contemplated the Atlantic. The temptation refused to be stilled. Nungesser and Coli were missing only three months when the beckoning finger of Dame Fortune lured another plane over the sea, and the Atlantic took its toll again. This time it was two men and a woman.

On August 31, British fliers Colonel Frederick Minchin and copilot Captain Leslie Hamilton took up the challenge to make the first east-west crossing. In an effort to succeed where the Frenchmen had failed, they decided to reduce the flying distance by starting from Cornwall, England. Their passenger was Princess Loewenstein-Wertheim. She was not a young woman, one who could take in stride the rigors of thirty-six hours over the Atlantic in a cramped cabin. She was sixty-two, but she wanted to be the first woman to cross the ocean by air. As the principal backer of the flight, she had no trouble making the arrangements, and the plane was equipped with a wicker armchair and an army cot to provide her the most comfort under the confining conditions. Outfitted in a blue leather flying outfit and suede boots, she traveled light, taking two handbags, a basket of food, and two hatboxes.

At Upavon, a small flying field on Salisbury Plain, the mechanics finished their last-minute check of the nine-cylinder, 450-horsepower engine that was to power the blue and yellow Fokker monoplane 3,600 miles to Ottawa. They stood back and waited, but the trio gave no sign they were ready to go.

A light steady drizzle was falling when a car drove onto the muddy field, carrying the Roman Catholic Archbishop of Cardiff and his acolytes who, at the princess' request, were to be in attendance. The archbishop blessed the plane, the *Saint Raphael,* and sprinkled it with holy water as the princess bowed her head and prayed silently. The ceremony was short, farewells were quickly said, and within ten minutes the Fokker lifted itself without difficulty and disappeared low into the ragged wispy clouds.

Over the water, Minchin and Hamilton settled G-EBTQ onto a steady course for Newfoundland. Droning along at 100 miles an hour, the six-and-a-half-ton aircraft handled well with its 800 gallons of fuel. Although the weather was squallish, the monoplane alternately broke into clear patches of air over the churning whitecaps, then into low-hanging "scud" again. They carried no wireless equipment, so their only contact with the world below was a visual one.

Occasionally, they sighted a fishing boat or a freighter near the coast, but after an hour the surface vessels thinned out. Several hours later the *Saint Raphael* was sighted well out to sea by a lone tanker that radioed the Fokker's position to London. It proved to be the last contact with the plane, for it was never reported again. After forty-five hours, hopes faded in Ottawa.

Then a curious phenomena was reported on the night of September 3, when the Fokker's fuel tanks would have been empty over twenty-four hours, something that makes all the more puzzling the record of the lighthouse keeper at Belle Isle, Labrador. So rarely is the monotonous splash of the sea broken by an alien sound that this man could not have imagined what he saw and heard. Shortly after midnight, he saw a red light in the southeastern sky, with a steady white light behind it, obviously the navigation lights of an airplane. Since aircraft carry a red light on the left wing and a white light on the tail, the man was looking at the left rear of the plane.

"Then I heard the engine," he said, "and watched the lights until they disappeared in the vicinity of Battle Harbor about 12:30 A.M."

Every attempt to track down the identity of the midnight flier ended in failure. Just who—or what—was moving over the barren stretch of isolated loneliness was never discovered.

A few days later, scraps of a broken airplane were found off the coast of Iceland. Among them was a wicker chair. There was no doubt this was all that remained of the *Saint Raphael,* despite the fact that the bodies of the crew and passenger were never recovered. Thus, instead of being the first of her sex to cross the Atlantic by air, Princess Loewenstein-Wertheim earned instead the dubious distinction of being the first woman to perish on a transatlantic flight.

Old Glory

Lloyd Berthaud, one of Columbia Aircraft Corporation's long-time pilots, planned the next transatlantic flight. He proposed to fly nonstop from New York to Rome, a distance of 3,850 miles. His plane, *Old Glory,* was also a single-engine Fokker monoplane with a 450-horsepower Jupiter engine.

On September 7, 1927, the long-awaited news flash came. Berthaud had hopped off from Orchard Beach, Maine, and was on his way. With him was his navigator, J. D. Hill, and Philip Payne. Payne was managing editor of the New York *Daily News,* one of the directors of the Hearst chain, and was personally selected by William Randolph Hearst to accompany them.

The *Old Glory* was better equipped than most of the early transatlantic contenders. It carried a wireless as well as a newly developed automatic apparatus to send continuous distress signals in case of a forced descent at sea. The radio transmitter worked so well that soon after take-off the steamer *Berlin,* 1,200 miles out of New York, picked up clear signals. Another innovation was a device for distilling sea water. Well-selected provisions and an inflatable rubber dinghy were stored in the fuselage, and in the rear of the cabin was a wreath. On its ribbon was written: TO NUNGESSER AND COLI—YOU SHOWED US THE WAY; WE ARE FOLLOWING. Although the gallant Frenchmen flew in the opposite direction, the sentiment was understood. "We intend to drop it in mid-Atlantic in honor of the two French airmen," Berthaud told reporters before takeoff.

Their Rome destination allowed Berthaud to plot their course farther south than Lindbergh's. This enabled him and his crew to fly along well-traveled shipping lanes, which increased their chances of survival in the event of a crash at sea. Several hours out of his jumping-off point, Berthaud was seen by a number of ships that reported all was well. The Fokker plodded steadily on course. It passed within 300 feet of the SS *California* plowing along 350 miles east of St. John's, Newfoundland, and the plane's identification letters, WHRP were clearly seen. Berthaud, it appeared, had a winning combination.

Then, toward nightfall, the seas turned heavy. By early morning, strong westerlies churned the waters into heavy swells. Wireless operators aboard ships whose course through the rough weather was close to *Old Glory* heard nothing but static. Bridge lookouts scanned the dark and blustery skies for the telltale colored navigation lights. But in the low cloud cover, nothing showed itself.

On board the *Transylvania*, the wireless operator kept close vigil. It was foul weather indeed, and he thought Berthaud and his crew would be having a rough time of it if they were within 250 miles of the ship.

He twisted the dials, picked up a time signal, scraps of a message from London, then turned back to the *Old Glory's* transmitting frequency. Suddenly out of the racket and noise, he heard the wavering dot-dash of "Old Glory calling . . . Old Glory calling . . ." Then came their position, followed, to the operator's dismay, by the emergency signal of the air: SOS. The garbled message was so broken with static he could make out "Newfoundland east . . ." and their position of Latitude 48:03 North and Longitude 41:15 West. He scratched the message on his pad and raced to the bridge. The weather was growing worse.

When Captain Bone read the message, he ordered the ship to alter course immediately. Other vessels were already hurrying to the position Hill transmitted, for the SS *California* and the SS *Carmania* picked up the distress call simultaneously. They were converging at full steam on the *Old Glory*.

The *Transylvania* was nearest the transmitted position of the plane, and after six hours in the rough seas it reached the spot. But in the growing light of dawn there was no trace of the plane. Captain Bone quartered, zigzagged, and circled the area in a systematic pattern. Other vessels appeared on the dim horizon and joined the search. There was still no sign of the *Old Glory*. Another six hours passed without result.

There was no misunderstanding about the distress position Hill transmitted. At least not among the ships that heard it. Six in all confirmed it, converged upon it, and marked the area well, but once the section was thoroughly combed, there was no hope that the plane was still afloat or that the fliers had escaped a watery death in their inflatable boat—if they had had time to launch it.

At twilight, after more than twelve hours of search, the captains reluctantly turned back to their courses and continued to port.

Did the weather force *Old Glory* down? Or was it engine trouble, a broken fuel or oil line? The world wondered. Berthaud definitely was not lost; he could not have given a position report. But was he certain of his position when he transmitted his latitude and longitude?

In the weeks that followed, tankers, liners, and naval ships found scattered bits of floating debris that could only have been the remains of the Fokker. The wreckage was generally found 100 miles north of Hill's position report. Thirty-four feet of wing was recovered, on which was painted the Stars and Stripes. Fuselage and tail fragments were also fished from the water. They were the first sizeable parts of any of the overwater planes to be found, and they told the story only too well. Berthaud had been unable to ditch the monoplane successfully, and on impact with the mountainous waves it had broken up within seconds, splintering into hundreds of pieces. No one held hope of finding the crew, and no one knows why they were forced to ditch.

The wreath intended for Nungesser and Coli now marked two graves. All had perished in the same fashion —trying to span the Atlantic.

The Sir John Carling

The tragic end of Berthaud and his crew failed to dissuade two other Britishers, pilot J. D. Metcalfe and navigator Terence Tully. The newspapers were still carrying headlines of *Old Glory's* disappearance when they departed on September 10, 1927. Their destination was London; no one had yet flown there from New York nonstop.

Their plane was the *Sir John Carling*, a monoplane that was to carry them from Roosevelt Field, Long Island, over

Harbor Grace, Newfoundland, and thence to England. Hours passed, then came the message that they had been sighted over Newfoundland, on course. But when Metcalfe and Tully left the last bit of coastline behind and headed over the waiting Atlantic they disappeared forever. At Croydon Aerodrome outside London, the fog rolled in and the watch waited in vain.

Two days later at Newquay, Cornwall, bits of silver-gray wreckage washed ashore and were identified as parts of the wing and rudder of the *Sir John Carling*. The plane was expected to cross the Galway coast that Thursday afternoon about the time a strong gale hit the Irish coast. They had come down at sea, just short of the shore of Britain. The sea had won again.

A Gambler's Chance

A month later, a lieutenant-commander in the Royal Navy, who had served with distinction during World War I, made the next attempt. H. C. McDonald was convinced he could fly from Newfoundland to Croydon in a tiny 85-horsepower De Havilland biplane that was modified for an incredible 3,600-mile range. His announcement stunned veteran airmen. "Foolhardy. Absolutely foolhardy," was their reaction to the press. McDonald, it appeared, had a total of eighty hours in the air, only a half hour of which was night-flying experience. Some months earlier, with only sixteen hours to his credit, he flew to India. Remarkably, he arrived safely, but on his return flight from Baghdad he was forced down in the Sahara and was seized by hostile Arabs. Only the timely arrival of an Italian armored car saved him from death. McDonald was thrilled; to him all life was a grand adventure, and the Atlantic only whetted his appetite for new experiences. Before he sailed for Newfoundland, his friends tried to dissuade him. All he said was, "I know I'm taking a gambler's chance."

At Harbor Grace, on the crisp morning of October 18, McDonald double-checked the instruments in his open-cockpit biplane. The small group of spectators had watched transatlantic hopefuls come and go, but never in a plane as small as this one. The tiny De Havilland's wingspan was only twenty-six feet. A few men shook their heads as they conversed quietly in small groups. McDonald was ready; he stored some sandwiches and a thermos of coffee in the cockpit. Grinning, he said, "I'll finish these in London tomorrow." He climbed into the cockpit and signaled a mechanic to swing the propeller. The engine sputtered, coughed to life as its four exhaust pipes popped away.

The biplane was so burdened with its extra fuel tanks that the undercarriage sagged and the tires bulged. The mechanic helped get the plane moving, and McDonald slowly taxied to the takeoff point. He turned his plane into the teeth of a twenty-five-mile-an-hour wind and paused briefly. Then the Gipsy engine roared full out, as full out as 85 horsepower can roar. With its exhaust crackling in the chill air, its pistons strained to get the airplane rolling. With a normal load, the light aircraft could pop into the air within a hundred feet, but now it took a lumbering run of 600 feet before it staggered into the air.

McDonald climbed slowly and steadily. He circled the aerodrome twice as he gained altitude; then, with a final dip of a wing, he headed over the water at 11:51. After that, he was sighted once or possibly twice as he flew eastward. Seven hundred miles out of St. John's he was sighted by the Dutch steamer *Hardenberg*. He was airborne seven-and-a-half hours. He was making good his planned track, was right on schedule, and was averaging almost 100-miles-an-hour ground speed. McDonald said before takeoff he would probably reach the coast of Ireland the following morning about seven o'clock. But without wireless, it was impossible for ship and shore stations to get a bearing on him to check his progress during the long night.

The British liner SS *Montclare* was steaming 150 miles off the coast of Northern Ireland, late in the evening of the second day, when several passengers saw a light moving in the distant sky. It was too far off for them to hear the sound of an engine.

In Kensington, London, Mrs. McDonald, a slim brunette, waited anxiously with their son, Ian, five. The boy knew of his father's flight and happily told callers: "My daddy's in an aeroplane . . . over the . . . the Al . . . Al . . . anic!" Mrs. McDonald put him to bed at 7, and continued her vigil.

"My husband has wanted to do this for a long time," she told a newsman. "He worked hard to make the arrangements, even had his machine dismantled and

114

shipped to America in boxes." As she spoke, police from Malin Head to Dingle Bay on the west coast, and Cape Clear to Land's End on the southwest coast, were keeping beacon fires alight and ears alert for the De Havilland. The weather over England turned wet and stormy as the expected hour of McDonald's arrival drew near. When 11:00 P.M., Friday, came and passed, hopes waned that the handsome naval officer would reach his goal.

Mrs. McDonald refused to believe the worst. She clung fast to the hope that her husband had been picked up by a vessel at sea, for he had reminded her that Hawker and Grieve were missing five days before they reached port. "Don't give up hope," he had said in parting. Then, two close family friends, Sir Herbert Barker and another, told her of their identical dreams. They each said they saw a rocky island about 200 miles off the west coast of Scotland. Mrs. McDonald hastened to check the charts. She said she believed the island was Rockall, and immediately contacted the Admiralty. The Admiralty was sympathetic, but carefully explained that Rockall was a small, high rock, cold and exposed to the sea winds. Anyone there could not survive long, they said.

Mrs. McDonald was not convinced. She tried again by telephoning Croydon Aerodrome and asking for a plane to be sent there to search. But the Admiralty intervened and refused to sanction the flight. So, whether or not McDonald crashed near Rockall will never be known.

The Endeavor

At 8:35 on the morning of March 13, 1928, Captain Walter Hinchliffe and his attractive copilot, the Hon. Elsie Mackay, took off from Cranwell, England, for Mitchell Field, Long Island. The thirty-four-year-old aviatrix, daughter of Lord Inchcape, had a small financial interest in the flight and had quietly driven to the airfield before sunup. The departure was without fanfare, spectators, or reporters, for Miss Mackay knew her aging father would have forbidden this foolhardy adventure. As it turned out, she was well on her way across the ocean when he learned of their departure.

The plane, named the Endeavor, was a Stinson Detroiter with a forty-five-foot wingspan, a 225-horsepower Wright Whirlwind, and a 500-gallon fuel capacity. Steady and reliable, it was a favorite with distance fliers.

115

At 11:30 A.M., with the news services already humming, the *Endeavor* was seen passing over Kilmeadan, Ireland. A storm was raging over Cork at 12:30 when the Stinson was observed heading westward, battling out the elements and heading into uglier weather. Observers were certain Hinchliffe and Mackay would turn back, but the plane pushed through the rough clouds safely and was again sighted at 1:30 that afternoon over the Irish coast at Mizen Head, about 465 miles from Cranwell. Later in the day it was sighted at sea by a ship, still maintaining a fair ground speed of ninety-three miles an hour, despite stiff headwinds. To all appearances, the *Endeavor* was off to a fine start.

The next day no ships reported seeing the Stinson, and at Mitchell Field the waiting crowd thinned out and drifted homeward. A few hopefuls lingered long into the night, scanned the eastern sky, and strained to hear the sound of an engine. Several false reports came in but only one, from Old Orchard, Maine, sounded plausible. At 1:05 A.M. Wednesday morning, the 16th, at a time when the *Endeavor* could have been approaching the Continent, the engineer of a passenger train looked out of his cab and saw the lights of a low-flying plane. If it was the British pilot and his companion, they could have crashed just offshore, lamentably close to their goal. The most prevalent theory has it that head winds slowed the Stinson until its fuel was exhausted from repeated battles with Atlantic squalls and the plane was swallowed by the turbulent sea without a trace.

The Secret Flight of the Mail-Route Pioneers

Unnoticed and unheralded, a graceful Bellanca floatplane lifted from Detroit's seaplane port on July 28, 1931. It swung to the northeast and settled on to a great-circle flight to Copenhagen. At the controls was Parker D. Cramer, an American World War I pilot and former member of Sir Hubert Wilkins Antarctic Expedition. Cramer had tried twice before to fly the Atlantic and had failed each time. In 1928, he and his companion, Bert Hassell, were forced to walk out over the Greenland ice cap after being forced down. In 1929, when the *Chicago Tribune* sponsored Untin Bower's Chicago-Berlin dash, Cramer was the copilot. The flight ended in the ocean and, luckily, both pilots were rescued.

116

Cramer's companion and copilot on this unannounced flight was Oliver Pacquette, a Canadian wireless operator. The well-planned air journey was not undertaken to break records or to establish a distance mark. Although it was still a challenge, the glory of the transatlantic dash was fast fading. Cramer and Pacquette were adventurers of a different sort; visionaries of a far-reaching dream. They were off to chart the first transatlantic air mail route on a course north of the Artic Circle. It would connect the United States with the land of the Vikings.

For seven days, Cramer and Pacquette droned northward over the Canadian wilds. Except for one bad day at Hudson Bay the weather was good. On August 3, they arrived at Hosteinborg on the west coast of Greenland. Thus far their flight had not attracted the attention of the news services; the pair smiled at the idea of having "put one over on the news boys."

The following day, in a brisk five-hour flight at 9,600 feet, they crossed the Greenland ice cap, en route to Angmagsalik, from where they planned to jump off for Iceland. As they soared high above the inland ice fields shimmering in the bright sunlight, Cramer thought the sun-illuminated snow fields were wonderful. "They'll be a great tourist attraction someday," he remarked to Pacquette. The most hazardous leg of their journey, or so they thought, was behind them.

News of the air venture hit the presses before they left Greenland. The full meaning of the flight was revealed by E. G. Thompson, president of the Thompson Aeronautical Corporation of Cleveland, who had selected the men to chart a proposed route for future air-mail pilots. "The route will be over the Greenland ice cap and the North Atlantic," Thompson told reporters. "Cramer's flight is the first ever undertaken and completed across the ice cap. Naturally, we're pleased with the success of their trip thus far, but we anticipate that much remains to be done in the way of study and preparation before we shall feel qualified to apply to the Post Office Department for a mail contract."

Thompson told the newsmen that another plane was being readied and would take off as soon as Cramer and Pacquette had finished their flight. It was to be followed by other flights on a monthly schedule. "Their purpose will be to determine just what we must face in all seasons," Thompson concluded. "We want to fly over these little-known regions during both freeze-up and break-up periods." •

Encouragement for the airmail flight came from Washington, where Assistant Postmaster-General Glover predicted the day was not far away when planes carrying mail to distant points would be a common occurrence.

Meanwhile, Cramer and Pacquette pushed on, winging their way toward Iceland. Almost as revolutionary as their journey was the fact that their aircraft was powered with a highly unusual engine—a diesel. This unconventional power-plant was developed three years earlier by the Packard Motor Car Corporation and was, to say the least, unique. It was the first air-cooled diesel and the success of the flight with this type of power would not only be a notable first-time feat in itself, but would boost the small group of aviation diesel proponents. Later, in the thirties, the huge Dornier flying boats of Germany, with their liquid-cooled in-line diesels, would make regular South American runs, but thus far only America had produced a successful air-cooled radial.

The engine had many advantages. It consumed less fuel and allowed a greater range. It required no carburetor and no ignition system, thus eliminating the majority of engine troubles. The absence of the engine's electrical system permitted Pacquette's coded transmissions to be free of radio ignition interference caused by high-voltage magnetos. Fire hazards were practically nonexistent. The fuel oil could not be accidentally ignited; it would burn only when properly atomized by the high-pressure fuel pump. Above all, the engine seemed perfectly adapted to high-altitude, cold-weather flying. The fuel and air mixture would not preignite or detonate in the cylinders as it could in a gasoline engine, and carburetor ice—the dreaded hazard of North Atlantic flying—was nonexistent in an intake system that didn't have a carburetor. Except for the slight additional weight of the engine, which was designed to withstand greater combustion pressures, it seemed to be the ideal answer—a troublefree, reliable powerplant.

In the early morning of August 6, the Detroit-to-Denmark fliers approached the coast of Iceland. They were able to contact Reykjavik radio when only two hours out of Angmagsalik, at which time they requested a

118

report on visibility and weather conditions along the northwest coast. Reykjavik informed them that their intended destination of Isafjordur was covered with fog. Cramer altered course for Reykjavik, 200 miles farther south where the weather was clear. At 3:20 A.M., the men flew the Bellanca over the capital city at 9,000 feet without seeing it. A few minutes later they discovered their error, turned back, and landed the floatplane near the beach.

After they moved the monoplane into the harbor and supervised the refueling, the men slept. At 2:10 on the afternoon of the 7th, they were off again, this time for the Faeroes, a small cluster of islands 250 miles north of Scotland. They faced 900 miles of treacherous water over a route rarely traveled by ships, even in the summer season. Quick help to a downed plane in this region was out of the question.

The first hint of trouble was received at Thorshavn, the only town on the islands. Late in the afternoon a radio message crackled through the wireless station on the desolate, windswept outpost.

> Forced to go down owing to engine trouble.
> Should like to obtain exact bearings. Can
> you assist, please?

Thorshavn could and did. After taking a bearing on the plane at sea, they also sent a dispatch to the London *Daily Mail*, informing them of the forced landing. Public concern for the daring men spread. When veteran fliers heard the news, they shook their heads. Cramer and Pacquette were doomed, they said, knowing full well the perils of coming down on the ocean in a small floatplane.

What caused the forced landing at sea was never known, but the remarkable feat that followed aroused the admiration of aviators on both sides of the Atlantic. After skillfully setting the Bellanca down on the choppy water, Cramer made the necessary adjustments, crawled back into the bobbing plane, and lifted it masterfully from the rough water. It was a narrow and dramatic escape from death.

When they reached Sydero Island in the Faeroes that night, the surveyors rested only long enough to refuel and to gain strength for the final two "easy stages" of their voyage. Early next morning, August 8, they departed for Norway, with their destination either Bergen or Stavanger, depending on the weather.

Cramer and Pacquette were tired from their long hours in the air, but their spirits were lifted by the thought that this very night they would dine in Copenhagen. Unknown to them, the city was preparing a gala celebration during which they would be presented with the gold medal of the Aeronautical Society.

A few hours out of Sydero, the weather over the North Sea turned foul. An ominous fog bank closed over the ocean, and the Bellanca was buffeted by rough winds and squalls. Wisely, Cramer turned toward the Shetlands and landed at Lerwick to await clear weather. The next day conditions improved, and they decided to push on for Bergen.

When the graceful float plane slipped easily into the sea spray off Lerwick and turned south toward Norway, it was the last time Cramer and Pacquette were seen. Somewhere east of the Orkney Islands something tragically ended the great dream of these men. Whether they had engine trouble, wing ice, or structural failure due to a sudden violent squall, was never known. The dots and dashes of Pacquette's telegraph key gave no hint. Only one thing is certain. The end was quick and violent; they had no time to tell their plight before they smashed into the icy waves of the North Sea. Five weeks later the British trawler, *Lord Trent*, came upon some drifting fragments of a plane wreckage, but no bodies. They fished one of the floats from the water and sent a wireless to London with the serial number of the float. The Associated Press relayed the data to New York, where K. D. Vasler of the Edo Aircraft Corporation consulted his files and announced: "This was the serial number of the floats on Cramer and Pacquette's Bellanca."

It was six months later, in March of 1932, that the final chapter was told. The crew of Dutch Trawler 130, plowing along at Latitude 59.38 North, Longitude 3.42 East, spotted a floating packet in the water. It was not far from where the earlier wreckage had been seen. On opening the waterlogged package, they found Cramer's pilot's license, the permit for his transatlantic flight, the Bellanca's registration papers, and a letter from his mother. The contents were turned over to the American Consulate in Amsterdam.

Thus, the flight that began in secrecy ended in secrecy, and the North Sea keeps its secret well. If Parker Cramer and Oliver Pacquette could look today on the great air-transport system of silver jets that carry mail and passengers over the very route they had blazed across the icy Arctic blue, they would say with pride: "We were first."

CHAPTER 8

The Dole Derby

Back in 1927, aviation's wildest gamble was the 2,400-mile dash to the Hawaiian Islands. When it was over, five aircraft were wrecked, three were lost at sea, and ten persons were dead. It proved to be little more than a mad dash for money and glory. And not a trace of the pilots and planes downed between California and Hawaii on the nights of August 16 and 17, 19 and 20, was ever found.

A year earlier the Atlantic claimed the world's attention, for both 1926 and 1927 had been tragic years for ocean crossings. Most of the planes and pilots that plunged into its icy waters were never seen again. It was a time of financial inducements and promises of quick fame. Any pilot who could get his hands on an airplane and could muster the courage to head it eastward over the water, was in the running. It didn't matter whether he had had any overwater navigation experience. Most of the pilots did not comprehend the meaning of the word. Europe, they reasoned was a big continent. So, if they could carry enough gas, hit the right weather, and fly long enough without going to sleep at the controls, they figured that sooner or later they would hit it.

At least thirty persons had crossed the Atlantic in airplanes and dirigibles before the Lone Eagle made the first solo crossing in May of 1927. To Lindberg went the coveted $25,000 first prize offered by Raymond Orteig. In Paris, Ambassador Myron T. Herrick offered another $25,000 to the first person who would fly from Paris to his home city, Cleveland, Ohio. In Dallas, William E. Easterwood, Jr. offered a similar sum for the first Dallas-to-Hong Kong flight.

One other man of prominence was interested in a certain long-distance ocean attempt. He was forty-nine-year-old James Drummond Dole, the Hawaiian pineapple tycoon. While in California on business, he head of Lindbergh's success. Precisely what Jim Dole hoped to accomplish when he announced a $25,000 purse for a California-to-Hawaii dash is argued to this day. Was it a desire to speed air transportation to the islands? Or a publicity stunt to open Hawaii as a tourist land? Whatever his reason, his sponsorship of the transocean marathon, the greatest air race of its time, resulted in financial tragedies, frustration, and sudden death.

Twenty-five thousand dollars pitted against any reasonable hazard is still enough of a challenge to send today's air adventurers scrambling to the starting line. Back in 1927, it sent them wild. Even the $10,000 second-place money sounded good. Dole bettered Orteig's offer.

From the beginning, several things went awry in the Dole Derby. The hazard was not reasonable nor did the prize money offset the risk to men and machines. True, the Pacific fliers only had to cover 2,400 miles (compared with Lindbergh's 3,600), but Hawaii wasn't as easy to find as the continent of Europe. And for most of the trip, they would be bucking head winds. When it was all over, aviation authorities claimed the Dole Derby had set aviation back twenty years.

Attempts to reach Hawaii by air were not new. In 1925, Navy Commander John Rodgers tried it in a flying boat and was forced down 300 miles short of his goal. After drifting for nine days, he and the crew of his disabled plane were sighted by a patrolling submarine and towed to the islands.

When Jim Dole notified the press of his offer four days after Lindbergh landed in Paris, pilots from all over the United States flocked to Oakland to plunk down the $100 entrance fee. There were over forty of them—barnstormers, ex-war pilots, Hollywood stunt pilots, and airmail pilots—all eager to cop the "easy money." They were unperturbed that Lloyds of London did not think much of the venture. Normally, this insurance firm would insure almost anything, but now it refused to underwrite any of the Dole contenders.

122

In California, none of the Dole pilots was giving much thought to the overwater dangers. Several were inexperienced in long-range navigation over land, with all its identifying landmarks, and most of them had never been over the water and out of sight of land. A scant two or three had radio equipment and the knowledge of how to use it. And what a motley assortment of flying machines they brought to the starting line! One plane was so ridiculously slow it couldn't carry enough fuel to fly the distance. It nosed over on every landing, so Tex Lagrone wisely withdrew his Air King biplane, *City of Peoria*.

The breakneck rush to California and the rash eagerness of the entrants to tackle the Pacific on the early August starting date worried officials of the newly formed Bureau of Air Commerce. They feared that tragic consequences would result over the open water. They intervened and insisted on rigid examinations for both planes and pilots. This had some safety value since the shortsighted entrants who were long on courage and short on judgment were forced to drop out. By August 8, only fifteen entrants remained. These men pulled numbers from a hat to determine their takeoff order, while James Dole, undismayed, happily commented: "It's shaping up to be a regular free-for-all." It certainly was.

At the very height of the preparations, four pilots stole some thunder from the Dole Derbyists. On June 28, Lieutenants Maitland and Hegenberger of the Army became the first men to fly nonstop to Hawaii. Then, on July 14, airmail pilot Ernie Smith and his navigator, Emory Bronte, duplicated the feat. None of them were Dole contenders, and the racers who worked frantically at Oakland airport could only salve their hurt pride with the philosophy, "It just proves it can be done." They overlooked the fact that Maitland and Hegenberger flew a trimotored Fokker, and Smith and Bronte, who barely reached the island, crash-landed into the treetops of Malokai when their fuel ran out. And both planes carried radios, the greatest single aid in transocean travel.

The race was plagued with misfortune from the beginning. In the hectic, tension-filled days before the starting gun sent them lumbering down Oakland's 7,000-foot runway, three planes crashed during tests and three men were killed. Death struck first on August 10. George Covell and Dick Waggener, U.S. naval officers, took off from

San Diego in their Tremaine *Humming Bird* to fly to Oakland for the start two days later. Their monoplane was heavily loaded with fuel and the engine was not operating well. Within minutes after the takeoff, they crashed into a dune at Point Loma and burned to death. Covell had picked number thirteen from the hat.

The next day, the 11th, Jim Griffin flew his huge two-engine triplane, the *Pride of Los Angeles*, from Long Beach to Oakland. As he throttled back to begin the landing approach, spectators saw his glide was too flat. Suddenly, off the edge of the field and over the mud flats, the plane stalled and flopped awkwardly into the swamps, breaking into splinters. No one was injured, but the plane sponsored by cowboy star Hoot Gibson was definitely out of the running.

August 12 was set as the starting date for two reasons: On that day in 1898, Hawaii became a territory, and, too, a full moon was scheduled to rise at sunset—a moon that would light the fliers' way through the long night. This was the best possible night-flying condition that could be had at a time when instrument and radio navigation was still an undeveloped art. When the big day arrived, however, no one was ready. Several planes were still being modified, and government officials had not finished their tests of the pilots' fitness. Race officials re-established the starting date as August 16.

At Vail Field, outside Los Angeles, another entrant, the *Angel of Los Angeles*, underwent tests before leaving for Oakland. Arthur Rodgers took off in his two-engine Bryant monoplane and began a curve around the field. While still at a low altitude—125 feet—the plane started into an uncontrollable slipping turn to the left. Rodgers fought to bring it level, then he abandoned the attempt, too late and too low. He stepped into space and pulled the ripcord. The canopy of his parachute caught in one engine and part of the tail section and pulled him to his death as the plane plummeted to earth. The death toll now stood at three.

The *City of Oakland*, a Travelaire, withdrew. So did the *Miss Hollydale*, an International owned by Frank Clarke and Charlie Babb.

By noon of the 16th, only eight of the forty-odd original contenders were ready at the starting line. A crowd of 50,000, sparked by the publicity, crashes, and excitement of the past two weeks, lined the field to cheer them off. Everything was in readiness. Ten merchant vessels and eight destroyers were spread out along the length of the course. They were to blink identifying lights to the planes when they passed overhead and relay their positions to the mainland. The four planes with radio equipment planned to home in on a radio beam transmitted from Maui, but only one of these planes, the *Woolaroc*, had two-way communication with ship and shore. The latest weather data, pieced together from ships observing at sea, indicated the winds in this part of the Pacific would be moderate, northwesterly, and would swing about sharply to the east or southeast on the last lap, giving the racers a boost into Oahu.

The men climbed aboard their planes, and the engines of the Dole racers popped, banged, and vibrated to life. Slowly, according to their takeoff position, they taxied in single file to the starting circle and awaited the starter's flag. Scheduled to be first off was Benny Griffin's and Al Henley's blue-and-yellow Travelaire, *Oklahoma*. It paused inside the starting circle, its engine ticking over impatiently, and as the starting flag flashed down, roared to sudden life. The heavily-laden plane surged forward, slowly gained speed, and staggered cumbersomely into the air at two minutes past twelve. The race was on!

One minute later the starter's flag dropped again, and Goddard and Hawkins in their silver, high-wing, open-cockpit monoplane, *El Encanto*, started down the runway. As it gained speed, it began to swerve uncontrollably right and left. In a flash, it veered sharply to the right in a vicious ground loop. The landing gear collapsed and the plane skidded to a stop in a cloud of sand and dust. Neither pilot was injured, though both were emotionally shaken by their bad luck. The plane was a total washout and, fortunately, the gas tanks did not burn or explode.

At 12:08, the *Pabco Pacific Flyer*, a Breese monoplane with Livingston Irving at the controls, got the signal. With its tremendous load of 450 gallons of gasoline, it inched forward sluggishly. Then it began to move off the runway, and Irving, unable to control it, cut the switch and rolled to a stop. A tractor was used to pull the plane back to the starting circle.

Next, the *Golden Eagle*, a 100-mile-per-hour Lockheed Vega flown by Jack Frost and Gordon Scott, took easily into the air and roared past the wreckage of the *El Encanto* and over the Pabco Pacific Flyer being returned for a second takeoff attempt. The *Golden Eagle* was highly favored to win. It was without a doubt the fastest plane in the race, with the best instrumentation. One minute later, Augy Pedlar, Lieutenant Silas Knope, and their passenger, Mildred Doran, a pretty twenty-two-year-old Caro, Michigan, schoolteacher, roared skyward in the *Miss Doran,* a Buhl sesquiplane. Mildred Doran was the only woman in the race. The *Aloha,* another Breese monoplane piloted by Martin Jensen with ocean captain Paul Schluter as navigator, lifted easily and climbed westward. The seventh plane off was the *Woolaroc,* a Travelaire flown by Arthur Goebel and Bill Davis, and bringing up the rear were Bill Erwin and Alvin Eichwaldt in their green-and-silver *Dallas Spirit*. It later came to light that these two had dreams far beyond those of the other Dole fliers. They were out to capture two prizes, the Dole purse and the additional $25,000 for the first Dallas-to-Hong Kong flight. Added to these prizes was William E. Easterwood's promise of his personal check for $10,000, which would bring the total to $60,000. If ever two men had reason to set a distance record, this was it. After their Swallow monoplane became airborne, the huge crowd began to relax its tension and drift homeward. Each spectator wondered which plane was going to reach the islands first.

Then someone pointed over the bay. Coming in low, streaming a white-silver streak of raw gasoline, was the *Miss Doran.* Pedlar was dumping fuel overboard to lighten the plane for a landing. He touched down and taxied hurriedly to the line. "It's backfiring and missing!" Pedlar yelled over the engine noise. He could have saved his breath; the engine sounded like a bucket of bolts to the most inexperienced onlooker. Pedlar shut down the popping machine and his mechanics scrambled over the cowling.

The crowd shouted again. A second plane, the *Dallas Spirit*, was coming back. Even before it landed, the trouble was obvious—a large fabric tear along the side of the fuselage. Much of the covering was ripped away and shreds were whipped briskly in the slipstream. Erwin and Eichwaldt were out of the race; the damage would take hours to repair. The *Dallas Spirit* had barely come to a standstill when the *Oklahoma* roared low over the crowd, its engine popping and trailing black smoke. As it landed and turned in beside the other two, Griffin's mechanics shook their heads. It was all over for the *Oklahoma*, too. Its overworked engine had blown five cylinders and was a total loss.

While mechanics worked frantically to change plugs on the *Miss Doran's* hot engine, Livingston Irving climbed back into his *Pabco Pacific Flyer* and tried for a second takeoff. He was already an hour and twenty minutes late, but he believed his chances were still good. Halfway down the runway he lifted the monoplane briefly. Then it settled on one wheel, bounced, lifted painfully, and settled again. It started into a wide, skidding ground loop. Finally, it toppled over on its side in a cloud of dust. The crowd gasped and tensed for an explosion. It never came, and Irving, physically unhurt but crushed in spirit, clambered out as screeching fire trucks and ambulances pulled to a stop beside him.

At the opposite end of the field, pretty Mildred Doran, shaken and pale over their aborted start, was nevertheless determined to go on. Several in the crowd shouted out demands that she be removed from the race. But she smiled faintly and climbed back aboard the Buhl as the mechanics snapped the final piece of cowling in place. Shortly after 2:00, the trio lifted off again and headed into the gusty mists beyond Fort Point and the Golden Gate. It was not until some time later that one of the mechanics thought to ask whether the *Miss Doran's* tanks had been refilled to replenish what Pedlar had dumped. They had not, and many of those who sat up all that night to ponder the progress of the fliers wondered if this little oversight was really important. No one would ever know for certain.

Now began the vigil. Those who waited throughout the night in the darkened airport hangars discussed the probable hazards awaiting the pilots. Darkness would overtake them at about 8:00, then would begin the long night. Every pilot carried life belts and a life raft as well as emergency food supplies. Jack Frost's Vega, the *Golden Eagle*, had cork slabs fitted into the wings, a sealed fuselage, and compressed-air cylinders to inflate flotation bags. It alone could remain afloat for days if forced down. The big worry, they all agreed, was the weather. A spin or a spiral dive while flying blind would be fatal.

One hour and twenty-eight minutes out of Oakland, the *Aloha* passed over the SS *Silver Fir*. Working a time-distance problem, navigator Schluter established their speed at a steady eighty miles per hour. A few minutes later the radio operator aboard the vessel heard another engine above the clouds and tapped out an inquiry. The *Woolaroc* replied, and as daylight faded, Bill Davis began to send out hourly position reports while simultaneously homing in on the directional beam transmitted from Maui. At eight o'clock, the SS *Wilhelmina,* 500 miles out of San Francisco, picked up a strong signal from the *Woolaroc's* key as it passed nearby.

After sunset, problems began to develop rapidly for the aviators. Things went somewhat better for the crew of the *Woolaroc* than for the *Aloha's* team. Arthur Goebel was more experienced in instrument flight than was Martin Jensen, who had difficulty finding his way blindly through the night and the thick fog. At one time during the night, as he groped through the inky blackness, Jensen felt the underside of the *Aloha* slap into a whitecap. He fought off the panic, pulled up, and gave the engine full power. When he leveled off he was in a cold sweat. The night ticked slowly on with no reference points. and the plane fell into several spins. Each time Jensen recovered before the churning waves could reach them. It was during this night-long struggle to keep the *Aloha* reasonably level and on course that Schluter passed him a note. "Lost until I can get a fix on Polaris."

At two o'clock, Wednesday morning, The SS *Manulani* heard the distant drone of a plane engine to the south-west. Moments later, another. The ship's radio operator raised one, the *Woolaroc,* and passed the word to the mainland. But no one had any inkling of who was flying the second plane or the whereabouts of the remaining two still unaccounted for.

Meanwhile, Honolulu was wide awake. Long before dawn 30,000 spectators jammed the road to Wheeler Field. Only the position of the *Woolaroc,* which had trans-mitted faithfully every hour, was known. It was dead on the directional beam, and at 6:00 A.M. was reported 600 miles out. But where were the others? The *Miss Doran?* The *Golden Eagle?* The *Aloha?*

Just before noon the *Woolaroc* raised land. Manuai! A short time later Molokai and Diamond Head slipped under its wings and a military escort of planes roared out to meet it. At 12:20, Goebel and Davis landed to the thunderous roar of the crowd, first-place winners. Their time: twenty-six hours and seventeen minutes. Now the big question was who would follow them.

During the black hours over the Pacific, Martin Jensen struggled to keep the *Aloha* on course. Vertigo and sensory illusions confused him. Below him was inky blackness; above, a solid cloud layer. The only thing he knew for certain was that they were lost somewhere between California and Hawaii, and as the night wore on, their hopes grew darker. Then, the nightmare broke into a beautiful dawn. Schluter, who had been unable to get a star fix once during the night, was certain from the record of his elapsed time that they were on a line (north or south) of the islands at 8:30. At 9:00 Jensen passed a note to Schluter. "Where from here?"

Schluter scribbled on a pad an passed the answer forward. "Circle till noon."

Until the sun was at its zenith, Schluter, who was accustomed to surface ship navigation, couldn't get a celestial fix. For the next three hours the pair flew in wide cirles as their gas began to run dangerously low. One after another the tanks ran dry. At noon, Schluter quickly made a sun shot. His report: 200 miles north of Hawaii!

Leaning out every ounce of gasoline, Jensen reached out for Diamond Head. After what seemed an interminable time they spotted the island, hopped over Koolau Range, and let down for Wheeler Field. They landed with four gallons of fuel remaining, twenty-eight hours and sixteen minutes out of Oakland, as second-place winners.

By late afternoon, hope was fading fast for the remaining two planes. At 4:20, Frost's *Golden Eagle* would have exhausted its fuel; at 8:20 that evening the last tank of the *Miss Doran* was dry. No one knew when or where their flight was stilled or what fate befell them over the Pacific on that long night of overcast, swirling fog, and darkness. Somewhere in that empty sky they met trouble, and somewhere in that empty sea they crashed. And the whitecaps rolled over them and smoothed away all trace of their graves.

The next day, the 18th, Jensen and Goebel searched

with Army and Navy planes for signs of wreckage. Reports of a signal flare on Mount Mauna Kea came in during the night, but it turned out to be a rancher testing a new type of gasoline lantern. Then a red, white, and blue object was reported afloat in the water east of Maui. Hopes arose that it was the *Miss Doran*. It wasn't; it was only a sampan.

Acting Secretary of the Navy Eberle authorized a sea search for the missing planes. It covered 540,000 square miles and lasted a week. The seven destroyers, submarine tenders, cruisers, and aircraft carriers—forty navy vessels in all—comprised, up to that time, the largest fleet to be used in a search in naval history. Jim Dole personally put up a reward of $20,000 for the finding of either plane, Bill Mollaska offered $10,000 for the *Miss Doran*, and George Hearst, Jr., put up another $10,000 for the *Golden Eagle*. No one collected.

Death was to touch its icy fingers on two more daredevils before the full account of the Pacific marathon would be closed. On Friday morning, August 19, Bill Erwin flew his repaired *Dallas Spirit* around the bay to test his two-way radio. It had been given the call letters KGGA and was installed while the repairs were being made to the Swallow's fuselage. When Erwin landed he was in excellent spirits. He reported everything fine and ordered his fuel tanks topped to their limit of 450 gallons.

Bill Erwin was no beginner to flying. He learned to fly in 1917 with the Signal Corps, went to France with the first Aero Squadron, and rose to the rank of captain. Flying Spads, he shot down eight enemy planes, was decorated, and awarded the Distinguished Service Cross. Lone Star Bill and his navigator, Alvin Eichwaldt, were thwarted in their try for the Dole prize, but now they declared themselves in the running for the Easterwood prize. Though they claimed they were off to search for the *Miss Doran* and the *Golden Eagle*, everyone knew otherwise. Hong Kong was their destination.

Five thousand spectators turned out to see them off. And although neither the Navy Department nor the National Aeronautics Association approved of their flight, the two would-be record makers would not be turned aside.

Ted Dealy, who is today the publisher of the *Dallas Morning News*, was a reporter at the time and a personal friend of Erwin. In looking back on that fateful date, he

130

says: "Erwin was thirty-one years old, the son of a Presbyterian preacher. He had no premonition he would lose his life in the Pacific. Before he took off he left a written message for his mother and a second letter for his sponsors. Each one evidences his deep religious beliefs and his confidence in the outcome of his flight. In the letter to his sponsors, Erwin wrote:

Tomorrow begins the great adventure. Flying personifies the spirit of man. Our bodies are bound to the earth; our spirits are bound by God alone, and it is my firm belief that God will guide the course of the *Dallas Spirit* tomorrow over the shortest route from the Golden Gate to the Isle of Oahu . . . If we succeed, it will be glorious.

If we fail, it will not be in vain, for a worthy attempt could never result in a mean failure.

I believe with my whole heart that we will make it. I believed it when I first conceived it, and I believe it more strongly now. We will win because *Dallas Spirit* always wins.

But if it be His will that we should not make it, and from the exploration of the Pacific we should suddenly be called upon to chart our course over the Great Ocean of Eternity, then be of good cheer. I hold life dear, but I do not fear death. It is the last and most wonderful adventure of life. If something should happen to me I know I don't have to ask you to look after Mrs. Erwin. It broke her heart that she could not accompany me. She is my life, gentlemen, and the sweetest, finest, truest girl the Almighty ever created.

Knowing that she is safe gives me confidence and vigor for the trial. We will make it because we must, but whatever comes, I am the master of my fate, and God willing, the Captain of my soul.

"The Mrs. Erwin he mentioned was his wife, Constance Ohl Erwin. She wanted to accompany her husband on the flight, but was ruled out because she was under twenty years of age. It was just as well, for the Erwins were expecting a child.

"When Captain Erwin left Oakland airport on his last voyage into the air," Dealy concluded, "he had a small

Bible in the right-hand pocket of his sack coat. He didn't mention it, but I saw it there as I was helping him into his flying suit."

Shortly after two in the afternoon, Erwin and Eichwaldt made an uneventful takeoff and headed out the Golden Gate. Twenty minutes later they began to transmit code messages. At 3:49 they reported the ceiling at 700 feet; they were flying at 500. At 5:10 they passed over the SS *Mana,* and at 6:53 they reported their position at 35.30 North Latitude and 130 West Longitude—about 450 miles out. At 7:12 the key crackled: "We have thirty miles visibility and are flying at 900 feet. Have seen nothing [of the *Miss Doran* or the *Golden Eagle*]."

At 8:00: "It is beginning to get dark."

8:51: "SOS. [pause] Belay that. We were in a spin, but came out of it O.K. We were sure scared. It was sure a close call. The lights on the instrument panel went out and it was so dark Bill could not see the wings."

9:02: "We are in an—"

Silence.

As the half-finished message broke, off radio operators on ship and shore waited anxiously. Several tried to tap out a message to KGGA. "Come in . . . Come in KGGA . . . Do you hear us, KGGA?"

KGGA did not hear. Apparently, Eichwaldt was trying to transmit "We are in another spin" and never finished it. And so the *Dallas Spirit* changed its course and headed into the Great Ocean of Eternity that Bill Erwin had mentioned.

At dawn, ships converged on the place where the *Dallas Spirit* made its final call. They searched the area for a week without finding a sign of anything—not a trace of wreckage, not a scrap or fragment of anything resembling an airplane. Like the others, the Pacific had swallowed the aircraft completely. The flight paths of the three missing planes were over the most traveled sea lanes between the islands, crossed almost constantly by passenger liners, freighters, tankers, and naval vessels, yet not a scrap of floating debris from any of the aircraft was ever found.

In the weeks that followed, the public protested and critics blasted the Dole Derby as a blow to aviation's progress. James Dole came in for a major share of the blame, accused of thinking only of publicity for his pineapple empire. Dole admitted he felt an indirect responsibility. Newspaper and magazine editorialists who a few weeks before had praised his gesture as a milestone in aviation pioneering, now decried just as loudly his thoughtless encouragement of stunt flying.

Perhaps everyone was partly right, but the fact remains that by hurrying to meet the starting deadline, many aviators who normally practiced safety in flight did dangerous and foolhardy things. In taking the short cuts they normally shunned, air safety took a back seat with several of the contenders. That it should have been riding as copilot was realized too late. Five planes were wrecked, three were lost at sea, and ten persons were killed—Waggener, Covell, Frost, Scott, Rodgers, Erwin, Eichwaldt, Pedlar, Knope, and young Mildred Doran, the first woman to be lost in a Pacific air crossing.

At noon on September 16, 750 miles out of San Francisco, the SS *Maui* cut its engines and drifted to a stop. The passengers and crew quietly assembled on deck and with heads bowed, listened as someone read from the Scriptures: "The Lord is my Shepherd . . . I shall not want . . ." Then the voice of another, a member of the ship's crew, drifted across the Pacific waters. "Going home, going home . . . I'm going home . . ."

The engines rumbled to a slow idle as the steamer made a huge circle. A shower of wreaths and floral pieces were dropped over the side. One of them, in the form of a Holy Bible, carried a message from the sixth-graders of Caro, Michigan. They had saved their pennies and nickles to send this parting prayer to those daring fliers who had gambled and lost all, and to Mildred Doran, their beloved teacher.

It said: "God Bless You Every One."

CHAPTER 9

South to Rio

The mystery of Paul Redfern's disappearance in 1927 remains today as puzzling as it was when the slim, handsome young adventurer climbed into the cabin of his monoplane and flew into—what?

Years after the green-and-gold Stinson Detroiter *Port of*

Brunswick vanished somewhere over South America, newspapers kept the story alive. Journalists were asking as late as 1961: Did Paul Redfern find his Shangri-la in the uninhabited wilds of British Guiana? Is he living as a white god somewhere along the snakelike Amazon? Someday, will he step out of the South American jungles as he allegedly said he would?

It is unlikely. Over a dozen searches have penetrated the dense brush of the Amazon Valley in the hope of finding a clue to the whereabouts of the missing pilot. Not one expedition has been even remotely successful. Not one scrap of evidence has ever been uncovered to indicate that Redfern survived his unknown rendezvous with Destiny.

The mystery, then, is not whether Paul Redfern is alive but where his green-and-gold monoplane disappeared and why.

The Roaring Twenties was in its seventh turbulent year. This was "the year the world went wild." Surely it seemed so. Lindbergh soloed the Atlantic; Chicago reeled under murderous gang wars. Anyone crazy enough to put up fifty-eight dollars could fly from Los Angeles to Seattle on a Pacific Air Transport plane. Hundreds of young eagles with dreams of adventure were planning and doing the feats that would shape aviation history.

A twenty-five-year-old former music student who had turned flier was among them. Born in Rochester in 1902, Paul Redfern was too young for World War I, but not for the postwar Jennies that barnstormed the country. Before he operated his own airport in Toledo in 1925, he had flown 60,000 miles in forty states.

In 1924, Redfern was a pilot for J. F. Reichard Cigar Company of York, Pennsylvania. He spent some time in Toledo, Ohio, on an advertising campaign directed by C. C. Hillabrand, the company's Toledo distributor. In one of the first attempts at aerial advertising, Redfern flew over the city and dropped miniature parachutes with sample cigars attached.

Paul met and married Hillabrand's attractive auburn-haired daughter, Gertrude, in January 1925. After a honeymoon combined with an advertising campaign, they returned to Toledo where Paul leased some land and operated his own airport.

This lasted only a few months, for Redfern was restless.

He had taken a position as a U.S. Government "dry sky scout" stationed at the famed old Customs House in Savannah. His job was to locate stills from the air, signal their locations to ground parties, and to chase rumrunners at sea.

Redfern's young wife noticed her husband's restlessness. "Paul was determined, romantic, and adventuresome," she reflects today. "In his early flying days many newspapermen referred to him as Daredevil Redfern."

In 1926, Redfern outlined plans to win the Dole purse but changed his mind in favor of a more difficult goal, a nonstop solo flight from Brunswick, Georgia, to Rio de Janeiro. Early in 1927, on a leave of absence from his job with the Customs Office, he turned his efforts toward convincing several prominent Brunswick businessmen that the next air route to be conquered was one linking North and South America. They agreed to back the venture and underwrote $25,000 for the plane and equipment.

Paul selected a Stinson Detroiter for the long-distance attempt. Although it was a single-engine aircraft, it had a highlift wing, could fly at a moderate airspeed, and was equipped with the finest engine of its day—the proved 225-horsepower Wright Whirlwind—the same model engine that powered Lindbergh's *Spirit of St. Louis*. Special fuel tanks installed at the Stinson factory could be emptied in forty-five seconds if it suddenly became necessary to lighten the load.

In midsummer, Paul flew his Stinson from Detroit to Glynn Isle Beach, Georgia, to complete preparations for his solo flight. In a brief ceremony just prior to his departure, Mrs. Eugene A. Lewis, wife of a prominent Detroit business leader, christened the plane *Port of Brunswick*, in honor of the Brunswick, Georgia, businessmen who backed the flight. The plane bore the registration-number NX773 on its wings.

Early in August, Redfern and his assistants began final preparations. J. J. B. Fulenwider was Redfern's nautical advisor; Paul J. Varner, chairman of the flight committee and one of the backers, assisted in selecting the equipment to be carried; and Captain D. M. Scaritt of the U.S. Department of Commerce was the official starter.

Redfern's survival equipment was more than adequate, provided he could set the airplane down in a clear area without injury to himself. He carried a small, inflatable raft, in case he was forced down at sea, emergency rations for ten days, fishing tackle, a collapsible rifle with 100 rounds of ammunition, quinine and other medicines, hunting knives, matches, flares, a small distilling outfit, boots, and a parachute, one item most of the other distance fliers omitted to save space and weight. Redfern made no effort to conceal his belief that his greatest danger would be a crash landing in the unexplored wilds of the Amazon.

At the Stinson factory, Redfern had the Detroiter modified to carry 550 gallons of gasoline, enough to reach Rio if an average ground speed of ninety-two miles an hour could be held. It did not allow much of a reserve. After two days and two nights aloft, Redfern planned to land at Camp Affenso near Campo, outside Rio. He knew a fuel shortage or bad weather would seriously cut his flying distance, so he wisely selected Pernambuco on the easternmost tip of Brazil as his alternate destination. A fact frequently overlooked in studying Redfern's trip is that the intrepid young man's carefully planned flight would have outdistanced all previous ones. The 4,600-mile span would, if successful, outdistance Lindbergh's flight of three months earlier by 1,000 miles.

The trial flights were made to confirm the airplane's balance, load-carrying ability, and airspeed. When Redfern finished, he was satisfied the plane would do the job, as were Government officials and the Stinson representatives who carefully cross-checked every mechanical and aerodynamic detail.

When Gertrude Redfern received a wire from her husband that preparations for the flight were almost completed and that he was "rarin' to go," she left Toledo immediately for Brunswick to be with Paul for a few days prior to the take-off scheduled for Saturday, August 20. Having flown with Paul many times she was fully confident of his flying ability.

When news came of the lost Dole contenders and of Erwin and Eichwaldt's disappearance in the Pacific, it failed to shake Redfern's confidence. He said little about it and busied himself with last-minute details on the *Port of Brunswick*.

The departure date was changed several times. A tropical storm was reported to be brewing to the south, in line with the flight path. Impatient, Redfern pushed plans for an early Monday morning takeoff. But the weather grew worse and by Tuesday the horizon was dark and gloomy. On Wednesday a hurricane swished up the Atlantic seaboard and sent its skirting waves almost to the hangar doors. Everything was battened down tight.

Thursday saw a welcome improvement in the weather and Redfern made a final check of his route. The line drawn across his air charts to show the flight path cut across the extreme tip of Puerto Rico, passed directly over Grenada and Tobago islands. He hoped to make his South American landfall at St. Andrew's Point, British Guiana, then fly over Dutch Guiana and the northeastern part of Brazil until he reached Macapa on the north bank of the Amazon estuary. From here, it was 1,300 miles to Pernambuco on the east coast (his alternate), and 1,650 to Rio. Over Macapa, Redfern was scheduled to drop a colored flare; red if his gas was running low and he planned to land at Pernambuco, green if everything was satisfactory and he intended to proceed to Rio.

If the possibility of a forced landing in the jungle haunted Redfern, he failed to show it. In one of his final interviews he told the press: "Don't lose hope of my return for at least six months or more. If I should be forced down in the Amazon Valley, I believe I can live for months with the equipment I'm carrying."

On Friday morning, the dark-haired 138-pound aviator announced that "barring another hurricane—and God willing, I'm going on to Brazil." Officials shook their heads; the weather picture was still doubtful in the Caribbean and over the Atlantic. He sent a last-minute telegram to his mother, Mrs. Blanche Redfern, who waited in Rochester, New York. The message read: "Goodbye Mother dear. Will cable you from Brazil. Heaps of love."

Shortly after noon—a gloomy overcast midday—Redfern climbed into the cramped cockpit of his monoplane. His wife slipped into the cabin beside him. They talked for a few brief moments. Paul Redfern's final words to his wife were: "Goodbye, my darling, and don't worry—I'll see you real soon." (Gertrude was to meet him in Rio or wherever he might land, if it was necessary to change course due to weather or low fuel.) There was a lingering last-minute kiss and then the young girl stepped unhesitatingly to the ground and walked away from the plane. One of the flight-committee members handed Redfern a sealed packet containing letters to the President of Brazil and the Mayor of Rio from the Governor of Georgia and the Mayor of Brunswick.

It was low tide. The waters had floated back from the marshes of Glynn and it was time to go. Redfern opened the throttle and began a slow, lumbering run down the long, eight-mile Sea Island Beach. As the heavily loaded plane, 5,500 pounds in all, struggled to become airborne, a stiff crosswind from the sea threatened to flip it on its side. Redfern cut the engine, rolled to a quick stop, turned and taxied back to the hangar. The crowd of 3,000 wondered if he would call the flight off.

Paul Varner ran to the airplane and conversed with Redfern. "I couldn't take the chance, Paul," Redfern shouted above the engine noise. "When I lifted the tail, the wind pushed me toward the water. Pull me higher onto the beach. I'll get off next time."

He did. A quarter of an hour later, with the Wright Whirlwind straining full out and the airplane now quartered into the wind, Redfern thrust it forward again and slipped heavily into the air amid the shouts of the crowd. It was 12:46. Paul Redfern, Brunswick's adopted son, was on his way south to Rio.

News of the successful takeoff was flashed to Rio, where excited Brazilians were already preparing a gala welcome for the "Lindbergh of South America." Although Redfern was not due to arrive until late Sunday, the streets were already humming with emotional Latins anxious for the celebration to begin. At Campo the United States Navy was ready with powerful searchlights to guide Redfern in if he arrived at night. Naval officers thought it would be even better if they could use their radio transmitters to direct him, but the *Port of Brunswick* carried no radio.

After the tiny speck disappeared low over the southern horizon, its position was reported several times. Shortly before midnight the monoplane was sighted overhead at 2,000 feet by a steamer 300 miles east of the Bahamas. It was droning steadily along in a southerly direction. The news was radioed to Station 4AQF in Nassau, which relayed the report to Brunswick by way of a radio operator in St. Petersburg, Florida.

In Brunswick, Redfern's wife and friends maintained a tense vigil. At Rio, Brazilians scanned the hourly bulletins while crowds began to congregate at Campo in anticipation of their hero's arrival. But even as Redfern winged over the Caribbean, armchair prophets were gloomily predicting his failure. One pointed out that the winds were sure to be unfavorable; naval navigators and hydrographers predicted he would miss his mark by 450 miles. They contended he would have to fly a total of twenty-four hours at night with no moon and that he would not have enough gas for what they were sure would be a sixty-two-hour flight.

About three o'clock on Saturday afternoon, ship's master Captain I. A. Hamre watched from the bridge of his Norwegian merchantman, *Christian Krogh,* as a lone plane, flying low, appeared over the northern horizon. As it circled his vessel, the crew could clearly make out the bold black letters on the fuselage: BRUNSWICK TO BRAZIL.

Three times the plane swooped low overhead as the pilot dropped messages in waterproof containers through the cabin window. The first one disappeared in the waves. As the second note fell, fireman W. T. Notweet dived into the churning water and grasped the container. The message asked the captain to point his ship toward the nearest land. Hamre complied and swung the prow toward Venezuela, 165 miles away. Redfern zoomed low again and dropped a third note which was recovered. It asked the crew to "blow the ship's whistle once for each 100 miles—Redfern, Thanks."

As the thunderous steam bellowed from the ship's whistle, the plane lined up with the *Christian Krogh's* path, wiggled its wings in thanks, and disappeared toward the Venezuelan coastline. Later that afternoon, excited natives watched the plane pass over the village of Tucupita, just north of the Orinoco Delta. Still later, it was seen crossing over the Canamacoreoa River, headed for Boca Grande. A heavy storm broke over the village of Macareito in the Orinoco Delta, but according to reports it occurred an hour before Redfern passed overhead, apparently unscathed.

This was the last time the plane was ever seen by white men—heading into the green nightmare of British Guiana and the Amazon River Valley.

As the hours moved up to the projected time of Redfern's arrival in Rio de Janeiro, Gertrude Redfern and Dr. Frederick C. Redfern, Paul's father, gathered with anxious members of the flight committee to hear, hopefully, the message flashed from Rio that the aviator had landed safely.

Long minutes slipped into even longer hours. There were no reports at all on Sunday; no word of any sighting along the proposed flight path. He had not flown over Macapa as planned. That evening Paul Varner solemnly announced to the press: "At 4:30 this afternoon we were certain that Paul Redfern was no longer in the air. His fuel would have been exhausted at that time."

Redfern had been forced down somewhere in the South American jungles. But where? Where in the hundreds of thousands of square miles of the wild continent? Did he crash in the Pacaraima Mountains of British Guiana? The Orinoco? The Amazon Basin? Or had he drifted westward, pushed by the prevailing easterlies, until he ran out of fuel in the unexplored heartland of central Brazil?

At Georgetown, British Guiana, the governor ordered a seaplane to patrol the jungles. A few days later, in an interview at the Great Northern Hotel in New York City, a commercial pilot, Robert Moore, claimed Redfern "was forced down before he flew 500 miles from Brunswick. He was struck by a waterspout." Moore claimed to have seen Redfern dodging waterspouts in the Bahamas near Great Abaco Island on Friday afternoon. Moore's theory was proved wrong when the messages dropped to the *Christian Krogh* were received in Brunswick and positively identified as having been written by Redfern.

The first expedition for the missing aviator got under way in September when Redfern's uncle, Richard Redfern, joined a search party headed by Richard O. Marsh of Rochester. Marsh, using two planes, started his search in the Delta of the Orinoco and worked south. After several grueling weeks they returned without finding a trace of the missing plane. The following June (1928), the citizens of Brunswick dedicated Redfern Field, in honor of their missing adopted son and his ambitious flight.

Between 1928 and 1937, expedition after expedition probed the South American jungles, tracking down every lead that could be found. None of them led anywhere. Art Williams, the naval pilot who had taught Redfern to fly, made extended flights over the route while he was working in South America, but like the others, his efforts were in vain.

In the years since Redfern's disappearance, thousands

of words have poured from the pens of imaginative newsmen and feature writers. The romantics of aviation had a heyday. Some pictured Redfern as a crippled white god among the savages; others as a dazed, white-haired man stumbling aimlessly through the steaming jungles. There has not been one fragment of fact to substantiate these weird tales or any evidence whatsoever that Redfern even survived the crash of his Stinson.

The final and most elaborate expedition was arranged in 1937 by Colonel Theodore Waldeck, a friend of the Redfern family. One member of the party, Dr. Frederick J. Fox, died on the trip, and a second member, William Astor Chandler, almost lost his life. Colonel Waldeck eventually emerged from the jungles of British Guiana "convinced that Redfern crashed and died on the continent."

Until his death in 1941, the aviator's father steadfastly clung to the hope that his son might still be alive. But Paul's sister, Mrs. Ruth Sanders of Sumter, doubts that this could be. In recent years she has said: "In spite of the many rumors . . . that Paul is alive, I don't believe it's possible that he could be after so many years without tangible evidence."

The last flurry of interest in the Redfern mystery occurred in December 1939. A Uruguayan seaman, Gustavo Adolpho Lentulus, who was temporarily stranded in Bayonne, New Jersey, told reporters this story. Clearly it is at variance with Colonel Waldeck's findings.

Shortly before he sailed from Argentina a few months earlier, Lentulus met a recluse, a Swiss resident of Buenos Aires, by the name of Hans Seigerst. He told Lentulus about a four-year expedition that he and three other men made into the jungles in 1932. According to Lentulus, Seigerst showed the sailor certain articles salvaged from the wreckage of a plane they found 800 miles from Buenos Aires. The items included a wrist watch, a buckle, and some papers, all taken from the remains of the pilot, who was still wearing a leather jacket. The papers, Lentulus claimed, were personally examined by him, and he identified a note that contained the abbreviation: "U.S.A." and the word "Cal." It was signed "Redfern."

Seigerst was the only man to return alive from the expedition.

Following her husband's disappearance, as the expeditions all failed, Gertrude Redfern gradually resigned herself to accept that Paul had perished on the flight. In 1937, after ten years of futile searching, elevated hopes, and saddening disappointments, she petitioned the Circuit Court at Detroit to declare her husband presumably dead. Today, Gertrude Redfern retains much of the charm and grace of the young girl who once stood on Glynn Isle Beach and waved to her husband in the green-and-gold monoplane fast disappearing into the mists. She is administrative assistant to the president of a Detroit corporation, which she joined twenty-one years ago. In looking back to those few short years when the world awaited news of her husband's fate, she reflects:

Many articles have been written about the Redfern flight, and most of them have been more fiction than fact. But there's no need to go into that now, for much water has gone over the dam since Paul's ill-fated flight and one cannot live in the past. My position is interesting and challenging and with my many outside interests I am always wishing for more hours in the day.

Paul's father never lost hope. Paul was quite resourceful and didn't want us to give up hope if he had a forced landing in the jungle. Dr. Redfern was very fervent in following the progress of the searches for his son; together we pored for hours over chart after chart of the Amazon River Valley. I think I know every town and village by heart. In all, thirteen expeditions were made, all with high hopes—but without success.

Of course, a number of stories have come out of the jungles about Paul's disappearance. Of these, the general consensus is that his crash was caused by a tropical storm.

Frankly, I believe we may never know the truth of what happened.

CHAPTER 10

"I'm Going On!"

The Sahara keeps its secrets well; still, it must relax its grip sometime. Proof of this was shown in French Algeria. What happens to those who gamble single-handedly with the desert's vastness—and lose—was dramatically brought to light in the discovery of the body and plane of a Royal Air Force Reserve pilot in the untrodden Algerian wastes. On the night of April 13, 1933, ten years to the month before the *Lady Be Good* crashed in the Sahara, the pilot took off from Reggan in a small De Havilland biplane. His destination was Gao, a small town on the banks of the Niger River, in what is today the Republic of Mali. Deep in the loneliest part of the Algerian Sahara, something happened, and the world lost contact with him for half a lifetime.

When the Algerian War flared in North Africa, French Army patrols ranged farther than ever before into the desert. One motorized patrol departed from isolated Reggan in February of 1962 and probed into the sun-scorched uninhabitable region, 150 miles to the south. Forty miles off the Trans-Saharan Road, in a stretch rarely seen by living beings, the motor carrier came to an abrupt halt. In their path lay strange skeletal remains. A closer inspection showed them to be the twisted, upturned wreckage of an old De Havilland biplane.

Under the bare framework of a wing that had once offered some shade from the glaring sun, one of the soldiers found the huddled corpse of a man. The mummified remains lay among empty water bottles and meager survival equipment: a flashlight, matches, some personal belongings.

Another man discovered one fuel tank that still held gasoline. Someone removed a weather-beaten, faded logbook that had been crudely wired to a wing strut. This was probably the pilot's final act before he died. It proved to be a diary that told the full story of the crash in painfully written paragraphs—eight days in the world's most merciless inferno. The brittle pages, remarkably intact after weathering twenty-four years in the Sahara, revealed that the pilot had been Captain William Newton Lancaster, RAF Reserve. He crashed on April 13, 1933, while attempting a night crossing of the Sahara.

Lancaster was thirty-four at the time of the crash, a formidable, square-jawed aviator who had flown with the RAF in World War I and later won long-distance flight laurels. He was no fledgling when it came to spanning continents. In 1927, he and Mrs. Jessie Miller teamed up for a successful 13,000-mile England-to-Australia flight in a tiny Avro Avian. Early in 1933, the air adventurer made plans to beat aviatrix Amy Mollison's England-to-Cape Town dash of four days, six hours, and fifty-four minutes.

In England, Lancaster purchased a used De Havilland, a blue biplane with a 100-horsepower engine, and modified it so it could fly 1,600 miles nonstop at ninety-five miles an hour. He named it the *Southern Cross Minor*.

With years of long-range flying under his belt, Lancaster was not the least deceived by the magnitude of his venture. "I propose to fly over the inhospitable Sahara, a distance of 1,500 miles in one flight. I've been warned to expect very bad weather on parts of the trip." It soon developed that his absolute determination to succeed had pushed aside rational thinking at a time when he needed it most.

At 5:30 A.M. on April 11, he kissed his mother and father goodbye at Lympne Airport in Kent and climbed into his heavily-laden plane. He took off on the first leg of his journey, circled heavily and slowly around the airfield, and waved to his only well-wishers on the ground—his parents and a lone reporter from the London *Daily Express*.

Lancaster covered the punishing 1,100-mile flight to Oran, Algeria, in sixteen hours. He landed in a state of exhaustion, rested as his plane was refueled, then prepared for immediate takeoff. French officials tried to detain him; they saw he was in no condition to go on. Stubbornly, Lancaster resisted. They reminded him that regulations required Sahara fliers to deposit £800 to defray search costs. Lancaster did not have it. Irritated, distraught, he shouted, "I'll take my chances. I don't expect you to look for me!" The French colonial shrugged and stepped aside.

Lancaster flew directly to Reggan, a distance of 700 miles, near the heart of the Sahara. In those days it was only an oasis, the post of the Trans-Saharan Company, but today it is France's atomic test site. Lancaster planned to make a daylight crossing of the desert, using the Trans-Saharan Road and a few landmarks to point the way to the Ahaggar Mountains in the south. If he arrived at Reggan early, he reasoned, he might be able to spend a few hours resting before a predawn takeoff for Gao.

The flying schedule went badly for the determined aviator. Head winds cut his ground speed to under seventy miles an hour. As a result, he did not reach Reggan until late in the afternoon of the 12th. Then a threatening sandstorm clouded the skies around the airstrip. Lancaster made a quick check of his schedule while his plane was being refueled. He was running well behind time. He knew at that moment there was only one way to break the record to Cape Town: to take off immediately on a night flight across the Sahara and navigate solely by compass.

The French officials at the post were disapproving when Lancaster told them of his decision. He had been in the air almost thirty hours without rest and could barely stand, much less fly and navigate simultaneously. They tried to disuade him; reminded him that the weather was growing worse, that he had no cockpit lights, no reserve rations, and only one extra gallon of water—a day's supply in the desert. They also pointed out that with head winds his ground speed would be reduced to seventy or seventy-five miles an hour. He might not make it to Gao, even though the plane's range was 1,600 miles. The margin for error was too critical; it was clearly touch and go all the way. But with sleeplessness beginning to show its effects, Lancaster stubbornly refused to listen.

"I'm going on," was all he said.

The French official in charge of the post realized Lancaster meant what he said, so he shrugged his shoulders, sighed, and signed the clearance papers. Lancaster climbed clumsily into the plane's small cockpit and signaled for the propeller to be pulled through. The engine sputtered to life and as the pilot was about to taxi away for takeoff, the Frenchman rushed up to the plane and handed Lancaster a box of matches and a flashlight. Lancaster nodded his thanks; now he would be able to see the compass in the darkened cockpit.

The takeoff was a mad grab for altitude; the lack of sleep was beginning to have its effects on Lancaster's reaction time. For several minutes the dazed pilot headed in the wrong direction, then, realizing his error, he turned southeast on course. Slowly, the sound of the Gipsy engine faded into the distant darkness. The men of the barren desert outpost listened until they could hear it no longer. They who longed for civilization did not envy Lancaster's way of getting there. They turned back to their huts, arguing about the "crazy Englishman's" chances of reaching Gao. Some said he might make it if he could stay awake. In any event, radio confirmation from Gao in a few days would settle the matter. The message never came; they were the last people ever to see William Newton Lancaster alive.

The desert night air grew blustery and strong as Captain Lancaster headed southeast from the oasis. Cold blasts flew against his face. He welcomed the chill air; it kept him awake. He leveled off at 1,000 feet and occasionally took a quick look at his compass with the flashlight.

Except for the rough air and the constant struggle to stay awake, the flight proceeded on course. Then, an hour and a half out of Reggan, the *Southern Cross Minor's* engine began to act up. Immediately Lancaster was wide awake . . . listening. There it was again—a misfire. He checked his power settings. Everything seemed normal. Sand perhaps . . . in the carburetor? A moment later and the engine cut out completely. In the lonely sky over the Sahara the only sound was the low whistling rush of wind past the struts of a small, powerless airplane and the muffled ticking of its windmilling propeller. Lancaster peered into the darkness below. He was determined to set the gasoline-laden biplane down in one piece. Then he could repair the damage and continue on.

But Lancaster's tired eyes played tricks on him. He misjudged the ground and the plane hit hard on the desert floor, bounced, hit again, and plowed into a mound of soft sand. The flimsy gear gave way, and the biplane flipped over on its back with a splintering crunch of wings and propeller. Lancaster pitched violently forward and slammed against the instrument panel.

Dazed and bleeding from face wounds, he crawled from the machine and surveyed the damage in the darkness. It was the end of the line for the *Southern Cross Minor*.

146

Half stumbling, half crawling, Lancaster burrowed under a wing where he slept until morning. He awakened with a compulsion to check his two-gallon water tank. He staggered to the broken fuselage. The tank was intact.

He took stock of his supplies. In all, things weren't too bad, he figured. He had two gallons of water, a thermos partly full, another thermos of coffee, and some food rations. Seven or eight days, he estimated. He looked at his map and judged he was about twenty miles off the Trans-Saharan Road.

He was wrong. Dead 'wrong. He was nowhere near the Trans-Saharan Road. Lancaster was lost, an insignificant speck in the world's largest unmapped desert.

He began to realize his weakness from loss of blood and rest. His head wound pained him and to pass the time he jotted down his thoughts in his logbook. He was confident his loss would be noted soon and searchers would start from Reggan that evening. He elected to remain with his plane; he had informed his parents and friends that this would be his plan if forced down. Too, he may have thought a passing caravan of friendly natives would rescue him.

He stripped fabric from the wings and made crude flares out of gasoline-soaked cloth wrapped around wire. He kept a lonely vigil all the next night, lighting the flares at regular intervals.

The nights as well as the days were agonizing. He wrote in his log:

The contrast in temperature is ghastly. In the day it's so hot it's like being in an oven; at night I need every bit of clothing I have with me—vest, shirt, sweater (thick one), coat, flying jacket (light), muffler of wool, flying trousers over them, socks, underpants. In spite of all this, I am still chilly.

The water tank gets cold at night, so by morning, if I fill the thermos flask, I have an ice-cold drink all day. I take a sip every half hour.

Not getting lost in the desert much, I don't know the technical method for conserving one's water. I do know this. When I lift the flask for my sip I have to fight with all my will power to prevent my tipping it up and having a good drink . . .

As the hours passed, Lancaster became more concerned about the absence of search parties. As early as the night of the 13th, however, the French authorities at Reggan had sent a desert vehicle along the Trans-Saharan road to look for flares. The following morning, two search planes left Gao, heading north. Other military aircraft based on the fringes of the barren wastes and at scattered outposts were alerted as the air-ground search was put into motion.

Sometime during the fifth night, one of the ground convoys came maddeningly close to finding Lancaster. The dazed pilot wrote that he saw a flare in the distance. Elated, he struggled to his feet and lighted several torches, then sat back to await the party he was confident would soon appear. He even took the luxury of drinking a little extra water. But his celebration was premature. No one appeared. His lights were not seen.

The next morning he wrote:

> I am resigned to my fate. I can see I shall not be
> rescued unless a miracle happens . . . I have no food
> of course. Only feel thirsty.

On the sixth day, the effects of prolonged desert exposure and loss of blood from his wounds began to tell. His skin was drying fast; his face swelled and his eyes ached. Now his writing was becoming illegible and he concentrated on sitting in the sheltering shadows of the plane's wings. He tried to conserve his energy to hold out as long as possible. He wrote that the only living things he saw were a small bird and a circling vulture that decided not to stay. That evening he stripped almost all of the fabric from the *Southern Cross Minor's* frame and made the final torches. These he set alight after dark. Doggedly, he still clung to a thread of hope. His writing now was of memories of earlier, happier times. He reminisced to pass the time and bolster his fast-fading spirits.

On the seventh day, he could barely move, but he managed to scratch out the final log entry. He bade his friends farewell, wrapped the book in a scrap of fabric and tied it to a wing strut with a piece of wire. Then he lay down to sleep, knowing the next day's water was gone.

The morning of the 20th dawned. Lancaster raised himself on one elbow and stared blankly at the far horizon through swollen eyelids. On a card, he painfully scratched some last words, early, before the sun rose in the heavens.

So the beginning of the eighth day has dawned. It is still cool. I have no water. No wind. I am waiting patiently. Come soon, please. Fever racked me last night. Hope you get my full log.

BILL

The desert claimed him sometime that day, or perhaps it was sometime during the night, when he slipped into welcome death—still waiting. The search party finally came, twenty-nine years too late, and found him in a position that appeared as though he was expecting them. No passing caravans, friendly or hostile, had passed this way since the day he crashed. The French soldiers who found him carried his body and his personal effects to the place of his last departure—Reggan.

CHAPTER 11

Amelia Earhart

On the morning of March 19, 1937, a twin-engine Lockheed 10 began its takeoff run at Honolulu. Halfway down the 3,000-foot runway, a wing dipped and the pilot frantically chopped an engine to straighten the veering plane. When the uneven shear crumpled the right landing gear, the heavy monoplane, carrying 1,150 gallons of gasoline, ground-looped in a cloud of dust and sparks. Near the hangars a small group of spectators waited tensely for the explosion. It did not come.

The pilot, a slender 39-year-old woman, cut the switches and jumped to the ground as her navigators, Harry Manning and Frederick Noonan, stepped shakily from the passenger compartment of the broken machine. Tiny Howland Island, 1,940 miles in the western Pacific, would have to wait. Amelia Earhart would not get there with her $80,000 "flying laboratory" in that condition.

In three months, America's First Lady of the Air was ready for a second attempt to circle the globe, this time along an easterly route to benefit from prevailing tail winds. With Noonan as navigator, she took off from Miami on June 1, bound for California—the hard way. The mystery of their fate, destined to grip the imaginations of millions has never been solved.

The flight down the east coast of South America was uneventful. For Noonan, an experienced Pan American Clipper navigator, it was a familiar run. After a brief rest at Natal, the pair jumped off for Africa. During the final hour of the tiring 1,900-mile leg over the South Atlantic, Amelia Earhart disregarded Noonan's course correction and deliberately altered her course to the left, instead of right. Forty-five minutes later they crossed the continent's coastline at Saint-Louis, French West Africa. Because of the aviatrix' disregard of Noonan's compass correction, they were 160 miles off course for Dakar, their intended destination.

After putting 4,400 miles of African wasteland behind them, they pressed on to Assab, then to Karachi. Dodging and fighting monsoons that threatened to ground them for months, they battled their way to Rangoon, Bangkok, and Singapore. It was between Bandung and Surabaya that Noonan found a malfunction in their long-range navigation instruments. Reluctantly they turned back to Bandung, where Dutch technicians worked on the mechanisms for two days. When they reached Port Darwin, they unloaded their parachutes, crated them, and shipped them home. The next day they flew to Lae, New Guinea, the departure point for the most grueling leg of the flight, 2,556 miles to Howland Island.

Forty days of flying, 22,000 miles, thirty stops, nineteen countries, and five continents began to exact their price. Pilot and navigator were on the verge of exhaustion. Added to this was a growing uneasiness about possible difficulty with their instruments on the long flight. There were no landmarks in the vast stretches of the South Pacific, and Howland was so small that dead reckoning was out. There was only celestial navigation and a special radio homing station to guide them in. The weather would have to be clear for Noonan to take fixes from the stars at night and the sun by day. After they were a few hundred miles out, they would be out of touch with Lae and too far from Howland for radio contact. But Amelia Earhart was confident that if she could keep an exacting course all night, early the next morning they could home in on radio signals from the Coast Guard cutter *Itasca*, anchored off Howland for that very purpose.

Even before their takeoff from Miami, a fateful conspiracy appeared to threaten the pair. It amounted to a myriad of seemingly unimportant details that culminated in disaster and in the controversial mystery that followed. To begin with, Amelia Earhart had had the plane's 250-foot reel-type trailing antenna removed before the flight to avoid the trouble of reeling it in and out. At Lae she and Noonan realized this was a mistake. The trailing antenna would have enabled her to contact the *Itasca* much farther out than would the small loop antenna. She wished she still had it; now that they were facing the broad Pacific, the fifty-watt transmitter seemed woefully inadequate. Then, too, no one had told them of another more powerful radio homing aid on the island. A Navy high-frequency direction finder had been installed to assist them, but neither Commander Thompson of the *Itasca* nor Richard Black of the Department of Interior had informed them of this.

Fred Noonan had trouble calibrating his chronometers. If they read slow or fast, he could not get an accurate celestial fix. Fifteen seconds of error in the precision dials meant an error of one mile from their actual position. A one-minute error would steer them four miles off. His pilot would have to navigate much of the distance at night with the magnetic compasses, but even here a one-degree error in longitude would mean missing the island by forty miles. In the face of these uncertainties, Earhart and Noonan set out to find a sand and coral speck in the Pacific.

At 5:20 P.M., Friday, July 2, 800 miles out of New Guinea and on course, Amelia Earhart radioed their position to Lae. Everything was going well. She began to feel better about the trip, despite her growing weariness. Noonan dozed intermittently. Both were confident the *Itasca* was waiting and listening, and that in the morning they would pick up its signals.

Aboard the cutter that night, everything hummed with expectation. Radio equipment on board and at Howland had been checked in preparation for the Electra to come within range. Coast Guard radiomen were prepared to broadcast weather and homing signals on the hour and half hour by voice and code. As a final check of their transmitting power, they called San Francisco and from a third of the way around the world came the reply: "Receiving you O.K." The Electra, using its call letter KHAQQ, was to report by radio at fifteen and forty-five minutes past the hour.

Shortly after midnight, the *Itasca* made its first attempt to contact the Electra, first by voice, then by key with their homing signal. At 12:15, there was no return call. The *Itasca* tried again at the 12:30 schedule. It also radioed the *Ontario* standing by near Samoa and asked if it had heard the Electra's reply. The *Ontario* said it had not. At 12:45 A.M., KHAQQ again failed to respond.

Transmissions continued from the *Itasca*, but by 1:15 they had not raised the fliers. Commander Thompson was not dismayed; the plane was still an estimated 1,000 miles out. His radio operators continued to broadcast the weather on schedule, but their messages were not acknowledged at the Electra's scheduled reporting times.

Then at 2:45 A.M., with the plane tentatively fixed at 800 miles, Amelia Earhart's voice was indistinctly heard through heavy static. The only intelligible words of her low monotone were "Cloudy and overcast . . ." then, nothing. Spirits soared aboard the cutter. They had heard them! They were coming in! Frantically the excited radiomen worked to hold the contact. They checked their own signal strength again. Yes, the *Itasca* could be heard clearly by ships, including Japanese vessels, throughout the Pacific.

At 3:00 A.M., the *Itasca* transmitted the weather by key and voice. A pause, then they sent out the homing A signal ". . . *dit-dah* . . . *dit-dah* . . ."

No response from the Electra.

At 3:45 A.M., the aviatrix made voice contact but the message was still garbled. She said she would listen for the homing signal. Again the *Itasca* tried to make contact but failed. It continued to transmit on the hour and half hour but, except for another garbled message at 4:45, the Electra was not heard again until 6:15, when Amelia called for a radio bearing. She said she would whistle into the microphone so the *Itasca* could get a steady sound. She added that she figured she was "200 miles out." Commander Thompson called the watch on the island and instructed them to get a bearing when the Electra transmitted. With two stations receiving—the *Itasca* and Howland —chances for a more accurate pinpointing of the plane

Proposed course of the Electra. 1. Standby position of the
fleet tug. Ontario. The Electra was scheduled to pass this
point about midnight. 2. Position of the Coast Guard cutter
Itasca. 3. Saipan, where Mrs. Akiyama saw Japanese soldiers bringing two American flyers ashore after an aircraft
ditching. 4. According to reports, two fliers came down
between Ailinglapalap and Jaluit atolls.

should be good. The whistle went out but the attempt to get a bearing on it was a failure. Then, at 6:45, Amelia Earhart's voice, strong, clear, but with an unmistakable undertone of urgency, broke through the crackling static. "Please take a bearing on us," she begged, "and report in half hour. We're about a hundred miles out!" Again the Howland direction finder swung for a bearing, and again it failed. This time she hadn't transmitted long enough.

At 7:00 A.M., the *Itasca*, certain that the plane could not be far away, transmitted a fifteen-minute homing signal. Then, at 7:18 the radioman called to inform the aviatrix that they could not take a good bearing on her. They asked if she wanted to take a bearing on them. They waited a full minute for her to reply. There was no acknowledgment. In the radio room of the cutter, the officers had the same question. Was Amelia Earhart having radio receiver trouble?

At 7:19, the *Itasca* transmitted: "Go ahead on 3,105 [kilocycles]."

No reply.

Six minutes later they tried again.

No reply.

At 7:42, the woman's voice broke across the distance. "We must be on you but cannot see you . . . gas is running low. . . . Been unable to reach you by radio . . . flying at altitude of 1,000 feet!"

The cutter acknowledged immediately. "Received your message, signal strength five [maximum]. Go ahead." Then it sent out the homing signal. It waited five minutes. No answer.

The *Itasca* repeated: "Your message O.K. Please acknowledge." Nine minutes later Amelia Earhart called again, and by now it was obvious that she had heard none of the previous messages from the Coast Guard vessel, since she had failed to acknowledge any of them.

Her voice came through again. "KHAQQ to *Itasca*. We're circling, but cannot hear you. Go ahead on 7,500 now or on schedule time of half hour." Her voice was loud and clear.

The Coast Guard radioman sent out a long homing signal on 7,500 kilocycles. Then, momentary success. She called back: ". . . receiving your signals, but unable to get a minimum. Please take a bearing on us and answer with voice on 3,105." She whistled into the microphone again while the *Itasca* and the Howland station worked frantically to get a radio fix. But the whistling could barely be distinguished from the mingled static and once again the attempt failed. If she had only counted slowly into the microphone, or if Noonan had transmitted with his key, the radiomen could have taken an accurate bearing. But the fliers failed to do so.

It was now 8:00 A.M., Howland time. The fliers had been airborne for twenty hours. The men at Howland figured it was possible for the twin-engine plane to remain aloft for a maximum of twenty-six hours, or until 2:00 P.M. that afternoon *if* the pilot had leaned the fuel mixture sufficiently. Unfortunately, the waiting men had no way of knowing this.

At 8:33, the *Itasca* called again and informed the Electra they were transmitting constantly on 7,500 kilocycles.

No response.

Considering the elapsed time from Lae, the plane should have been in the general area. The *Itasca* asked for a reply on 3,105. In a few moments, at 8:45 A.M. to be exact, Amelia Earhart's voice broke through. It sounded broken, hesitant, yet urgent. Clearly, she was tired, and very worried. "We are in a line of position 157-337. Will report on 6,210 kilocycles. Wait, listen on 6,210 kilocycles. We are running north and south!"

Nothing came through on 6,210. Suspense mounted in the *Itasca's* radio room. The frustrated operators tried again and again to make contact, alternately transmitting and listening on all frequencies until ten o'clock. But the vast Pacific was ominously still.

Amelia Earhart had made her last call.

Radio officers and navigators tried to fathom the meaning of her last call, especially: "We are in a line of position 157-337." They assumed she had finally managed to take a bearing on them. "We are running north and south" —her final words—suggested that she did not know whether she was north or south of the line and was flying a zigzag search pattern for the island. That she asked the *Itasca* to take a bearing on her, appears to confirm their theory. Communications officers estimated from her signal strength that she was no farther than 250 miles, or closer than thirty miles, from Howland.

Commander Thompson acted promptly, realizing if the Electra were not already in the water, it soon would be.

At 10:15, he ordered the *Itasca* north, reasoning that if the plane had flown to the south, it would have spotted Baker Island, thirty-eight miles away. The "337" line, he decided, was the one to search. If the fliers ditched without mishap, the Electra's empty tanks would keep them afloat, but they would not be able to use their radio; it depended on the right engine for power. Still, on the chance that they might yet be aloft, the *Itasca* continued to call, despite fading hopes that contact could be made.

In Washington, Admiral Leahy, Chief of Naval Operations, ordered four destroyers, a battleship, a minesweeper, a seaplane, and the carrier *Lexington*—with its full complement of planes—into action. During the next sixteen days they set up search patterns around Howland and through the Gilbert and Marshall chains as well. They covered 250,000 square miles. Navy planes scanned 150,000 square miles and logged 1,600 hours. Planes and ships found nothing.

A stunned America listened at its radios, hoping that each news broadcast would tell of the rescue of Lady Lindy and her companion. In a few days the usual false reports began to come in. One of the search ships reported a green flare to the north. The missing fliers had flares and when the *Itasca* veered north to investigate, it radioed, asking if Earhart and Noonan were signaling. If they were, it instructed, they should send up another flare. As though their message were heard, another green light appeared a few seconds later. Twenty-five witnesses saw it, and Howland reported flares in the same area. Another ship saw them, then they faded. The Navy decided that perhaps they had not been flares after all, but a meteor shower.

There were radio reports. All the way across the Pacific, from Hawaii to the West Coast of the United States, radio operators claimed they heard SOS signals from Amelia Earhart. Strangely, none of them were heard by naval radiomen on any of the Pacific islands or aboard the search ships, and so they were dismissed as imaginary.

Meanwhile, in California, a search of another kind was getting under way. It did not involve men, planes, or ships, but the unfathomable power of a gifted mind. Amelia Earhart's husband, George Palmer Putnam, called upon a close family friend, famed woman flier Jacqueline Cochran, who was later to head the WASPs during World

War II. She and her husband, Floyd Odlum, had helped in financing Amelia's world flight.

The two women had often discussed extrasensory perception. During one of Amelia's visits, they heard that a plane had crashed somewhere in the mountains between Los Angeles and Salt Lake City. Miss Cochran gave a location, details of the terrain, and roads leading to the wreckage. Amelia Earhart checked with Paul Mantz, a friend and famed Hollywood stunt pilot. He confirmed the features on a map. She made a three-day search over the area but failed to find the plane. That spring, when the snows melted, the wreckage was discovered two miles from the spot Miss Cochran had indicated. On another occasion Jacqueline Cochran found a missing airliner that had smashed on a mountain peak and was pointed downward. It was located exactly as she had described it. Again, she used her strange powers to record—and later had verified—the exact dates, times, and locations of stops made by Amelia and her husband during a trip in the Electra. It was inevitable that the two women should make a pact. If Amelia should go down and get lost, Jacqueline was to tell the searchers where to look.

It was a worried and distraught George Putnam who now asked Jacqueline Cochran: "Where are they?"

Calmly, she told him the fliers had been forced to ditch. She gave the location. Fred Noonan, she said, had injured his skull in the landing. The Electra was still afloat. Although she did not know the name of the ship waiting for them at Howland, she identified it by name as the *Itasca*. Then she named a Japanese fishing trawler in the same area. "Tell the ships and planes to go there," she said. "The plane is drifting, but I'll try to follow it." The Navy combed the area, zigzagged, and doubled back over it again. No luck. This proved to be one of the heaviest disappointments in Jacqueline Cochran's life. She never again tried to use her unusual gift.

On July 19, the Navy called off the search, the cost of which now exceeded a million dollars. They had failed to find as much as an oil slick. Speculation and the following rumors, none of which appeared to be founded on fact, continued to flourish:

Amelia Earhart and Fred Noonan had inadvertently flown over Japanese islands that were being illegally fortified, and were shot down.

The fliers had been requested by the United States Navy to "look over" and photograph islands in the Japanese Mandate and had been captured as spies.

The two were in love and had used the flight as an excuse to escape from the world. They had landed on a remote Pacific island and were living happily together.

The second rumor found support from Dr. M. L. Brittain of the Georgia Institute of Technology, as well as others who were guests of the battleship *Colorado*. The vessel was one of those pressed into the search. As late as 1944, Dr. Brittain believed the aviatrix and Noonan were Japanese prisoners and would be freed by advancing U.S. Marines. "We got the definite feeling that Miss Earhart had some sort of understanding with Government officials that the last part of her world trip would be over Japanese islands, probably the Marshalls," he said.

Someone else believed this rumor, too. She was Amelia Earhart's mother, Amy Otis Earhart. Although her belief had no official basis, she affirmed that her daughter was on a highly secret Government mission and had been captured by the Japanese. In 1949, she said: "Amelia told me many things. But there were some things she didn't tell me. I am convinced she was on some sort of Government mission, probably on verbal orders."

The deeper one probes into the Earhart mystery, the more the Marshall Islands keep popping into the picture. The accounts of two naval officers are a case in point. Eugene Bogen, now a Washington, D.C., attorney, was Senior Military Government Officer there in 1944. He was in a position to hear much local history from the natives. Several of them told him that in 1937, "two white fliers— one a woman—came down between Jaluit and Ailinglapalap atolls [southeastern Marshalls]. They were close by Majuro, where they were picked up by a Japanese fishing boat. Later they were taken away on a Japanese ship bound for Saipan.

"Elieu, a missionary-trained native, was my most trusted native assistant," Bogen said. "He said the Japanese were amazed that one of the fliers was a woman."

Former LTC Commander Charles Toole of Bethesda, Maryland, confirmed Bogen's statement. He operated between islands in the Marshalls and said: "Bogen's absolutely correct. I've come across the same story myself."

Was the Japanese ship bound for Saipan? Some significant discoveries occurred in July of 1944 on that little twelve-by-five-mile island in the Marianas Group. Thanks to the Japanese interest in cameras and photography, invading U.S. Marines found a photograph album filled with pictures of Amelia Earhart. It is a fact that she carried a camera on her last flight, but no album. If there were any connection between the last flight and the album, it means that either the film in the aviatrix' camera was developed after her capture, or the pictures were taken by the Japanese. When Dr. Brittain was asked about the Saipan album, he said, "Yes, I believe a definite relationship exists between the album and Amelia Earhart's disappearance."

Two Pacific combat veterans would agree with Dr. Brittain. During the Saipan invasion, Sergeant Ralph Kanna, now of Johnson City, New York, was with an intelligence and reconnaissance platoon. His job was to capture and interrogate prisoners. One enemy soldier captured near "Tank Valley," carried a photo of Amelia Earhart standing close to a Japanese aircraft. It was sent through channels to S-2 Intelligence. Through the nisei interpreters, the prisoner explained that "this woman had been taken prisoner with a male companion." Eventually, "both had been executed."

Robert Kinley of Norfolk, Virginia, found another photograph of the aviatrix on Saipan. Probing ahead from Red Beach One, his Marine squad came across a house near a small cemetery. While Kinley, a demolition specialist, was inside checking for booby traps, he saw a picture on the wall. "It was of Miss Earhart and a Japanese officer," remarked Kinley. "It had been taken in an open field with hills in the background. The officer's fatigue cap had a star in the center." When the Marine was wounded soon afterward, the picture was lost with all his other belongings.

When World War II came to a close, there was another surge of rumors, claims, and denials and the U.S. Navy made an official statement. Amelia Earhart was not on a mission of espionage. She was not on a naval cloak-and-dagger operation. Her Electra had not been shot out of the skies by Japanese gunfire. She had not been captured, held prisoner, or shot as a spy. The rumors still flourish, however, because of certain singular events that came to light after World War II.

159

They began when General Hap Arnold sent Jacqueline Cochran to the Japanese Imperial Air Force Headquarters after the surrender to report on the activities of Japanese women pilots during the war. She found many records on famous American pilots and uncovered several files on her late friend, Amelia Earhart. Clearly, the Japanese Government once had more than a casual interest in America's most famous aviatrix. Those documents cannot be located today. Not one department of either the United States Government or the Japanese Government claims to have them. They have vanished.

Next came the story that made the first breakthrough in plausibility. It began in 1960, when Operation Earhart was formed by three Air Force captains. They operated without Government sanction or backing. Theirs was a private and independent organization formed to answer one question: What became of Amelia Earhart? Captain J. T. Gervais, a pilot with the 817th Troop Carrier Squadron, and Captain R. S. Dinger, Public Information Officer of Naha Air Base, Okinawa, had read Major Paul Briand's biography of the aviatrix, published in 1960. It contained a startling account that purported to explain her fate.

Major Briand's story came from a woman now living in California, Mrs. Josephine Blanco Akiyama, who was on the Japanese-held island of Saipan in the summer of 1937. A Chamorro native girl of eleven, she was bicycling along the harbor road at noon, delivering lunch to her Japanese brother-in-law, J. Y. Matsumoto, who worked inside the military compound. The area was under the strictest security, but she had a special pass to be admitted to the restricted zone. She had passed beyond the gate when she heard an airplane low overhead. She looked up and saw a silver twin-engine plane. It ditched in Tanopag Harbor.

When Josephine Blanco reached her brother-in-law, there was much excitement in the compound. They joined a crowd that witnessed Japanese soldiers bringing two American fliers ashore. One was a woman dressed like a man, in khaki trousers and a sport shirt. Her hair was cut short. The man was tall and thin, similarly dressed. Both were pale, weak, and exhausted. Their plane, if indeed it was the Electra, had come down in an illegal and extensive military installation, for Saipan, as well as other Japanese-mandated islands, was being heavily fortified.

In a few minutes a file of Japanese soldiers pushed the natives aside and led the couple away. At a nearby clearing in the jungle a volley of shots cracked out. It was all over in a second. The squad returned without the prisoners; presumably the fliers were executed and buried on the spot. Mrs. Akiyama later stated, after having studied a picture of Earhart and Noonan taken during the last flight, that they were the two she and her brother-in-law had seen on Saipan. At the time, she said, the Japanese would have killed anyone whom they suspected of spying on their secret operations.

When the news services heard Mrs. Akiyama's story, they queried Japanese Government officials. Was it true? Were Amelia Earhart and Fred Noonan executed on Saipan? The officials wouldn't say yes and they wouldn't say no. They did say: "Records pertaining to the Imperial Army and Navy were either destroyed by us or taken away by American officials at the end of the war. The report would be difficult to verify." Why, after twenty-three years, would the Japanese not want to admit the detainment and death of the Americans? The answer, perhaps, lies in the inscrutable Japanese mind. To admit to an incident involving Earhart and Noonan before the war would be to admit that in direct violation of international law they did indeed deliberately fortify the mandated islands. This would involve a shattering loss of face, especially since the Japanese had already testified at the Tokyo War Crimes trials of 1946 and 1947 that the air bases and installations were for cultural purposes and to aid fishermen in finding schools of fish. It seems unlikely that Josephine Akiyama would deliberately fabricate the story; she had no reason. Since she first related the story to Dr. Casimir Sheft, a Navy dentist on Saipan in 1946 (for whom she worked as dental assistant), she has had many opportunities to capitalize on it. She did not.

Meanwhile Operation Earhart was hard at work in other quarters, digging deeper to verify Mrs. Akiyama's story. Here's what they found:

Four Saipan natives remembered seeing a plane crash-land in Tanopag Harbor in the summer of 1937.

They watched Japanese troops take its two pilots to jail after rescuing them from the bay. (This does not agree with Mrs. Akiyama's account but, instead, ties in with later discoveries.)

161

One native recalled being invited by the Japanese to see a white woman hanged. She declined.

The general consensus of the island natives is that the two Americans were executed out of sight and hearing of the local population in order to keep the secret of Japanese activities secure.

While Captain Gervais was busy on Saipan, a team from Columbia Broadcasting System questioned Japanese Diet member Zenshiro Hoshina, who was Chief of Japan's Naval Affairs Bureau at the time of the alleged execution. His reaction was one of surprise and shock. "I absolutely deny it!" he replied brusquely. "No such execution could have taken place without my knowledge and approval."

Some late information found by Major Briand did not agree with Hoshina's indignant denial. Briand heard from Gervais on Saipan; on the very day the former Imperial war lord voiced his denial, July 6, 1960, Briand stated in Los Angeles: "Captain Gervais has obtained Japanese photographs [the photo album pictures?] showing that Miss Earhart and Noonan were captured and killed on Saipan as spies. He also has affidavits from seventy-two eyewitnesses of this capture and execution." He continued from the Gervais letter, which gave the details of the fliers' imprisonment as well as the locations of their graves "untouched and undisturbed for twenty-three years, not even by war." The next day Captain Dinger, at a news conference at Fuchu Air Station, Japan, echoed Briand's and Gervais' charges.

Operation Earhart was becoming of interest to the Air Force as well as to the Japanese Government. Gervais and Dinger were ordered to report to Fifth Air Force Headquarters at Fuchu to present their evidence. After evaluating the information, the Air Force stamped it "incomplete and inconclusive," and tucked it away in a classified file. Their action, coming as it did when Communist anti-American riots were being staged in Japan, was thought by some to have been designed to avoid incidents that could embarrass the Japanese at that time. Nevertheless, Operation Earhart was told to stop its investigation and the CBS team returned to the United States.

Much of Operation Earhart was talk, theorizing, conjecture, and countercharges. Although it took a step forward in clearing the way for later investigations, it did not establish that (1) the "Americans" were indeed Earhart and

Noonan; (2) it was their Electra at the bottom of Tanopag Harbor; and (3) the bodies in the alleged graves were those of the missing world fliers. And still unanswered were the questions:

What could have happened during the night of July 2, to cause the fliers to head for Saipan instead of Howland?

How could Noonan, veteran of eighteen Pacific crossings, navigator of the *China Clipper,* have been so much in error?

Many persons involved in the final phase of the flight claim it could not have happened.

Curiously, this most famous woman pilot of all time was not an exacting flier. She flew mainly for the fun of it, or because flying was a personal challenge. Many of her record-breaking flights were happy-go-lucky adventures. There were times during her career when she failed to pay attention to instructions. She had a firm confidence, perhaps a touch of overconfidence, in her flying abilities. For example, when Noonan directed her to turn right a few degrees in order to hit Dakar, she turned left. As a result they were 163 miles off course when they reached the African coast.

Saipan lies 1,650 miles north of Lae; Howland lies 2,550 miles west. If the Electra's magnetic compasses functioned normally (and there was nothing to indicate they did not), Amelia Earhart would have had to have made an incredible course error of almost 100 degrees. Even though the sky could have been completely overcast all during the night and prevented Noonan from making even one star fix, at dawn the sun would have come up off their right wing instead of over the nose—dead ahead. True, they were tired, but hardly so exhausted as to ignore the obviously misplaced position of the most reliable reference in the entire Pacific.

There are other arguments against the pair having flown the Electra to Saipan. Almost 800 miles out of Lae, at 5:20 P.M., July 2, Amelia Earhart reported their position by latitude and longitude. It was determined by a celestial fix. She said she was "proceeding on course," so if they altered course for Saipan after this time, when they were almost a third of the way to Howland, they would have to have flown west to reach the Japanese island. Then, too, when the Navy called off their search after having carefully swept the area northwest and southeast of Howland, they decided that the Electra's position of 157–337 could not have been a radio line after all, but a sun line. Considering the time and latitude differences between Saipan and Howland (factors in plotting a sun line), the numbers still came closer to the Howland position.

Chief Petty Officer J. D. Harrington is a Navy journalist and member of the Navy Institute. He does not believe the two fliers ever turned toward Saipan but, instead, that they got at least halfway to Howland, possibly as close as fifty miles. While researching information for his book on Japanese human torpedoes in World War II, Harrington investigated the log of the fleet tug *Ontario*, at the National Archives. The *Ontario* was stationed halfway between Lae and Howland. It had been previously arranged that Miss Earhart was to signal the *Ontario* around midnight, when she was due to pass over the ship. At 2:15 A.M., the commander of the *Ontario* ordered the ship to steam for nearby Samoa.

"The *Ontario*'s skipper must have been satisfied that they had passed over, otherwise he wouldn't have left his assigned position," remarked Harrington. "And if they passed over the *Ontario*, they wouldn't have had enough gas to make it to Saipan."

Harrington believes the Electra went down somewhere northwest of Howland. He speculates:

> They might have been saved if high brass in Washington hadn't interfered with the *Itasca*'s rescue attempt. Radio contact showed that the plane was near the island. Commander Thompson set out to search in the most logical area they could have ditched in, but Washington called the ship back to the island to serve as a seaplane tender. Bad weather kept the planes from searching for several days. Washington then released the *Itasca* to investigate false reports of the plane's location [the green flares]. By the time it arrived back in the area where the plane probably went down, it was eight days later.

The *Itasca* heard nothing after 8:45 on any frequency, by voice or key. An hour earlier the aviatrix transmitted: ". . . gas is running low . . ." She meant precisely what she said. If she had had another four hours' flying time—until noon Howland time—it seems unlikely she would have said this. Those who reject the Saipan story believe the Electra came down shortly after 8:45. They point out the two-hour time difference between Howland and Saipan. Eight forty-five Howland time is 6:45 Saipan time. This does not support the Saipan natives' story that the plane pancaked in Tanopag Harbor about noon.

"During the summer" covers three months; "1937" could have been 1936 or 1938. No doubt Saipan natives witnessed something, but what? During the Pacific struggle, many planes must have ditched in Tanopag Harbor. After twenty-three years the memory dims; events run together.

For those who waited in vain on Howland Island, however, the last flight of Earhart and Noonan remains a vivid memory. Dr. David J. Zaugg, a medical officer of the San Francisco Merchant Marine Hospital, recalled:

She was due to reach Howland around 7:00 A.M. It was a bright, sunny day and we were waiting on Howland to service her plane when it landed. We began to pick her up quite clearly on the radio, but the trouble was, she made voice transmissions when we needed Morse code to triangulate her position. She was flying directly into the morning sun and might not have seen Howland at all. I think she just went into the drink.

I never knew of any espionage work she was asked to do, and I never put any credence in the statements of the Saipan natives. It seems highly improbable to me that they [the fliers] could have gotten to the Marianas.

Another mystery. Why did Noonan not use his telegraph key?

Two other retired naval officers are in accord with Dr. Zaugg. Rear Admiral Hoeffel was gunnery officer aboard the *Lexington*. "Regarding her possible landing on another island—there simply aren't any. I've never accepted the idea that she may have been captured and executed by the Japanese. I've always believed they crashed and drowned." Vice Admiral Beary, then executive officer of the battleship *Colorado*, said, "It's been my guess that Amelia Earhart ran out of fuel, crashed in the Pacific, and drowned."

When asked about the secret mission, Paul Mantz, who outfitted the Lockheed for its world dash, replied:

I won't say yes or no. It was so long ago—it makes a man think hard about it. I installed one large vent which was channeled to all the gas tanks. If the plane pancaked on the water in one piece, all they had to do was pull a lever to seal the tanks for flotation. It could have floated indefinitely. They had all the survival gear they needed for a mid-ocean rescue: a rubber life raft, two-way radio, and other items. At the last minute she left some of it behind—I don't know why.

Naturally I've wondered about what happened to them. Perhaps they didn't have enough gas to find Howland. . . . Perhaps Amelia Earhart's still alive. . . . I don't know.

Late in 1961, there was a renewed flurry of interest in the mysterious mid-Pacific disappearance. From shallow unmarked graves on Saipan, Fred Goerner, a San Francisco radio newsman, sifted bone fragments and teeth of what he believed to be the remains of the two fliers. Goerner, a most persistent sleuth in the Earhart puzzle, has made three trips to Saipan for CBS. During his 1962 trip, he stopped off at the Marshalls and found Elieu, the native who had given Bogen and Toole information about the American fliers. Now a schoolteacher on Majoro, Elieu told Goerner the same story.

Goerner reasoned that there might be a few natives still on Saipan (during his first trip in 1960) who would have remembered Amelia Earhart if they had once seen her; workers at Tanopag Naval Base, natives who had worked for the Japanese military police at Garapan garrison. He was right; after questioning almost a thousand Saipanese with the help of Monsignor Oscar Calva, Father Arnold Bendowski, and Father Sylvan Conover of the island's Roman Catholic Mission, Goerner pieced together this intriguing story:

In 1937, two white fliers, a man with a bandaged head and a woman with close-cropped hair, dressed in man's clothing, were brought ashore from Tanopag Harbor in a motor launch. The man was taken to a prison stockade at Punta Muchot; the woman was taken into town (Garapan) and kept at a hotel where political prisoners were detained.

The woman was kept under close guard. A native woman testified that, as a young girl, she lived across from the hotel and saw the woman prisoner almost every day when she was allowed a short exercise period in the yard. About six months after she was brought to Garapan, the white woman died of dysentery. Goerner found a native laundress who had worked for the Japanese and who had "many times washed the clothes of the white lady." Another woman, who worked at the Japanese crematorium near Garapan's native cemetery, said she saw the body of the woman being taken to a place just outside the cemetery along with the man who had also been imprisoned. There the man was beheaded and both were buried in a shallow grave. Goerner's assiduous search even ferreted out the woman whose father had supplied the black burial cloth for the dead woman, and a former dentist whose Japanese-officer patients talked too much about the "two American-flier spies."

With the help of native divers, the Navy veteran went down for parts of a two-engine plane in thirty feet of water. He recovered a generator he assumed was from the Electra. It was slime- and coral-encrusted from many years in the water. In the States, Bendix Aviation officials and Paul Mantz examined it and identified it as a Japanese copy of an American generator.

After Goerner returned to the States he continued to track down leads. He got a tip from Thomas E. Devine of Westhaven, Connecticut, who was stationed on Saipan after it was captured from the Japanese. The natives told Devine of a white couple held captive there in July of 1937. The woman allegedly died of dysentery and the man was beheaded. According to a native woman, both were buried at Garapan Cemetery. In fact, she showed Devine the unmarked grave of a man and a woman who had come before the war. This was in 1945. Testimony from nineteen other islanders supported the woman's story.

Goerner was certain his months of work were about to pay off. He believed, however, that the pair had actually crashed near Jaluit Island in the Marshalls, where the Japanese were constructing illegal fortifications. It was Commander Paul Bridwell of the Navy Administration Unit on

Saipan in 1961, who convinced Goerner. Bridwell admitted to the newsman that a Naval Intelligence officer who followed up Goerner's earlier leads was unable to find flaws in the natives' statements. And Bridwell had a theory of his own.

I think they went down near Alingalapalap, Majuro, and Jaluit atolls in the Marshalls. A Japanese supply ship took them to Yap in the Carolines and probably a Japanese naval seaplane [the one Mrs. Akiyama saw ditch in Tanopag Harbor?] flew them on to Saipan—that's why some witnesses think they came from the air. Back in 1937, four U.S. logistic vessels were supplying the Far East Fleet. The *Gold Star, Blackhawk, Chaumont,* and *Henderson.* I understand they intercepted some coded Japanese messages.

In Bridwell's opinion, their radio logs should make fascinating reading. Goerner tried to get copies of them. The Navy informed him they were among records declared missing or destroyed.

Why would Earhart and Noonan be sent to Saipan, 2,000 miles to the west? Possibly the Japanese garrison at Jaluit did not want the responsibility of disposing of the white "spies."

The six-and-a-half pounds of bones and skeletal fragments were taken from a grave at Garapan Cemetery and sent to San Francisco. University of California anthropologist Professor Theodore McCown examined the bone fragments and thirty-seven teeth. He undertook the task with no preconceived opinions. Until he reconstructed the skeletons from the bones, Dr. McCown discussed the case with no one who had known the aviatrix personally, nor did he care to see photographs or become in any way personally involved. McCown said that in some cases it was possible to identify individuals from only one or two bones, but he made no such promise in this instance.

A tense week followed as the world awaited Dr. McCown's decision. It came—in the negative. His careful analysis showed the remains to include teeth from four individuals and bones from two. The tooth structure, the doctor revealed, showed them to be from Orientals.

Here the mystery stands. The vast Pacific still holds fast to the key, and speculation still flourishes.

Amelia Earhart Light—a lonely memorial lighthouse—stands on Howland Island. The Japanese Navy shot the top off during the war and it was never repaired. Once a year a Coast Guard cutter visits Howland. In 1962, crewmen from the *Buttonwood* painted the base of the structure white, to serve as a day navigation marker. A plaque on its foundation reads: AMELIA EARHART, 1937.

"Someday," Amelia once told her husband, "I'll probably get killed. There's so much fun in life and so much to do; I don't want to die. But when I do, I want to go in my plane—quickly."

Perhaps she did; perhaps she did not. Until there's more definite evidence, we shall never know.

CHAPTER 12

The Lost Levanevsky Fliers

August 13, 1937, marked another air disappearance. On that day six Soviet airmen were swallowed up somewhere in the great barren stretch between the North Pole and the Alaska Range. Over a quarter of a century has passed since they lifted their H-209 from Schelkove airfield outside Moscow and headed nonstop for Fairbanks, since the one brief, broken distress call crackled through the crisp Arctic air from somewhere near the Pole.

It was a year of great Soviet air achievements. In June a Russian plane with a crew of three flew from Moscow to Oregon. The fliers turned back and landed at Vancouver because they found the weather over the Oregon ranges more hazardous than the skies over the Pole and the Arctic Sea. A month later another Russian three-man team flew the same route and reached Mexico, from where they turned to land at San Jacinto, California. Their flight of 6,295 miles broke the long-distance-flight record.

There was little thought of failure in the minds of the H-209's crew as they readied their four-engine passenger plane in early August. The two earlier flights of greater distances were made easily in small, single-engine airplanes; the H-209 was completely equipped and would be piloted by the most skilled airmen in all Russia. Thirty-five-year-old Sigismund Levanevsky was the aircraft commander; Victor Levchenko, the navigator. Nikolai Kastanayen and Nikolai Galkovsky were copilot and radio operator, and the party's two mechanics were Gregory Pobeykimon and Nikolai Godivikov. Three of the six were veterans of Arctic-flight explorations, so plans were well laid to this aerial survey to trailblaze a polar passenger route to the United States.

Levanevsky was no stranger to air-minded America. In 1933, when Jimmy Mattern cracked up in the Siberian wilds during his round-the-world dash, it was Levanevsky who located his plane. With Levchenko navigating, the Russians flew the injured pilot from Anadir to Alaska. A year later the American people heard Levanevsky's name again when he led the rescue operations to the stranded Chelyuskin party that was adrift on an ice floe in the Chuktotsh Sea off Arctic Siberia.

Later summer is the most dangerous time to cross the Arctic region. Only if an aircraft can stay above the cloud layers, out of icing weather, where the midnight sun shines continually, is it safe from weather hazards. During this warm season, temperatures hover between thirty and forty degrees Fahrenheit, the critical range for carburetor and fog ice. Paradoxically, winter, with its bitter cold, rarely causes serious icing problems.

Every other day in summer the northern ice pack hangs heavy with fog; in winter it is almost always clear. Summer brings the Arctic rain season and by the middle of August, when Levanevsky and his crew would cross the Pole, the thawing would be at its worst. The huge ice islands of the polar sea, earmarked as emergency landing fields, would be a crisscross of deep ditches and rivulets made by the rain and sun. The worst dangers the Russians could face would be a long flight through the overcast and a forced landing on a scarred and broken ice field. The Levanevsky fliers knew the hazards, but they were confident of their ability and the stoutness of their machine. They had reason to be; the combined knowledge and experience of these six men in Arctic flying was greater than that of airmen in all other countries of the world at that time.

After takeoff the flight proceeded on schedule. At 1,050 miles the Russian fliers crossed Cheshkaya Bay, from which they altered course to skirt the eastern shore of Novaya Zemlya. At its northern tip they headed over the great ice ocean to Graham Bell Island, then struck a straight course for the Pole, 600 miles beyond. During this first 2,000 miles, wind and clouds swept across their path, but because of their heavy fuel load they were unable to rise above the weather. Fortunately no ice collected on the plane. When they were within 300 miles of the Pole, Levanevsky decided their luck might not hold as increasingly dense cloud layers loomed ahead, so he tried to climb above them. The H-209 responded slowly. It lifted above the billowing cottonlike peaks until, by the time Levchenko announced they were passing over the Pole, they had reached 20,000 feet. Here they found bright sun and cold, dry air. Levanevsky was delighted until Levchenko made another calculation. The wind here was stronger than he had expected. It was almost a direct head wind. Levchenko judged it was cutting their ground speed at least sixty miles an hour. Since takeoff, Galkovsky kept radio contact with Russian, Alaskan, and Canadian stations. The progress and position of the H-209 was continually recorded as the Russian sent regular transmissions with his crackling key. During the two hours after they crossed the Pole, everything went smoothly. The great passenger plane held a steady course on longitude 140 degrees (the Fairbanks meridian) for the north coast of Alaska.

Then came a distress call. Galkovsky hurriedly tapped out their plight. One of the four engines had quit when the sub-zero cold burst an oil line. When the H-209 descended to the warmer air level at 13,000 feet, it was forced to fly in the cloud layer. Ice was forming on its wings and the other engines were running rough. Radio operators at three stations in the northland waited expectantly and pressed their earphones against their heads to hear:

"Do you hear me? . . . Do you hear me? . . ." Then, "We are landing in . . ." followed by garbled signals that were never understood. The news was soon flashed around the world: The Levanevsky fliers were down!

During the first hours of silence after the distress call, it was thought that perhaps they had not landed after all; perhaps they had only had radio trouble and would continue to Fairbanks at a reduced speed. Bush pilots plotted the H-209's new speed and estimated its time of arrival at Fairbanks. But when the hour came and passed, the Soviet Embassy in Washington put in a call to the Explorers Club in New York, an organization formed to assist explorers and scientific expeditions. Club spokesmen were quick to give the opinion that a search should be started without delay. The chances for success, they thought, were good. They believed Levanevsky might well have made a safe landing on the broken polar sea. If the six men landed unhurt, even with damaged radio gear, there were better than average chances for survival. They had food for three months, rifles and ammunition to hunt for more. They were wellclothed, had camping gear, tents, and stoves, and for three of the men, the Arctic was no stranger. They could survive Eskimo style. Authorities agreed if all survived the landing without serious injury, they could last six months. And since their last-known position—approximately 300 miles from the Pole—was well established, searchers believed they had an excellent starting point.

For several days after the disappearance, strange "radio messages," which might have come from the H-209, were reported from a number of northern stations. The plane carried no spare radio; the one installed in the cabin was the only one, so hope rose that Galkovsky had got it working again. To support this, a new item in the Moscow newspaper said of the radio operator: "Even at home, during his spare hours, he continued to work on emergency radio apparatus." Perhaps this was happening now, perhaps not. How many times after the disappearances of famed aviators have the radio waves been filled with devilish hoaxes? The faked Earhart distress messages were part of this morbid psychology, as were the "actual sightings" of Andrée's 1897 polar balloon thousands of miles from where it was actually carried. But no one would say for certain this was now the case in the Levanevsky disappearance. From these garbled and wavering signals (that were never deciphered into anything resembling a reliable position report), there came only one distinct pattern. Every day the signals grew weaker until finally they faded completely. It was as though the strength of the radio storage batteries was slowly diminishing. Some listeners said this proved the messages were genuine, and that they came from a survivor of the landing who must have had only a limited knowledge of radio code.

The messages spurred the Explorers Club into faster action. The day after the fliers were reported overdue, they had a plan in operation. The U.S. Government agreed to co-operate with the Canadian and Soviet governments in the search. Captain Sir Hubert Wilkins, the one man widely experienced in both Arctic exploration and polar flying, accepted command of the search operation. Given free reign in his choice of men, he telegraphed pilots Herbert Hallick-Kenyon and S. A. Chessman. "Will you accept the challenge?" Back came the replies: "Yes!"

Next, to find a suitable airplane. They needed a flying boat with an extended range. The U.S. Navy had them, but, for security reasons, could not release them. The trio found a similar type, a Consolidated PBY boat, owned by club member Richard Archbold. Archbold had plans to take his amphibian on a scientific exploration of New Guinea in three months, but when Wilkins convinced him that this plane was the only one suitable for the Levanev-sky search, Archbold turned it over. Immediately, the work in outfitting the flying boat for the tropics stopped, and it was refitted instead for Arctic operation.

The U.S. Weather Bureau ordered two of its crack forecasters to Fairbanks to prepare weather data in support of the flying team. Canada set up a radio and telegraph network to channel weather reports to that remote station, and Russia sent an English-speaking forecaster to Fairbanks to translate Russian weather data and funnel it in from 150 observing sites in Siberia and the Soviet Arctic. The U.S. Army Signal Corps responded to the call, setting up extra lines and radios to handle the overload of weather data that would soon stream into Fairbanks.

While these hasty preparations were under way in the United States, pilot Robert Randall, in a hired MacKenzie Air Service plane, made an air search westward from Aklavik. Between August 15 and September 1, he flew 500 miles along the north Alaskan coast, landed whenever he saw natives, and talked with them. Wisely, Randall refrained from asking the Eskimos point-blank if they had seen or heard a plane on August 13. He knew that part of their friendly makeup was to tell traveling strangers only what they thought would please them. So Randall acted unhurried and relaxed. He chatted aimlessly about the summer hunting and fishing, inquired which of their neighbors had powerboats, what steamers had visited them, how much they knew about airplanes, and when they had last seen one. He had no luck at all until he reached Barter Island, about halfway between Aklavik and Point Barrow, a little east of the Fairbanks meridian. Here he learned that on August 13, while some Eskimos were busy corralling a small herd of reindeer, they had been interrupted by engine noise. Some of the natives thought it was a power launch, but a few seconds later they realized that from the direction of the sound in the overcast, it was a plane. They all stopped to listen as the noise passed from the north and died away south, inland. This was the only place Randall got a clue. When he returned from Barrow a few days later, he curved inland to search the mountain foothills near Barter Island. He found nothing.

Joe Crosson, manager of Pacific Alaska Airways in Fairbanks, heard of Randall's clue and believed he would find the H-209 down somewhere between Barter Island and Fairbanks. Several other planes joined him in searches north to the Brooks and Endicott ranges. For several weeks the bush pilots zigzagged in loose search patterns without sighting anything resembling wreckage or tracks. They heard stories about some strange lights and signals on the mountain peaks, but after trying to track the reports down, Crosson and his companions finally wrote them off as imaginative aftermaths of the Randall story.

By August 21, just eight days after Levanevsky was reported missing, Wilkins, Kenyon, and Chessman were in the air over the Northwest Territory, ready to begin a search of the polar seas. With them were radio operator Raymond Booth and mechanic Gerald Brown. From August 22 until September 21, they flew the *Guba* 10,000 miles over the great icecap. The care they took in planning these flights, with the help of the weather data from Fairbanks, paid off. Hundreds of miles from their Aklavik base in the MacKenzie River delta, they found fog and rain within a few miles of where it was predicted. This accurate forecasting allowed them to fly almost every day, at a time when icing conditions were most severe. They penetrated deep into the northernmost regions of barren ice and snow, and the *Guba* contributed a striking chapter in the history in Arctic flying. Wilkins proved that a capable crew, a sound aircraft, and reliable weather reports could cope with the worst the polar sea could offer. Only their failure to find any trace of the missing H-209 marred the success of their extended operations.

The polar freeze-up starts in early September, and on the 23rd the *Guba* headed back to New York. Now another plane, one fitted with skis for operating from the frozen sea, would have to be used. The season of perpetual darkness was fast coming on when a Lockheed Electra (similar to the one used by Amelia Earhart and Fred Noonan four months earlier on their ill-fated round-the-world flight) was fitted with ski gear. By November the sleek metal monoplane was at Aklavik, 150 miles north of the Arctic Circle. Brown and Booth, who remained with the *Guba* as it left with the Archbold Expedition, were replaced with A. T. L. Dyne, mechanic, and radio engineers Wilson and Cooke, whose job was to set up radio homing stations at Aklavik and Point Barrow for the roaming Electra. Wilkins hoped to pierce the innermost traces of the unexplored North and be able to know his exact position at any time by simple radio triangulation. But suitable radio equipment proved hard to find. When the November weather took an unusual freakish turn along the coast, a month and a half passed before the men were able to start new flights. Finally, on January 14, 1938, all was ready and the Electra warmed its engines for takeoff. As it began its run down the frozen MacKenzie River—*crack!*—the left propeller struck a pole that had been thrust upright in the fresh snow. When the Electra slipped into the subzero air and curved to the north, the crew noticed the left engine was not operating normally. They made power and trim adjustments and decided the trouble was temporary. They focused their attention on the search ahead and forgot about it.

Moonlight is the only illumination of the Arctic winter, and it proved to be more than adequate over the frozen sea. Everything below was white in the clear cold atmosphere where the moonlight was reflected to double its normal intensity. It was then that Wilkins and his party made the discovery that a pilot could see farther with a half moon in the Arctic than with a full moon in the tropics.

This flight took them to 76 degrees north and 140 degrees west before ominous weather forced them back to base. They were satisfied that if the Levanevsky camp were in the area they searched, they would have been sighted as easily by Arctic moonlight as by daylight.

Encouraged by the effectiveness of moonlight for aerial searching, the made plans at Aklavik for its full use during

February, the clearest of the Arctic months, when the ice-cap is practically cloudless. Dyne checked the engines before he left the plane and found their earlier engine trouble to be a bent propeller tip. He straightened it and assumed the condition was corrected.

More search patterns were plotted for the remaining days in January, but one troublesome delay followed another. The weather turned foul along the coast and the twin-engine search plane was grounded. On February 6, when the searchers were making plans to get airborne for the full-moon period, Dyne made a heartbreaking discovery. As he warmed the engine for takeoff, he found the left engine so badly damaged from the vibration of its earlier 1,420-mile flight with the bent propeller tip that it was ruined. Another month passed before a MacKenzie Air Service plane delivered a new engine.

Sir Hubert Wilkins decided to change his search plans and follow an earlier prospect. He was acquainted with several Eskimos of Barter Island and knew them to be completely reliable. He was convinced the information they had given Randall the preceding August was true, and on March his party scanned 3,000 miles of the Endicott and Brooks ranges. They flew the length of the awesome mountain chain several times, crisscrossing back and forth every ten miles. Still they saw nothing of the missing men or their airplane. Wilkins knew the chance of finding a wreck on one of the mountains was slim, but not impossible. If the Russians had lived, they could have walked to safety, but if the H-209 had slammed into one of the peaks, it would have been buried under an avalanche of ice and rock. Fifty years could come and go, hundreds of planes could pass within a thousand feet of its grave, and no one would be the wiser. To this day the only men who cross the ranges are trappers or a lone prospector or trader. They use pack animals in summer and dog sledges in winter, and they rarely stray from the passes and trails.

On March 15, the Wilkins-Explorers Club search was halted, but with another summer coming on, air activity out of Point Barrow continued. Jimmy Mattern made a flight to the ice pack and returned, unable to report a trace of the missing plane of men. In late August and September, Soviet float planes based at Point Barrow, fanned out in a final great search of the area without success.

Meanwhile, on the Russian side of the Pole, the Soviets were banking on the possibility that the Levanevsky fliers, if they actually had come down near their last reported position, would drift eastward during the summer, into the North Atlantic to the Old World side of the Pole. Rudolph Island, north of the Arctic Circle on longitude 60 degrees, was the Russians' base of operations. From here they sent planes west and northwest into the ice ocean, zigzagging back and forth between latitudes 82 and 84 degrees. Much of their search was over parts of the earth never before crossed by man, but by spring their operation came to a reluctant close.

The Levanevsky disappearance changed ideas on Arctic flying. Before the H-209 disappeared, no one had lost his life in the thousands of flights over the northern sea, although several dozen forced landings had occurred there. The great ice floes of the Arctic are markedly different from the liquid seas farther south. On the ice fields the survivors can walk out to safety, something that cannot be done on water. From 1919 to 1937, nineteen descents were made in the Atlantic Ocean; nine planes were lost. The survivors were lucky enough to come down in fair weather within sight of a ship or could radio one nearby. In this same period, 100,000 polar air miles were flown. There were fifty-six descents, forced and intentional, in all kinds of weather with no lives lost. None, that is, until the H-209 carried its crew into mystery and conjecture. No one can say for certain the four-engine passenger plane had come down soon after it sent out its distress call. If it had crashed on the pack, how long had it been stationary before the shifting ice moved it and in what direction? The Russians asserted the ice pack would drift the party eastward; Americans disagreed. They believed the ice pack would float the fliers southeast toward Borden Island, along Prince Patrick and Banks islands, then westward along the north coast of Alaska to arrive finally in the North Atlantic, where the floe would melt in the warm North Atlantic Current seven or eight years later.

On one thing however, the authorities agreed: no part, fragment, or clue of the Levanevsky survey expedition was ever found by anyone.

In August of 1938, as Sir Hubert Wilkins left New York for Antarctica, he told the press he was still hopeful that Levanevsky and his men "would eventually come through to an inhabited region." Perhaps Wilkins was thinking of Levanevsky's ragged predecessors—four Russian sailors stranded on an island off Spitsbergen in 1743. Three of them survived on a few pounds of flour and tobacco, but mainly by hunting and fishing. When rescued six years later, they were in good health and fine spirits, having adapted themselves to Arctic survival.

But if it actually was the H-209 that the Barter Island Eskimos had heard coming in from the sea on August 13, 1937, then its crumpled remains lie somewhere in the Alaska mountains. Perhaps one day some lone prospector, wandering off the beaten trail during the spring thaw, will see a curious sight protruding from the melting snow of a mountainside—the remains of a Russian airplane and its crew from another time.

PART THREE

FAMOUS

CONTROVERSIES

CHAPTER 13

The Great Floating Palace

Air Transportation came to a grim crossroads on May 6, 1937. The path it took on that fateful day at Lakehurst, New Jersey, eventually broadened into the global airlanes paced by today's sleek 600-mile-an-hour passenger jets.

If the *Hindenburg* disaster had not occurred, world aviation would have continued to develop the great rigid airships—the dirigibles. But in the twilight of that spring evening, the death of the airship era was close at hand as disaster stalked the giant that droned softly over the Jersey pinewoods. The mammoth LZ-129, mightiest and most successful lighter-than-air transport ever built, was about to die.

As it drifted majestically toward the mooring tower, none of the thousand spectators knew they were about to see the end of an epoch. The *Hindenburg* would burn into the public's mind an indelible picture of what could happen to people who traveled on a hydrogen-filled airship.

Although there had been a number of dirigible disasters since 1921, the *Hindenburg*'s safety record was flawless. In fact, not one paying passenger had, as yet, died in a dirigible disaster.

The *Hindenburg* was the most luxurious airship ever built, the pride of Nazi Germany. Its imposing form measured more than 800 feet. Nothing on America's airways could match its performance or range, 8,800 miles nonstop. Inside the floating aluminum lacework were seventy staterooms, a lavishly decorated staircase leading from one deck to another, a lounge with an aluminum piano, a dining room, and a bar. Meals were cooked on board by a Continental chef, sumptuous servings of lobster, fowl, and roasts with any wine you could name. The $400 fare gave passengers a few unique days aloft. In fair weather the huge windows were left open, affording a panorama unmatched by today's commercial airliners. It was called the Great Floating Palace.

Three days earlier, thirty-six passengers had boarded the 240-ton airship at Frankfurt and, except for head winds, the Atlantic crossing was uneventful. Nothing, exclaimed the *Hindenburg's* passengers, could match travel by dirigible. The four 1,200-horsepower diesel engines in their aft locations could barely be heard. Flight was vibrationless. A famous passenger, ghosting along at eighty-four miles an hour, once poetically ventured that the sky giant was "held aloft by angels."

The huge transport was said to be the safest aircraft ever built, even though its sixteen balloon-cloth gas cells held 7,000,000 cubic feet of hydrogen, one of the hottest-burning gases known. An article in the current issue of *Collier's* had said: ". . . only a stroke of war or an unfathomable Act of God will ever mar this German dirigible's safety record." So stringent were fire precautions that Lloyd's of London had insured it for £500,000 at the low figure of 5 per cent. The low-vapor fuel oil was so safe it could quench fire. Every one of the vigilant sixty-one-man crew was trained to spot hazards. Heinrich Kubis, the chief steward, took custody of a sparking windup toy that the Doehner children ran across the deck. "We don't tempt hydrogen," he said firmly.

Each crewman wore antistatic asbestos coveralls and hemp-soled shoes as he moved about his duties inside the cavernous skeleton. Ladders and catwalks were rubber covered. All matches and lighters were confiscated on boarding, and below the hydrogen bags was a specially insulated smoking room with a double-door entrance. This room was pressurized to keep stray hydrogen out, and a steward was constantly in attendance to light the passenger's cigars and cigarettes and to make certain no fire left the room.

The *Hindenburg* was running ten hours late. It had been due to moor at Lakehurst Naval Air Station at 8:00 A.M., but it did not arrive over Boston until 11:40. Then ominous black clouds over New Jersey prompted Max Pruss, the airship's captain, to hold out for better landing conditions. It was raining at Lakehurst when the airship was first sighted through the gloom at 4:00 in the afternoon. Lightning flashed in the nearby storm clouds. Veteran airship commander Charles Rosendahl radioed Pruss that he approved of his decision to wait. The *Hindenburg* droned low over the crowd of waiting friends and relatives, and its hoarse, throbbing engines added to the awesome sight. It swung over New York City to wait out better landing conditions.

With Captain Pruss in the control gondola was Captain Ernst Lehmann, a senior airship officer who had commanded the LZ-98 during World War I and who was the *Hindenburg*'s captain the year before. Both Pruss and Lehmann had commanded the *Graf Zeppelin*. Lehmann was along to advise Pruss on his first command crossing with the newer airship. His son had died only a few days earlier and he had not really wanted to come, but he thought he might have an opportunity to talk with officials in Washington about helium. The new and larger *Graf Zeppelin II* was under construction in Germany, and the Germans wanted and needed this rare gas that would not burn and that was commercially manufactured only in the United States. Lehmann probably knew what Washington's answer would be; they had no intention of giving Hitler a military advantage.

Over New York City, the *Hindenburg* circled the Empire State Building and headed south again, where a wet disgruntled crowd waited impatiently. One bored newsreel photographer went to a movie in Toms River; another reporter waited in a New York bar. Both missed the greatest aviation disaster of the thirties.

It was raining at the air station at 6:12. The wind steadied at eight knots. The ceiling was still low, 200 feet, but the visibility had widened to five miles. Rosendahl radioed the *Hindenburg* "All clear and waiting."

Still Pruss was cautious. He held off. At seven o'clock, with darkness coming on, Rosendahl recommended an immediate landing. The rain slackened to a drizzle, the wind died to two knots and the ceiling lifted to 2,500 feet. The milling spectators, newsmen, and custom officials became even more restless and irritable with the approaching darkness. Many had been roused from their beds twelve hours earlier, expecting the landing on schedule. A landing crew of ninety-two Navy men and 138 civilian "dollar detail" volunteers huddled in the drizzle as the *Hindenburg* flew overhead, made a tight turn, and headed into the wind.

Pruss ordered hydrogen valved at 7:19. The big ship weighed off and began to settle. Then Pruss called for water ballast to be dumped, and the *Hindenburg* smoothly steadied its descent in the cool, wet air and leveled off under perfect control. Lehmann watched approvingly. Pruss, he knew, could handle the giant during this exacting and final part of the flight.

At 360 feet, the *Hindenburg* weighed off again and nudged onto the field. Seven hundred feet from the mooring mast, Pruss ordered the engines reversed to "idle astern," and the dirigible drifted slowly to a near standstill. Spectators and passengers shouted and waved, but one of the crowd, a former airshipman, thought there was "something wrong" with the airship's approach.

At 7:21, the starboard-bow line was dropped 200 feet to the waiting ground party and the port line followed. They landed just inside the mooring circle and Lieutenant Raymond Tyler, chief mooring officer, saw dust puff up from the dry rope coils as they struck the wet sand. He began to direct the landing operation.

At that precise moment, one spectator was about to draw his companion's attention to what he thought was a small spark flickering above and below the tail assembly.

Then it happened.

Inside the structure two crewmen, Sauter and Lau, were the first to see it. They heard a *pop!* and a *whuff!*, and looked up as Number Four cell near the tail broke into a brilliant flash of red, blue, and yellow light. At that moment observers on the ground saw a deep-red glow in the belly of the huge silver monster. A split second later the crowd froze in horror. Rosendahl gasped as he saw flames spurt up just forward on the top fin. "I knew the ship was doomed," he said later.

Most of the passengers heard and felt nothing at first. In the control room Pruss and Lehmann felt only a mild shock. "What is it?" Pruss asked, thinking a landing line had snapped. Then he looked aft, saw the rosy glow at the tail, saw the ground crew scatter, and knew.

The fire rushed quickly forward through the superstructure to burst one gas bag after another and to feed the already white-hot inferno. The muffled detonations were heard fifteen miles away at Point Pleasant.

As the landing party scattered and the crowd fell back, the *Hindenburg*'s nose lifted to 500 feet. Passengers on the promenade deck were tumbled by the lurch. Relatives on the ground screamed. They were certain no one would survive the fire, even as they saw passengers hurl themselves through the huge windows, plummeting to the ground, some to die, some to live.

Pruss's first instinct was to valve the gas in the forward cells, but wisely he decided to let the burning stern fall first.

The bust of Field Marshal von Hindenburg toppled from its pedestal, and passengers grabbed for whatever supports they could reach. Over the pandemonium and hysterical screaming, Mrs. Doehner kept her head and saved two of her four children by throwing them out the window.

John Pannes and his wife had become separated during the airship's approach. Although they were not far apart when the fire broke out, he left his window—through which he could have jumped—to join her. Both perished.

Margaret Mather reached the boarding ramp as the flames collapsed its supports, and stepped down to the ground practically unscathed.

A cabin boy looked up to see the fiery wreckage descending on him, then a water-ballast tank let go, soaked him, and spared his life.

James O'Laughlin, who had survived an earlier airplane crash, later said of the airship's death throes: "I never flew in a craft that traveled through the air as easily. Even in breaking up, the *Hindenburg* was gentle to its passengers—those who lived."

Miraculously, during the thirty-two seconds that elapsed since the explosion, some did survive in the melting, white-hot framework that crashed to the ground. Rescue men from the landing crew ran repeatedly into the twisted, glowing wreck. Max Pruss dashed clear at the last moment, then rushed back again and again to help his crewmen. Badly burned and dazed, he had to be forcibly restrained from reentering the glowing wreckage.

Captain Lehmann did not fare so well. His clothes had caught fire and he was badly seared over much of his body. He stumbled back and forth mumbling, "I don't understand . . . I don't understand . . ." At Paul Kimball Hospital he was placed face down on a table, bare from the waist up. Thoughtful, polite, and fully composed, though in great pain, he realized how badly he was burned. Passenger Leonard Adelt paused in the hallway and stepped inside the room.

"What caused it?" he asked.

Painfully, Lehmann looked up. He did not answer right away. Finally, he said, "Lightning." Their eyes met and in that brief moment told each other that this was not really the cause.

Word of the disaster traveled quickly around the world. In the early morning hours Dr. Hugo Eckner, director of the Zeppelin Company, was roused from his bed by a telephone call. It was Berlin correspondent Weyer. Eckner was drowsy and annoyed. "Yes," he snapped, "what is it?"

"I thought it my duty to inform you of some bad news we have just received from New York," Weyer said.

"Yes?"

"The *Hindenburg* exploded at Lakehurst and crashed in flames."

"No! . . . No! . . . it isn't possible!" Eckner stammered.

Weyer pressed him for a statement. "Do you think there is a possibility of sabotage, Doctor?"

"If it was in the air . . ." the dazed airship pioneer faltered, ". . . then it must have been sabotage."

The following day Commander Rosendahl visited Captain Lehmann. The airship veteran lay motionless on his bed. He never complained, and he knew he did not have much longer to live. As carefully as possible, the two men reviewed every possible cause of the fire. Each one—from a static spark to a gas cell ruptured by a shattered propeller blade—led them in circles. "No . . . no," moaned Lehmann, shaking his head. "It must have been a *Hollenmaschine* [an infernal machine]." Then he added hopefully, "But, of course, no matter what the cause, the next airship *must* have helium." He died later that afternoon without realizing there would never be a "next" airship.

The death toll stood at twenty-two crewmen, thirteen passengers, and one ground crewman. On May 11, 10,000 spectators and mourners gathered at Pier 86 in New York to witness the services for the twenty-eight European victims. Germany declared two weeks of official mourning, and as the SS *Hamburg* steamed out of port, the ghost of the airship era sailed with it. The hope of the rigid airship was laid to rest with the *Hindenburg's* victims.

Two unnatural occurrences found their way into the *Hindenburg* picture. The first happened exactly one month to the day before the airship went to its catastrophic destruction. In Milwaukee, a German citizen had a frightening dream. In it he saw a dirigible drifting toward the mooring mast at Lakehurst. Then it burst into flames so suddenly and so completely that the man was sure all aboard had perished. The dream preyed on his mind and seemed so real he felt compelled to warn someone of the approaching disaster. Because he was an illegal alien who'd jumped ship in 1928, he lived in constant fear of being discovered and deported. He asked his landlady to write to the German Ambassador. She did.

To Dr. Hans Luther, the woman's "friendly warning" and assurance that this was "no joke" was but one of many letters he received warning of the destruction of either the *Graf Zeppelin* or the *Hindenburg*. There was something special about this one, however, so he sent it on to Captain Lehmann, who put it in his coat pocket. It was there when fire scorched his coat as he fled the burning airship. It went back to Germany with the remanants of his personal belongings. There, Max Pruss saw it a year later.

The second curious incident involved Lehmann's wife Marie, who was fearful over this season's first *Hindenburg* crossing. Grief-stricken over the recent loss of their son, Frau Lehmann would have preferred that her husband remain at home for a while. A clairvoyant in Vienna had recently told her that her husband would die in a burning dirigible.

It was strange that the bulk of the *Hindenburg* letters and phone calls received by Dr. Eckner and Dr. Luther did not warn the ship away from Rio, Frankfurt, or Friedrichshafen, but only from Lakehurst.

Even before the charred and twisted wreckage cooled, aeronautical experts and technicians flocked to Lakehurst to find the cause of the disaster. Investigators arrived during the night and began to question witnesses. One young line handler said he watched a boy and a dog jump from the front of the dirigible as it settled. They landed safely, he said, and ran into the pinewoods.

The Navy Department assembled a board of inquiry to convene the following Saturday, but the group of Navy officers adjourned when the Department of Commerce reminded them that this was a civilian air disaster, not a military one. On Monday, a civilian board of the Bureau of Air Commerce met in an empty hangar of the air station. It was the same huge, drafty room that had been a waiting room and, more recently, a morgue for the airship's victims.

Rosendahl, gruff and outspoken, was the first to testify. He stated that when the *Hindenburg*'s bow lines hit the ground, they had "definitely grounded the airship" by discharging whatever static electricity it held. However, in later testimony, Lieutenant Tyler seemingly contradicted the commander when he claimed the trailing ropes could not have discharged any static electricity.

The controversy began from the first day. Nothing was firmly established then or in the days of inquiry that followed. The evidence accumulated, reams of it. And unknown to the board at that time, intrigue to match the enigma of the *Hindenburg*'s destruction was being brewed in Berlin. Hermann Goering, Germany's Number Two man, sent orders to the airship officers that there was to be no speculation as to the cause; they "should not try to find an explanation." Obviously, the death of the *Hindenburg* was a blow to the pride of Nazi Germany. If it were ever established that the airship had been destroyed by an enemy faction, the disgrace would have been unbearable. Thus the crew, many of whom were party members who feared Nazi power, complied. The conspiracy of suppression muzzled them. The commission, unaware of Goering's orders, did not learn until much later what the airshipmen suspected about the cause.

Electrical malfunctions were logically ruled out. Definitely, there had been no short circuits or overloads. Major structural failure was also ruled out; no lines or brace wires had snapped. A sticking gas valve? One had stuck on the South American run the previous season. Sparks from the engines? They were under the airship and well away from the buoyant hydrogen that would have risen far above them. An incendiary bullet? Bullets fired in tests failed to ignite identical gas cells. Besides, no one knew in advance which approach the *Hindenburg* would use when it came onto the mooring mast. Static electricity? Perhaps, but how, or why, would a static spark travel from the bow lines all the way to the tail before causing an explosion? Some technical reports deny that St. Elmo's fire and static electricity are strong enough to ignite even sensitive hydrogen. Dr. Eckner ruled out ball lightning and exhaust sparks. A broken propeller blade? No evidence.

What about a radio bomb, a device smuggled aboard with a single frequency matched to a transmitter that had been triggered by an accomplice watching the landing from the pinewoods? Highly unlikely for many reasons. The tiny transistor and the printed circuit were electronic dreams in 1937; such a bomb in that day would have been too large and bulky to escape detection. Something of an electrical nature was found, however. Something that was not seriously considered at the time, despite its having come to the attention of the board. A small, unidentified part of the wreckage came under the scrutiny of Detective George McCartney of the New York City Police Bomb Squad. He had it analyzed. It proved to be a cotton container of manganese dioxide, zinc oxide, and graphite —the elements of a dry battery. No one, crew or passenger, was permitted to have such an item in his possession. Gestapo agents in Frankfurt had thoroughly searched all passengers' belongings as well as the airship before take-off.

One other strange finding was made in the wreckage, something that probably belonged to one of the *Luftwaffe* officers who was carried as a passenger. It was a Luger pistol. One shot had been fired.

On the stand, the Germans who were able to testify were cautious and reticent. Captain Witteman, one of the five qualified captains aboard, had emerged from the incandescent blob of fire practically unscathed. He had rushed up to Rosendahl soon after the crash and told him he wanted to talk privately with him as soon as possible. But to the board he simply said, "The whole affair is a complete mystery to me."

At one point in the proceedings it was suggested that during the tight final turn toward the mast, a brace wire had snapped and whipped into cell Number Four, where leaking gas was ignited by static electricity. Chief Engineer Sauter and Helmsman Lau, who were in the vicinity of the initial explosion, both said No.

In Lennox Hill Hospital in New York, *Luftwaffe* Major Frank Witt could not appear to testify, but from his bed he told of threats and an anonymous letter his brother and a representative of the Zeppelin Company knew about.

Hans Freund, a rigger in the tail section at the time of the explosion, had to be coaxed to talk. He was recalled for questioning the following Monday. Yes, he said, gas valves could stick. No, he did not believe hydrogen was leaking. He also established that Ludwig Knorr, the chief rigger who was killed, had relieved another rigger, Eric Spehl, at Number Four gas cell at 6:00—one hour and twenty-one minutes before the explosion. This information later proved helpful to the Gestapo, although it was inconclusive.

Steward Nunnenmacher took the stand, as tight-lipped as his predecessors. He said nothing of a distraught passenger's unusual behavior in the dining saloon during the landing delay. The *Hindenburg* was maneuvering about the air station, preparing for the approach, when the man began to pace nervously back and forth near an opened window. This was twenty minutes before the explosion.

"I don't want to go around the field again," he mumbled. "I want to go down!"

Nunnenmacher made an effort to calm the passenger by explaining that the airship had to await better conditions. When Chief Steward Kubis entered the room a few minutes later, the man was even more upset.

"My watch," he cried out ". . . my watch! Can I find it when we go down?"

In his nervous state he had removed his wrist watch and dropped it over the side. Nunnenmacher and Kubis knew no reason for the man's hurry.

When Kubis took the stand, he was questioned at length but, like Nunnenmacher, he said nothing of the jittery passenger. Later, the FBI investigated and found the man to be passing himself as an American citizen, although he was traveling on a foreign passport.

Kubis also omitted another important point of which he had full knowledge. It concerned Rigger Knorr, who at seven o'clock looked over Number Four cell and thought it somewhat light of gas. A leak perhaps? Perhaps not. They had reduced altitude and this might account for it. Knorr decided to look at the other cells for comparison. As he worked his way forward along the catwalks and labyrinth of ladders, he passed Kubis' door. He paused, mentioned his discovery, and suggested that some quick repairs might have to be made before the turn-around trip. Kubis must have thought it strange that a leak had occurred so quickly, but he said nothing about it to the board.

As the possibilities were examined and considered, the

theory of sabotage persisted. The board was anxious to investigate this avenue thoroughly. They failed, and to this day the deliberate destruction of the *Hindenburg* has never been proved, disproved, or eliminated.

The board adjourned on May 28. Their official finding: "Most probably" St. Elmo's fire—a type of static electricity. Twenty-five years after the accident, with the fear of Gestapo reprisal gone, the scraps of information given by the surviving passengers and crewmen reject this finding and confound the mystery even more. And still the truth has not come out.

The dirigible's destruction by sabotage was not unlikely. Look at the record. Time bombs were planted on two postwar passenger zeppelins, the *Nordstern* and the *Bodensee*. Another was found under a chair in the lounge of the *Graf Zeppelin*. America's own *Akron* was involved in a sabotage plot in 1931, but the damage was discovered and repaired before flight. When the *Hindenburg* was on its South American schedule the year before, this plot was uncovered; a passenger's strange behavior had attracted the Gestapo's attention. While this man was absent from his Frankfurt hotel room, the agents found detailed interior sketches of the *Hindenburg* and *Graf Zeppelin* in his belongings. There were several Xs marked at the top of the gas cells and along critical places in the fuel lines. Somehow the suspect got warning of the search and escaped.

Late in 1938 the Hamburg-American liners *Reliance* and *Deutschland* were also involved in unexplained fires.

Dr. Ludwig Duerr, designer of the *Hindenburg*, was absolutely convinced of sabotage of the dirigible.

Who had reason to destroy the giant airship? A crank? A pyromaniac? A member of the *Gegen-Nazi Wiederstand*—the anti-Nazi resistance? How much did the Gestapo know of the plot beforehand? Years after the disaster, when the German-Russian military pact was made, the Gestapo quietly confided to Max Pruss that their search had led them quite close to the Communists. Pruss himself had long suspected a certain passenger, but although the Gestapo never uncovered more than circumstantial evidence, they did narrow their investigation down to one man, rigger Erich Spehl.

No one knew much about the tall, fair-haired crewman, He was a moody and introverted young man, aloof and quiet. He did his job well, bothered no one, and occupied his spare time with photography. Shortly before the *Hindenburg's* scheduled departure, Spehl was seen hanging around one of the drinking places frequented by Communists. He was keeping company with a somewhat plump woman several years his senior. His crewmates remarked to one another that this behavior was quite unlike him, but Spehl, obviously enamoured of the woman, explained that it was just a farewell party.

Little else is known of the mysterious woman except this: As the *Hindenburg* drummed over the Atlantic, she visited the Frankfurt terminal of the Zeppelin Company three times. She was clearly apprehensive and highly curious. Each time she inquired about the airship's position. On her last visit she wanted to know the hour of its landing at Lakehurst.

Spehl's position near the tail was in the area where the explosion occurred. He had been relieved by Knorr, and at the time of the landing approach was in the farthermost part of the nose. He perished in the holocaust, so we shall never know if he played a part in setting a fire device in the crevices of gas cell Number Four. Purely circumstantial evidence suggests that he may have hidden a flashbulb filled with aluminum foil, near the center catwalk under the aft bag. It would have to have been connected to an electrical source (the small battery?) and a timing device. Here is what supports this theory:

1. Spehl associated with known Communists who were active in trying to destroy the Nazi myth of invincibility.
2. He had full access to the cavernous interior of the airship, much opportunity to work alone and undetected, and could have placed the device in position before he was relieved of his watch at 6:00 P.M.
3. With his knowledge of photography, he knew the potential of flashbulbs, that they contained their own oxygen, could instantly reach 6,400 degrees Fahrenheit, and could be made to explode when fired by simply nicking the glass with a small file.
4. He was among the few crewmen who were farthest from the explosion when it occurred.
5. Crewmen in the tail aft of cell Number Four said the fire started as a brilliant flash (like a photoflash

bulb), and sounded like a *pop* (as when one is accidentally shattered because of faulty construction).

True, it is all circumstantial. And it seems to lose significance when we remember that the airship was scheduled to land at 8:00 A.M., and its destruction occurred twelve hours later. Logically, a bomb would be timed to explode over the Atlantic where its quick work would leave no trace of the crime.

We shall probably never know for certain who, or what, destroyed the *Hindenburg*. Or why or how. The disaster could not have happened had helium been used. In the enigmatic ending of the short but brilliant day of the giant rigid airship, the dirigible had shown its unfitness to everyone but the most devoted lighter-than-air airshipman. The insurance companies paid the Zeppelin Company two-and-a-half million dollars, with the announcement that never again would they underwrite a hydrogen-filled airship.

The *Graf Zeppelin* was near the Canaries on its return run from Brazil when Captain Schiller received the news of the *Hindenburg*'s death. After he arrived át Frankfurt his airship was put into its shed and never flown again.

Work on the *Graf Zeppelin II* continued at Friedrichschafen, where it was tested in September 1938. But Hitler forbade even one commercial flight with the new giant. This was his revenge for Dr. Eckener's earlier refusal of the Friedrichschafen hangar for a Nazi mass meeting. Work on another superzeppelin, the LZ-131, was halted at the outbreak of the war. Then, in March of 1940, after bitter words between Max Pruss and Reichmarschal Goering, both *Grafs* were dismantled. Two months later, on May 6, 1940, the massive airship shed at Frankfurt was blown up. It happened three years to the day after Lakehurst.

Like Rosendahl, Pruss never lost faith in the dirigible as the best means of air transportation. In 1957 he journeyed to Brazil and the United States, trying to raise capital for another airship company. He was unable to arouse enough interest and the dream never materialized. Pruss died in 1960, still satisfied that the cause of the *Hindenburg*'s destruction was sabotage.

The thirteen passengers who died aboard the *Hindenburg* were the first and last commercial casualties in airship history. Not a single rigid airship has carried another paying passenger since May 6, 1937.

In the words of Dr. Eckener when he discussed the *Hindenburg*'s end with newsmen in Berlin: "It is over."

CHAPTER 14

The Mystery of Flight 19

Throughout the history of manned flight, aircraft have disappeared without a trace. Pilots are reluctant to discuss these cases with outsiders, and will only guardedly talk about them among themselves.

They can understand crashes. As shocking as wreck sites are, the planes, or at least parts of them, are still in evidence to offer clues on the probable causes. But in the case of an airplane simply vanishing, a deep-seated, almost superstitious dread replaces the power of reason.

The disappearance of a squadron of torpedo bombers off the east coast of Florida remains one of the most incredible mysteries of our time. To confound the puzzle, a huge PBM-5 Mariner flying boat sent to search for the missing planes vanished minutes after takeoff. Twenty-seven men were plucked from the skies under circumstances so unusual that twenty years later the sea has not given up a single clue as to their fate, nor has one fragment of wreckage been washed ashore or found afloat.

Soon after daybreak on Wednesday, December 5, 1945, a cloud cover moved out of the Gulf of Mexico and drifted across the Florida Peninsula. It crossed the west coast between Tarpon Springs south to Sarasota and by midmorning the cloud bank reached the Atlantic shore between Daytona Beach and Melbourne. At one o'clock in the afternoon the overcast had all but dissipated over the open water east of Canaveral. Except for a few scattered clouds, most of the Florida peninsula was clear. Flight conditions improved rapidly. The warm Gulf Stream again became a bright blue and the sun lighted the sandy shorelines and lush, semi-tropical forests.

The stage was set for Flight 19 to make its never-to-be-forgotten journey to oblivion.

This unlikely story began that afternoon at the Fort

Lauderdale Naval Air Station. Although the war had been over for three months, patrol flights were still conducted as part of training exercises in coastal defense. A squadron of five Grumman Avengers waited on the operations ramp as fourteen airmen strolled from the briefing room with navigation gear and flight charts, and climbed into their cockpits. Each chart was marked with a triangle, one leg of which extended east to sea for 160 miles. At the end of this line, which would put the patrol in the vicinity of the Bahamas, they would follow the second line due north for forty miles, then swing southwestward toward the air station on the final course for home. It was to be a routine training exercise.

At 2:02 P.M., the flight leader closed his cockpit canopy, poured the power to the 1,750-horsepower Wright engine, and led the other four TBMs down the runway. This was the lead Avenger, FT-81, piloted by Marine First Lieutenant Forrest J. Gerber. Marine pfc William E. Lightfoot was his only crewman. Normally a TBM carried a crew of three: pilot, gunner, and radio operator. But one crewman failed to report, and at 2:08 the five planes closed into a right formation at 150 miles per hour over the sparkling blue Atlantic—one man short.

Aircraft FT-28 was piloted by Navy Lieutenant Charles C. Taylor, with E-4 Walter R. Parpart as radioman and E-4 Robert F. Harmon as gunner. Marine Captain Edward J. Powers was in command of FT-36, with Marine Staff Sergeants H. O. Thompson and G. R. Paonessa as crewmen.

Torpedo bomber FT-117 was flown by Marine Captain George W. Stivers with crewmen Private R. P. Gruebell and Sergeant R. F. Gallivan. The remaining patrol plane was FT-3, piloted by Ensign Joseph Bassi. Seamen H. A. Thelander and B. E. Baluk, Jr., made up his crew.

All the planes were mechanically sound; engines, controls and navigation systems were in normal working order. Their tanks were full and all of the bombers carried self-inflating life rafts. Each crewman wore a life jacket and a parachute. All fourteen men had had flight experience ranging from thirteen months to six years. The weather was clear and a somewhat cool sixty-five degrees for south Florida, even for December. A moderate to fresh breeze blew from the northwest but the usual afternoon buildup of cumulus clouds, a characteristic of that semitropical climate, was absent.

One hour and thirty-five minutes later, at 3:45 P.M. to be exact, when the five-plane patrol should have been homeward bound on its final leg, the control tower at Lauderdale Naval Air Station heard a distress call.

"Flight 19 to Lauderdale Naval Air Station, this is an emergency," an uneasy voice radioed. "We appear to be off our course . . . cannot see land . . . repeat, cannot see land."

"What's your position?" the tower requested.

"Not certain of our position," the patrol leader replied. "We aren't sure . . . we seem to be lost. . . ."

The tower operators were puzzled. How could five experienced pilot navigators be lost at the same time, less than an hour's flying time from base in clear weather? The tower ordered the leader to perform the standard emergency procedure for all aircraft lost off Florida's east coast. "Fly due west," the operator instructed, knowing the planes must sooner or later cross the coastline.

The tower waited for an acknowledgment from Flight 19 and when one came, radioed: "Go ahead, Flight 19." There was a long pause before the squadron replied. The men in the tower were stunned by the flight leader's words.

"We don't know which direction is west. Everything is wrong . . . the sky looks strange. We aren't sure of any direction. Even the water doesn't look as it should!"

Naval officers at the air station were unable to understand how an unusual appearance of the sky and water could cause the flight to become lost. Although a small magnetic storm in the local area might cause their magnetic compasses to go awry, the radio navigation gear in the planes would have given them a radio fix on Lauderdale Naval Air Station and, above all, the late afternoon sun was boldly visible on the western horizon. At Lauderdale it remained bright in the sky. What could be shielding the sun from the pilots' view 200 miles at sea?

A hectic hour and forty-five minutes followed. While the tower operators listened to an exchange of confused chatter between the planes, they heard conversations that ranged between anxiety and near hysteria. Then, a few minutes after 5:00 P.M., the flight leader did a strange thing, he turned command of the patrol over to another pilot. At 5:25, fifteen minutes after the time schedule for the squadron to be safely on the ground, the new patrol leader contacted the tower with this final, wavering call:

"We're still not certain of our position . . . have gas for seventy-five minutes more . . . can't tell whether we're over the Atlantic or the Gulf of Mexico . . . we think we must be about seventy-five miles northeast of Banana River and about 225 miles north of base. . . . It looks like we are . . ."

Abruptly, the message broke off. When the tower operators failed to re-establish contact, they alerted the Banana River air-sea rescue unit. A huge gull-wing Martin PBM-5 Mariner flying boat, commanded by Lieutenant W. G. Jeffrey, nosed out of its berth with thirteen men, full rescue equipment, and survival gear, and headed for the patrol's last assumed position. Once the twin-engine aircraft was airborne, Lauderdale tower radioed a message to the squadron that help was on the way. It was not acknowledged.

The twenty-eight-ton search plane had exchanged several radio messages with Lauderdale NAS as it taxied out for takeoff, but twenty minutes en route, when it was presumed near Flight 19's probable position, the tower requested a report. There was no reply—then or ever.

In the gathering dusk it became disturbingly apparent that something frightening was happening out there. Flight operations at Lauderdale NAS flashed an alert to the Miami Coast Guard Station. A rescue plane took off, retraced the PBM's path and reached the position where it had apparently disappeared. It returned after darkness and reported search results negative.

Officially, the last message was received at 5:25 P.M., but unofficially, another call was heard at the time the Avengers' five-hour fuel supply would have been exhausted. One bomber was heard trying vainly to call another at 7:04 P.M. Its signal was so faint that little could be understood except the flickering call letters "FT . . . FT . . . FT . . ."

Through the long winter night the Navy and Coast Guard put ships to sea from ports along the east coast of Florida. Watch officers scanned the horizon for signal flares from life rafts, but at dawn, no lights had been reported anywhere. In the early morning hours the Chief of Naval Advanced Training at Jacksonville Naval Air Station appointed a board of inquiry as the escort carrier

USS *Solomons* nosed into the alert area with thirty planes. By now, twenty-one vessels were fanning out in an ever-widening search, and by midday three hundred airplanes formed systematic grid patterns between Bermuda and Florida. The Royal Air Force dispatched two search planes from Windsor Field at Nassau, as the methodical crisscross of air and sea intensified during the afternoon. As the hours passed without a clue, search officers had growing doubts about being in the proper sector. Six planes down and not a scrap of wreckage? Impossible! But nightfall came and nothing was sighted by the air-sea flotilla.

All of the next day, Friday, the growing search spread outward to include a 200-mile penetration of the Gulf of Mexico. Low-flying reconnaissance planes made sweeps from Key West to Jacksonville, while twelve large parties made an onshore search of 300 miles of coastline between Miami Beach and St. Augustine. The Everglades were surveyed. After each high tide and offshore blow, the outlying coastal islands and beaches were scanned for clues. Every life raft, bit of flotsam, and remnant of clothing washed ashore was examined until it was ruled out.

Military commanders could not believe that six planes could suddenly vanish without a trace over a relatively small area of the Atlantic. Commander Howard S. Roberts, executive officer of the Fort Lauderdale NAS, reported that although the flight was under the direction of an experienced combat navigator, his pilots could have been blown off course by high winds. Miami weather reports listed freak winds with occasional gusts of forty miles an hour and higher, as well as showers and thunderstorms over the Banana River sector, when the 5:25 call was made to Lauderdale NAS. But the patrol pilots had made no mention of adverse weather. Although the Avengers could have been blown off course, they were tough combat aircraft that would be unaffected by rough weather. Structural failure was ruled out. And even if the TBM was not the most buoyant combat plane in the Navy's inventory, Commander Roberts assured the press that when ditched, the planes would remain afloat long enough for each life raft to be launched and inflated.

"Each man has been so well trained in emergency ditching at sea," he explained, "They shouldn't even get their feet wet."

Each TBM had a two-way radio. How could all five planes disappear in one swoop without one radio operator sending a last-minute SOS, or a hint of approaching disaster? Did all five go down en masse in a mid-air collision while flying wing to wing in "dead man" formation? Were they in a blinding storm?

What about the Mariner? Did it disappear before the TBMs were lost? It was last heard from twenty minutes after it departed Banana River—about 5:45—but the last "unofficial" call from one TBM was an hour and fifteen minutes later, at 7:04, when its weak and faltering "FT . . . FT . . ." call letters were picked up. Did the flying boat meet the same fate as the patrol? An unusually mild sea was running, making it feasible for the Mariner to land. It also carried an emergency radio transmitter that it never used.

Waterspouts were unlikely. Widespread debris would have littered the surface of the water.

Every theory failed to account for the weird sky conditions described by the pilots and their failure to orient themselves. One possibility after another was tracked down and crossed off.

On the night of the disappearance, the merchant steamer *Gaines Mills* was at sea off Florida's east coast. It radioed the Navy that its crew had seen an explosion in the air about 7:50 P.M., and what appeared to be an airplane spin down into the sea off New Smyrna Beach. This coincided with the approximate time the TBM's tanks would have run dry. Could this have been the Mariner? The planes that combed the area at daybreak were unable to answer the question; they reported no wreckage, no fragments, no oil slicks.

If the patrol had flown west, it would have crossed the Florida coast or the Keys. Flying east, the pilots would have sighted the Bahamas with its twenty-five-mile-long Grand Bahama Isle. To the southeast were Andros and Great Abaco Islands, land masses impossible to ignore. Had the patrol struck out north or south over open water, the Florida mainland would have been visible at times. Despite high winds, the squadron could not have flown in one direction for an hour and forty-five minutes—from the time they declared their state of confusion until their last radio call—without sighting one familiar landmark. The compasses of all five planes must have been erratic, for if the error was identical, all five would have flown in a straight line and crossed land somewhere. Conclusion: the patrol flew in circles between the Bahamas and Florida.

The search, which covered 380,000 miles over land and water, ended on December 11, but Navy ships and aircraft that traveled the area regularly were ordered to remain on indefinite alert. Months later the Navy delivered its final report. They had not found a single clue as to the fate of the twenty-seven men. Not a scrap of the six planes was recovered. The board of inquiry reluctantly admitted that its members "were not able to make even a good guess as to what happened."

Over the past two decades, scientific discoveries have thrown some light on the once-baffling reports connected with the squadron that vanished. The blacking out of the sun and the strange appearance of the sea described by the naval aviators is now believed to have more bearing on the strange disappearance than was originally believed. Some careful research brings to light past cases where sudden darkness occurred on bright sunshiny days and no eclipse was noted. For example, on September 24, 1950, a large area of the United States saw a weird purple-blue sun filtering through an eerie atmosphere. An official explanation was released to the uneasy populace. The unnatural appearance of the sun was attributed to widespread forest fires in Alberta, Canada. Smoke and haze had lifted to a very high altitude and altered the color of the sunlight. On September 26, the high "smoke and haze" appeared over Britain and the sun was seen as a blue-green ball.

The smoke theory had one serious flaw. While the prevailing winds were moving the alleged clouds eastward across the United States, the haze was almost moving westward across the state of Washington and obscuring the sun. No follow-up theory on how a wind could blow in opposite directions at the same time was forthcoming.

At ten o'clock on the morning of December 2, 1904, darkness fell on Memphis, Tennessee. The sun simply failed to shine. Fifteen minutes later the unearthly blanket of darkness lifted. A similar thing happened at Aitkin, Minnesota, in April of 1889.

In 1886, there was a ten-minute pitch-blackout on the afternoon of March 19. It occurred as a thick cloud mass carried an area of darkness across the United States from west to east. The small circle of intense gloom—a semisolid body moving between the sun and earth—blocked out the light as it passed from coast to coast in little more than three hours.

What is the significance of sudden midday darkness? Astronomers tell us that space is not so empty as it was once thought to be. Our earth is gaining weight daily as billions of microscopic particles are swept into our atmosphere. Some experts have suggested that there are great masses of opaque gas and dust drifting in outer space and that our planet, hurtling through these cosmic clouds, causes a sharp decrease in sunlight over a limited area. If this condition is cosmic in origin, it could point to a rare and little-understood phenomena that electronic experts call "reduced binding" or, more commonly, "a hole in the sky."

Magnetic disturbances from above have occurred before in erratic, wavelike pulses. Special instruments show these anomalies to be roughly circular, usually no more than a thousand feet in diameter, and extending upward an indefinite distance. A magnetic tornado of sorts.

The late Wilbur B. Smith of Ottawa, former electronic consultant for the Canadian Government, was once in charge of investigating these deviations. He used an instrument of his own design to trace and plot the magnetic patterns. In 1950 and 1951, he produced evidence that correlated sudden localized areas of magnetic twisters with certain unexplained plane crashes. He also showed the binding to be more common in the southern lattitudes. Whether they weave about or merely drop down and fade away is still unknown. "When we looked for some of them a few months later, we could find no trace," Smith reported. "Some planes, of course, would not be affected by the conditions, others might fly to pieces in a storm of turbulence."

Although the U.S. Navy believes that there is not enough evidence to support any such "unlikely theory" as an atmospheric aberration, its classified operation, Project Magnet, plots them on a world-wide scale. Super Constellations with highly sensitive magnetometers—instruments that measure the earth's magnetic fields—have discovered that erratic magnetic forces from space frequent the Caribbean-Key West area.

The fact that a substantial number of military aircraft and commercial flights regularly pass unscathed through this region has not lessened the haunting threat. The five Avengers and the Mariner were only six of several aircraft that were lost in this general area. The Deadly Triangle, as it is called, lies roughly within a line drawn from Bermuda to Puerto Rico to the Florida coast (through the Bahama chain) and back to Bermuda. What makes the disappearances so incredible is the simple fact that the area is by no means an isolated one. The Caribbean and Florida coasts are well populated. So are the offshore islands. Day and night a stream of air and sea traffic shuttles between the islands and the mainland, over relatively short distances.

In December, 1948, another mysterious disappearance was recorded in the triangle. Captain Robert Linquist of Fort Meyers and copilot Ernest Hill of Miami were about to complete a thousand-mile flight from San Juan, Puerto Rico, to Miami. Their DC-3, a charter plane of Airborne Transport, Incorporated, carried thirty-two passengers, including two infants. Shortly after takeoff, stewardess Mary Burks served coffee and cookies to the passengers, all of whom were returning from Christmas holidays on the island. The mood was light. Early in the flight, Linquist reported by radio that the passengers were singing Christmas carols. Now, hours later, they neared the mainland with the tired passengers lulled to sleep by the monotonous drone of the engines and the half-light of the darkened cabin. At 4:13 A.M., Linquist contacted the Miami control tower. Ahead, dimly, the glow of the great city's lights edged the horizon.

"Approaching field. Fifty miles out. South. All is well; we'll stand by for landing instructions."

Seconds after Linquist made this call, it happened, and it was over quickly. There was no time for a distress call; the DC-3 had simply vanished.

What happened to the airliner, so near its destination? It was not forced down by bad weather; the Weather Bureau reported good flight conditions. Both pilots were experienced over the route, and there was no hint of mechanical trouble in flight.

There was a search, of course. Planes fanned into the area and scanned the water for debris and telltale packs of sharks and barracuda. Forty-eight vessels swept the region over seas so clear and shallow that anything as large as a transport plane could be seen on the bottom. After scouring 310,000 miles of the Everglades, the Keys, the Caribbean, and the Gulf of Mexico, the search was called off. To this day nothing has been found.

Twenty days later, on January 17, 1949, a British South American Airways plane vanished under equally baffling circumstances. It was the *Star Ariel*, an Avro Tudor IV en route from Bermuda to Santiago via Kingston. It carried thirteen passengers and a crew of seven commanded by Captain J. C. McPhee. The transport departed Bermuda at 7:30 A.M. and climbed into a brilliantly clear morning sky. At 8:25, Bermuda tower heard this call: "This is Captain McPhee aboard the Ariel en route to Kingston, Jamaica, from Bermuda. We have reached cruising altitude. Weather fair. Expected time of arrival Kingston as scheduled."

This was the last call. Again, there was no wreckage, oil slick, clothing, or bodies. Nothing.

In the early 1950s British Overseas Airways Company absorbed BSAA, and all records of the uncanny disappearance of the *Star Ariel* were turned over to the British Ministry of Aviation for thorough investigation. Their conclusions, not surprisingly, were almost identical with those of the U.S. Navy Board.

Six years later, in October of 1954, doom struck another aircraft, this time just north of the triangle. A Navy Constellation disappeared without sending an emergency call, despite having two powerful radio transmitters aboard. Several hundred planes and ships covered the area but, again, nothing was found. When questioned about the Constellation's disappearance, Commander Andrew Bright, director of the Navy's Aviation Safety Section, admitted officially there was "no explanation."

Two years passed before the invisible, lurking mantle of death visited the triangle again. On November 9, 1956, another Navy plane, a patrol bomber, disappeared off Bermuda. Again there was no radio call to warn of an impending disaster.

An Air Force KB-50 tanker left Langley Air Force Base, Virginia, on January 8, 1962, and headed for the Azores. The four-engine plane carried eight men under the command of Major Robert Tawney. A short time out of base, Langley tower heard a weak and wavering radio call from the tanker. Then the message drifted into silence. Contact could not be re-established and the plane was presumed down at sea. Search units went into operation immediately, but, again, after 1,700 man-hours of combing the Atlantic, no trace of wreckage or bodies was found.

The next strike swallowed up two planes—KC-135 jet strato-tankers. On August 28, 1963, they took off in clear weather from Homestead AFB, Florida, to fly a classified refueling mission over the Atlantic. The crews totaled eleven men. At noon the planes radioed their position as 800 miles northeast of Miami and 300 miles west of Bermuda. The KC-135s failed to make scheduled follow-up position reports and airway radio communications centers tried in vain to raise them. An air-sea search was ordered and the next day search planes sighted floating debris 260 miles southwest of Bermuda, but no survivors or bodies. A midair collision was first thought to have caused the crash, despite the statement from an Air Force spokesman who said the tankers were not flying in close formation and were in constant contact with one another. He was proved correct the following day when debris of the second tanker was found 160 miles from the first. No bodies were recovered.

Shortly before midnight on March 23, 1965, an air disaster again struck within the triangle. It happened during the joint Canadian-U.S. Exercise, *Maple Spring*.

One of three long-range RCAF sub hunters, a four-engine Argus, was operating sixty miles north of San Juan. It carried a crew of sixteen, which included three pilots, three navigators, two flight engineers, and seven electronic-equipment operators. One civilian, a scientific consultant to the Maritime Air Command, was also on board. The Argus, out of the U.S. Navy Base at Roosevelt Roads, San Juan, was on patrol four hours when the target submarine *Alcide* reported a flash on the horizon. She got under way immediately along with Canadian Navy destroyers *Gatineau* and *Terra Nova*.

When the *Alcide* reached the scene, the crew recovered aircraft wreckage, rubber dinghies, and life jackets. An RCAF observer identified them as the type carried by the Argus.

A C-119 "Flying Boxcar," with ten men aboard, took off from Homestead Air Force Base at 7:47 P.M., the following June 5, to deliver a replacement engine to another C-119 stranded on Grand Turk Island. The 580-mile flight

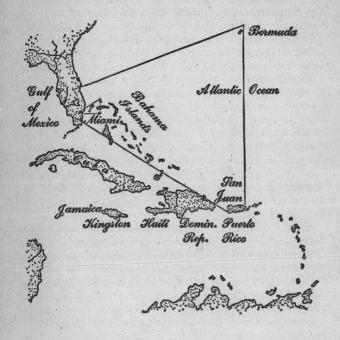

The Deadly Triangle. The small triangle shows the proposed
flight path of the five Avengers of Flight 19.

to the Bahamas was expected to take three-and-a-half hours, and for Major Louis Giuntolli, the pilot, it was another routine mission. The flight path took them southeast along a heavily-traveled air corridor called the "Yankee route." The copilot, Lieutenant Lawrence Gares, settled the ungainly plane on the course plotted by navigator Captain Richard Basset and made the usual radio-position reports. At 10:04, they reported their position as over Crooked Island, about ninety-five miles northwest of their destination. This was about an hour before they were to touch down on Grand Turk. It was a routine call; no trouble was reported.

When the cargo plane was overdue at 11:23 P.M., Grand Turk control tower tried to raise them but failed. At 5:30 A.M., when the C-119's nine hours of fuel would have been exhausted, search units were already in action. Twenty-two Coast Guard, Navy, and Air Force planes swept the Bahama chain while the cutters *Aurora* and *Diligence* plowed through seas that grew rougher by the minute. Squalls and low visibility impaired search efforts for several days. By the time the unsuccessful search was called off five days later, thirty-three planes were involved. On June 10, the Coast Guard announced: "Five days and nights of searching. Results negative. There are no conjectures." The Air Force concurred with a statement that the ten men were "presumed dead."

A paradox was the report of another C-119 that passed over the same route in the opposite direction within an hour of Major Giuntolli's 10:04 call. The crew agreed they encountered their best weather in the area where the C-119 was missing.

Although the waters in the deadly triangle are well patrolled by elements of the Coast Guard, Navy, and Air Force, there is no reason to believe the weird disappearances of planes and ships will cease.

Over this relatively small area of the Atlantic an impressive fleet of aircraft has vanished without apparent cause. All were flown by experienced airmen and directed to their destinations by trained navigators. All carried radio and survival equipment and all disappeared in good weather. Almost all were daytime disappearances.

Until a survivor can tell the tale of what happens out there, the unpredictable whims of this strange force will remain a threat to seamen and airmen alike.

CHAPTER 15

Heaven's Intruders

Is something alien roaming about our airways?

Since 1947, elusive aerial objects have been reported over every country on earth. They have been clocked by radar, observed through telescopes, photographed and paced by pilots at close range. They have been watched, it is claimed, by hundreds of ground observers at one time. Military pilots have fired on them at close range; one jet fighter discharged its air-to-air rockets—and missed.

Are unidentified flying objects—flying saucers—fact or fantasy?

Here is the greatest aerial mystery of all time—a mystery that has stirred the attention of officials from every nation.

Were there reports of UFOs sighted before 1947? Yes, many times.

When science writer J. Stubbs Walker of England tallied history's recorded observations of UFO sightings as of February 1954, he found them to total 10,000. Over 300 occurred before the twentieth century.

For hundreds of years students of the Old Testament believed the Hebrew prophet, Ezekiel, described a mystical happening in Chaldea in 593 B.C. "And I looked, and behold," he recorded, "a whirlwind came out of the north, a great cloud and a fire infolding itself, and a brightness was about it . . ." Today, some historians are taking another look at this landing near the Chebar, and wondering about the fiery "wheel" Ezekiel reported in Chapters One and Ten of his Book.

Alexander the Great found the sky visitors troublesome. In 329 B.C., two strange flying objects harassed his tired army as it tried to cross the Jaxartes River. His historian wrote of "great shining silvery shields spitting fire around their rims" that dived again and again at his columns until men, horses and war elephants panicked and refused to cross the water. Among the ancients, we find that Aristotle mentioned these same discs in his *Meteoroloigica*.

Latin author Pliny noted a certain type of comet he named *"disci"—discs.* He wrote that in 100 B.C., "when L. Valerius and C. Marius were consuls, a fiery shield flashed across the sky from west to east at sunset."

Gregory of Tours, France's first historian, wrote of "globes of fire" that moved about the sky in A.D. 583.

A document discovered at Byland Abbey in Yorkshire, England, tells of an event in 1290. Something resembling a flat, silvery disc flew over the monastery and caused much alarm.

In 1478 a fireball was seen maneuvering through the skies over Switzerland. The sight so inspired the Swiss mountain troops that they descended on the Milanese army and soundly defeated them.

The sightings before 1700 were scattered and vague; from the 1760s to the 1860s reports were less frequent.

1873. A large, silent, silvery flying machine terrorized field hands at a farm near Bonham, Texas. One workman said it came from the sky, zoomed low over them several times, and caused a team of horses to stampede. The driver was jerked under the wagon's wheels and killed. An hour later an object strikingly similar to the Bonham visitor streaked from the heavens over Fort Riley, Kansas, and turned an orderly cavalry drill into chaos.

1878. John Martin, a farmer, was hunting six miles from Denison, Texas, when he noticed a small, dark object high in the southern sky. It was round, and in his words, "traveled at a wonderful speed."

1885. A large disc was sighted over Adrianople, Turkey.

1897. As the North people looked skyward for a glimpse of Salomon Andrée's *Eagle,* observers reported instead several "high-speed balloons" that had an "electric sheen," gave out "considerable light," and "rose quickly and disappeared." Earlier that year, on April 9, people from St. Louis to Denver were said to have watched the most spectacular aerial show ever recorded. For seven spellbinding days and nights the celestial performance was uninterrupted. The star of the show was a machine that moved across the heavens at an extremely high altitude. Red, white, and green lights blinked from it at night. All across the Midwest, telescopes showed it to be cigar-shaped with broad, stubby wings. It disappeared temporarily on April 16.

Then, in the predawn glow of the 19th, at the little

hamlet of Sisterville, West Virginia, the urgent blast of the sawmill whistle roused sleeping townspeople from their beds and turned them out on the streets. What they saw swelled church attendance for weeks. Overhead, a great tubular flying contraption was slowly circling the countryside and sweeping the ground with brilliant searchlights. Red and green lights blinked along its two-hundred-foot length. It gave out an ominous, humming sound, but after ten minutes it clicked off its lights and sped away to the east.

1904. The crew of the USS *Supply* watched a brilliant light pass rapidly over the Atlantic.

1907. An "aerial spindle" was watched as it moved across Vermont.

1910. One crisp morning in January a cigar-shaped object moved over Chattanooga at twenty miles an hour. The townspeople who watched it agreed it made a distinct chugging sound. It flew away, and fifteen minutes later appeared over Huntsville, Alabama, seventy-five miles distant. The next day it returned to Chattanooga, which it circled the city again, lifted itself into the sky over Missionary Ridge, and disappeared.

1913. A large round disc hovered above a thin cloud layer and cast its shadow over Fort Worth. Then it rose out of sight.

1926. A team of American explorers led by Nicholas Roerich was crossing a remote part of Mongolia when a porter drew their attention to an object in the sky. Roerich watched it through his binoculars. It proved to be a huge, hovering object, noiseless, oval in shape, and silver-gray in color. After a few minutes it flew out of sight.

1944-1945. During the final months of World War II, scores of Allied fliers said that they had encountered what appeared to be intelligently controlled fireballs—"foo fighters." They paced bombers and pursuits during missions in Europe and the Pacific, especially after large-scale incendiary bombings left wide areas burning. Allied Intelligence thought they were a type of secret weapon, but after the war they learned that the Germans and Japanese had been as puzzled about them as they were.

One of the most dramatic news stories about UFOs broke on the quiet afternoon of June 23, 1947. It attracted scant attention at the time. A railroad engineer telephoned the city editor of the Cedar Rapids, Iowa, newspaper to report some strange flying objects. "They looked like ten shiny, disc-shaped things," he said. They were "very, very high, fluttering along in a string." They vanished toward the northwest, the engineer concluded, traveling at an estimated 500 miles an hour, "faster than any plane I've ever seen."

The newsman thanked him and scribbled a few lines for the news tickers. Then, on the following day, flying businessman Kenneth Arnold reported that he had seen nine shining "piepans" over Mount Rainier. An experienced pilot, Arnold estimated their speed at over 1,000 miles per hour plus. The story was published in newspapers from coast to coast.

In the weeks that followed, reports of sightings swamped news offices. The same silvery discs were seen in Alaska and Canada. The U.S. Air Force said they would investigate. Several days later, while people in Portland, Seattle, Spokane, and Vancouver reported seeing the saucer-shaped things maneuver overhead at tremendous heights and unbelievable speeds, the Air Force released the results of their investigation. There was no mystery at all, they announced. People were seeing things.

The crew of a United Airliner over Emmett, Idaho, said they saw five flying objects team up with four more. They watched the show for ten minutes before the formation suddenly streaked to an unbelievable speed and vanished.

In June of 1947, the Air Force said: "We have no idea what they are." The next month, Air Force officers at Wright-Patterson said: "The Air Force is making a serious investigation." That same day in Washington the press was told: "The saucers are hallucinations—no investigation is needed."

In April of 1949, the Air Force said in a Project Saucer report:

. . . observations based on nuclear power plant research in this country label as "highly improbable" the existence on Earth of engines small enough to have powered the saucers.

Intelligent life on Mars . . . is not impossible but is completely unproven. The possibility of intelligent life on the Planet Venus is not considered completely unreasonable by astronomers.

The saucers are not jokes. Neither are they cause for alarm.

Then, the following December, the Air Force again issued a statement that the flying objects did not exist.

In February 1950, Key West Naval Air Station locked on two discs fifty miles *over* Key West. The Air Force said: "No comment."

In March, F-51s and jets reportedly chased a large, metal disc over Wright Field, Ohio, the home of Air Technical Intelligence Center. The pursuit was watched by more than a hundred officers and men. A few days later the Air Force told the public the flying objects were not real. Colonel Watson, Chief of ATIC, publicly asserted: "Behind nearly every report tracked down stands a crackpot, a religious crank, a publicity hound, or a malicious practical joker."

The most revealing photographs ever made of a UFO were taken in the early evening of May 11, 1950. Although the sun had set in McMinnville, Oregon, there was enough light along the rim of the horizon to clearly record its unmistakable shape and details.

Mr. and Mrs. Paul Trent drove into the yard of their small farm about 7:30. As they got out of the car, Mr. Trent decided to check on some of his stock behind the garage. He rounded the corner of the building and stopped dead in his tracks. A hundred feet over his field an odd-shaped metallic object was suspended in mid-air. It was circular, with a low, flat-topped dome on top. The bottom appeared to be perfectly flat. It was absolutely silent as it rocked lazily from side to side over one spot.

As Mrs. Trent stopped beside him, Paul Trent noticed the small camera in his wife's hand. They had taken pictures of some children that afternoon and Paul was not sure there were any exposures remaining on the roll. Mrs. Trent lifted the camera to her eye and snapped a picture of the object. Then, as she quickly advanced the film for another exposure, their mysterious aerial visitor began to move. Silently, it banked toward them, and as it swung passed at close range, Mrs. Trent snapped another picture. The disc accelerated at a fantastic rate and in a matter of seconds passed out of sight.

The farmer and his wife did not know what they had photographed. As usual, they took the film to a drugstore to be processed, and when it was returned, they sorted out the children's pictures and put the others aside.

Six weeks passed before Paul Trent happened to mention the pictures to a newspaper editor. The man asked to see them, and a search began for the misplaced negatives at the farm. They were finally located under a sofa, where the children had tossed them. The enlargements proved to be so outstanding that they were printed world-wide in newspapers and in *Life* magazine.

One man, airline captain Willis Sperry, was especially pleased to see the photos in print. For the past three weeks he had taken the good-natured jibes of his fellow pilots because of a strange object he reported nineteen days after Mrs. Trent had snapped the picture in her back yard. Captain Sperry was at the controls of an American Airlines DC-6, on a night flight from Washington, D.C., to Tulsa, when the incident occurred. After a routine takeoff from National Airport, he nosed the airliner into a steady climb at slightly under 200 miles per hour. When they were only a few minutes clear of the runway and in the vicinity of Mount Vernon, the copilot grasped Sperry's arm and pointed excitedly over the nose. A large, dark object, its form outlined in the moonlight, was directly in their path—motionless. Sperry broke his climb by lowering the nose for better control, and as the airliner rapidly closed on it the object accelerated and zipped several hundred yards to the left. Both men noticed that it glistened in the pale moonlight.

The thought struck them that this might be a military aircraft running without lights. If so, regulations were being flagrantly violated. Sperry radioed a report to National's control tower. The tower confirmed the object; they had it on their radarscope. Then the shape swung around behind the left wing of the transport plane, where the pilots got a clearer look as it was silhouetted against a moonlit cloud bank. A few minutes later it circled the airliner and perched off the copilot's wing. National Airport's radar reported: "We're still watching it . . . and there are no other planes in the area." Sperry acknowledged, "It's certainly not a plane. It's like nothing we've ever seen. It looks to us like the conning tower of a small submarine."

A few seconds later the mystery object swept nonchalantly across the path of the plane, streaked over the Atlantic, and disappeared into the night sky. When newspapers carried the weird description of the thing, Sperry and his copilot became the subject of much derision. But then the McMinnville photos appeared in print a few weeks later and some readers drew a parallel between the conning-tower shape over Virginia and the object over the Trent farm.

It was at this time that thirty-four sightings (many reported simultaneously by pilots, ground observers, and radar operators) were recorded over the nation's capital. The objects returned on several nights that month of July 1952. For six hours on the morning of the 20th, ten unidentifiable objects were reported over the city. Their gyrations on the radarscopes indicated that they were not ordinary aircraft. They made right-angle turns and complete instant reversals in formation. The Air Force told reporters the sightings were "reflections and temperature inversions." In other words, illusions.

Many airline pilots took UFO sightings seriously and still do. But in the early fifties some were so discouraged by the Air Force's habit of passing off their sightings as "windshield reflections, fatigue, or weather balloons," they vowed they would not report another sighting, no matter how extraordinary. They thought it strange, however, that the Air Force had not grounded their pilots because of fatigue or hallucinations, and that Government radar operators were not relieved of their duties—guiding millions of dollars' worth of airliners with their priceless human cargoes into passenger terminals.

At the end of 1947, Project Saucer came into being. Coordinated with the Air Technical Intelligence Center at Dayton, its job was to evaluate reports of unidentified flying objects (the Air Force rarely calls them flying saucers). In 1949 the name was changed to Project Grudge, and early in 1952 changed again to Project Blue Book, which stands today.

There were hoaxes of course, attempts to cash in on the sensationalism. Some of them paid off; many did not.

An early hoax was the Maury Island Mystery of June 1947. It concerned two Tacoma, Washington, "harbor patrolmen," one of whom had watched six noiseless silver discs hover over his patrol boat near Maury Island. Five of the objects circled around the sixth, which threw off light-metal particles and chunks of rocklike material. Some of the pieces landed on the beach and were picked up by the patrolmen and their crew. They took pictures of the entire sky display. The next morning, when they docked at Tacoma, a mysterious visitor told them to forget what they had seen.

Two Air Force officers heard of the incident and flew to Tacoma to question one of the men. On their return to Hamilton Air Force Base, their B-25 caught fire and crashed, killing them. The newspapers hinted that saucers had played a part in the bomber's crash. A rumor started that the men who watched the saucers at Maury Island had mysteriously "disappeared."

The final investigation showed that the Maury Island affair began as a joke and mushroomed into a gigantic hoax. The parties finally admitted the fragments had nothing to do with saucers; they were bits of slag. They had sent the fragments to a magazine editor as a joke, stating they were part of the saucers, which didn't exist either. The editor sent a $200 check to the men and asked them to investigate the case and come up with a story. Thus obligated, the conspirators came up with a good one, but were unable to find the pictures they had said were made. They had misplaced them. The mysterious visitor was imaginary and the harbor patrolmen turned out to be lumber-salvage men who owned some decrepit boats used on Puget Sound.

The mysterious B-25 crash? It was totally unrelated. An engine caught fire, burned off, and before the pilots could bail out, the wing and tail separated and trapped them. The crew chief and a passenger parachuted to safety.

In 1950, *Behind the Flying Saucers* was published. It told a fantastic tale of how three different types of saucers (which had crash-landed in the southwestern desert) were recovered by Government scientists. The machines were made of an amazingly strong metal unknown on earth. It was said to have resisted 150 tests and 10,000 degrees of heat at an unnamed laboratory. The dimensions of the space ships were patterned after a "formula of nines." Inside, the scientists found little men ranging in height from thirty-six to forty-two inches, dressed in blue uniforms. All were dead. The author, Frank Scully, got the information from "millionaire oilman" Silas Newton. Newton got the story from one of his employees, Government scientist "Dr. Gee" who had been present at the examination of the little men and their mysterious machines.

It was a great story. So convincingly did Scully tell it, some readers were satisfied that extraterrestrial visitors had indeed landed. Then J. P. Cahn of the San Francisco *Chronicle* revealed that not only was Silas Newton not a millionaire oilman but that superscientist Dr. Gee was Leo Gebauer, owner of a TV-parts house in Phoenix.

In Kearney, Nebraska, a man claimed a spaceship had landed near the Platte River for repairs. Two men and a woman invited him aboard. They were friendly, but would not tell him where they came from. A few months later the man claimed four more contacts and a couple of rides in the flying saucer, on one of which he was allowed to take his car. When an investigation showed the man had a prison record, he was locked up pending a mental examination. There have been many similar weird, UFO claims put forward by cultists, crackpots, and sensation seekers.

Something that was not a hoax happened on January 7, 1948, when Captain Thomas Mantell met his strange, and still unexplained death in the skies over Frankfort, Kentucky. The incident began early in the afternoon when state police and Army MPs alerted Godman Field, outside Fort Knox. A huge, shining disc was sighted at Madisonville, ninety miles away, and was moving slowly toward the air base. Half an hour later it appeared overhead, south of the base, and hovered over a layer of thin clouds, its weird, pulsing red glow showing through the veil of vapor. Spectators watched it for almost thirty minutes. Captain Mantell and two other pilots scrambled for their P-51 Mustangs, took off, and climbed toward it. In a few minutes Mantell, well ahead of his wingmen, radioed: "It's directly ahead of me and still moving at about half my speed. The thing looks metallic and of tremendous size!" Then he passed through the thin cloud layer, still climbing.

"The thing's starting to climb," Mantell called again. "It's still above me, making my speed or better. I'm going to 20,000 feet. If I'm no closer, I'll abandon chase."

That was all Godman tower ever heard. A few moments after this message a witness saw the P-51 disintegrate in mid-air as though by a terrible force. The falling fragments were scattered over thousands of square feet. There was no fire.

At first, intelligence officers admitted they did not know

what the object was or what had caused Mantell to crash. Their findings at the wreckage became top secret. Two years later, the Air Force brought out the official solution. Captain Mantell was chasing Venus, had blacked out due to oxygen starvation, and his plane fell apart in the power dive that followed. Venus, however, was a pinpoint of light barely discernible that day, hardly the "metallic" thing of "tremendous size" that Captain Mantell had reported.

On the night of July 22, 1956, an Air Force C-131 Convair was cruising at 16,000 feet, near Pixley, California, with Major Mervin Stenvers at the controls. There was a sudden impact at the tail section. The plane nosed into a steep dive and Stenvers struggled to level the cargo carrier. Finally, after losing several thousand feet of altitude, the pilot pulled the Convair out of its plunge and made an emergency landing at Bakersfield. With his crew he surveyed the damage and found the tail section badly battered and crumpled. It was a miracle the major was able to control the plane, much less land it safety.

A UFO had been reported near Fresno a few hours earlier, so it was inevitable that a connection would be made with the mysterious collision. The object had been described as an oval-shaped disc with a greenish light at the rear. But the Air Force explained the plane's failure was caused by sudden metal fatigue. This model aircraft, however, had been flown for millions of miles on civil airways without a similar failure. At least the Civil Aeronautics Board was unable to find a case in their accident records when they sought to prevent a like failure on the commercial version of the Convair. Some aeronautical engineers theorized that such a failure might happen in extremely turbulent air, but the C-131 was cruising straight and level in smooth air.

It later developed that Major Stenvers had stated he had seen a UFO shortly before the collision.

An Air Force C-118 crashed in flames near Tacoma, Washington, in April 1959. Before the plane struck the ground, the pilot radioed: "We have hit something—or something hit us!" The Air Force first announced the crash was obviously caused by a mid-air collision. But when they were unable to locate the second plane, they decided the pilot had flown too low and had struck the crest of a ridge. Reports of ground witnesses said a UFO was in the area shortly before the crash.

If UFOs downed these planes, does it mean they are hostile? Certain retired military strategists and officials have pointed out that the UFOs have had every opportunity to attack thousands of civilian and military airplanes. But to all indications they have always come and gone swiftly, silently—and in peace.

Radar tells the tale of their terrific speeds, their breathtaking and almost unbelievable performances. When a blip appears on a radar screen, it means a *solid* body is bouncing back a radio wave. Radar can determine the number, distance, and approximate size of bodies in flight. By timing the passage of the blip between gridlines on the screenscope, radar operators can tell an object's speed with amazing accuracy.

There have been many reports of the fantastic speeds of UFOs. At Kirksville, Missouri, a radar sighting picked up an object the size of a B-36. It was traveling at 1,700 miles an hour. A month later a station in Columbia, South Carolina, recorded a blip that clocked across the scope at 4,000 miles an hour. During a practice mission of a B-29 at 18,000 feet, one hundred miles off the Louisiana coast, the radar operator started to pick up blips that were traveling at 5,000 miles an hour. At that moment the pilot and crew sighted several UFOs in groups, all of them glowing with an eerie bluish light. The UFOs quickly joined up with a larger disc and all passed off the screen at 9,000 miles an hour. This "joining up" has occurred so often that many investigators suspect the large "mother ships" to be a type of aircraft carrier of the sky.

It is claimed that at White Sands, New Mexico, a radar set clocked UFOs at 18,000 to 20,000 miles an hour. This is orbital speed for our earth satellites. And they are still being sighted by radar scanners. On December 29, 1964, at 8:30 P.M., naval operators at Patuxent Naval Air Station, Maryland, observed "two objects on their scope approaching at approximately 4,800 miles an hour from thirty to forty miles south of the base." Then the objects executed a tight turn and disappeared from the scope.

In 1955, John Badby of the Chicago Planetarium announced his discovery of a number of "moonlets"—satellites of unknown origin—circling the earth at a distance of

475 miles. This was two years before the Russians launched the first artificial earth satellite, Sputnik I. Dr. Clyde Tombaugh, the discoverer of the planet, Pluto, conducted a special search for years, trying to find natural earth satellites, but at the conclusion he announced he had found nothing.

Dr. Walter Reidel, a developer of the German V2, said he believed we had visitors from outer space. Meteorologist Dr. Seymour Hess of Florida State University, and Dr. Clyde Tombaugh gave accounts of sky objects that were neither planets, suns, nor satellites. Former Secretary of the Navy Dan Kimball, on a night flight between Hawaii and Guam in 1952, watched an aerial object buzz his plane, race with it a few seconds and then whiz out of sight. A few minutes later, another plane, several miles behind, radioed that a flying saucer had just come down on them and was flying alongside their wingtip. Then it zoomed out of sight. Admiral Arthur Radford was in the second plane; he watched the object from his window.

The man most closely involved in the systematic study of the UFO is a tenacious retired Marine Corps major, Donald E. Keyhoe, the Director of the National Investigations Committee on Aerial Phenomena (NICAP) in Washington, D.C. NICAP is a private, nonprofit organization formed in 1956 to serve as a collecting point for UFO sightings. In explaining NICAP's views on the UFO, Assistant Director Richard Hall says: "Briefly, we consider the extraterrestrial answer a very reasonable hypothesis. We don't insist on this answer, and prefer to pose the problem in terms of the need for a scientific investigation to determine whether this *is*, in fact, the answer."

Today, NICAP has 7200 members and a board of governors composed of retired admirals and generals, writers, columnists, and clergymen. Its special advisers are physicists, aeronautical engineers, rocket and space experts, astronomers, and pilots. Members include Congressmen, Government officials, newsmen, physicians, and lawyers, who provide regular channels of information from almost every state. They have discovered that people, hesitant to report sightings to newspapers or the Air Force, have reported to NICAP. And NICAP also receives unclassified reports from individuals in many government agencies. Because many of these people are in sensitive positions,

NICAP respects their confidence and will not identify them, except in private to a Congressional committee.

Ever since 1949, Major Keyhoe has been determined to slug it out with the Air Force. He stated in an article in *True* magazine that the saucers were interplanetary, and nothing has happened in the interim to cause him to change his contention. In three books that followed the article, he denounced Air Force censorship and presented data to document his claims.

Although UFO reports slowed somewhat in the late 'fifties, there was a new rash of sightings between 1961 and 1964. On January 10, 1964, a Polaris missile was fired from Cape Kennedy. The missile was well on its way when it was reported that an "unidentifiable flying object" zipped in over the tracking range. It was of such mass and drew so near the Polaris that the ground automatic-tracking radar locked onto the UFO in error. Eventually, the object left the radar's sight, and fourteen minutes later the trackers found the Polaris again. This event was not carried by the news services, but NICAP has a photo copy of the official tracking log that tells the story.

Near Sunnyvale, California, on July 18, 1963, four Air Force jets attempted an air intercept with a disc-shaped craft. A NICAP observer said "the UFO pulled up in a short arc and shot out of sight in three seconds."

How are these strange machines propelled? Why, except for a slight whistle or whine at low altitude, are they practically silent? Why do they rarely, if ever, leave a vapor trail as do our high-altitude jets? How can they accelerate to instant 20-G forces plus—with the accompanying pressures that would kill a human? Why don't they create a sonic shock wave as do our high-speed military aircraft? Why don't they burn up in the earth's atmosphere when they travel at thousands of miles an hour? Who—or what—is aboard?

Long-time observers are willing to admit the aerial phenomena are powered by a principle beyond the range of our present-day scientific knowledge. There's no shortage of theories, however.

Some believe that the UFOs use a source of power as yet undiscovered by our scientists. One theory supports magnetism (magnetic compasses spin crazily when near the objects); another, cosmic transformation (some atomic scientists claim to have detected radiation when certain types of UFOs were near their station). Because the objects have, under radar monitoring, changed their course 90 or 180 degrees instantly, at thousands of miles an hour, they lend support to the Plantier Theory—that they carry their own force field around them, which they vary and direct at will. Thus, the occupants themselves would be unaffected by the tremendous acceleration forces. And something about the UFO force field (or whatever) interferes with car-ignition systems, radios, and lights.

Applying the cosmic field theory to the UFO explains the mysteries of their silence, their fantastic course changes, the absence of vapor trails and sonic booms, and their ability to resist friction in the earth's atmosphere. The force field, centered on the UFO's power plant, would also act on the surrounding air. The air molecules would be carried along at speeds in proportion to their distance from the craft.

Perhaps it is because many people fail to comprehend the enormity of the universe that they doubt the possibility of life on other worlds. Consider the 200-inch reflecting telescope on Mount Palomar. Pointed in the night heavens, its lens covers a narrow area about the size of our moon, but it can observe in those few degrees over one billion gallaxies beyond. There could well be a vast number of planets much like our own in the heavens, each with an individual history from its fiery birth to its ice-cold death. Has earth been the subject of random space probes?

Within the past sixty years, since man made the first powered flight at Kitty Hawk, his strides toward space and the use of new forms of energy have been tremendous. Where will he be a hundred years from today? Are there life-supporting planets out there that are a hundred —or a thousand—years ahead of us?

In February 1962, the *Air Force Times* came out with an updated UFO report. After fifteen years of probing, they repeated their original statement of July 1947. UFOs do not exist.

Three years later, on March 3, 1965, they added:

> No evidence has been submitted to or discovered by the Air Force that sightings classed as unidentified represent technological developments or principles beyond the range of present-day scientific

knowledge. . . . There are no films, photographs, maps, charts, or graphs of unidentified flying objects . . . . The only photographs that have been submitted have been determined to be a misrepresentation of natural or conventional objects, or hoaxes.

Has every one of the thousands of UFO witnesses been in error? Observe the objective words of a noted astronomer who neither believes nor disbelieves in UFOs; who does not accept that they are interplanetary, but who seriously considers them as a scientific phenomenon. He is Dr. J. Allen Hynek, an Air Force consultant on UFOs, who says in the *Yale Scientific* magazine of April 1963:

The intelligence of the observers and reporters of UFOs is certainly at least average, in many cases above average, in some cases embarrassingly above average.

He adds:

Flying saucers have by no means died out. There are more UFO reports per year rather than less. For every puzzling report that reaches Air Force attention there are many more that do not.

Although the elusive silvery discs and cigar-shaped "things" have been around for a long time, they have never been reported in such growing numbers or in such close contact. Only during the past eighteen years have the sightings provided interest for continued news coverage. They have built a faithful following and they are still good for a space in newspapers. No show in the heavens has ever matched their fantastic antics.

Almost twenty years have passed since Kenneth Arnold reported the string of "pie pans" over Mt. Rainier. During this time, the Air Force has investigated every sighting brought to its attention. Its March, 1966 report revealed a total of 10,147 sightings, and claimed that most of them had been checked out to be such things as "meteors, stars and planets, or planes, balloons and satellites."

Then the report said that 646 of these sightings could not be identified.

What were they?

Just as the feeble beam of a flashlight is swallowed up

in the night sky, the real depths of the UFO mystery absorbs attempts at enlightenment. Real or unreal? Hallucinations or interplanetary visitors? Natural atmospheric phenomena or observers from space? The answer to these questions may come tomorrow, or in the next generation—or never.

Perhaps somewhere in the dark skies are those who know.

MEN AT WAR

TOWER HISTORY BOOKS
OF EXCEPTIONAL INTEREST

Secretos de cama
Yvonne Lindsay

Editado por Harlequin Ibérica.
Una división de HarperCollins Ibérica, S.A.
Núñez de Balboa, 56
28001 Madrid

© 2016 Dolce Vita Trust
© 2017 Harlequin Ibérica, una división de HarperCollins Ibérica, S.A.
Secretos de cama, n.º 2103 - 3.8.17
Título original: Arranged Marriage, Bedroom Secrets
Publicada originalmente por Harlequin Enterprises, Ltd.

I.S.B.N.: 978-84-687-9796-0
Depósito legal: M-15504-2017
Impresión en CPI (Barcelona)
Fecha impresion para Argentina: 30.1.18
Distribuidor exclusivo para España: LOGISTA
Distribuidores para México: CODIPLYRSA y Despacho Flores
Distribuidores para Argentina: Interior, DGP, S.A. Alvarado 2118.
Cap. Fed./Buenos Aires y Gran Buenos Aires, VACCARO HNOS.

Capítulo Uno

–Angel, ¿esa no eres tú?

Mila, a quien todo el mundo allí, en Estados Unidos, conocía por el diminutivo de su segundo nombre, apartó un mechón de pelo negro de su rostro y levantó la vista, irritada, de las notas que estaba repasando en su cuaderno.

–¿Eh?

Su amiga y compañera de cuarto, Sally, que estaba viendo las noticias del corazón, señaló el televisor.

–Esa de ahí –respondió–. Eres tú, ¿no?

El corazón le dio un vuelco a Mila. En el programa que estaba viendo su amiga, y que se retransmitía en todo el país, estaban mostrando las espantosas fotos oficiales de su compromiso con el príncipe Thierry de Sylvain, siete años atrás. En ellas se la veía con dieciocho años, sobrepeso, aparato de dientes y un corte de pelo que se había hecho en un intento desesperado por parecer más sofisticada, aunque lo único que había logrado era parecer un payaso, pensó estremeciéndose.

–No me lo puedo creer… –murmuró Sally fijando su mirada en ella–. Esa eres tú hace unos años, ¿no? –insistió en un tono acusador, señalando de nuevo el televisor–. ¿Eres la princesa Mila Angelina de Erminia? ¿Es ese tu verdadero nombre?

De nada le serviría negarlo. Sally había descubierto

3

su secreto. Milla contrajo el rostro y se limitó a agachar la cabeza, volviendo a las notas de su tesis, la tesis que seguramente no le permitirían que completara.

–¿Vas a casarte con un príncipe? –le preguntó Sally indignada.

Lo que no sabía era si le indignaba que estuviese comprometida con un príncipe o que le hubiese ocultado quién era durante todo ese tiempo. Suspiró y soltó el bolígrafo. Como procedía de un minúsculo reino europeo, había pasado desapercibida desde su llegada a Estados Unidos, siete años atrás, pero era evidente que le debía una explicación a su amiga.

Se conocían desde el primer año de universidad y, aunque al principio Sally se había mostrado algo sorprendida de que tuviera carabina, de que no tuviese citas, y de que cuando iba a algún sitio fuese acompañada de escoltas, nunca había cuestionado esos detalles porque era hija de un millonario y vivía, como ella, constreñida por normas.

Mila exhaló un pesado suspiro.

–Sí, soy Mila Angelina de Erminia, Y sí, estoy prometida a un príncipe.

–O sea que… ¿es verdad?, ¿eres una princesa?

Mila asintió y contuvo el aliento, esperando la reacción de su amiga. ¿Estaría enfadada con ella? ¿Perdería por aquello a la amiga a la que tanto apreciaba?

–Ahora mismo siento como si no te conociera, pero… ¡madre mía, qué pasada! –exclamó Sally.

Mila puso los ojos en blanco y se rio con alivio.

–Siempre tuve la sensación de que había cosas que no me contabas –murmuró Sally, yendo a sentarse en el sofá, junto a ella–. Bueno, háblame de él. ¿Cómo es?

–¿Quién?

Entonces fue Sally la que puso los ojos en blanco.

–El príncipe. ¿Quién va a ser? Venga, Angel, puedes contármelo; no se lo diré a nadie. Aunque, la verdad, me molesta que hayas estado ocultándome esto durante todos estos años.

Sally suavizó sus palabras con una sonrisa, pero era evidente que estaba dolida. ¿Cómo iba a explicarle que, a pesar de llevar años comprometida con el príncipe Thierry, apenas lo conocía? Solo se habían visto una vez: el día en que se habían conocido y se había hecho público el compromiso. Luego el único contacto que habían mantenido había sido por cartas de carácter formal enviadas por valija diplomática.

–La… la verdad es que no lo sé –admitió–. Pero lo he buscado en Google.

Su amiga se rio.

–No te imaginas lo raro que ha sonado eso. Es de locos… Es como en un cuento: una princesa prometida desde la niñez, bueno, en tu caso desde la adolescencia, a un príncipe de otro reino… –Sally suspiró y se llevó una mano al pecho–. Es tan romántico… ¿Y lo único que se te ocurre decir es que lo has buscado en Google?

–De romántico no tiene nada. Si me voy a casar con él es por el deber que tengo para con mi país y mi familia. Erminia y Sylvain han estado al borde de una guerra durante la última década. Se supone que mi unión con el príncipe Thierry unirá a nuestras naciones… aunque no es algo tan simple.

–Pero… ¿no te gustaría casarte por amor?

–¡Pues claro que me gustaría!

Mila bajó la vista y se quedó callada. Amor… Siempre había soñado con llegar a conocer el amor, pero desde la cuna la habían criado para servir a su país, y sabía que el deber no era algo que conjugase bien con el amor. En lo que se refería a su compromiso, nadie le había pedido su opinión. Se lo habían expuesto como una responsabilidad y, como tal, ella la había aceptado. ¿Qué otra cosa habría podido hacer?

Conocer al príncipe había sido una experiencia aterradora. Seis años mayor que ella, era culto, carismático, guapo y rebosaba confianza en sí mismo… todo lo contrario que ella. Y no se le había escapado la cara de consternación que había puesto, aunque hubiese disimulado de inmediato, cuando los habían presentado.

Cierto que entonces su aspecto había dejado mucho que desear, pero aún la hería en el orgullo pensar que no había estado a la altura de sus expectativas. Además, tampoco podría haber dicho al verla que había cambiado de idea y no quería casarse. Él, al igual que ella, no era más que un peón al servicio de los gobiernos de sus países en aquel plan que habían ideado para intentar aplacar la animosidad entre ambas naciones.

–¿Y por qué viniste a estudiar aquí? –inquirió Sally–. Si lo que se busca con vuestra unión es la paz, ¿por qué no se celebró la boda de inmediato?

Mila volvió a recordar la expresión del príncipe Thierry al verla. Aquella expresión había hecho que se diera cuenta de que, si quería llegar a ser para él algo más que una mera representación del deber hacia su pueblo, debería esforzarse para convertirse en su igual, empezando por mejorar su educación. Por suerte, su hermano Rocco, el rey de Erminia, había llegado a la misma conclusión que ella, y había dado su consentimiento cuando le había expuesto su plan de completar sus estudios en el extranjero.

–El acuerdo al que llegamos era que nos casaríamos el día en que cumpla los veinticinco.

–¡Pero eso es a finales del mes que viene!

–Lo sé.

–Si ni siquiera has acabado el doctorado…

Mila pensó en todos los sacrificios que había hecho hasta la fecha. No completar su tesis doctoral sería probablemente el más duro de todos. Aunque ante la insistencia de su hermano se había matriculado en algunas asignaturas sueltas de Ciencias Políticas, pero la carrera que había escogido había sido Ciencias Medioambientales. La razón era que se había enterado de que al príncipe Thierry le apasionaba todo lo que tuviera que ver con la naturaleza, y después de todos esos años de estudio a ella le había ocurrido lo mismo.

Le dolía pensar que tal vez no podría presentarse ante él con el título de doctora, pero tendría que apretar los puños y aceptarlo. No había planeado pasar tanto tiempo como estudiante, pero por su dislexia, los primeros años de universidad habían resultado más difíciles de lo que había esperado, y había tenido que repetir varias asignaturas.

–¡Madre mía, es guapísimo! –exclamó Sally, que había vuelto a centrar su atención en la pantalla.

Mila resopló mientras cerraba su cuaderno.

–A mí me lo vas a decir… –murmuró–. ¡Y eso que esas fotos son de hace siete años! Supongo que estará muy cambiado y…

–No, mira, estas imágenes son de ahora –la interrumpió Sally impaciente, agarrándola por el brazo con una mano y señalando con la otra–. Está en Nueva York, en esa cumbre medioambiental de la que nos habló el profesor Winslow hace unas semanas.

Mila giró la cabeza tan deprisa que le dio un latigazo en el cuello.

–¿Está aquí?, ¿en Estados Unidos? –preguntó aturdida, masajeándose el trapecio con la mano.

Fijó la mirada en la pantalla. Sí que estaba bastante cambiado, y aún más guapo, si es que eso era posible. El corazón le palpitó con fuerza y sintió que una mezcla de emociones contradictorias se agolpaba en su interior: miedo, deseo, melancolía…

–¿No sabías que iba a ir a Nueva York? –le preguntó su amiga.

Mila despegó los ojos de la pantalla y tuvo que hacer un esfuerzo para que pareciera que no le importaba.

–No, pero me da igual.

–¿Que te da igual? ¿Cómo que te da igual? –chilló Sally–. Ese tipo viaja miles de kilómetros para venir al país en el que llevas viviendo siete años… ¿y ni siquiera es capaz de llamar para decírtelo?

–Bueno, probablemente solo esté aquí en visita oficial y vaya a quedarse poco tiempo –replicó Mila–. Y seguro que tiene una agenda muy apretada. Además, yo estoy aquí, en Boston; no estamos precisamente a dos pasos –se encogió de hombros–. Y tampoco importa, la verdad. No falta nada para que nos veamos: nos casamos dentro de poco más de cuatro semanas.

La voz se le quebró al decir esas últimas palabras. Aunque intentara mostrarse indiferente, lo cierto era que sí le dolía. ¿Tanto le habría costado hacerle saber que iba a ir a Estados Unidos?

–Pues a mí me parece increíble que no vayáis a veros, ya que está aquí –continuó Sally, que no parecía dispuesta a dejarlo estar–. ¿En serio no quieres verle?

–Como te he dicho, lo más probable es que no tenga tiempo para que nos veamos –repuso Mila.

Prefería no entrar en lo que quería o no quería en lo tocante al príncipe Thierry. Había intentado convencerse muchas veces de que el amor a primera vista no era más que un invento de las películas y las escritoras de novelas rosas, pero desde el día en que se habían conocido no había podido dejar de pensar en él. ¿Podría ser amor?

–Bueno, pues si fuera mi prometido –apuntó Sally–, aunque no me hubiera dicho que venía, iría a verlo yo.

Mila se rio, y respondió como su amiga esperaría que respondiese:

–Ya, pues no es tu prometido, sino el mío, y no pienso compartirlo contigo.

Sally se rio también, y Mila volvió a girar la cabeza hacia el televisor. En ese momento estaban hablando de ella. La reportera estaba diciendo que se sabía que estaba estudiando en el extranjero, y especuló acerca de su paradero, que la Casa Real de Erminia había mantenido celosamente en secreto durante todos esos años. Claro que, si Sally la había reconocido al ver esas imágenes, ¿no la reconocerían también otras personas?

Confiaba en que nadie más estableciese la conexión entre ella y aquellas fotos del patito feo que había sido. Ya no era aquella chica apocada con una boca demasiado grande para su cara y mejillas y piernas regordetas. Porque por suerte, en algún momento entre los diecinueve y los veinte años, se había producido una transformación milagrosa en ella.

Había perdido los diez kilos que le sobraban, sus facciones se habían hecho más finas, la permanente que lucía en aquellas fotos ya solo era un recuerdo humillante, y por fin tenía la elegancia y la desenvoltura que le habían faltado en su adolescencia.

¿La encontraría atractiva ahora el que pronto sería su marido? Detestaba pensar que pudiera causarle rechazo, y más con lo atraída que se sentía ella por él.

Dentro de solo unas semanas regresaría a Erminia. Había llegado el momento de volver a echarse sobre los hombros el manto de responsabilidad que durante aquellos siete años había dejado a un lado, y asumir de nuevo su posición de princesa.

Aquel matrimonio era muy importante para Erminia y para Sylvain. La frágil paz entre ellos se había hecho añicos varias décadas atrás, a raíz del escandaloso idilio entre la reina de Sylvain, la madre del príncipe Thierry, y un diplomático de Erminia.

Cuando la reina y su amante habían perdido la vida en un terrible accidente de coche, los gobiernos de ambas naciones se habían acusado mutuamente, y la exhibición de fuerza militar por una y otra parte en la frontera había generado inquietud entre sus gentes.

Mila comprendía que se esperaba que su enlace con el príncipe Thierry fuera el comienzo de una alianza duradera entre Erminia y Sylvain, que pusiera fin a aquella tormenta diplomática, pero ella quería algo más que un matrimonio concertado. ¿Era desear demasiado que el príncipe pudiera llegar a amarla?

Mila alcanzó el mando a distancia y le quitó la voz al televisor, decidida a volver a su tarea, pero Sally aún no había dado el tema por zanjado.

–Deberías ir a Nueva York y encontrarte con él, plantarte en la puerta de la suite de su hotel y presentarte –la instó.

Mila soltó una risa amarga.

–Aunque consiguiera salir de Boston sin que se enteraran mi carabina y mis escoltas, no podría llegar hasta él porque sus guardaespaldas me lo impedirían. Es el príncipe heredero de Sylvain.

Sally puso los ojos en blanco.

–Y tú eres su prometida, ¡por amor de Dios! Seguro que sacaría tiempo para verte. Y en cuanto a Bernadette y los gorilas –dijo refiriéndose a su carabina y sus dos escoltas–, creo que podría ocurrírseme un modo de darles esquinazo… si estás dispuesta, claro está.

–No puedo hacer eso. Además, ¿y si mi hermano se enterara?

Sally no sabía que su hermano era el rey de Erminia, pero sí que había sido su tutor legal desde la muerte de sus padres, muchos años atrás.

–¿Y qué haría?, ¿castigarte sin salir? –se burló Sally–. ¡Vamos!, tienes casi veinticinco años y te has pasado los últimos siete aplicada a los estudios y tienes por delante toda una vida de cenas de estado mortalmente aburridas y actos oficiales. Tienes derecho a divertirte un poco, ¿no crees?

–En eso tienes razón –contestó Mila con una sonrisa traviesa–. ¿Qué sugieres?

–El profesor Winslow dijo que si queríamos podía conseguirnos entradas para la serie de charlas sobre sostenibilidad en la cumbre de Nueva York –respondió Sally–. ¿Por qué no aceptamos su oferta? La cumbre empieza mañana y hay una charla a la que podríamos… «asistir» –dijo entrecomillando la palabra con los dedos– pasado mañana. Nos alojaríamos en un hotel céntrico, cerca de donde se aloja el príncipe. Podríamos salir mañana por la tarde en el jet privado de mi padre. Si le digo que es por mis estudios no me pondrá ningún problema. Pediremos una suite de dos habitaciones: una con dos camas que compartiremos tú y yo, y otra para Bernie. Cuando hayamos hecho el *check-in* subimos a la suite, y una vez allí tú te sientes «indispuesta» –añadió entrecomillando de nuevo con los dedos–. Puedes decir que te duele mucho la cabeza y te acuestas. Bernie y yo nos quedaremos en el salón leyendo o viendo la televisión. Cuando pase una hora o así le diré que voy a salir a dar una vuelta y entraré un momento en la habitación con la excusa de ir a por mis gafas de sol o algo así. Y entonces será cuando hagamos el cambiazo: nos llevaremos una peluca rubia para que parezcas yo y un sombrero. Te pones mi ropa, yo me meto en la cama para que si entra Bernie crea que soy tú. Los chicos estarán montando guardia en el pasillo, pero cuando te vean salir también pensarán que soy yo. ¿Qué te parece?

–No se lo tragarán.

–Por intentarlo no perdemos nada, ¿no? Venga, Angel, ¿qué es lo peor que podría pasar?

Mila sopesó la idea. El plan de Sally parecía tan absurdo, y a la vez tan simple, que tal vez sí funcionara.

–Está bien; lo haremos.

No podía creerse que hubiera dicho eso, pero un cosquilleo de emoción la recorrió.

–¡Estupendo! –exclamó Sally, y añadió con una sonrisa perversa–: Esto va a ser divertido.

Capítulo Dos

Muerto… El rey había muerto… Larga vida al rey…

Ajeno al hermoso atardecer que estaba cayendo sobre la ciudad de Nueva York, Thierry, que aún estaba aturdido por la noticia, se paseaba arriba y abajo por la suite del hotel.

Ahora él era el rey de Sylvain y todos sus dominios, pues al haber exhalado su padre su último aliento, la corona había pasado automáticamente a él.

Una ráfaga de ira lo invadió. Su padre había tenido que morirse justo cuando él estaba fuera; no podía haber esperado a su regreso… Claro que era algo típico de él, andar siempre fastidiándolo. Hasta había insistido en que hiciera aquel viaje, sabiendo que estaba muriéndose. Quizá incluso lo hubiera hecho con toda la idea, porque sabía que no podría volver antes de su fallecimiento. Los arrebatos de emoción siempre lo habían incomodado.

Aunque habría sido difícil que se hubiese puesto sensible, teniendo en cuenta lo distante que su padre se había mostrado siempre con él, y cuando no estaba reprendiéndolo por la más mínima falta, se había encargado de recordarle a cada ocasión su deber para con su pueblo.

Sin embargo, más allá de la frustración y la ira que se agitaban dentro de él, Thierry sentía una honda pena,

13

tal vez más por la relación padre-hijo que nunca habían llegado a tener que por los desencuentros entre ellos.

–¿Señor? –insistió su secretario, sacándolo de sus pensamientos–. ¿Hay algo que…?

–No –lo cortó Thierry antes de que pudiera volver a preguntarle si había algo que pudiera hacer por él.

Desde que habían recibido la noticia, todos los miembros de su personal, conscientes de que ya no servían al príncipe heredero, sino al nuevo rey, habían estado asfixiándolo en su empeño por mostrarse más serviciales que nunca. Se sentía como un león enjaulado allí dentro; tenía que salir, necesitaba respirar aire fresco y disfrutar de los pocos momentos de libertad que le quedaban antes de que la noticia saltara a los titulares de todo el mundo, cosa que ocurriría en solo unas horas. Se volvió hacia su secretario.

–Perdona, Pasquale. Es que esta noticia… aunque estábamos esperándola…

–Lo sé, señor. A todos nos ha impactado, a pesar de que sabíamos que era inminente.

Thierry asintió.

–Voy a salir –le dijo.

Su secretario puso cara de espanto.

–¡Pero, señor…!

–Pasquale, lo necesito. Necesito disfrutar de una última noche de libertad antes de que todo cambie.

Ya estaba empezando a sentir la presión de lo que sería su nueva vida. De pronto se sentía como si se hubiese convertido en Atlas, el titán de la mitología griega, con el peso del mundo sobre sus hombros.

–Está bien, siempre y cuando se lleve a sus guardaespaldas.

14

Thierry asintió, consciente de que eso no era negociable, aunque no era algo que le molestase, porque sus escoltas sabían ser discretos. Aparte del equipo de televisión que lo había pillado al llegar el día anterior al hotel, hasta ese momento ningún otro medio de comunicación había informado de su visita a los Estados Unidos.

En comparación con los otros jefes de estado que se habían reunido en la ciudad para acudir a la cumbre él no era más que un personaje real de poca monta, pero al día siguiente, para cuando la noticia de la muerte de su padre ocupase las portadas de los periódicos, eso habría cambiado. Solo esperaba que, para entonces, ya estuviese a bordo de su avión privado de regreso a Sylvain.

Se desanudó la corbata, se la quitó de un tirón y fue al dormitorio. Su anciano ayuda de cámara, Nico, que estaba allí sentado, hojeando un periódico, se levantó de inmediato.

–Nico, unos vaqueros y una camisa limpia, por favor.

–Enseguida, señor.

Minutos después, tras una ducha rápida, Thierry ya estaba vestido y esperando en el salón de la suite a sus guardaespaldas, listo para salir.

–Hace un poco de fresco, señor; necesitará esto –le dijo Nico, saliendo del dormitorio con una chaqueta informal colgada del brazo.

Le ayudó a ponérsela y le tendió unas gafas de sol y un gorro de lana.

–Nico, ¿querrás preparar mi equipaje para mañanas? –le pidió Thierry–. Creo que salimos a las ocho.

Adriano, el jefe de su equipo de escoltas, entró en la suite con sus tres hombres.

–Cuando quiera, señor.

Thierry le dio las gracias a Pasquale y a Nico con un asentimiento de cabeza y salieron.

–Hemos pensado que lo mejor sería utilizar la salida lateral del hotel, señor –le dijo Adriano, que iba a su lado, mientras avanzaban por el pasillo–. Así podremos evitar el vestíbulo. Además el servicio de seguridad del hotel ya ha rastreado las inmediaciones para asegurarse de que no hay paparazzi.

–Estupendo.

Se sentía como una oveja conducida por un grupo de perros pastores cuando llegaron a la planta baja y salieron del ascensor.

–Un poco de espacio, caballeros –les pidió en un tono firme, apretando el paso para ponerse solo al frente.

Sabía que no les haría mucha gracia, pero si iba por las calles con ellos rodeándolo, llamaría la atención y prefería parecer solo un transeúnte más.

–¡Que iba a ser divertido, dijo! –masculló Mila entre dientes mientras daba la sexta vuelta a la manzana que formaba el hotel.

Una vez pasados los nervios de haber burlado a Bernadette y a sus guardaespaldas, se había sentido expectante ante la posibilidad de volver a ver a Thierry, pero ahora que ya estaba allí, dando vueltas como una tonta, estaba empezando a preguntarse si aquello no habría sido un error.

Tomó un sorbo de la infusión que se había comprado en un Starbucks para intentar calmarse y se resguardó

16

en el portal de la entrada lateral del hotel porque estaba empezando a llover. «Genial», pensó mientras miraba distraída a la gente abrir sus paraguas y apretar el paso. De pronto alguien le dio un empujón por detrás. El té hirviendo le salpicó el dorso de la mano, y el dolor hizo que soltara el vaso, que rodó por el pavimento mojado, derramando su contenido.

–¡Eh, tenga más cuidado! –protestó sin volverse, mientras sacaba un pañuelo para limpiar la mancha de su… bueno, del abrigo de Sally.

¡Menuda impresión le iba a causar al príncipe con aquella mancha! Debería volver al hotel… Aquella había sido una idea ridícula desde el principio, y si su hermano llegase a enterarse se metería en un buen lío.

–Mis disculpas.

La voz del hombre que se había chocado con ella era tan profunda y aterciopelada que un cosquilleo le recorrió la espalda. Se giró, y casi volvió a chocarse con él, porque estaba más cerca de ella de lo que había pensado.

–Perdón –murmuró.

Los sensuales labios del hombre se curvaron en una sonrisa. Llevaba un gorro de lana oscuro que le tapaba el pelo, y también gafas de sol, lo cual resultaba un poco extraño, siendo como era de noche, pero… bueno, estaban en Nueva York.

Se las bajó un poco, como si quisiera verla mejor, y al ver sus ojos, aquellos inconfundibles ojos grises, todo pensamiento racional la abandonó. Era él… el príncipe Thierry… allí, en carne y hueso, delante de ella… Se estremeció de deseo.

–Le compraré otro… bueno, lo que estuviera tomando –dijo quitándose las gafas y señalando el vaso de papel tirado en la acera.

–No, yo… era té, pero… es igual –balbució ella atropelladamente.

«¡Piensa!», se ordenó. «Preséntate. ¡Haz algo! ¡Lo que sea!». Pero cuando alzó la vista y sus ojos se encontraron de nuevo, volvió a quedarse aturdida.

Cuando se dio cuenta de que se había quedado mirándolo fijamente, lo cual era bastante grosero, se apresuró a bajar la vista, pero su corazón desbocado no se apaciguó.

–Señor, no debería…

Un hombre había aparecido junto a ellos, pero en cuanto el príncipe le dijo unas palabras en su idioma, se calló y retrocedió un par de pasos. Debía ser uno de sus escoltas, y parecía que no le hacía mucha gracia que se mezclase con la gente del lugar. Solo que ella no era de Nueva York. Y entonces cayó en la cuenta de que el príncipe no parecía haberla reconocido.

Thierry volvió a centrar su atención en ella y le dijo en un tono preocupado:

–¿Seguro que está bien? Parece que se ha quemado.

Mila dio un respingo cuando tomó su mano para examinar más de cerca la piel enrojecida por el té caliente que la había salpicado. Se le cortó el aliento cuando su pulgar rozó suavemente los bordes de la quemadura.

–No es nada, de verdad –le dijo.

Debería apartar la mano, pero de pronto era como si se hubiese quedado paralizada y no pudiese moverse.

–Por favor, deje que la invite a otro té –insistió él, soltándole la mano al fin.

Mila escrutó su rostro, sorprendida de que no la hubiera reconocido. Obviamente no habría imaginado que fuese a encontrarse precisamente con su prometida en las calles de Nueva York, se dijo intentando ser racional, pero no pudo evitar una punzada de decepción.

Claro que quizá podría utilizar aquello en su provecho... El plan que había ideado con Sally era presentarse a él diciéndole quién era, pero... ¿y si no lo hiciera? ¿Y si se hacía pasar por una chica cualquiera de Nueva York?

Sin el peso de su compromiso, que no haría sino incomodarlos y que se comportasen con excesiva formalidad, podría aprovechar para conocerlo mejor, podría conocer al verdadero Thierry y ver cómo era el hombre con el que iba a casarse.

–Gracias –murmuró, haciendo acopio de la serenidad y la fortaleza interior que le habían instilado desde su nacimiento. Era absurdo que estuviese hecha un manojo de nervios–. Me encantaría.

Los ojos de Thierry brillaron de satisfacción, y una de las comisuras de sus labios se arqueó. Mila volvió a quedarse embobada, pero de inmediato se obligó a apartar la vista y echaron a andar calle abajo.

Unos metros por delante de ellos, uno de sus guardaespaldas ya había comprobado el Starbucks en el que se había comprado el té, y le indicó a Thierry con un gesto discreto que estaba despejado. Lo hizo de un modo tan sutil que ella no se habría dado ni cuenta si no fuera porque conocía esas señales.

Cuando entraron y fueron a la barra a pedir, Mila pensó en lo surrealista que era aquello. Thierry se comportaba como si fuese algo que hacía todos los días, entrar en una cafetería llena de gente corriente para tomar algo. Sus guardaespaldas se habían apostado en distintos sitios dentro del local: dos junto a la puerta y uno cerca de la mesa a la que la condujo el príncipe cuando les sirvieron lo que habían pedido.

–¿Son amigos tuyos? –le preguntó, señalando con la cabeza a los que se habían quedado junto a la puerta.

Él resopló.

–Algo así –murmuró con humor–. ¿Te molestan? Puedo decirles que se vayan.

–Ah, no, no te preocupes. No me importa –contestó tomando asiento.

Thierry se sacó del bolsillo un pañuelo, y envolvió en él un cubito de hielo del pequeño cuenco que había pedido que les pusieran en la bandeja.

–Dame tu mano –le dijo.

–No hace falta; apenas me molesta –protestó Mila.

–¿Tu mano, por favor? –insistió él, fijando sus ojos grises en los de ella.

Y Mila claudicó de inmediato.

El príncipe le sostuvo la mano mientras aplicaba con suavidad la improvisada compresa fría, y Mila intentó en vano ignorar los rápidos latidos de su corazón mientras lo observaba.

–Te pido disculpas otra vez por mi torpeza –añadió él–. No estaba mirando por dónde iba –alzó la vista y le dijo–: Me llamo Hawk. ¿Y tú?

¿Hawk? De modo que no iba a revelarle su verdadera identidad…

–Angel –respondió Mila. Si él iba a usar un nombre falso, bien podía ella recurrir al diminutivo por el que la conocían sus profesores y compañeros allí, en Estados

Unidos. Sí, podía hacer como que eran dos extraños que acababan de conocerse.

—¿Has venido a Nueva York por negocios? —le preguntó, aunque sabía muy bien el motivo de su visita a la ciudad.

—Sí, pero me marcho mañana por la mañana —contestó él.

Mila no se esperaba esa respuesta. La cumbre duraba cuatro días y empezaba al día siguiente. Acababa de llegar… ¿y ya iba a marcharse? Quería preguntarle por qué, pero no podía hacerlo porque se suponía que no sabía nada de él.

Thierry levantó el pañuelo y asintió satisfecho.

—Ya tiene mejor aspecto —dijo.

—Gracias.

—¿Y tú? —le preguntó él, soltándole la mano.

Mila alzó la vista y lo miró aturdida.

—¿Yo qué?

—Pues que si has venido a Nueva York por trabajo o vives aquí —contestó él, reprimiendo una sonrisilla.

Mila recordó lo inepta que se había sentido el día que se habían conocido, la vergüenza que había pasado, y cómo se había sentido indigna de un hombre tan atractivo y seguro de sí mismo.

Pero ya no era aquella adolescente tímida y patosa, se dijo con firmeza. Esa noche iba de incógnito, y podía ser quien quisiera ser. Hasta alguien capaz de encandilar a un hombre como el príncipe Thierry de Sylvain. Aquel pensamiento la animó y le dio coraje. Sí, podía hacer aquello.

Capítulo Tres

Se quedaron mirándose a los ojos, y a Thierry le pareció como si el ambiente se cargase de electricidad. Las finas y perfectas cejas de Angel eran de un color oscuro, como las pestañas que bordeaban sus ojos ambarinos, en discordancia con su largo pelo rubio, pero ese contraste no le restaba ni un ápice de belleza. De hecho, quizá precisamente por eso llamaba más la atención.

Sus pómulos eran elevados y parecían suavemente esculpidos; y su nariz corta y recta; pero eran sus labios carnosos los que parecían haberlo atrapado bajo un hechizo. Un hechizo que solo se rompió cuando alguien pasó junto a su mesa y la golpeó sin darse cuenta, derramando parte del té de Angel.

–Parece que el destino no quiere que tome té –comentó ella riéndose, mientras secaba la mesa con una servilleta de papel–. Y en respuesta a tu pregunta: no, vivo en Boston. Solo estoy aquí de visita.

–Ya me parecía que tu acento no era de aquí –observó Thierry.

Angel tomó el vaso de papel con sus elegantes dedos y bebió un sorbo. Cada uno de sus movimientos lo cautivaba, hasta el modo en el que se lamía los labios con la punta de la lengua al acabar de beber. Tragó saliva. No debería estar allí con aquella joven; estaba

22

comprometido… con alguien a quien apenas conocía, y con quien iba a casarse a finales de ese mes.

Pero es que jamás había sentido una atracción así. Tenía una sensación extraña, como si hubiese visto a Angel antes en alguna parte, como si ya se conociesen.

–En realidad –añadió ella dejando el vaso en la mesa–, he venido para asistir a una conferencia que se celebra mañana sobre iniciativas sostenibles.

Thierry parpadeó.

–¿En serio? ¡Qué coincidencia! Yo también iba a ir a esa conferencia.

–¿Y no puedes retrasar tu vuelta?

La fría realidad le tiró de la manga, recordándole que al día siguiente, tras un vuelo de ocho horas y media hasta Sylvain, y veinte minutos en helicóptero hasta el palacio, le esperaba una reunión con el consejo de ministros. No volvería a ser dueño de su tiempo hasta que su padre hubiese sido enterrado en el panteón familiar. Y quizá, ni siquiera entonces.

–¿Hawk? –lo llamó Angel, sacándolo de sus pensamientos.

–No, tengo que volver; se trata de un asunto urgente. Pero no hablemos más de eso; dime, ¿qué se le ha perdido a una chica tan bonita como tú en un auditorio?

A ella pareció ofenderle su pregunta.

–Eso ha sido un poco sexista, ¿no?

–Perdona –se apresuró a disculparse él–. No pretendía menospreciar tu inteligencia ni parecer un machista.

Al final iba a ser verdad eso de que «de casta le viene al galgo», pensó, avergonzado de sí mismo. Su padre había tenido una visión anticuada de que la mujer no servía más que para dar hijos al hombre, y que tenía que reverenciarlo y serle fiel.

Su madre, la reina consorte, había «fracasado» estrepitosamente en lo segundo y su padre, en vez de plantearse que tal vez se hubiera equivocado en cómo la había tratado, se había reafirmado en su opinión sobre el rol secundario de la mujer en la monarquía.

De hecho, Thierry había empezado a preguntarse si su madre no le habría sido infiel, en parte, por cómo había minado su autoestima con su condescendencia hacia ella. Tal vez esos actos de su madre no habían sido otra cosa más que un modo desesperado de dar sentido a su vida. Pero poco importaba eso ya, cuando su amante y ella habían muerto en un accidente de coche años atrás.

El escándalo que aquello había provocado había estado a punto de llevar a ambas naciones a la guerra, y había sido uno de los motivos por los que él se había propuesto mantenerse virgen hasta el matrimonio y, cuando se hubiese casado, permanecer fiel a su esposa hasta su muerte. Y esperaría lo mismo de ella, por supuesto. Ya que no podía casarse por amor, al menos se esforzaría por que su matrimonio durase. Tenía que lograrlo, tenía que cambiar el curso de generaciones y generaciones de fracaso e infelicidad conyugal.

Angel aceptó su disculpa con un breve asentimiento de cabeza.

–Me alegra oír eso –dijo–, porque bastantes actitudes machistas le aguanto ya a mi hermano –suavizó sus palabras con una sonrisa, y añadió–: Y en respuesta a tu pregunta, voy a asistir a esa conferencia porque me interesa, y porque me la recomendó un profesor de la universidad.

Se pasaron la hora siguiente hablando de sus estudios, y en particular de su interés por el desarrollo de soluciones sostenibles mediante energías renovables que contribuyeran a reducir la pobreza. El entusiasmo de Angel al defender esas causas, que teñía sus mejillas con un suave rubor, haciéndola aún más bonita, lo fascinaba. Además, aquel era un tema que para él también era importante y que quería promover en su reino. Hacía tiempo que no tenía una conversación tan estimulante.

La cafetería se había ido vaciando poco a poco, y Thierry se dio cuenta de que sus guardaespaldas, que se habían sentado en mesas distintas, estaban empezando a moverse incómodos en sus asientos. Angel también pareció darse cuenta, porque le dijo:

–Ah, perdona por quitarte tanto tiempo. Cuando empiezo a hablar de algo que me apasiona me dejo llevar –se disculpó.

–En absoluto –replicó él–. He disfrutado mucho con esta conversación. No tengo muy a menudo la ocasión de intercambiar opiniones con alguien tan elocuente y tan versado en estos temas como tú.

Angel miró su reloj, que tenía una delicada pulsera de platino y, si no le engañaban sus ojos, adornada con diamantes. Aquel sutil pero evidente signo de que pertenecía a una familia adinerada, lo intrigó aún más.

–Se está haciendo tarde; debería volver a mi hotel –dijo, como a regañadientes–. Lo he pasado muy bien, gracias.

Thierry no quería despedirse tan pronto de ella.

–No te vayas. Todavía no –le rogó, poniendo su mano sobre la de ella. Aquellas palabras lo sorprendieron tanto como parecieron sorprenderla a ella–. A menos que tengas que irte, por supuesto.

Maldijo para sus adentros. No quería parecer desesperado, pero después de la noticia de la muerte de su padre y de lo que se le venía encima, la compañía de aquella joven era una agradable distracción. La miró a los ojos, maravillándose una vez más con ese color ambarino que tenían. Estaba seguro de haber conocido antes a alguien con unos ojos así, pero no podía recordar cuándo, ni dónde.

–Bueno, no es que tenga que estar a una hora en ninguna parte –murmuró ella.

–¿No tienes a un novio esperándote? –inquirió él desvergonzadamente, acariciándole el dorso de la mano con el pulgar.

Angel se rio suavemente.

–No, no tengo novio.

–Estupendo. ¿Damos un paseo? –le sugirió él.

–Me encantaría.

Angel se levantó de un modo tan grácil que no pudo evitar quedarse mirándola embobado, y tomó su bolso y su abrigo. Thierry se levantó como un resorte para ayudarla a ponerse el abrigo, y cuando las yemas de sus dedos rozaron la suave piel de la nuca de Angel, un cosquilleo lo recorrió. Sabía que estaba mal que se sintiese tan atraído por ella cuando estaba comprometido con otra mujer. Tal vez tampoco fuera muy distinto de su madre, que había sido incapaz de respetar sus votos matrimoniales.

Dejó caer las manos para metérselas en los bolsillos y apretó los puños, avergonzado de sí mismo, pero cuando Angel se volvió hacia él y le sonrió, supo que, fuera cual fuera a ser su futuro, tenía que aprovechar aquel momento, aquella noche.

Salieron de la cafetería y se encaminaron a Séptima Avenida. Sus guardaespaldas se mimetizaron con la gente que los rodeaba, vigilantes, pero discretos.

Había dejado de llover, y Thierry empezaba a sentirse más animado. De hecho, aquello resultaba tan natural, tan normal… Era algo completamente distinto de su día a día.

–Háblame de ti –le pidió a Angel–. ¿Tienes hermanos?

–Un hermano –contestó ella–. Ahora mismo está en Europa –añadió en un tono extraño–. ¿Y tú?

–Soy hijo único.

–¿Te sentiste solo en tu infancia por no tener hermanos?

–Algunas veces –admitió Thierry–, aunque siempre estaba rodeado de gente.

–¿Gente como tus «amigos»? –preguntó ella, señalando con la cabeza a uno de sus guardaespaldas.

Él asintió. Cuando se pararon al llegar a un cruce, Angel levantó la barbilla y, mirando hacia delante con aspecto pensativo, murmuró:

–A veces, cuando tienes a un montón de gente a tu alrededor, es cuando te sientes más solo.

Sí, él conocía muy bien esa sensación. Y por el modo en que lo había dicho, le daba la impresión de que Angel hablaba por propia experiencia. Al pensarlo, sintió una punzada en el pecho, y deseó poder borrar la tristeza que había destilado su voz.

«¿Y qué más?», le espetó su conciencia. Thierry apartó aquel pensamiento de su mente. Era absurdo que pensase esas cosas cuando a la mañana siguiente se convertiría oficialmente en rey y aquellos momentos no serían más que un recuerdo.

–¿Y qué haces? –le preguntó Angel cuando llegaron al otro lado de la calle.

–¿Que qué hago?

–Para ganarte la vida. Bueno, supongo que trabajas, ¿no?

Sí, trabajaba, aunque seguramente en su idea de trabajo no entraría ser jefe de Estado de un país.

–Ocupo un puesto de dirección –contestó. No era del todo mentira.

–Eso es bastante vago –lo picó ella con un brillo travieso en la mirada.

–Es que tengo un abanico muy amplio de responsabilidades. ¿Y tú, qué tienes pensado hacer cuando acabes tus estudios?

Angel se puso seria, pero en un instante esa repentina solemnidad se desvaneció.

–Pues… no sé, cosas –contestó encogiéndose de hombros.

–¿Y me acusabas a mí de vaguedad? –la picó él, divertido.

–Bueno, ya que lo preguntas… quiero hacer algo importante. Quiero que la gente me escuche, que me escuchen de verdad, y que me tomen en serio en vez de ignorarme solo porque soy mujer.

Thierry enarcó las cejas.

–¿Eso pasa a menudo?

–Tú me lo has hecho antes –le espetó ella.

–Es verdad, y vuelvo a pedirte disculpas por mis prejuicios –le dijo él–. Espero que consigas hacer reali-

28

dad tus sueños –se detuvo junto a un puesto ambulante de comida–. ¿Ya has cenado?

–Pues no, pero…

–Me han dicho que no puede uno irse de Nueva York sin probar estos bocadillos de entrecot de ternera –la interrumpió él, señalando el puesto.

Angel inspiró profundamente.

–Desde luego, huelen que alimentan.

–Tomaré eso como un sí.

Se volvió hacia uno de sus guardaespaldas y se dirigió a él en su lengua natal. El hombre asintió con una sonrisa y se puso al final de la cola de gente que esperaba para comprar.

Poco después reanudaron su paseo mientras comían, prorrumpiendo en risas a cada bocado por lo difícil que era darle un mordisco al bocadillo y evitar que se desparramaran los trozos de filete, champiñones laminados y tiras de cebolla que llevaba dentro.

Cuando se lo terminaron, Angel se miró las manos, todas manchadas, con espanto.

–Debería haberte llevado a un restaurante –se disculpó Thierry.

–¡Ni hablar! –replicó ella–. Ha sido divertido… aunque acabes con las manos pringadas –comentó riéndose.

Sacó con cuidado un paquete de pañuelos del bolso para limpiarse y le tendió uno a él.

Thierry sintió que sus labios se curvaban en una sonrisa, como le había ocurrido tantas veces esa tarde. ¿Qué tenía aquella chica que lo hacía sentirse tan bien, cuando todo lo demás en su vida parecía ir tan mal?

–No me cansaré nunca de esta ciudad –comentó Angel–. Es tan vibrante…

–Sí que lo es –asintió él–. Oye, ¿te gusta bailar?

Angel se rio.

–¿Quieres sabes si me gusta, o si me gustaría ir a bailar contigo? –le preguntó con picardía.

Thierry se encogió de hombros.

–Las dos cosas –respondió, riéndose también.

La verdad era que se moría por tenerla entre sus brazos, y se le había ocurrido que probablemente ese sería el único modo de hacerlo sin faltar a sus principios.

–Pues, no sé, es que… no voy vestida para ir a bailar –respondió ella vacilante.

–Estás preciosa –replicó él–. Hay un club nocturno, no lejos de aquí, que no es grande y bullicioso como la mayoría, sino un sitio tranquilo donde puedes bailar si quieres, o simplemente sentarte a charlar y tomar algo, si lo prefieres.

–Suena perfecto.

–Entonces, ¿quieres venir?

Ella asintió con una sonrisa.

–Me encantaría.

Thierry la tomó de la mano y echaron a andar de nuevo. Tampoco tenía nada de malo bailar con una mujer que no fuera su prometida, ¿no? Al fin y al cabo, era algo que hacía cada vez que celebraban un acto oficial en palacio. Además, la noche aún era joven, y no quería que acabase tan pronto.

Tenerla entre sus brazos mientras bailaban resultó ser tan increíble como había imaginado. El único problema era que de pronto se encontró deseando más, deseando algo que se había vetado a sí mismo hasta el matrimonio. No se había mantenido célibe por puro masoquismo. A veces había sido un auténtico tormento negarse a reconocer las necesidades de su cuerpo, pero se había jurado que no permitiría que el deseo le nublase la razón. A diferencia de distintos miembros de su familia, que durante siglos habían estado varias veces a punto de perderlo todo por su falta de autocontrol.

Siempre había visto como una debilidad esa propensión de sus predecesores a los placeres de la carne, y en sus treinta y un años de vida nada le había hecho dudar de la decisión que había tomado. Hasta ese momento.

Sin embargo, se dijo era un tormento que podía soportar: el roce de los senos de Angel contra su pecho, la caricia de su cálido aliento contra su cuello… Cuando estuviese sentado a bordo del jet privado que lo llevaría de vuelta a Sylvain en solo unas pocas horas, lo haría con la tranquilidad de haber mantenido la promesa que se había hecho a sí mismo, y de no haberle faltado al respeto a la mujer con la que iba a casarse. Pero, hasta entonces, disfrutaría de aquella noche robada al tiempo tanto como se lo permitiese su sentido del deber y del honor.

Aquella había sido una noche mágica, algo más increíble de lo que jamás pudiera haber soñado. De hecho, estaba segura de que ni a Sally, con lo romántica que era, podría haber imaginado algo tan perfecto. Se sentía como Cenicienta, solo que en su cuento de hadas no había salido corriendo del baile, sino que el príncipe

la había acompañado a su hotel, y era más de media-
noche.

Cuando la limusina, que había estado esperándolos
a la salida del club, se detuvo frente a su hotel, se giró
hacia Thierry para mirarlo. Esa noche había visto una
faceta de él que no se había esperado, y la había cautivado por completo.

Quizá fuera el champán que habían bebido en el
club, o quizá simplemente el saber que a finales de ese
mes estaría a su lado frente al altar de la catedral de
Sylvain, prometiendo amarle y serle fiel durante el resto de su vida, pero en ese momento se sentía como si
estuviera flotando.

Aquella noche había tenido la oportunidad de conocer mejor al hombre que había tras el título real, el
hombre con el que compartiría sus días y sus noches y,
después de haber experimentado la poderosa atracción
que había entre ellos, estaba deseando conocerlo aún
mejor; en todos los sentidos.

Se había comportado como un auténtico caballero,
y por primera vez en su vida ella se había sentido de-
seable, y había sentido que por fin tenía la suficiente
confianza en sí misma como para ser la mujer que pudiese hacerlo feliz.

–Gracias por esta maravillosa velada, Hawk –le
dijo–. Nunca la olvidaré.

Él le tomó la mano, y cuando le besó los nudillos
una ráfaga de deseo la atravesó.

–Ni yo –murmuró.

Thierry se inclinó hacia delante para besarla en la
mejilla, pero en el último segundo ella volvió el rostro
y sus labios se encontraron. El contacto no pudo ser

más leve, más inocente, pero Mila sintió que una ola de calor la invadía.

Incapaz de articular palabra, se dio la vuelta, abrió torpemente la puerta y se bajó del coche, tambaleándose ligeramente. No miró atrás. No habría podido hacerlo porque, de haberlo hecho, tal vez le habría pedido más, y no era el momento, ni el lugar.

Entró en el hotel y cruzó a toda prisa el vestíbulo. Ya en el ascensor se quitó la peluca rubia y se miró en el espejo. Esa noche había fingido ser una extraña y Thierry había disfrutado de su compañía, pero... ¿cómo reaccionaría cuando supiese que era la misma chica regordeta y desmañada a quien había mirado con desdén años atrás?

Capítulo Cuatro

–¿Cómo has podido hacer algo tan estúpido e irresponsable? ¿Y si los medios se enteran de esto? ¿Te paraste siquiera a pensar en eso? Te crucificarán, y esto puede poner en riesgo tu compromiso.

Mila estaba esperando en silencio y con la cabeza gacha a que terminara el rapapolvo de su hermano, que se paseaba de un lado a otro de su despacho, aunque parecía que no fuese a terminar nunca.

–No has sido educada para comportarte así –continuó Rocco, con una mezcla de enfado e indignación–. ¿Cómo se te ocurrió salir a escondidas del hotel para irte por ahí? Eres una inconsciente.

Ya estaba empezando a exasperarla.

–Oye, espera un momento, yo no... –empezó a protestar, pero Rocco la cortó con una mirada fulminante.

–Eres una princesa. Las princesas no salen sin su escolta y se quedan por ahí de juerga en compañía de extraños hasta el amanecer.

Thierry no era un extraño para ella, habría querido decirle Mila –bueno, no exactamente–, pero no le quedaba otra que soportar el sermón de Rocco. Por el momento prefería no decirle a su hermano con quién había estado; se pondría histérico y empezaría a preocuparse por las repercusiones políticas que podría tener aquello y estropearía el recuerdo de aquella noche mágica.

Rocco se detuvo frente al ventanal, de espaldas a ella. Se quedó mirándolo y, al ver a un pájaro pasar volando sobre las copas de los árboles, pensó en la libertad que probablemente no volvería a experimentar. El anonimato del que había disfrutado en los Estados Unidos había sido una bendición, pero ahora que estaba de nuevo en Erminia eso se había acabado. Volvía a estar bajo el dictado de las estrictas normas de protocolo de la Casa Real, y se encontró preguntándose si no habría sido mejor no haber salido nunca de su país, porque ahora que había saboreado la libertad, la falta de ella se le haría aún más dura.

—¿Y qué vas a hacer? —le espetó a su hermano—, ¿arrojarme a las mazmorras?

Rocco se volvió, y a Mila le sorprendió ver cómo había envejecido desde la última vez que lo había visto, un año atrás. Era como si el estrés y la preocupación, que se habían convertido en una constante en su vida, hubieran dejado huella en su rostro y hubieran hecho aparecer las primeras canas en sus sienes. Quería muchísimo a su hermano, y no quería hacerle daño ni darle problemas; solo quería que, al menos por una vez, la escuchara.

—No creas que no lo haré —gruñó—. Supongo que esa insolencia es lo único que puedo esperar después de haberte atado demasiada libertad durante los últimos siete años. Jamás debería haber sido tan indulgente contigo. Mis consejeros me recomendaron que te casara con el príncipe Thierry cuando cumplieras los dieciocho. ¿Y lo hice? No, dejé que me persuadieras y te dejé que fueras al extranjero a estudiar… para que tuvieras una educación mejor; no para traer la deshonra a nuestra familia –se pellizcó el puente de la nariz, cerrando los ojos un momento, e inspiró profundamente antes de continuar–. Sentí compasión por ti entonces, Mila, porque no eras más que una colegiala que acababa de comprometerse con alguien mayor que tú y a quien no conocías de nada. Imaginé que debías sentirte agobiada, y me atrevo a decir que hasta aterrada ante la idea de lo que aquello implicaba, porque eras aún tan joven, tan inocente... – exhaló un suspiro y se volvió de nuevo hacia la ventana.

Aquella descripción que había hecho de ella irritó a Mila. ¡Pues claro que era inocente! ¿Cómo iba a saber nada del mundo y de la gente cuando se había criado en un ambiente tan estricto y con tantas normas? Ese era otro de los motivos por los que le había suplicado que la dejara estudiar en el extranjero. ¿Qué clase de reina sería si no supiese nada de los problemas y el día a día del pueblo, de la gente común?

–También te di mi consentimiento cuando me pediste aplazar la boda hasta que cumplieras los veinticinco –continuó Rocco, girándose de nuevo hacia ella–. Pensé que sería lo mejor para ti, y que tal vez contribuiría a que tuvieras un matrimonio más feliz. Debería haber imaginado que esto acabaría así, que la falta de orden y disciplina durante estos años fuera te corromperían y te desviarían de tu camino.

¿Falta de orden y disciplina? Mila se mordió la lengua para no responder. Las buenas calificaciones que había obtenido en la universidad las había conseguido precisamente gracias a una buena dosis de esfuerzo y autodisciplina. Y difícilmente podría haberse «corrompido» cuando estaba constantemente vigilada por sus guardaespaldas y por su carabina, que le había vetado prácticamente cualquier oportunidad de relajarse o de tratar de hacer amigos. ¡Si apenas había podido socializar con otros estudiantes en el campus!

Pero su hermano estaba que echaba chispas y, aunque intentase explicarse, no la escucharía.

–Tu boda es dentro de cuatro semanas –prosiguió Rocco–, y en ese tiempo no quiero oír ni la más mínima queja de ti. ¿Me has entendido? La estabilidad de nuestra nación depende de ti, de que demuestres que eres capaz de desempeñar el papel para el que has sido educada.

El papel para el que había sido educada… Sí, a eso se reducía todo, a que la única razón de su existencia era convertirse en la esposa apropiada del hombre que habían elegido para ella.

–¿Y el funeral del rey de Sylvain? –inquirió–. ¿No se supone que debería asistir contigo en señal de respeto?

Al regresar al hotel, tras la reprimenda de su carabina, se había enterado por las noticias de la muerte del padre de Thierry y había comprendido el motivo de su apresurado regreso a Sylvain.

–No, te quedarás aquí.

Mila habría querido replicar, decirle que tenía todo el derecho a ir para estar al lado de su prometido cuando le diera el último adiós a su padre, pero sabía que de nada le serviría, y pronunció las palabras que Rocco quería escuchar.

–Lo comprendo; haré lo que me pides.

Pero no se lo había pedido; se lo había ordenado. En ningún momento durante aquella audiencia con él, porque no podía considerarse otra cosa, había sentido que se alegrara de que hubiera vuelto. Más bien todo lo contrario: se sentía como si se hubiese convertido en una gran decepción para él, en una carga de la que quería deshacerse, o en un problema que tuviese que solventar.

No la había felicitado por los buenos resultados que había cosechado en la universidad: ni por su matrícula de honor, ni por la publicación de su ensayo sobre la *Igualdad de oportunidades y el desarrollo sostenible en las naciones europeas*. A él solo le importaba que fuera capaz de desempeñar debidamente su papel, como le había dicho. No era más que un peón en su partida de ajedrez.

Al oír su respuesta la tensión del rostro de Rocco se disipó, sus hombros se relajaron y su mirada se suavizó.

–Gracias. Lo entiendes, ¿no? No te pido que hagas esto por mí, sino por nuestro pueblo. Y también por ti, porque es indispensable que te ganes la confianza y el respeto del hombre que va a ser tu marido.

–Lo entiendo –respondió ella con una inclinación de cabeza.

Sin embargo, en su interior se agitaba una desazón que no podía acallar. Era evidente que lo único que le importaba a su hermano era que su honra permaneciese intacta hasta su matrimonio. Comparada con su reputación, poco valor tenían sus conocimientos, la confianza en sí misma que había adquirido en esos últimos años, o las ideas que tenía para mejorar su país y la vida de su pueblo.

Nada había cambiado. Erminia seguía anclada en

el pasado: el lugar que debía ocupar la mujer no era al lado de su marido, sino detrás de él, o de su padre, su hermano, o cualquier otra figura masculina que fuese el cabeza de familia.

Hasta en el parlamento de Erminia había pocas mujeres. Era algo que esperaba que cambiase, que se reconociese al fin el valor de las mujeres como miembros de la sociedad, pero sabía que esos cambios serían muy lentos… si es que llegaban a producirse.

–No te veo muy entusiasmada con la boda –comentó su hermano–. Creí que no harías más que hablar de eso.

Mila suspiró.

–Rocco, no soy una niña pequeña a la que han invitado a una fiesta de cumpleaños en casa de una amiga. Soy una mujer adulta capaz de pensar por sí misma, que está a punto de casarse con un hombre al que apenas conoce.

Su hermano se acercó y le levantó la barbilla con el índice para mirarla.

–Has cambiado.

–Por supuesto que he cambiado. He crecido.

–No, es algo más que eso –su hermano frunció el ceño y entornó los ojos–. ¿Aún eres…? ¿No habrás…?

Mila estuvo a un paso de perder los estribos.

–No puedo creer lo que estoy oyendo. ¿Me estás preguntando si sigo siendo virgen? ¿De verdad piensas que comprometería mi futuro solo por una noche de sexo?

Su hermano palideció.

–No consentiré que me hables en ese tono. Aunque sea tu hermano, antes que eso soy tu rey.

–Os ruego que me perdonéis, majestad –dijo ella con retintín, haciéndole una reverencia.

–Mila, no te burles de mí.

–No me burlo, alteza –replicó ella–. Soy perfectamente consciente de mi posición en el mundo. Cumpliré con mi deber y podéis estar tranquilo: llegaré al día de mi boda sin que ningún hombre me haya tocado, o besado siquiera, antes de que mi futuro marido lo haga. Aunque, si no me creéis, podéis hacer que el médico de la corte me examine para aseguraros de que soy una mujer de palabra.

–Mila, ya está…

–¡Vaya, qué tarde es! –lo interrumpió ella, mirando su reloj y levantándose–. He quedado con la modista para probarme el vestido y hacerle los arreglos necesarios, así que si me disculpas…

Estaba segura de que su hermano también detestaba haberse visto obligado a tener con ella esa conversación. Lo movía el deber, y eso implicaba anteponer siempre las necesidades de su país. No podía seguir siendo el cariñoso hermano mayor que le había evitado en lo posible todos los golpes y obligaciones durante su adolescencia.

Cuando salió del despacho para dirigirse a sus aposentos, aunque seguía molesta por lo que le había dicho su hermano, no pudo evitar sentir lástima por él. Al fin y al cabo Rocco, que era diez años mayor que ella, tampoco lo había tenido nada fácil: había tenido que ocupar el trono prematuramente a los diecinueve años, tras el asesinato de su padre, y eso lo había cambiado.

Más tarde, subida a un taburete mientras la modista le arreglaba el elegante vestido de novia, acudió a su mente el recuerdo del beso accidental con Thierry y no pudo reprimir una sonrisa. Si cerraba los ojos casi podía sentir la suave presión de sus labios, oler el sutil aroma de su colonia… Un cosquilleo de excitación la recorrió, pero se disipó de inmediato cuando notó un pinchazo en la pantorrilla.

–Lo siento, alteza, pero si no dejáis de moveros… –la reprendió la modista, con evidente frustración.

–No, soy yo quien debe disculparse –se apresuró a decir Mila–. Perdón, es que estoy un poco distraída.

Así que se quedó lo más quieta que pudo, girándose y levantando o bajando los brazos cuando se lo pedía la modista, como una marioneta. Y eso era, en esencia, lo único que era para su hermano, pensó con tristeza. Una marioneta cuyos hilos movían sus consejeros y él «por el bien de Erminia».

No estaría bajo tanta presión si él ya se hubiese casado, se dijo, aunque tampoco era culpa suya. Había estado saliendo con una chica durante años, pero cuando le había pedido que se casara con él, lo había rechazado porque de repente se había dado cuenta de que lo de ser de la realeza no iba con ella. Y desde entonces su hermano no había querido saber nada más de las mujeres.

Bueno, al menos para ella las cosas parecía que pintaban un poco mejor, pensó Mila. Ahora que había conocido un poco a Thierry había descubierto que estaban al mismo nivel en lo intelectual, y la había agradado ver que respetaba sus opiniones. Si la había escuchado cuando se había hecho pasar por una extraña, ¿por qué no habría de tratarla con la misma cortesía cuando fuese su esposa?

Eran las dos de la madrugada y Mila seguía despierta. Siempre le costaba acostumbrarse a los cambios de horario cuando viajaba, pero es que había sido un día agotador, con todas esas horas de vuelo seguidas de aquella espantosa reunión con su hermano. Apartó las sábanas con un suspiro, se bajó de la cama y se puso la bata. Quizá un vaso de leche caliente la ayudaría.

Sí, podría haber usado el intercomunicador para pedir que se lo llevasen a sus aposentos, pensó mientras se dirigía hacia la escalera del servicio, pero no quería molestar a nadie a esas horas, y las cocinas del castillo le evocaban recuerdos felices de su niñez.

Sus zapatillas apenas hacían ruido al descender por los antiguos escalones de piedra, y estaba todo en silencio, no como durante el día, cuando el castillo bullía de actividad.

Al llegar abajo oyó voces al fondo del pasillo a su izquierda. La puerta del despacho de Gregor, el mayordomo de palacio, estaba entreabierta, y por ella salía luz. Siempre había algún miembro del servicio asignado al turno de noche, pero era inusual que Gregor aún estuviese levantado a esa hora. Pero no había duda de que una de las voces era la de él. La otra era de una mujer joven.

Mila iba a seguir su camino, pero al oír que mencionaban a Thierry la curiosidad le pudo, y se acercó sigilosamente a la puerta para escuchar.

–¿Y estás segura de eso? –le preguntó Gregor a la joven.

Su tono severo sorprendió a Mila. Aunque tenía un puesto de gran responsabilidad, Gregor era un hombre amable y cercano.

–Sí, señor. Mi primo segundo es el ayudante del secretario del rey de Sylvain, y vio el documento en que solicitaba los… –la joven vaciló un instante– bueno, los servicios de esa mujer.

–¿Y qué pretende tu primo al ir divulgando tan indiscretamente esa información?

–Ay, señor, no piense mal de él. No me lo contó porque sea un chismoso.

–Entonces, ¿con qué intención lo hizo?

Mila oyó un gemido ahogado, como si la joven estuviese conteniendo las lágrimas.

–Por favor, señor, no quiero meterle en problemas. Le preocupaba que el rey requiriese los servicios de una cortesana estando tan próxima la fecha de su boda, sobre todo cuando es cosa sabida en la corte de Sylvain que el príncipe… es decir, el rey, ha estado «reservándose» para la noche de bodas.

¿Los servicios de una cortesana? A Mila el estómago le dio un vuelco, y de pronto sintió náuseas. Cuando oyó que Gregor y la joven se dirigían hacia la puerta, se coló apresuradamente en la sala contigua y cerró despacio tras de sí.

Se quedó allí de pie, en la penumbra, con los brazos apretados con fuerza en torno a la cintura, mientras los pensamientos bullían en su mente.

¿Thierry había contratado los servicios de una prostituta? ¿Por qué iba a hacer algo así? ¿Tan equivocada había estado al juzgarlo? Durante las horas que habían pasado juntos en Nueva York, se había mostrado tan encantador, tan respetuoso… Y en ningún momento había intentado besarla ni propasarse con ella. Le había ilusionado pensar que tal vez no lo hubiese hecho por respeto a su compromiso, y nada de todo aquello tenía sentido con lo que acababa de oír.

Oyó unos pasos ligeros alejándose, probablemente de la joven criada, y se quedó esperando a que Gregor se marchara también. ¿Qué debería hacer?, se preguntó aturdida. No podía negarse a casarse con Thierry; eso causaría un revuelo enorme a ambos lados de la frontera.

Pero… ¿cómo iba a casarse con un hombre que estaba a punto de instalar a una prostituta en el hogar que habían de compartir? Y pensar en todo lo que se había esforzado para ser una esposa digna de él… ¿Se había equivocado con él?, volvió a preguntarse. Tal vez solo veía su matrimonio como una fachada, como tantos otros enlaces de la realeza. ¿Tan pocas esperanzas tenía de que pudiera hacerle feliz?

Los ojos se le llenaron de lágrimas, pero parpadeó furiosa para contenerlas. No, no iba a comportarse como una mujer débil. Tenía que haber alguna forma de impedir que llevara a la corte a aquella fulana.

De pronto se le ocurrió una idea, una idea tan absurda, tan descabellada, que no pudo creerse que se le hubiera pasado algo así por la cabeza. ¿Sería capaz de llevarlo a cabo? Pensarlo era una cosa, pero hacerlo era otra muy distinta, y necesitaría la colaboración de otras personas.

¿Hasta qué punto era importante para ella tener un matrimonio feliz? ¿Iba a aceptar una unión en la que ella solo fuera un mascarón de proa, en la que los dos llevasen vidas separadas? ¿O quería un matrimonio de verdad? La respuesta era bien simple. Sí, quería que al menos se diesen una oportunidad. Abrió la puerta con decisión, salió al pasillo, y se dirigió al despacho de Gregor.

Capítulo Cinco

–¡Pero, alteza…! –protestó Gregor–. Lo que estáis sugiriendo… roza lo delictivo. ¿Qué digo?, ¡el rapto es un delito!

Mila había imaginado que se mostraría reacio a su plan, y se vio obligada a jugar una baza que habría preferido no tener que emplear.

–Gregor, ¿has olvidado con quién estás hablando? Soy la princesa de Erminia –le dijo en un tono imperioso. Detestaba tener que actuar así, porque nunca se le había dado bien mandar, ni era de la clase de personas que trataban con superioridad a aquellos a su servicio–. Y no estoy dispuesta a ser segundo plato cuando me reúna con mi prometido frente al altar –le dijo, tomando el toro por los cuernos.

El pobre Gregor se puso rojo como un tomate. Por un momento le dio la impresión que iba a protestar de nuevo, pero Mila se mantuvo firme y no apartó los ojos de los de él. El hombre tampoco titubeó, sino que le sostuvo la mirada, como si con ello esperara poder hacerla cambiar de opinión, pero pareció comprender que estaba decidida a hacerlo… con su ayuda, o sin ella.

–Entiendo, alteza.

Y estaba segura de que así era. De todos los que vivían y trabajaban entre aquellos muros, nadie podría entender su dilema mejor que él, que había sido testigo del pésimo resultado de las alianzas matrimoniales de la familia real generación tras generación. Claro que difícilmente se podría esperar otra cosa cuando aquellas uniones se hacían pensando solo en el linaje de las dos partes, y no en si serían compatibles el uno con el otro. Pero su corazón le decía que Thierry y ella podían aspirar a algo mejor; se merecían algo mejor.

—Entonces, ¿me ayudarás? —insistió.

—Vuestra seguridad es lo que más preocupa, alteza. Si os ocurriera algo…

—No me pasará nada —lo interrumpió Mila—. Aunque primero debemos averiguar quién es esa… cortesana —dijo torciendo el gesto al pronunciar la palabra—, y cuáles son sus planes de viaje. Todo depende de eso.

—No será fácil, alteza.

—Pero es imprescindible que consigamos esa información —respondió Mila—. Y gracias, Gregor.

—Vuestros deseos son órdenes, alteza —dijo Gregor con una reverencia—. Vuestro pueblo solo desea que seáis feliz.

Mila solo esperaba que su plan de raptar a aquella cortesana y ocupar su lugar funcionase, porque si no… los dos se meterían en un lío muy gordo.

Thierry desabrochó el cincho de su espada ceremonial y arrojó ambas cosas sobre la cama sin el menor miramiento.

—¡Nico! —llamó—. Échame una mano con esto, ¿quieres?

Su ayuda de cámara salió a toda prisa del vestidor y le ayudó a quitarse el uniforme militar de gala que había llevado en el funeral de su padre esa tarde. El peso del ceñidor, las condecoraciones, los cordones trenzados y demás adornos del traje lo estaban sofocando, y estaba ansioso por despojarse de toda aquella parafernalia.

El día se le había hecho interminable. Primero la larga procesión desde el palacio hasta la catedral, siguiendo a pie el féretro de su padre por las calles de la ciudad, en cuyas aceras se agolpaban sus súbditos. Primero un pie y luego el otro; en eso se había centrado durante todo el trayecto, rodeado de pompa y ceremonia. Era lo que lo había ayudado a aguantar hasta el final, hasta que su padre había sido enterrado en el panteón familiar, allí en palacio. Todo aquello le había hecho pensar en los años de entrega y dedicación al deber que tenía por delante, y en lo que se esperaba de él.

Era para lo que había sido educado; lo mismo que se esperaría de sus hijos después de él. Si es que los tenía. Nunca se había parado a pensar cómo sería ser padre. Era un concepto que para él no tenía connotaciones positivas por su propia infancia disfuncional, con unos padres distantes a los que siempre se había esperado que tratase con el mayor respeto y devoción. Incluso a su madre, que se había desentendido por completo de su posición y sus responsabilidades mucho antes de embarcarse en el romance que había terminado con su muerte.

—¿Necesitáis algo más, majestad? —inquirió Nico cuando hubo terminado su tarea.

—No, gracias, Nico. Y disculpa mi mal humor.

—No hay nada que disculpar, señor. Ha sido un día difícil para su majestad.

Difícil, sí, esa era la palabra, pensó Thierry mientras entraba en el enorme cuarto de baño anexo a su dormitorio. Se quitó los boxer, entró en la ducha y abrió el grifo. Tenía una reunión con el rey Rocco de Erminia dentro de una hora. Obviamente era un encuentro dictado por el deber, aunque, si consiguieran dejar a un lado sus diferencias, podría resultar muy provechoso para ambas partes. Al fin y al cabo los dos ansiaban lo mismo: una paz duradera entre Erminia y Sylvain y la apertura de su frontera, lo que se esperaba que mejorase la economía de ambos países.

El problema era que todavía había miembros de sus respectivos gobiernos que se negaban a ese entendimiento y querían mantener el *status quo*. Thierry comprendía su desconfianza, pero pertenecían a una era que había que cerrar. Había llegado el momento de avanzar con cambios positivos en vez de empecinarse en los errores del pasado.

Querría poder escapar a su cabaña en las montañas, pensó mientras el chorro de la ducha le aliviaba la tensión acumulada en el cuello y los hombros, pero aquella reunión era ineludible. Además, dentro de tres semanas el rey de Erminia se convertiría en su cuñado.

Thierry levantó el tapón de cristal tallado de la licorera y miró al corpulento hombre de pelo negro sentado en un sillón junto a la ventana de la biblioteca.

–¿Brandy? –le preguntó.

–En realidad, mataría por una cerveza –respondió su invitado, el rey de Erminia, con una sonrisa.

Thierry sonrió también.

–¿Vaso o botellín?

–Botellín –contestó Rocco.

Thierry abrió el mueble bar y sacó un par de botellines. Sin duda a sus respectivos asesores de protocolo les daría un patatús si los vieran bebiendo a morro, pero le daba igual. Le quitó el tapón a los dos botellines y le tendió uno a Rocco, que tomó un trago y le preguntó:

–¿Es de aquí?

Thierry asintió.

–Creo que no la importamos en Erminia. Y quizá deberíamos hacerlo; es buena.

Se quedaron en silencio mientras tomaban otro trago. Thierry sabía que, con la boda a solo unas semanas, debería preguntarle por su hermana, pero había pasado mucho tiempo de su primer encuentro, y no había ido demasiado bien.

No, se reprendió, estaba siendo injusto. Por aquel entonces la princesa Mila aún era apenas una chiquilla, y era normal que, habiéndose criado entre algodones, hubiese estado nerviosa aquel día ante la idea de que iba a conocer a su futuro marido. Además, ¿qué había esperado?, ¿una hermosa mujer de mundo? ¿Alguien con quien poder conversar largo y tendido de temas que lo entusiasmaban?

Y entonces se acordó de Angel. Hacía menos de una semana de aquello, pero parecía que hubiese pasado una vida entera. Por un instante deseó ser un ciudadano de a pie para haber podido... ¿Pero qué estaba pensando?, se dijo irritado, apartando esa idea de su mente. No era como los demás, ni su vida era como la de los demás. Tenía una serie de obligaciones para con su país, y pronto iba a casarse con la princesa de Erminia.

El cosquilleo que lo había invadido al recordar a Angel se disipó de inmediato. Tomó otro trago de cerveza y se volvió hacia su invitado con resignación.

–¿Cómo está Mila? –le preguntó–. ¿Disfrutó de su estancia en el extranjero? Si mal no recuerdo se fue a estudiar a Estados Unidos, ¿no?

Fue decir esas palabras y ¡bum!, lo asaltó de nuevo el recuerdo de Angel: el aroma de su perfume, la caricia de sus labios cuando se habían despedido en el coche…

De pronto se dio cuenta de que Rocco había hablado y estaba esperando una respuesta.

–Perdona –se apresuró a disculparse–. ¿Podrías repetir lo que has dicho?

–¿Soñando despierto con tu prometida? –lo picó Rocco con una media sonrisa–. Te decía que está muy cambiada. Ha pulido tanto su carácter como su educación. Si cuidas de ella como se merece, será una excelente reina consorte.

En el tono de Rocco había un inequívoco matiz protector, pero a ese respecto podía estar tranquilo. Jamás le haría daño a su hermana, y estaba dando los pasos necesarios para asegurarse de que la haría feliz –por lo menos en la cama–, solo que no era algo que uno trataría con el hermano de su prometida.

Por fortuna la conversación pronto derivó en temas más amplios sobre la relación entre sus reinos y cómo esperaban solventar las desavenencias entre ellos.

En general fue una reunión cordial, aunque a Thierry le quedó bastante claro que, de fracasar la relación entre su futura esposa y él, la frágil paz entre las dos naciones se quebraría, volvería la inestabilidad económica y podría llevar a nuevos enfrentamientos.

Cuando su visitante se hubo marchado, Thierry se sirvió una copa de brandy y fue hasta la ventana, que miraba al país vecino. Confiaba en que su prometida estuviese preparada para la vida a la que pronto tendría que enfrentarse. Ya se había concretado la agenda de eventos a los que tendría que asistir o presidir cuando regresaran de su luna de miel, y a partir de ese momento ya no estaría bajo la protección de su hermano, sino bajo el escrutinio constante de los medios.

Pero quizá debería preocuparse menos por Mila, que contaría con la ayuda de sus asesores para aclimatarse, y más por lo que tenía que hacer para que se sintiera a gusto a su lado. Por eso había decidido tomar lecciones sobre las «artes amatorias» para aprender a satisfacer plenamente a su esposa. Por supuesto, para no faltar a la promesa que se había hecho de mantenerse célibe hasta la noche de bodas, dicha instrucción sería estrictamente teórica. Es decir, que no tendría relaciones íntimas con su instructora. Pero estaba seguro de que, aun sin demostraciones prácticas podría aprender mucho para empezar su matrimonio con buen pie. Quería saber qué tenía que hacer exactamente para seducir a una mujer –y no solo físicamente, sino también en el plano emocional y en el espiritual–, y conseguir una unión duradera.

Y para ello había contratado los servicios de una discreta cortesana. ¿Quién si no podría instruirlo en los detalles sutiles relativos al placer de una mujer? Para él siempre había sido esencial estar preparado. Detestaba las sorpresas y los imprevistos, y si iba a casarse lo haría bien informado de todo lo que necesitara saber.

Capítulo Seis

–¡Esto es absurdo! Tengo un pasaporte diplomático; ¿por qué me han traído aquí?

Desde la sala en la que estaba escondida, Mila oía a la mujer discutir con un guardia de la frontera de Erminia en algún despacho. Cuando Gregor entró apresuradamente por la puerta, alzó la vista hacia él.

–¿Tienes sus documentos? –le preguntó levantándose.

–Los tengo –Gregor iba a dárselos, pero vaciló–. ¿Seguro que queréis seguir adelante con esto, alteza? Los riesgos…

–Soy consciente de los riesgos, pero no puedo quedarme de brazos cruzados –lo cortó Mila con firmeza.

Tomó los papeles de la mano de Gregor y estudió un momento la fotografía en el pasaporte de la mujer. Tenía el pelo largo y negro, como ella, y sus facciones no eran muy distintas. Mientras nadie se fijara muy de cerca en el color de sus ojos o en su estatura, podría hacerse pasar por ella sin despertar sospechas.

Un grupo del servicio secreto que seguía sus movimientos la había informado de su atuendo, y se había vestido de modo idéntico a ella, incluidas unas grandes gafas de sol que tenía en la mano, y un pañuelo de Hermès que le cubría el cabello. Pero, de cualquier modo, era un alivio saber que la documentación que le habían confiscado a Ottavia Romolo le permitiría atravesar la frontera con Sylvain sin problemas.

Sin embargo, estaba hecha un manojo de nervios cuando se puso las gafas, y rogó por que el chófer de Sylvain que había llevado hasta allí a Ottavia Romolo, y que estaba fuera, esperando a que los guardias terminaran de inspeccionar el maletero, no se diera cuenta, cuando subiera al coche, de que no era la misma mujer que había bajado de él.

–Deséame suerte –le dijo a Gregor.

–Buena suerte, alteza –respondió él, con expresión preocupada.

Mila le sonrió y le dijo:

–Anímate, Gregor. Aunque me descubrieran, no me fusilarán ni nada de eso.

–Supongo que no, pero puedo aseguraros que vuestro hermano no será demasiado magnánimo conmigo si se entera de lo que habéis hecho y de que os he ayudado.

–Entonces tendremos que asegurarnos de que eso no ocurra. ¿Has reservado esa suite de hotel para nuestra «invitada» y preparado al equipo de seguridad que se ocupará de ella?

–Sí, alteza. A la señorita Romolo no le faltará ninguna comodidad hasta vuestro regreso.

–Estupendo –dijo Mila–. Bueno, pues vamos a ello –murmuró irguiendo los hombros.

–Como acordamos, os acompañaré hasta que salgamos del edificio –dijo Gregor–. Y confío en que fuera todo el mundo estará demasiado ocupado como para fijarse en vos.

Ella asintió y salieron del edificio. Fuera el aire era

algo frío y olía a pino. Mila inspiró profundamente y avanzó con confianza hacia el coche negro que la esperaba. Gregor, que seguía a su lado, miró al agente que estaba supervisando el registro del maletero, y le indicó con un asentimiento de cabeza que estaban listos. El hombre dio una orden en erminiano a los guardias, que se apartaron al punto del coche y dijeron al chófer que podían proseguir su viaje.

Mila se subió al vehículo y cuando se abrochó el cinturón le sorprendió ver que no le temblaban las manos. Casi un milagro con lo rápido que le latía el corazón en ese momento, pensó. Alzó la vista hacia Gregor y se quitó las gafas un momento.

—Gracias, Gregor. No olvidaré esto —le dijo con una sonrisa.

Él asintió brevemente y cerró la puerta del coche.

—Perdone esta pérdida de tiempo, señorita Romolo —dijo el chófer, sentándose al volante—. No se puede confiar en estos erminianos. Pero le aseguro que cuando el rey se entere de esto rodarán cabezas.

Mila reprimió el impulso de defender a su gente, y se limitó a murmurar:

—Espero que no.

—Intentaré recuperar el tiempo que hemos perdido; deberíamos llegar a nuestro destino sobre las siete y media.

—Gracias. Creo que intentaré relajarme un poco.

—Por supuesto, señorita Romolo. La avisaré cuando estemos cerca de la cabaña.

En los últimos días los hombres de Gregor habían estado intentando descubrir dónde se encontraba la cabaña de Thierry, pero su localización era un secreto bien guardado. Pero precisamente por eso serviría muy bien a su propósito, porque allí nadie los molestaría. Lo único que la preocupaba un poco era que ni siquiera Gregor sabría dónde estaba exactamente. Había hecho jurar a sus guardaespaldas que mantendrían aquella «misión» en secreto, y se suponía que su hermano iba a estar fuera durante una semana, así que no tenía por qué enterarse de nada.

Aunque iba a casarse con Thierry y a convertirse en la reina de Sylvain, el comentario del chófer la había dejado algo intranquila. Había expresado de modo meridianamente claro su desprecio por la gente de su país, y Mila se preguntó cuánta gente en Sylvain compartiría ese sentimiento. Si así fuera, se le exigiría mucho más como reina consorte: no solo tendría que ganarse a su marido y a su pueblo, sino que tendría que hacerlo, sobre todo, por el bien de las gentes de Erminia a quienes dejaría atrás. Quizá había sido un error haberse quedado tanto tiempo en Estados Unidos. No solo se había distanciado de su pueblo, sino que también había perdido la oportunidad de hacerse un poco más cercana al de Thierry antes de su enlace.

Se mordió el labio, pensativa, y miró el paisaje por la ventanilla. Había estado tan empeñada en mejorar su educación para convertirse en la persona que creía que debía ser para su futuro esposo, que había desatendido otras igual de importantes. Lo único que podía hacer era intentar, en adelante, tomar mejores decisiones.

¿Se habría equivocado también con aquel plan descabellado? Solo quería un matrimonio sólido, y para eso lo primero era asegurarse de que Thierry no querría a otra mujer en su cama más que a ella. Además, aunque hubiese cometido un error, ya no había vuelta atrás. Su plan tenía que funcionar. Tenía que hacer creer a Thierry que era la cortesana a la que estaba esperando, y conseguir que se enamorase de ella para que no volviese a buscar en otros brazos lo que ella podía darle.

Llevaban un buen rato atravesando un desfiladero, donde la carretera, estrecha y serpenteante, ascendía por la montaña junto a un impresionante muro de roca . Mila se había quedado dormida a ratos, pero durante la última media hora había estado más que despierta, demasiado nerviosa para cerrar los ojos, a pesar del cansancio. Se notaba la boca seca y estaba empezando a dolerle la cabeza, pero estaba segura de que no era más que la tensión acumulada. En cuanto se reuniera con Thierry todo iría bien.

¿Por qué no habría de ir bien?, se dijo. Iba a ir allí para hacer lo que él le pidiera. ¿Qué hombre rechazaría eso? Una ola de calor la invadió al pensar en toda la información sobre sexo que había estado recabando esos días para poder hacerse pasar por una mujer experimentada.

Apretó los muslos al sentir una punzada de deseo en el vientre, y se deleitó con la suave presión de sus senos hinchados y sus pezones endurecidos contra el delicado encaje de las copas del sujetador. Se moría por sentir las fuertes manos de Thierry, o su pecho desnudo contra ellos.

Las mejillas le ardían. Si se excitaba así solo con pensar en lo que había aprendido esos días, no cabía duda de que sus investigaciones sobre el tema habían sido exhaustivas. Había pasado día y noche leyendo libros, tanto informativos como novelas de amor, y viendo películas románticas. Había intentado enfocarlo como la búsqueda de información que había llevado a cabo tantas veces para sus proyectos de carrera, pero no había imaginado la frustración que le generaría imaginarlos a Thierry y a ella haciendo las cosas que había leído.

Cuando el chófer disminuyó la velocidad, el corazón empezó a latirle más deprisa. Ante ellos se alzaba una verja de hierro que debía medir al menos tres metros, cuya puerta estaba flanqueada por sendos puestos de guardia. Uno de los guardias, vestido con el uniforme del ejército de Sylvain, se acercó al coche.

Mila contuvo el aliento mientras el chófer bajaba la ventanilla. Cruzaron unas palabras y el guardia dio orden a su compañero de que les dejara pasar. Las puertas de la verja se abrieron lentamente y, tras cruzarlas, iniciaron el ascenso por un empinado sendero de tierra.

Cuando vio a Pasquale entrar en el estudio, Thierry, que estaba sentado en un sillón junto a la chimenea encendida, se irguió en el asiento.

—Majestad, los guardias de la entrada nos han avisado de que el coche de la señorita Romolo acaba de entrar en la propiedad y estará aquí dentro de diez minutos.

Thierry se levantó.

—Gracias, Pasquale. Por favor, asegúrate de que nadie nos moleste. De hecho, quiero a todo el mundo fuera hasta nuevo aviso.

—¿A todo el mundo, señor?

–Todos; tú incluido.

–Pero… ¿quién le preparará las comidas?

–Creo que sabré arreglármelas sin que muramos de hambre durante una semana –contestó Thierry con una sonrisa socarrona–. Tenemos suficientes provisiones, ¿no?

–Como gustéis, señor –respondió Pasquale–, pero debo insistir en que se queden al menos los miembros del equipo de seguridad.

Thierry asintió.

–Por supuesto. Y, Pasquale…

–¿Sí, majestad? –inquirió el buen hombre, casi rogándole con la mirada que no le pidiese nada más que fuese en contra de su criterio.

Thierry, que sabía que a Pasquale no le agradaría lo que le iba a decir, esbozó una sonrisa y escogió con cuidado sus palabras.

–Ocúpate también antes de irte de desconectar todos los aparatos que puedan servir de distracción o como medio de comunicación con el exterior: la radio, la televisión, Internet…

Pasquale palideció.

–¿Los teléfonos también, señor?

–Los teléfonos también. Solo quiero que dejes un *walkie-talkie*, por si necesitara ponerme en contacto con el equipo de seguridad.

–Majestad, no creo que sea buena idea.

–Todo irá bien. Es solo que necesito privacidad absoluta. Si te parece puedes emitir un comunicado en mi nombre diciendo que me he tomado unos días de retiro para estar a solas y llorar la muerte de mi padre.

Pasquale dejó caer los hombros.

–Como queráis, majestad.

–Estupendo. Pues eso es todo. Gracias, Pasquale. Disfruta de tu permiso.

El secretario torció el gesto, pero finalmente le hizo una reverencia y se marchó.

Thierry fue hasta el ventanal, y al poco vio a través de ella al escaso personal de servicio y a Pasquale abandonando el lugar.

Minutos después reinaba el silencio. Inspiró profundamente. Para él quedarse a solas era un lujo al que estaba poco acostumbrado, y se le hacía raro. Pronto estaría allí su «instructora», pensó, algo nervioso.

Se apartó de la ventana y bajó a la planta inferior para esperar su llegada. Se le habían dado instrucciones al chófer de la señorita Romolo para que dejara en la puerta principal a su pasajera junto con su equipaje. Él mismo le daría la bienvenida y llevaría dentro sus cosas.

Aguardó impaciente en el salón, en cuya chimenea ardía un fuego acogedor. Aunque estaban en primavera, en las montañas hacía todavía bastante frío, y él iba bien abrigado, con un jersey de lana y unos vaqueros.

Le pareció oír el ruido de neumáticos pisando la grava de la rotonda frente a la cabaña. Luego escuchó una puerta de coche cerrarse, pasos, y de nuevo otra puerta cerrándose. Después, mientras oía el coche alejarse, las pisadas se dirigieron hacia la entrada y subieron los escalones de piedra.

Se dirigió al vestíbulo en cuanto la aldaba golpeó la puerta de madera. Al abrir lo cegó un instante la luz del atardecer que recortaba la silueta femenina frente a él, pero cuando la miró apenas pudo creer lo que veían sus ojos. ¿Angel?

Capítulo Siete

El corazón a Thierry le palpitaba con fuerza mientras la recorría con la mirada. No había esperado volver a verla, y menos allí, en su cabaña, su refugio del mundanal ruido. Tragó saliva. Una docena de preguntas se agolpaban en su garganta. No podía creer que la encantadora Angel a la que había conocido en Nueva York fuese la cortesana cuyos servicios había contratado por una semana.

Fue entonces cuando cayó en la cuenta de que ella aún no había dicho nada. De hecho parecía nerviosa, insegura. ¿Podría ser que estuviera equivocado, que no fuese Angel? Algunas diferencias sí que había. Por ejemplo tenía el cabello negro, y no rubio, y el atuendo no podía ser más distinto. La mujer frente a él llevaba un vestido ceñido, claramente ideado para seducir, y los zapatos, de al menos diez centímetros de tacón, hacían que sus torneadas piernas pareciesen interminables.

Pero cuando se quitó las gafas de sol y vio sus peculiares ojos ambarinos, los mismos que lo habían hechizado en Nueva York, supo que sí era ella. Pero aquello no era lo que él había planeado. Había solicitado los servicios de una cortesana que pudiera educarlo en las artes amatorias, creyendo que con una profesional no se sentiría tentado de romper su promesa de mantenerse virgen hasta el matrimonio. Sin embargo, a juzgar por el calor que se estaba extendiendo por todo su cuerpo, parecía que no le iba a resultar nada fácil. Dio un paso adelante y le tendió la mano.

–Bienvenida a mi cabaña, señorita Romolo. Espero que se sienta cómoda aquí durante su estancia.

Se le hacía raro hablarle de usted, y más llamarla «señorita Romolo», pero si quería que aquella fuese una relación estrictamente profesional, era lo más adecuado.

–Gracias, majestad. Estaba impaciente por llegar –contestó ella, estrechándole la mano antes de hacerle una reverencia.

Cuando volvió a erguirse, Thierry se dio cuenta de que su mano aún sostenía la de ella.

–Entre, por favor –dijo soltándola y haciéndose a un lado para dejarla pasar.

–Pe-pero mis cosas… ¿No las llevo dentro? –inquirió ella, señalando sus maletas con un ademán.

–No se preocupe; nadie se las va a llevar de ahí. Ya me ocuparé yo luego.

–¿Vos, ma-majestad?

De nuevo ese ligero tartamudeo. ¿Podía ser que estuviese nerviosa? La idea lo intrigó. ¿Por qué habría de estar nerviosa una cortesana? Sin duda debía estar acostumbrada a situaciones como aquella: reunirse con un nuevo cliente. ¿Podría ser que ella también se sintiese atraída por él?

–Solo son un par de maletas; creo que podré con ellas –le aseguró, con una sonrisa divertida.

Ella sonrió nerviosa, visiblemente tensa, y entró en la cabaña. Era extraño. Su ropa y el olor de su perfume le evocaban las palabras «pecado» y «seducción», pero la aprensión en su rostro insinuaba una ingenuidad que lo descolocaba.

Y luego, cuando cerró la puerta, el ruido de esta al cerrarse le hizo dar un respingo. Incapaz de disimular su contrariedad, su voz sonó algo áspera cuando le preguntó:

—¿Por qué no me dijo quién era en realidad cuando nos conocimos en Nueva York?

Mila tragó saliva y levantó la vista hacia Thierry.

—Pues… Es que cuando no estoy trabajando prefiero no revelar a qué me dedico, majestad —respondió, improvisando sobre la marcha—. Además, fuisteis vos quien os chocasteis conmigo y quien inició la conversación, no yo. Solo éramos dos extraños de visita en la ciudad. No tenía ni idea de que os encontraría allí.

—Pero me reconoció, ¿no es verdad? —inquirió él. Y, cuando ella asintió, le preguntó—: ¿Y no le parece que debería haberme dicho quién era, sabiendo que nos veríamos aquí una semana después?

—Porque me pareció que conoceros así, sin que supierais quién era, me daba la oportunidad de descubrir al hombre de carne y hueso detrás del título de rey, por así decirlo.

No era mentira.

—¿Y por qué «Angel»?, ¿por qué ese nombre?

—Bueno, es un nombre que… uso algunas veces —dijo. Tampoco era una mentira—. Y vos tampoco me dijisteis vuestro verdadero nombre.

Thierry la estudió en silencio, y Mila, aunque nerviosa por ese escrutinio, aprovechó para mirarlo también y recrearse la vista. Le encantaban sus anchos hombros, y el jersey de lana de color crema que llevaba resaltaba su piel aceitunada y también su barba de dos días, que le daba un aire algo salvaje, peligroso. ¿Un lobo con piel de cordero? Esa analogía le arrancó una sonrisa que reprimió a duras penas. Los vaqueros le sentaban muy bien, y cuando sus ojos se posaron en la bragueta no pudo evitar sentirse acalorada al pensar en lo que escondía y cómo sería hacer el amor con él.

Y si no fuera por los años que había pasado aprendiendo cómo debía comportarse en público, en ese momento no podría estar manteniendo una apariencia serena ante él. Porque se moría por ponerle las manos en el pecho, aspirar su colonia… Los imaginó desnudos en la cama, imaginó su barba arañándola, entre beso y beso, en el cuello, los pechos, los muslos… Tenía que parar o se derretiría a sus pies, se dijo, obligándose a levantar la vista y mirarlo a la cara.

–Debe estar cansada del viaje –dijo Thierry–. ¿Quiere refrescarse un poco antes de la cena?

Ella asintió.

–Gracias, me encantaría.

–Bien. La llevaré a sus aposentos.

Creía que iba a dormir con él. ¿No era para eso para lo que había contratado a una cortesana?, se preguntó Mila, confundida, mientras subía al piso de arriba detrás de él. Quizá prefiriera dormir solo e ir a su habitación solo para el sexo.

Thierry la condujo por un largo y amplio pasillo, de cuyas paredes colgaban cuadros o trofeos de caza. Se estremeció cuando pasaron junto a la cabeza de un ciervo con una cornamenta que intimidaba un poco.

–Sospecho que no es aficionada a la caza –observó Thierry cuando llegaron al final del pasillo.

–La verdad es que no, no cuando se caza por placer.

–¿He oído una nota de censura en su voz?

Ella se tensó. No sabía muy bien qué responder.

–No, jamás os censuraría, majestad.

Thierry cerró los ojos un instante y resopló, como irritado.

–Majestad, si os he molestado…

–No es eso –la interrumpió él–. Es que… es ridículo que nos tratemos como si fuéramos dos extraños, y eso de «majestad». Aquí soy Thierry, un hombre como otro cualquiera.

–Siento disentir, pero… no sois un hombre cualquiera.

Thierry apretó los labios, pero luego esbozó una sonrisa y respondió:

No, supongo que no, señorita Romolo, pero preferiría que nos tuteáramos y que nos tratáramos de un modo menos formal. Si se siente incómoda llamándome por mi nombre de pila, podría llamarme Hawk, como aquel día en Nueva York.

–De acuerdo, siempre y cuando a mí sigas llamándome Angel –sugirió Mila.

–Angel… –repitió él, alargando la mano para acariciarle la mejilla con el dorso de la mano–. Si, te pega más que Ottavia.

A Mila le alegró que pensara así, sobre todo porque no habría soportado que la llamase por el nombre de otra cuando estuvieran en la cama.

Thierry se volvió para abrir la puerta que tenían ante sí, y entraron en un saloncito elegantemente decorado.

–Es precioso –murmuró ella, acercándose al ventanal, que se asomaba al extenso jardín.

Parecía que era la única parte de la propiedad moldeada por la mano del hombre. Más allá, hasta donde se extendía la vista, era todo agreste, todo bosque.

Thierry cruzó el saloncito para abrir otra puerta.

–Y esta es la alcoba.

Ella sonrió al oír ese término anticuado, pero cuando cruzó el umbral tuvo que admitir que esa palabra se ajustaba mejor que dormitorio a la belleza y la elegancia de aquella habitación. Claro que a aquella casa, que disponía de todo tipo de comodidades, tampoco la llamaría una cabaña.

–Iré a por tus maletas –dijo Thierry–. El baño está ahí –añadió señalándole otra puerta–. Tómate el tiempo que necesites y baja cuando estés lista.

Cuando se quedó a solas, Mila se estiró un poco para desentumecerse. Se daría una ducha y se cambiaría de ropa… si Thierry subía las maletas, como le había prometido. Se le hacía raro no haber visto aún a ningún sirviente. Además, ¿por qué habría de ocuparse él de su equipaje cuando podría hacerlo cualquier miembro del servicio? Bueno, ya lo averiguaría, se dijo entrando en el cuarto de baño y cerrando tras de sí antes de empezar a desvestirse.

Después de la ducha se secó y se envolvió en un albornoz blanco que había colgado detrás de la puerta. Si Thierry no había subido todavía sus bolsas, tendría que bajar a cenar de esa guisa, pensó. ¿O habría sido esa su intención desde el principio?, se preguntó algo nerviosa. Pero cuando salió del baño, allí estaban sus maletas. Bueno, las de Ottavia Romolo.

Se sintió como una ladrona al abrir una de las maletas y empezar a mirar lo que había en ella. No se sentía cómoda hurgando en los objetos personales de otra mujer, pero no le quedaba más remedio que hacer de tripas corazón. No habría podido cambiar el equipaje de Ottavia Romolo por el suyo sin despertar las sospechas del chófer.

Suerte que al menos se había llevado su bolso más grande, donde había metido sus utensilios de aseo y la lencería que había comprado para la ocasión –prendas mucho más atrevidas que las que ella solía ponerse–, porque si hubiera tenido que usar la ropa interior de otra mujer, sí que se hubiera sentido verdaderamente incómoda.

Mila apartó a un lado la lencería de Ottavia y se concentró en sacar el resto de la ropa de las dos maletas. Allí había tal cantidad y variedad de modelos, que Mila no pudo evitar preguntarse cuántas veces habría pensado en cambiarse de ropa al día.

Escogió para la cena un conjunto de seda de pantalón y camisola de color morado. Los pantalones eran anchos, y la camisola tenía un bordado alrededor del cuello y manga tres cuartos.

Se estremeció un poco cuando, al meterse los pantalones, la seda le hizo cosquillas en las nalgas. No estaba acostumbrada a llevar ropa interior tan escueta como el tanga que se había puesto, y le sorprendió lo sensual que era el roce de la seda. Acabó de deshacer las maletas y las colocó en un rincón del vestidor.

Tras maquillarse y cepillarse el cabello, que se dejó suelto, se calzó unas sandalias negras con un fino tacón de aguja. Era una suerte que Ottavia y ella tuvieran el mismo número de pie…

Cuando se miró en el espejo una última vez, fue como si estuviera mirando a una extraña, pero el verse tan distinta, como más sofisticada, la hizo sentirse más fuerte. Su plan iba a tener éxito, estaba segura. Una ola de deseo la invadió al pensar en la velada que estaba a punto de comenzar y, con las mejillas encendidas y los ojos brillantes, se preguntó si harían el amor esa misma noche.

Capítulo Ocho

Cuando Mila llegó al salón, Thierry estaba de espaldas a ella, de pie frente a la chimenea y con las manos en los bolsillos, aparentemente hipnotizado por el baile de las llamas. Aprovechó para pasear la mirada por la habitación. Sobre el suelo de piedra se habían colocado varias alfombras en tonos rojizos para hacer el salón menos frío, y la distribución de los muebles creaba cómodos rincones para sentarse a charlar, o para acurrucarse y leer un libro. Y luego estaba la enorme chimenea, frente a la cual había una mesita alargada y sofás de cuero dispuestos en forma de herradura a su alrededor.

Al cruzar el umbral de la puerta Thierry oyó sus pasos y se volvió hacia ella.

–¡Ah, ya estás aquí! –la saludó con una sonrisa–. ¿Tienes hambre?

A Mila le hizo ruido el estómago, y los dos se rieron.

–Creo que puedes tomar eso como un sí –le dijo sonrojándose.

La verdad era que estaba hambrienta. Los nervios apenas le habían dejado probar bocado en el desayuno y el almuerzo.

–Tengo aquí una bandeja con entremeses –dijo Thierry, señalando la mesita. Quitó unos cuantos cojines de los sofás y los puso en el suelo, junto a la mesa–. ¿Te parece bien para empezar?

–Claro –contestó Mila. Y se quitó las sandalias antes de sentarse sobre los cojines–. Es casi como si estuviéramos de picnic.

–¿Preferirías que nos sentáramos en el sofá? –le preguntó él, agachándose para sentarse a su lado.

–No, me gusta la idea que has tenido. Es más distendido.

Thierry le dio un plato y le indicó con un ademán que se sirviera lo que quisiera.

–¿Qué te gusta más de lo que hay aquí? –inquirió ella, con su mano oscilando, dubitativa, sobre la selección de embutidos, quesos y hortalizas .

–No se trata de lo que me guste a mí –respondió él, contrariado.

–¿Eso crees? –le espetó ella, mirándolo a los ojos–. Pues permite que te diga que te equivocas. De hecho, creo que esta podría ser nuestra primera lección. ¿Alguna vez te han dado de comer?

Thierry frunció el ceño.

–No desde que era niño.

–Pues dar de comer a otra persona puede ser un acto muy íntimo, ¿sabes? Y simboliza el toma y daca que debe haber en una relación, además de que te ayuda a aprender y comprender qué le gusta al otro.

Envolvió en una loncha de salami un corazón de alcachofa y se lo tendió, acercándoselo a la boca. Thierry vaciló un instante, pero finalmente se inclinó hacia delante para tomar aquel bocado que le ofrecía. A Mila el corazón le martilleaba contra las costillas, y cuando los labios de Thierry rozaron las yemas de sus dedos, por un momento se olvidó hasta de respirar.

Un cosquilleo eléctrico la recorrió, haciéndola estremecer, y él, que pareció darse cuenta, la asió por la muñeca y murmuró:

–¿Estás bien? No tienes por qué estar nerviosa conmigo. Aquí no soy un rey, ¿recuerdas? Tan solo Hawk.

Mila liberó su mano al tiempo que asentía y, en un intento por concentrarse tomó un poco de hummus con una rodaja de pepino y se la ofreció a Thierry, que esbozó una sonrisa antes de acercar la boca. Mientras masticaba hizo un ruido gutural, como si le gustara la combinación de sabores, y procedió a darle también a ella a probar algo.

Mila se sentía desconcertada de que se hubieran invertido las tornas, pero tomó la pequeña rebanada de pan de ajo con salsa de tomate que Thierry le tendía y lo saboreó con gusto.

–¿Qué te apetece beber? –le preguntó Thierry–. ¿Prefieres tinto, o vino blanco? ¿O mejor champán?

–Creo que champán.

Thierry se levantó.

–De acuerdo; vuelvo enseguida.

¿Pero por qué no llamaba a algún sirviente para que se lo trajera?, se preguntó Mila. Y él debió notar su extrañeza, porque se detuvo y le preguntó:

–¿Ocurre algo?

–No, nada. Es solo que me estaba preguntando… ¿dónde está el servicio? ¿Les has dado la noche libre?

–Les he dado toda la semana libre.

–¿Cómo?

–Les he relevado de sus obligaciones durante tu estancia. Estoy seguro de que lo comprenderás. No quería que tuviéramos público, ni ningún tipo de distracciones.

¿Estaban completamente solos? La idea la excitaba y la aterraba a la vez.

–Bueno, puedo hacerme la cama; por eso no hay problema –dijo riéndose.

Pero se le cortó la risa al darse cuenta de que acababa de meterse ella sola en un terreno de arenas movedizas.

–De eso no me cabe duda. Estoy seguro de que eres una mujer tan capaz como hermosa. Bueno, voy a por el champán.

Cuando abandonó el salón, Mila apoyó la espalda en el sofá sin saber muy bien qué pensar. Por un lado se sentía como una tonta por haberse sorprendido: Thierry había pretendido engañarla con otra mujer y obviamente no había querido arriesgarse a que algún sirviente fuese luego contándolo por ahí.

Pero, por otro lado, aquella situación a ella le venía mejor que bien, porque ya no tenía que preocuparse porque alguien del servicio la reconociera. Claro que era difícil que eso hubiera ocurrido: durante su adolescencia había pasado inadvertida por ser la hermana feúcha y torpe del rey de Erminia, y luego había pasado siete años en el extranjero y había cambiado tanto que era poco probable que nadie la reconociese.

Bueno, había cambiado físicamente, porque en su interior seguía siendo aquella chica que solo quería complacer y sentirse aceptada. ¿La aceptaría Thierry tal y como era?

–Pareces pensativa –comentó este, que había aparecido a su lado con la botella de champán y dos copas.

–Lo estaba –admitió ella, alzando la vista–. La verdad es que me estaba preguntando qué esperas de mí.

Thierry, que acababa de descorchar la botella con un abridor especial, se quedó mirándola un momento antes de responder.

–Bueno, creo que eso quedó especificado con bastante claridad cuando contraté tus servicios.

Mila maldijo para sus adentros.

–Ya, pero es que… querría que me lo dijeras con tus propias palabras –improvisó, esbozando una sonrisa.

–Está bien. Necesito que me instruyas en el arte de la seducción. Quiero asegurarme de que sabré satisfacer a mi futura esposa en la cama –dijo Thierry mientras servía el champán.

Mila parpadeó. ¿Estaba haciendo aquello por ella?

–Eso es muy noble por tu parte, Hawk –le dijo, tomando la copa que le tendía–. Bueno, pues, entonces quizá deberíamos comprometernos a esforzarnos para que tengáis un matrimonio largo y feliz.

Thierry levantó su copa.

–Esa es la idea –dijo, y brindaron.

El cosquilleo de las burbujas del champán no era nada comparado con el que Mila sentía en ese momento en el estómago. Un pensamiento cruzó por su mente, y lo soltó sin darse cuenta.

–O sea que quieres hacerla feliz en la cama. ¿Y fuera de ella también? –le preguntó.

Thierry tomó un largo trago de su copa antes de asentir.

–Por supuesto. Para mí es muy importante que mi matrimonio tenga éxito. No quiero que la gente sienta lástima de nosotros, ni que chismorreen, ni quiero repetir los errores de mis padres y de quienes los precedieron.

Vaya, parecía que los dos querían lo mismo…

–Entiendo –dijo Mila–. Pero no has sido muy conciso. ¿Cómo esperas que te ayude a conseguirlo?

–Quiero que me digas qué debo hacer para que mi esposa sea feliz. Quiero que me enseñes a comprenderla como mujer: sus estados de ánimo, lo que desea, lo que necesita… Todo.

–¿Y no crees que habría sido más fácil que se lo hubieses preguntado directamente a ella?

Thierry sacudió la cabeza.

–Me ha sido imposible. Ha estado viviendo en el extranjero los últimos siete años, y cuando nos conocimos se comportó como un animalillo asustado, así que dudo que hubiera estado muy receptiva a hablar de sexo. Además, temo que considere nuestro matrimonio como un deber nada más.

–Pero los dos os vais a casar por deber, ¿no?

Se le hacía raro estar hablando de sí misma como si fuera otra persona.

–Sí, pero nuestro matrimonio no tiene por qué basarse solo en el deber.

–¿Y cuál va a ser tu enfoque? ¿Vas a ir despacio con ella?

Él soltó una risa cínica.

–¿Despacio? Nos casamos a finales de este mes.

–Puedes cortejarla cuando ya estéis casados.

Thierry negó con la cabeza.

–Desde el primer día estaremos sujetos a lo que se espera de ella y de mí. Sería difícil cortejarla con todas las miradas puestas en nosotros.

En eso tenía toda la razón. Desde su regreso había sentido esa presión, y le había resultado difícil salir de palacio para embarcarse en aquella «misión», aunque por suerte no imposible. ¡Y a Dios gracias que su hermano estaba fuera por asuntos de Estado! Después de mucho discutir con Gregor cómo explicarían que fuese a ausentarse, finalmente habían acordado que dirían que se marchaba una semana a la casa de verano de su familia junto al lago, para poder estar a solas y disfrutar de algo de calma antes de la boda. Por fortuna nadie había cuestionado su excusa, y su carabina y sus guardaespaldas habían accedido a respetar su deseo de viajar sola.

–Así que, como ves, tengo que pisar el acelerador –comentó Thierry–. ¿Qué tal si empiezas por instruirme en los juegos preliminares al sexo? –le propuso, seleccionando otro bocado de la bandeja.

Cuando se lo ofreció, Mila lo rechazó. De pronto se le había quitado el apetito. Su mente era un hervidero de pensamientos. Se había equivocado de parte a parte con Thierry; lo había juzgado injustamente. Claro que… ¿cómo podría no haber pensado mal de él cuando había contratado los servicios de una cortesana? Lo último que se le hubiera ocurrido era que lo hubiera hecho por ella.

Sin embargo, la fea marca de los celos no se desvaneció. Le dolía que hubiera cambiado de opinión con respecto a llegar al matrimonio virgen al cien por cien como ella, que, en vez de que descubriesen juntos los placeres del sexo, como marido y mujer, hubiese escogido que lo instruyese en ellos una extraña.

–Vas un poco deprisa –le dijo a Thierry–. Verás, creo que debes tener en cuenta que a las mujeres queremos que un hombre nos haga sentirnos especiales en todo momento, no solo antes de meternos en la cama.

Thierry ladeó la cabeza y la miró con fingida sorpresa.

—¿No me digas?, ¿de verdad? —exclamó, como si acabara de revelarle un secreto colosal.

Mila reprimió una sonrisa y le dio un manotazo de broma en el hombro.

—Sí, de verdad. ¿Vas a escucharme o no?

—Te estoy escuchando —contestó él con una sonrisa traviesa.

—Bien. Pues no basta con que sonrías a tu esposa de manera lasciva cuando estéis en la cama, y que le digas lo sexy que está.

—Entonces… ¿eso es algo que no debería hacer?

—No, me has malinterpretado. O a lo mejor es que yo me he explicado mal —Mila suspiró e intentó poner sus pensamientos en orden—. Lo que quiero decir es que puedes encontrar mil oportunidades a lo largo del día para seducir a tu esposa.

—¿Me estás diciendo que la manosee en cualquier momento? —le preguntó Thierry, con un brillo travieso en los ojos.

Mila reprimió una sonrisa y enarcó una ceja a modo de reproche.

—No, sabes perfectamente que no me refiero a eso. Lo que quiero decir es que tienes que «sazonar» vuestro día a día con muestras de cariño, con detalles que le demuestren qué piensas en ella. Puedes apartar un mechón de su rostro mientras hablas con ella, tomarla de la mano y entrelazar tus dedos con los de ella cuando salgáis a pasear… La intimidad comienza por esas pequeñas cosas. Puede ser algo tan simple como buscar su mirada cuando veas algo divertido que sabes que a ella también le hará gracia. O algo más concreto, como dejarle una nota sobre la almohada, o mandarle un mensaje al móvil cuando estéis separados para que sepa que te acuerdas de ella, o una foto de algo que crees que le gustará.

—O sea, hacerla partícipe de mi día a día. Y supongo que cuando ella haga lo mismo, debo hacerle ver que me siento afortunado de tenerla a mi lado. ¿Algo así?

Mila sonrió satisfecha.

—Exactamente. La seducción es algo que implica un esfuerzo constante, sobre todo cuando quieres enamorar a una mujer y no solo llevártela a la cama. En nosotras el deseo sexual no es algo que se active con un interruptor. Respondemos mejor cuando se nos corteja, cuando se nos muestra de forma repetida que nos desean y nos valoran.

—Entonces… ¿primero tengo que seducir mentalmente a mi esposa?

—Básicamente. Es una lástima que no hayáis tenido contacto desde que os prometisteis.

Thierry se encogió de hombros.

—¿Qué sentido habría tenido? Es un matrimonio concertado; no es como si tuviera que pedirle que se casase conmigo y convencerla para que me dijera que sí.

—Pero si quieres que el vuestro sea un matrimonio feliz, ¿no cree que se merece conocerte un poco mejor antes de la boda?

—Ella no parece que tenga interés. En estos siete años solo hemos cruzado algunas cartas en un tono formal. No me ha mandado ninguna foto suya, ni me ha llamado por teléfono. Los dos deberíamos poner de nuestra parte, ¿no?

Mila palideció. Tenía razón. Era injusto esperar que fuera él el único que se esforzase. Parecía que en los asuntos del corazón estaba tan verde como en el sexo.

–Por supuesto –admitió–. Y eso me lleva a otra pregunta: ¿cómo podría cortejarte ella?

Thierry se rio.

–¿Qué, es que también vas a instruir a mi prometida? –bromeó.

–Bueno, lo haría si pudiera –murmuró Mila, rehuyendo su mirada–. ¿Crees que funcionaría, como cuando los matrimonios van a terapia de pareja?

–Seguro que sí –respondió él, pero luego se puso serio y añadió–: Pero la princesa Mila y yo no somos una pareja normal. Somos dos extraños que van a iniciar una vida juntos, y temo que no funcionará.

–¿Por qué? ¿Piensas que no tendréis nada que deciros? Tu prometida… imagino que habrá recibido una buena educación, ¿no? Supongo que podrás hablar con ella de igual a igual…

Thierry se encogió de hombros.

–Claro. Su hermano me ha dicho que ha tenido muy buenas notas en la universidad.

–¿Entonces? ¿Es que no te atrae? –insistió ella con curiosidad.

–Su aspecto no es lo que más me preocupa. Es que… va a ser mi consorte, la madre de mis hijos, si es que los tenemos. Quiero que nuestra relación sea duradera, que nos respetemos el uno al otro, que compartamos nuestros sueños… Esas cosas son muy importantes para mí.

Para ella también lo eran.

—¿Y no crees que ella también querrá lo mismo?

—No lo sé. Apenas la conozco. De hecho, apenas sé nada de ella. Necesito saber cómo seducirla, y no solo físicamente, sino también en el plano emocional. No quiero que llegue un día en que al mirarla vea odio en sus ojos, como lo vi tantas veces en los ojos de mi madre cuando miraba a mi padre. Ni quiero acabar tratándola con el desdén que mi padre mostraba hacia mi madre. No quiero tener un matrimonio así —murmuró. Había angustia en sus ojos—. Por esa razón te he hecho venir aquí. Porque quiero que me ayudes a hacer que mi esposa se enamore tan profundamente de mí que jamás busque en los brazos de otro hombre algo que yo no le pueda dar. ¿Puedes hacerlo?

Capítulo Nueve

Thierry la miró a los ojos, ansioso porque le dijera que sí.

—A ver si lo he entendido —murmuró ella—: ¿quieres que te enseñe cómo seducir a tu prometida a través del intelecto y los sentidos, para después pasar a lo físico?

—Eso es.

Por un momento ella pareció sorprendida, pero luego se dibujó en sus labios una sonrisa.

—No es lo que esperaba que me pidieras, pero creo que podré hacerlo.

—¿Y por dónde empezamos?

—Bueno, cuando quieres ganarte a alguien, lo habitual es preguntarle qué cosas le gustan para ver si tienes con ella algo en común, ¿no? Por ejemplo, ¿a ti qué te gusta hacer en tu tiempo libre?

—¿En mi tiempo libre? No estoy muy seguro de saber lo que es eso.

Angel se rio, y el sonido de su risa hizo sonreír a Thierry.

—¡Perfecto! —exclamó Angel.

—¿El qué? —inquirió él contrariado.

—El humor es perfecto para romper el hielo cuando estás intentando conocer mejor a alguien.

Ya. Solo que él no intentaba ser gracioso; su día a día estaba siempre repleto de obligaciones.

–Entiendo. Entonces, ¿cómo lo hacemos? ¿Fingimos que no nos conocemos? No sé si voy a saber hacer esto.

Angel se giró para estar de frente a él y apoyó un codo en el asiento del sofá.

–Solo tienes que hacer lo mismo que cuando nos conocimos en Nueva York, Hawk. Y a mí entonces no me pareció que tuvieras ningún miedo a fracasar.

–Bueno, es que entonces no estaba hablando con mi prometida –apuntó él.

Al decir eso le pareció como si Angel se quedara aturdida, pero fue solo un instante, y pensó que tal vez se lo hubiera imaginado.

–Ya, tienes razón. Está bien, entonces finjamos que soy tu prometida –dijo ella–. ¿Qué querrías saber de mí?

Thierry, que no sabía por dónde empezar, titubeó, e hizo reír a Angel una vez más.

–¡Venga, no es tan difícil! –lo pinchó–. ¿Qué pasa?, ¿es que le tienes miedo? ¡Ni que fuera un dragón!

–No, claro que no.

–Pues entonces relájate. Seguro que no te morderá.

Angel sonreía divertida, y Thierry se encontró preguntándose cómo sería sentir el roce de esos blancos dientes contra su piel. A pesar de su capacidad de autocontrol, perfeccionada a lo largo de todos esos años, de pronto el deseo estaba desgarrándolo por dentro.

Aquello no había sido buena idea. Quería aprender a conquistar a su prometida, la princesa Mila, no sentirse desesperadamente atraído por otra mujer. Se levantó y fue hasta la chimenea.

–Esta noche no consigo relajarme –le confesó mirando las llamas–. Quizá deberíamos dejarlo para maña-na por la mañana, cuando los dos estemos descansados.

Oyó a Angel acercarse a él por detrás. El aroma de su perfume, aunque sutil, se coló a través de la barrera que su mente que, con tanto esfuerzo, estaba intentan-do sostener.

–Lo siento, Hawk. No pretendía…

–No es por ti. Tal vez me haya impuesto unas ex-pectativas demasiado altas. Tengo tan poco tiempo y…

–Sé lo importante que esto es para ti –lo interrum-pió ella–. No pasa nada; lo comprendo. Nos veremos por la mañana.

Mientras la oía alejarse, Thierry reprimió el impul-so de detenerla.

–Sí, por la mañana –murmuró–. ¿Sabes montar a caballo? –le preguntó abruptamente, volviéndose hacia ella.

–Hace bastante que no lo hago, pero sí, sé montar.

–Estupendo. Entonces saldremos a dar un paseo a caballo antes de desayunar. Reúnete conmigo en las cuadras, detrás de la casa, cuando te levantes.

–¿Seguro? Soy de las que se levanta temprano –le avisó ella con una sonrisa, enarcando una ceja y la-deando la cabeza.

¿Por qué tenía que ser tan encantadora? Thierry se sentía hechizado por cada uno de sus gestos y movi-mientos, por cada palabra que cruzaba esos carnosos labios. Únicamente los separaban unos pasos. Unos pasos y podría tomarla entre sus brazos, podría besarla, y no solo rozar sus labios por accidente, como aquella noche en Nueva York. No, tenía que contenerse, se re-prendió con firmeza. Carraspeó y contestó:

–Yo también; la mayoría de los días ya estoy despierto al alba, cuando cantan los pájaros.

Ella sonrió, ladeando la cabeza de nuevo, y su oscura melena cayó hacia delante, dejando al descubierto la suave curva de su cuello. Se moría por acariciarle el cabello, por besar la piel desnuda de su garganta… Thierry se metió las manos en los bolsillos del pantalón y tragó saliva.

La observó mientras subía la escalera con las sandalias colgando de los dedos. La fina tela de la camisola marcaba ciertas partes de su anatomía que sabía que no debería estar mirando, solo que no podía apartar los ojos de ella…

Maldiciendo entre dientes, se giró sobre los talones, abandonó el salón y no se detuvo hasta llegar al vestíbulo. Salió de la casa, y echó a andar hacia el bosque a la tenue luz de los últimos rayos del sol, que casi se había ocultado por completo. Lo que necesitaba era un poco de aire fresco y caminar, se dijo. Podía controlarse; podía controlarse…

La silueta plateada de la luna asomaba ya tras las montañas cuando regresaba a la cabaña. Hasta habían cesado las últimas notas del canto de los pájaros, que ya habrían vuelto a sus nidos para pasar la noche.

Solo había algunas ventanas iluminadas, un recordatorio de que había dado toda la semana libre al servicio, y únicamente quedaba una persona. Una persona a la que había pedido que fuese allí sin imaginar lo atraído que iba a sentirse por ella.

¿Cómo podía haber sido tan estúpido? Solicitar los

servicios de una cortesana, una maestra de la seducción, sin pensar en que acabaría cayendo bajo su hechizo, como los marineros por el canto de las sirenas…

Pero la solución era muy simple: a la mañana siguiente le diría que se marchase. Ni paseo a caballo, ni lecciones de seducción… ¡Al diablo con todo!

Estaba decidido… hasta que entró en la cabaña y, sediento tras la larga caminata, fue a la cocina, y allí sentada encontró a la mujer que, sin pretenderlo, se había convertido en su talón de Aquiles.

Envuelta en una bata de seda que apenas ocultaba la corta combinación de satén y encaje que llevaba debajo, estaba devorando una rebanada de pan con una loncha de queso y otra de fiambre de pavo como si no hubiera comido en una semana.

Al oírlo entrar levantó la vista, sobresaltada, y tragó la comida que tenía en la boca. Él, que se había quedado mirándola, comprendió de repente.

—Perdona. Sabía que tenías hambre y ni siquiera te he dado de cenar. Soy un anfitrión horrible.

Angel sacudió la cabeza.

—No pasa nada. Ya soy mayorcita; sé cuidar de mí misma.

—¿Quieres algo más? —le preguntó él, señalando la bandeja, que obviamente se había traído del salón.

—No, ya voy servida. ¿No quieres comer nada? Tú también debes tener hambre.

Su apetito no se saciaría con comida. Negó con la cabeza, sacó un vaso del armarito y lo llenó con el grifo del fregadero.

—El agua viene de un manantial de montaña —le dijo a Angel—. ¿No quieres un poco?

Angel sacudió la cabeza, levantando el vaso de leche que tenía en la mesa, tomó un trago y sonrió. Era una mujer de contrastes, pensó Thierry: se vestía con la lencería más fina, pero comía con el apetito de un jornalero tras una dura mañana de trabajo en el campo; antes la había visto tomar con elegancia sorbitos de champán, y ahora se bebía aquel vaso de leche con el entusiasmo de una niña.

Se había lavado la cara y así, sin maquillar, parecía más joven. Le gustaba más así, al natural, pensó, aunque preferiría que llevase algo más de ropa encima.

–¿Has disfrutado de tu paseo? –le preguntó Angel.

¿Que si lo había disfrutado? Había estado demasiado enfadado consigo mismo como para disfrutar nada.

–El bosque siempre está precioso en esta época del año –murmuró.

–No has respondido a mi pregunta –observó ella–. ¿Haces eso a menudo?

–Puede ser. A veces es más fácil evadir una pregunta que dar una respuesta sincera –admitió él a regañadientes.

–¿Y también piensas mostrarte evasivo con tu esposa?

–No –respondió él de un modo enfático–. Quiero que podamos ser sinceros el uno con el otro en todo. El engaño es la semilla del descontento, y no toleraré que haya mentiras entre nosotros.

Angel tomó otro sorbo de leche.

–Me alegra oír eso. Entonces, volveré a preguntártelo: ¿has disfrutado de tu paseo?

Thierry resopló de pura frustración.

–No. Apenas he mirado a mi alrededor mientras caminaba. Salí enfadado y no me he parado ni un segundo a admirar la belleza del paisaje, que seguramente podría haberme calmado, y ahora también estoy enfadado conmigo mismo por eso.

Angel se rio suavemente.

–Bien hecho. Aplaudo tu sinceridad. Bueno, no ha sido tan difícil, ¿no?

–Y un cuerno que no –replicó él, y se encontró riéndose con ella.

–Pues tendremos que trabajar eso –dijo Angel levantándose y tomando su plato y su vaso.

Thierry la siguió mientras lo llevaba al fregadero. Cada movimiento resaltaba las formas femeninas de su cuerpo: sus turgentes pechos, la curva de sus caderas y sus nalgas, sus muslos…

La sinceridad no era lo único que tenía que trabajar, pensó girándose para servirse otro vaso de agua bien fría. Sí, el autocontrol estaba al principio de la lista de cosas que tenía que mejorar, reconoció para sus adentros al notar lo tirante que empezaba a notarse la bragueta del pantalón.

–Deja, ya acabo yo –le dijo cuando vio que iba a recoger lo que quedaba en la mesa–. Es lo menos que puedo hacer como anfitrión –añadió tras terminarse el segundo vaso de agua.

–A mí no me lo digas dos veces – respondió ella con una sonrisa descarada–. Siempre se me ha dado mejor desbaratarlo todo que recoger.

–No sé por qué no me sorprende –contestó Thierry, enarcando una ceja.

Angel sonrió aún más.

–Ya, ya, pero seguro que no me equivoco si digo

que tú no habrás limpiado mucho en tu vida, ¿a que no? ¿Para qué vas a limpiar, cuando tienes a un montón de gente a tu servicio?

–No es tan maravilloso como parece: no tengo que mover un dedo, pero apenas tengo privacidad.

–Eso me lo creo –dijo Angel, poniéndose seria–. Bueno, te dejo; nos vemos por la mañana.

–Sí, por la mañana. Que duermas bien.

–Gracias. Tú también, Hawk, dulces sueños.

Cuando Angel salió de la cocina, se dio cuenta de que no quería que se fuera. Aquello era ridículo. Apenas la conocía y estaba obsesionado con ella…

Quizá no hubiera sido buena idea mantenerse célibe todos esos años. Quizá, si se hubiera permitido un poco más de libertad, ahora no estaría consumiéndolo el deseo. Siempre se había considerado un hombre paciente, alguien que había elevado a la categoría de arte el autocontrol, pero de repente parecía como si esa capacidad de autocontrol estuviera siendo puesta a prueba al límite. No sabía cómo, pero tendría que sobrevivir a esos siete días sin sucumbir a la tentación.

Capítulo Diez

Mila se levantó a las seis y se fue derecha a la ducha. Después de las emociones del día anterior, había creído que le costaría conciliar el sueño, pero se había quedado dormida en el momento nada más meterse en la cama, y ahora se sentía llena de energía y lista para afrontar el día.

Después de secarse el pelo, que se recogió en una coleta alta, y ponerse la ropa interior, se encontró rebuscando en los cajones y el armario, deseando recordar mejor dónde había puesto cada cosa.

Estaba segura de que había visto unos pantalones de montar entre las cosas de la señorita Romolo... ¡ah, sí, allí estaban! Se los enfundó, y se puso también una camiseta ajustada y un jersey antes de ir a por unos calcetines de lana y las botas de montar.

Desde luego la señorita Romolo había pensado en todo, se dijo, preguntándose si la cortesana se habría quedado tan sorprendida como ella al saber que a Thierry le preocupaba más cómo ganarse a su futura esposa que seducirla.

Apartó de su mente a aquella mujer. No quería pensar en ella en ese momento, ni tenía que preocuparse por ella. Estaría recibiendo las mejores atenciones, como le había indicado a Gregor que se hiciera, y seguramente le daría igual que le pagasen por tomarse unas vacaciones en un hotel de lujo en vez de estar con un cliente, se dijo mientras bajaba descalza la escalera.

Cuando llegó abajo se sentó en el último escalón para ponerse los calcetines y las botas, y fue a la cocina, donde tomó una manzana del frutero que había sobre la mesa. Mientras se la comía a mordiscos, deambuló por la planta baja hasta encontrar la puerta trasera de la cabaña y salió fuera. El aire de la mañana era fresco, pero el sol ya estaba ascendiendo por el despejado firmamento, y prometía ser un día cálido.

Cruzó el amplio patio, y caminó hasta las cuadras, un enorme edificio de madera. Dentro se oía el suave relinchar de los caballos y el ruido de sus cascos.

–Buenos días –la saludó al verla entrar Thierry, que salía de un cuarto a su derecha, con una silla de montar en los brazos–. Ya veo que no bromeabas cuando me dijiste que te gustaba levantarte temprano.

Él también llevaba pantalones y botas de montar, además de un polo ajustado de manga corta que dejaba al descubierto sus brazos fuertes y bronceados. Levantó la silla y se la colocó a un alazán castaño rojizo como si no pesara más que la manta sobre el lomo del animal.

–¿Por qué desperdiciar en la cama un día tan hermoso? –le contestó ella.

No lo había dicho con doble sentido, pero había sonado un poco raro. La verdad era que podría pasarse un día entero en la cama con él y no lo consideraría como un día desperdiciado. Al pensar eso se le encendieron las mejillas, y miró a su alrededor, buscando algo que hacer o sobre lo que hablar para que él no se percatara de su azoramiento.

–¿Quieres que te ayude a preparar a los caballos? –le preguntó.

–Casi he acabado –contestó él, mientras ajustaba la cincha y comprobaba los estribos–. He pensado que Henri sería una buena montura para ti. Es muy dócil.

Mila se acercó y alargó la mano para acariciar al alazán en la frente antes de ofrecerle lo que quedaba de su manzana.

–Gracias. Como te dije anoche, hace bastante que no monto. Unos cuantos años, de hecho.

–Henri cuidará bien de ti, no te preocupes –dijo Thierry, dándole unas palmadas suaves al caballo en la grupa.

Desenredó las riendas del poste y, seguido de Mila, condujo a Henri hasta la otra salida del establo, en el extremo opuesto. Allí esperaba otro caballo ya ensilla- do, un majestuoso corcel gris.

–¡Vaya, es precioso! –exclamó Mila.

–No le digas eso, o se le subirá a la cabeza –dijo Thierry riéndose.

Le dio unas palmadas en el cuello y le susurró algo al oído. El caballo relinchó suavemente por respuesta, y la escena enterneció a Mila. ¡Era tan fácil encariñarse con Thierry…!

–¿Cómo se llama? –le preguntó.

–Sleipnir. Es un nombre de…

–De la mitología nórdica, lo sé –lo interrumpió ella–. El caballo de Odín, nada menos. Un nombre muy noble para un noble corcel. ¿Hace mucho que lo tienes?

Thierry, que se había quedado anonadado al ver que sabía de dónde venía el nombre, respondió:

–Desde que era un potrillo. Tiene cinco años.

—Es justo la clase de caballo que habría imaginado que tendrías —observó Mila.

Seguro que sería una imagen magnífica: él a lomos de Sleipnir.

—¿Nos vamos? —le preguntó Thierry—. ¿Quieres que te ayude a subirte al caballo?

—Te lo agradezco. Hace tanto que no monto…

Thierry se colocó junto al flanco de su caballo y se inclinó, con las manos entrelazadas.

—Gracias —murmuró ella, poniendo el pie en ellas.

Thierry la impulsó y, ya encima del animal, Mila pasó la pierna al otro lado de la silla para sentarse a horcajadas. Metió los pies en los estribos y tomó las riendas.

—¿Está bien ese largo para ti, o quieres que las suelte un poco más? —le preguntó Thierry, con una mano apoyada en su muslo mientras comprobaba las riendas.

—S-sí —balbució ella, apenas capaz de concentrarse en la pregunta, con el calor de su mano—. Así está perfecto, gracias.

Thierry se subió a su caballo y se puso junto a ella.

—He pensado que podríamos tomar un sendero a través del bosque, y luego, cuando lleguemos al prado que hay al otro lado, les dejaremos rienda suelta a Henri y a Sleipnir. ¿Qué te parece?, ¿estás dispuesta?

—Me parece estupendo —murmuró ella—. Estoy dispuesta para lo que quieras.

Cuando Thierry se quedó mirándola, Mila se dio cuenta de lo que había dicho y apartó la vista, muerta de vergüenza. Iba a tener que cuidar más las palabras que salieran de su boca.

–Bueno, pues vamos –dijo Thierry, y se pusieron en marcha.

Mientras avanzaban por el sendero, solo los trinos de los pájaros en las ramas de los árboles rompían el silencio. Mila aspiró el aire fresco y el olor a bosque, y se relajó sobre su montura. Al día siguiente estaría algo dolorida, pero estaba disfrutando del paseo.

Al cabo de veinte minutos la espesura del bosque empezó a disminuir, y pronto llegaron al prado que Thierry había mencionado, un prado inmenso salpicado de flores silvestres.

–¡Venga, vamos a galopar un poco! –le dijo Thierry, agitando las riendas y espoleando a su caballo.

Mila lo imitó, y rio mientras Henri salía corriendo tras Sleipnir. Había olvidado la maravillosa sensación de libertad que se experimentaba al correr al galope a lomos de un caballo sintiendo el viento en la cara.

Sleipnir era mucho más rápido que su alazán, y cuando por fin les dieron alcance a Thierry y a él, se habían detenido junto a un arroyo y Thierry había desmontado. Era un lugar tan idílico que casi parecía salido de una fotografía, y mientras desmontaba ella también así se lo dijo a Thierry, quien acudió raudo a su lado para ayudarla, asiéndola por la cintura hasta que sus pies tocaron el suelo.

–Teniendo una cabaña en un sitio tan hermoso, ¿cómo lo soportas cuando tienes que volver a la ciudad? –le preguntó.

Thierry se quedó callado un momento.

–Este es mi sitio favorito –respondió finalmente–, y el saber que seguirá aquí, esperándome, es lo que lo que lo hace soportable.

Mila le puso una mano en el pecho y, mirándolo a los ojos, le preguntó:

–¿Tan difícil es ser de la realeza?

Ella sabía lo difícil que podía ser a veces, pero quería saber cómo lo vivía Thierry.

–Es mi vida –contestó él encogiéndose de hombros–; no conozco otra cosa.

A pesar de su respuesta, intuyó, por su mirada sombría, que las obligaciones de su cargo le pesaban tanto como a ella. Mila dejó caer la mano y optó por intentar aligerar un poco el tono de la conversación.

–Entonces, la vida de un rey… ¿no es todo fiestas y banquetes?

La comisura de los labios de Thierry se arqueó ligeramente.

–No, claro que no. Y menos mal, porque si no me pondría como un tonel.

–Cierto –dijo ella, mirándolo y fingiéndose pensativa. Le hincó un dedo en el estómago, que estaba duro como una piedra, y bromeó diciendo–: Me parece que os está saliendo tripita, majestad.

Una sombra le cruzó el rostro a Thierry, que se apartó de ella.

–Hawk. Aquí soy solamente Hawk –le recordó muy serio.

Contrariada, Mila escrutó su rostro.

–¿Has deseado alguna vez que todo Sylvain pudiera ser como este lugar? –le preguntó mientras llevaban a los caballos hacia el arroyo para que pudieran beber.

–Sí y no. Lógicamente un país necesita de la industria para avanzar y para que la economía funcione, pero sí animo al gobierno a considerar alternativas sostenibles cuando en el parlamento se discute alguna ley que puede afectar al medioambiente. Claro que por desgracia mis sugerencias suelen caer en saco roto. No es fácil persuadir a la gente para que pruebe energías alternativas, y más cuando eso implica costes mucho mayores.

–Yo creo que tendremos más posibilidades de concienciar a la gente si empezamos por educar a los niños en el colegio de que el desarrollo sostenible es esencial para la supervivencia de nuestro planeta –apuntó Mila–. Cuando eso se comprenda, será mucho más fácil.

–Sí, pero… ¿no será para entonces demasiado tarde? –murmuró Thierry, con la mirada perdida en las montañas.

–Puede que nosotros no lleguemos a ver grandes cambios en política medioambiental a nivel global –respondió ella–, pero tienes que pensar que estás luchando por el futuro, por tus nietos y los nietos de tus nietos.

–Nietos… –repitió él–. Eso me abruma un poco; ni me he casado todavía.

–Pero es lo que uno espera cuando se casa, ¿no?, tener hijos y nietos.

Ella tenía muy claro que quería tener hijos, tres o cuatro por lo menos. Rocco y ella se llevaban tantos años que nunca habían tenido la relación de hermanos que le hubiera gustado que tuvieran.

–Claro –admitió él–. Pero la verdad, hasta ahora ni me he planteado lo de los hijos. Sé que tengo la responsabilidad de dar continuidad a la línea sucesoria, pero cuando pienso en el pésimo legado de mis predecesores, a veces me pregunto si no sería mejor que permaneciera soltero y dejase que la monarquía muriese conmigo.

–¡No! –protestó Mila–. ¡No digas eso!

–Seamos sinceros: la monarquía es un concepto anticuado.

–Pero tú tienes un papel que desempeñar: sigues siendo un símbolo de la unidad del país, y el representante del pueblo. Todo el mundo conoce la labor tan importante que hiciste liderando esa campaña para reducir la contaminación de las vías fluviales en tu país –argumentó Mila con pasión.

–Bueno, fue un paso en la dirección correcta –concedió Thierry.

–Es más que eso. Tu pueblo ve que te implicas en las cosas que te importan, que no es algo que apoyes solo de boquilla. Te pusiste al frente y le diste a tu gente un ejemplo a seguir. No puedes tirar eso por la borda.

–Perdona si te he decepcionado con mi pesimismo –se disculpó Thierry–. Supongo que ya te habrás dado cuenta de que no soy más que un ídolo con pies de barro.

–No, me he dado cuenta de que eres un ser humano, y que como tal, como el resto de nosotros, tienes debilidades, pero también tienes cosas buenas.

Cuanto más conocía a aquel hombre, que pronto se convertiría en su marido, más claro tenía que lo amaría durante el resto de sus días. ¡Si tan solo consiguiera que él la amase a ella también…!

Capítulo Once

–Pero dejemos de hablar de mí –dijo Thierry–. Cuéntame más sobre qué debo hacer para conquistar a mi prometida.

–Muestra interés por ella; interés de verdad.

Thierry la miró sorprendido.

–¿Así de simple?

Angel gruñó y puso los ojos en blanco.

–Pues claro que sí. ¿Qué hace una mujer cuando conoce a alguien?

Él se quedó mirándola sin saber qué decir. ¿Cómo iba a saber lo que hacía una mujer cuando conocía a alguien si él era un hombre?

–Hacen preguntas –le dijo Angel en un tono irritado, como si fuera algo evidente–. Muestran interés hacia su interlocutor. Eso da lugar a un diálogo, que puede conducir a una conversación, y ayudarte a descubrir intereses en común con la otra persona. Y todo fluye a partir de ahí –le explicó–. Por ejemplo, ¿cómo te hiciste esa cicatriz que tienes junto a la ceja derecha? Apenas se aprecia… –lo tomó por la barbilla para hacerle girar un poco la cabeza–, excepto cuando le da la luz.

Thierry, que estaba haciendo un esfuerzo por ignorar el suave tacto de sus dedos, respiró aliviado cuando dejó caer la mano.

–Eres muy observadora. Pues me la hice un día que había salido precisamente a montar a caballo y no estaba prestando atención. Estaba tan distraído charlando con los amigos que me acompañaban, que no me fijé en una rama baja que había un poco más adelante. Me golpeé con ella y me caí del caballo. Todo el mundo se asustó al ver la sangre, pero, a pesar de la cicatriz que me quedó, solo fue una herida sin importancia, y la experiencia me enseñó a estar más atento.

–¿Qué edad tenías cuando ocurrió?

–Ocho años. Mi padre me echó una buena bronca por ser tan despistado, mientras que mi madre me besaba y me abrazaba como si hubiese estado a punto de morir. ¿Y tú? –le preguntó–, ¿tienes alguna historia interesante que contar de una cicatriz en alguna parte oculta de tu cuerpo? –le preguntó con picardía.

Angel vaciló.

–Bueno, yo… –comenzó.

Pero de pronto se apartó de él para ir hacia donde Henri estaba pastando, y agarró las riendas.

–Ya lo vas pillando –le dijo, esbozando una sonrisa.

–¿El qué? –inquirió él, confundido.

–Lo de hacer preguntas para entablar conversación y conocer mejor a alguien –respondió ella–. ¿Continuamos? Podemos seguir hablando mientras montamos.

¿Por qué de repente había puesto distancia entre ellos?, se preguntó Thierry. Era ella quien había sugerido que tenía que aprender a hacer preguntas para conocer mejor a su prometida, y se suponía que debía ensayar con ella. Y en cambio, ahora que le había hecho una simple pregunta, había zanjado la conversación como si le diese miedo contestar.

–Claro, si es lo que quieres… Podemos volver a la cabaña para desayunar –le propuso mientras la ayudaba a montar.

–Me parece bien –contestó ella.

–Tomaremos un sendero distinto –le dijo Thierry tras montar también, y fue delante para indicarle el camino.

Ya de regreso en las cuadras, Angel desmontó deprisa y se puso a desabrochar la cincha de la silla de montar. Thierry desmontó también y fue junto a ella.

–Deja, ya lo haré yo –le dijo agarrándola suavemente por la cintura para apartarla del animal.

–No soy de porcelana –replicó ella–. Puedo ayudar.

–Como quieras –contestó contrariado. Señaló con la cabeza hacia el cuarto donde se guardaban los aparejos–. Ve a por un par de cepillos; yo iré quitándoles la silla de montar.

Mila aprovechó ese momento a solas para recobrar la compostura. Aquellos días con Thierry estaban resultándole muy provechosos para conocerlo mejor, pero a la vez inmensamente difíciles. Ansiaba contarle la verdad, decirle quién era en realidad y dejar caer los velos de subterfugio con que los había envuelto a ambos, pero no podía.

Dudaba de que Thierry se tomase bien que estuviera engañándolo así, pero es que ansiaba tanto –¡Dios, cómo lo ansiaba!– poder ser ella misma con él… No, habría tiempo de sobra para eso cuando estuviesen casados, se recordó. Miró a su alrededor hasta encontrar los cepillos a por los que la había mandado y volvió con Thierry.

Juntos cepillaron a los caballos, los devolvieron a sus boxes y terminaron de recogerlo todo.

–¿Te parece que vaya y prepare algo para desayunar? –le preguntó a Thierry.

–¿No te fías de lo que pueda preparar yo? –inquirió él, enarcando una ceja.

–No es eso –protestó Mila.

–Bueno, como quieras. Soy lo bastante hombre como para aprovecharme de tu ofrecimiento. Iré a darme una ducha mientras tú te ocupas de la comida –respondió él, con una sonrisa burlona.

Mila lo miró con los ojos entornados.

–¿Ya estás otra vez comportándote como un machista?

–¿Otra vez?

–Como aquel día en Nueva York.

Thierry resopló.

–En absoluto. O al menos, no pretendía parecer machista –le aseguró sonriendo–. Y para compensarte, si te he ofendido, me ofrezco a preparar yo la comida y la cena. ¿Te parece suficiente castigo por mi metedura de pata?

Mila no pudo evitar sonreír, y asintió con la cabeza.

–Gracias, sería estupendo.

–Y eso es lo que debería haber respondido yo cuando me has preguntado si preparabas el desayuno –observó Thierry.

–Aprendes rápido –lo picó ella.

–No me queda otra si quiero aprovechar tus lecciones.

Y así, de repente, allí estaba de nuevo esa tensión sexual entre ellos que hacía que saltaran chispas. Mila sintió como si cada célula de su cuerpo la empujase hacia él. ¿Se estaba acercando Thierry? ¿O era ella la que se estaba acercando a él? Fueran uno de ellos, o los dos, de algún modo acabaron frente a frente.

Las manos de Thierry se posaron en su cintura, y las de ella, como si una fuerza magnética las moviera, subieron al pecho de él. Bajo sus palmas podía sentir los fuertes latidos de su corazón, y cuando Thierry inclinó la cabeza y tomó sus labios, sintió que se derretía contra él, como si su cuerpo estuviese diciéndole que debieran haber hecho aquello mucho antes.

Se arqueó hacia él, deleitándose con el contraste entre los duros músculos del pecho y el abdomen de Thierry y sus blandas formas, y casi ronroneó de satisfacción al notar lo excitado que estaba. Era la prueba palpable de que la encontraba atractiva.

En un instante se disipó la preocupación que la había acompañado todo ese tiempo de que para él jamás sería otra cosa más que la torpe y desgarbada adolescente a la que había conocido años atrás.

Las manos de Thierry se deslizaron hacia su espalda para estrecharla aún más contra sí. Sus senos quedaron aplastados contra su pecho, y Mila sintió cómo se endurecían sus pezones, como suplicando que Thierry los tocara. De pronto le sobraban el sujetador y el resto de la ropa.

Los firmes labios de Thierry asediaban los suyos de un modo muy sensual, y al claudicar finalmente y abrir la boca, se estremeció de placer cuando succionó suavemente su labio inferior. Le clavó las uñas en la camisa, presa del deseo, y de repente, en un instante, se encontró con que no había más que aire frente a ella.

Casi perdió el equilibrio al abrir los ojos y darse cuenta de que Thierry la había apartado de él y había retrocedido varios pasos.

–¿Hawk? ¿Qué…? –lo llamó, alargando el brazo hacia él.

–¡No! –la cortó él, y se pasó una mano temblorosa por la cara–. No me toques. No debería haber hecho eso. Te pido disculpas.

–Pero… ¿por qué no? ¿Qué tiene de malo? Contrataste mis servicios como cortesana, ¿no?

Mila no podía estar más confundida, y por más que trataba de comprender qué le pasaba, no lo conseguía.

–No puedo romper mi promesa –dijo él–. No puedo volver a tocarte de esa manera… Esto ha sido un error… Estar aquí, contigo… me está convirtiendo en un hombre débil.

Había angustia en su voz. Angustia mezclada con desprecio, no hacia ella, sino hacia él mismo.

–¿Qué promesa? ¿Tu promesa de casarte con la princesa? –aventuró, intentando dilucidar a qué se refería.

–Sí, mi promesa a ella, y a mí mismo.

–Háblame de esa promesa a ti mismo –le pidió ella.

–No puedo… Ahora no. Por favor, ve a la cabaña. Solo necesito estar a solas un rato –le dijo Thierry. Sus ojos grises la miraban turbulentos, como las aguas de un lago azotadas por un fuerte viento en un día nublado.

Pero ella no quería que las cosas se quedaran así. No cuando todo su cuerpo vibraba aún por el efecto de aquel beso.

–No, dime qué ocurre. Estoy aquí para ayudarte. ¿Cómo voy a poder hacerlo si te niegas a abrirte a mí?

–fue hasta él y lo tomó de la mano–. Hawk, por favor, ayúdame a entenderte. ¿Por favor?

Lo vio tragar saliva. Estaba tan rígido, haciendo un esfuerzo tan grande por reprimirse, que por un momento temió que volviera a apartarla de él, pero entonces sintió como, poco a poco, empezaba a relajarse. Inspiró profundamente y cuando por fin habló su voz sonó áspera, como si las palabras que pronunció le rasparan la garganta.

–La fidelidad lo es todo para mí.

–Como debería ser –murmuró ella.

–No, tú no lo entiendes –replicó él, sacudiendo la cabeza.

–Pues entonces explícamelo –lo instó Mila–. Háblame.

–Crecí viendo a mis padres vivir bajo el mismo techo, pero jamás como un matrimonio de verdad. Para cuando ya fui lo bastante mayor como para comprender, apenas se soportaban, pero no podían vivir separados por su posición. Durante años mi padre antepuso cualquier obligación y preocupación a la felicidad de mi madre, hasta que ella ya no pudo aguantarlo más. Se dejó llevar por su corazón e inició una relación con un hombre que creía que la amaría… y aquello acabó destruyéndola. No dejaré que mi esposa pase por algo así.

–¿Y tú? ¿Qué pasa con lo que quieres tú?

–Lo único que yo quiero es ser lo mejor posible como persona, en todos los aspectos, y asegurarme de que mi comportamiento no dañará a mi pueblo… ni a mi esposa.

–Hawk, eso es admirable, pero debes comprender que no puedes controlarlo todo.

Thierry se apartó de ella.

–Sí que puedo. Soy el rey de Sylvain. ¿Y de qué sirvo como rey si yo no soy capaz de controlar todo aquello sobre lo que tengo alguna influencia? No seré como mi padre. No dejaré que mis defectos como persona hagan infelices a otros. Haré que mi matrimonio funcione y que mi esposa me ame.

–¿Y tú la amarás a ella también?

Capítulo Doce

Thierry se sintió atacado por sus palabras.

—La respetaré y la honraré como mi consorte, y haré todo lo que esté en mi mano para hacerla feliz. ¿Acaso no basta con eso?

Angel lo miró con lástima.

—Si tú amaras a alguien y solo pudieras esperar a cambio respeto, ¿crees que con eso te bastaría? ¿No te parece que no es mucho más de lo que le ofreció tu padre a tu madre?

Thierry resopló.

—Él no la respetaba, y no le importaba nada su felicidad. Para él no fue más que un vientre con el que engendrar un heredero, y cuando lo rechazaba y no quería compartir su cama, se buscó a otras mujeres con las que reemplazarla.

Angel lo miraba espantada. Era evidente que no estaba al tanto de los rumores sobre las numerosas aventuras que había tenido su padre. No se había podido probar ninguna de ellas, por supuesto, pero Thierry sabía que habían ocurrido; con mucha discreción, eso sí.

¿De dónde iba a haber sacado él la idea de contratar los servicios de una cortesana sino de su padre? ¡Si hasta se había ofrecido en una ocasión a buscarle una él!

—Jamás trataría a mi esposa de un modo tan cruel —le aseguró a Angel—. Me aseguraré de tratarla siempre con la dignidad que merece como persona y como princesa.

–Pero tú esperas obtener de ella más que eso –replicó Angel–. Quieres obtener su amor, pero no estás dispuesto a ofrecerle a cambio el tuyo.

–Yo no… No puedo prometerle eso –contestó él, con un nudo en la garganta.

Había una honda decepción en los ojos de Angel cuando le respondió con una voz hueca:

–Pues entonces lo siento por tu esposa, porque yo no podría vivir sin amor.

Cuando Angel salió de las cuadras y se alejó hacia la cabaña, la siguió con la mirada sintiendo cada paso que daba como una puñalada en el corazón. ¿Que no podía vivir sin amor? Él ni siquiera sabía lo que era el amor. Jamás lo había experimentado. Pero sí sabía lo que era sentirse atraído por una mujer, y los problemas que eso podía acarrear.

Abandonó las cuadras, pero no se dirigió a la cabaña, sino al bosque, y solo se detuvo cuando se calmó y logró reprimir la necesidad imperiosa de ir tras Angel, de disculparse por las cosas que le había dicho, de decirle que… ¿Qué?, ¿que la amaba? Ridículo. Se sentía atraído por ella, pero eso era todo.

Debería haberse mantenido firme en su decisión y haber hecho que se fuera esa mañana. La idea con que había contratado sus servicios se había ido al traste. Aquello estaba siendo una pérdida de tiempo y no estaba cumpliendo su objetivo de aprender a ganarse a su prometida; solo complicando aún más las cosas.

Regresó a la cabaña, decidido a decirle que ya no necesitaba de sus servicios, pero cuando entró en el salón y Angel, que estaba de pie junto a la ventana de la cocina, se volvió, vio que había estado llorando.

Sintió una punzada en el pecho, y fue a su lado para tomarla entre sus brazos. Al principio ella se resistió un poco, pero terminó cediendo a su abrazo.

–Lo siento –murmuró él contra su cabello–. No pretendía hacerte sentir mal.

–No… no es culpa tuya –replicó ella sollozando–. La culpa es mía y de mis estúpidos ideales.

–No es estúpido querer ser amado.

Al pronunciar esas palabras, Thierry se dio cuenta de que lo pensaba de verdad, que no eran solo unas palabras vacías de consuelo. Sus padres habían hecho que dejara de creer en el amor, pero cuando estaba con Angel sentía que quería creer que el amor sí era posible, que no era solo un concepto sentimental e idealizado. Y, sin embargo, no podía enamorarse de Angel. Era una cortesana, y él estaba comprometido.

Angel se apartó de él y le dijo:

–Pues si lo crees así, ¿no te parece que deberías darle al menos una oportunidad a tu prometida, abrirte a la posibilidad de amarla? Es que… dices que quieres hacerla feliz, lo cual es admirable, pero… ¿no debería hacerte feliz ella también a ti?

Su pregunta planteaba una cuestión interesante.

–Bueno, la verdad es que hasta ahora no lo había considerado necesario –admitió.

–Entonces… ¿no vas a decirme que me marche? –le preguntó Angel.

–No –contestó él con una sonrisa–. Te contraté para que me ayudaras, y aún confío en que puedas ayudarme. Lo harás, ¿verdad?

Angel lo miró muy seria, y algo vacilante, pero finalmente asintió.

–Lo haré –le prometió. Fue a la nevera y después de echar un vistazo dentro, giró la cabeza y le preguntó–: ¿Huevos revueltos y beicon?

–Me parece bien. ¿Quieres que te eche una mano con algo?

–No, no hace falta.

–Bueno, pues yo recogeré luego y fregaré los platos –propuso él–. Entonces, si no te importa, creo que iré a darme esa ducha.

Angel sonrió, pero la sonrisa no se reflejó en sus ojos.

–Claro.

Thierry vaciló al llegar a la puerta. Quería preguntarle por qué había estado llorando, pero lo pensó mejor y decidió que quizá no fuera buena idea reavivar el tema. No podía establecer un vínculo emocional con ella, se dijo saliendo de la cocina y dirigiéndose a la escalera. Tenía que encontrar la manera de mantener las distancias entre ellos, de que su relación fuera solo la de maestra y alumno. No le quedaba otro remedio.

Habían pasado un par de días, y entre Thierry y ella se había establecido una especie de rutina. Por la mañana, por ejemplo, salían a montar a caballo o a pasear por el bosque. Habían hablado ya de una amplia variedad de temas, y a Mila le encantaba poder aprender más sobre él y que él quisiera escuchar sus opiniones, cosa que esperaba que siguiera haciendo cuando estuviesen casados. Seguía preocupándole cómo reaccionaría cuando descubriese su engaño, pero acallaba su mala conciencia diciéndose que solo estaba dándole lo que él quería: ¿quién mejor que ella para enseñarle cómo conquistarla?

Las tardes, en cambio, eran una auténtica tortura. Thierry había empezado a pedirle consejo acerca de la parte física de la relación de pareja, no explícitamente acerca del sexo, sino acerca de cómo propiciar el siguiente paso en esa dirección, y Mila había conducido sus «lecciones» a temas más íntimos y sensuales.

El problema era que la noche anterior, cuando se habían dado las buenas noches y había subido a acostarse, se sentía como una botella de gaseosa que alguien hubiese estado agitando. Había intentado aliviar su frustración dándose un baño relajante, pero no le había servido de mucho, y a juzgar por el mal humor de Thierry esa mañana, parecía que él se sentía igual.

Cuando le había dicho que no le apetecía salir a montar con él y que prefería quedarse a leer en la biblioteca, su respuesta no podría haber sido más áspera. Había dejado que se fuera sin hacer ningún comentario al respecto, aunque su contestación la había dejado más furiosa que un enjambre de abejas.

Al poco de marcharse Thierry había empezado a llover, pero habían pasado varias horas y aún no había regresado. Había encendido el fuego y no podía estar más a gusto, acurrucada en un sillón orejero junto a la ventana, pero no conseguía concentrarse en el libro que había escogido.

Fue entonces cuando se oyeron en el patio de atrás los cascos de Sleipnir. Miró por la ventana y vio a Thierry, empapado, desmontando y llevando a su caballo a las cuadras. Al poco rato se escuchó la puerta y oyó a Thierry irse derecho al piso de arriba.

Se levantó para devolver el libro a su estantería, se sentó en otro sillón frente a la chimenea, y se preguntó, mientras miraba las llamas, si a Thierry se le habría pasado el mal humor.

No tuvo que esperar mucho para averiguarlo, porque a los pocos minutos la puerta de la biblioteca se abrió y apareció Thierry. Se había cambiado de ropa, pero aún tenía el pelo mojado.

–Ah, ya has vuelto –dijo, intentando parecer despreocupada, como si no hubiese estado contando los minutos–. ¿Qué tal tu paseo a caballo?

–Mal –contestó él de un modo abrupto.

Se acercó a la chimenea y se plantó delante, extendiendo las manos para calentarse.

–Vaya, lo siento –balbució ella–. ¿Quieres que me vaya y te deje a solas? –inquirió, levantándose del asiento.

Thierry se volvió y la agarró por la muñeca para detenerla cuando estaba a punto de marcharse.

–No, no quiero que te vayas.

Mila no estaba segura de qué pasó después, pero de pronto se encontró pegada al cuerpo de Thierry y con sus labios sobre los de ella. Era un beso dominante, una expresión de su ira y su frustración, y Mila, que sabía que le sería imposible apartarse de él cuando sus brazos estaban sujetándola con la fuerza de un cepo, hizo lo contrario. Se quedó quieta, con los brazos caídos y los labios inmóviles, sin responder al beso.

No quería sino zafarse de su abrazo y abandonar la habitación, dejarlo a solas con su ira, pero al poco notó que un cambio sobrevenía a Thierry. Al momento sus brazos se aflojaron, dándole la libertad de apartarse, y despegó sus labios de los de ella. Sin embargo, en vez de alejarse de él, Mila se quedó donde estaba, y le hizo frente.

–¿Te sientes mejor ahora? –le espetó en un tono lo más calmado que pudo.

Él la miró avergonzado, y Mila sintió compasión por él.

–Perdóname, Angel, no debería haber hecho eso –murmuró Thierry–. Si quieres irte, no te detendré, y llamaré inmediatamente para que vengan a buscarte.

–Eso no será necesario –respondió ella–. Contrataste mis servicios, y no me marcharé hasta que no haya terminado mi trabajo. Aunque, si eso es lo mejor que sabes hacer… –esbozó una pequeña sonrisa–, parece que no estoy haciendo mi trabajo demasiado bien.

Thierry frunció el ceño, como herido en su pundonor, pero pronto su expresión se tornó humilde.

–Te pido disculpas de nuevo. Quizá podrías darme otra oportunidad para demostrarte cuánto he aprendido contigo.

Antes de que ella pudiera responder, Thierry la atrajo de nuevo hacia sí, esta vez con más suavidad, la tomó por la barbilla para mirarla a los ojos y le preguntó:

–Angel, ¿puedo besarte?

Ella asintió levemente, y esa vez, cuando los labios de Thierry tomaron los suyos, fue con una delicadeza infinita, y la besó de un modo tan sensual que la sangre que corría por sus venas parecía estar propagando calor y deseo por todo su cuerpo. Thierry deslizó la punta de la lengua por la unión entre sus labios, y Mila los abrió, al tiempo que tomaba su rostro entre las manos, y enroscó su lengua con la de él.

Thierry gimió y, cuando deslizó las manos por debajo de su jersey y acarició su piel desnuda, fue como si sus dedos dejaran a su paso un rastro ardiente. Sus labios abandonaron los de ella, y cubrieron con pequeños besos la línea de su mandíbula y la curva de su cuello. Mila se estremeció cuando la besó debajo del lóbulo de la oreja, antes de descender de nuevo por su garganta hacia el cuello en V del jersey.

Sus senos ansiaban sus caricias; sus pezones, tirantes, que los succionase su boca. Thierry cerró las palmas en torno a la parte inferior de sus pechos, y antes de que se diese cuenta le había desabrochado el sujetador y estaba masajeándoselos mientras le frotaba los pezones con las yemas de los pulgares.

Mila jadeó extasiada. Le temblaban las piernas, y en la unión entre sus muslos notaba un calor húmedo y una tensión que sabía que solo Thierry podría aliviar. Al arquear las caderas hacia él, notó la presión de su miembro erecto, y quitó las manos de sus anchos hombros para deslizarlas por su pecho y tirar de la camisa para sacársela de los vaqueros.

Cuando finalmente pudo sentir su piel, suave como el satén, notó un cosquilleo en las yemas de los dedos al encontrar el vello que asomaba por encima de la cinturilla de los pantalones. Se dispuso a desabrocharle el cinturón, guiada más por el instinto y el deseo que por la experiencia, pero antes de que pudiera hacerlo, él la agarró por las muñecas y le besó primero una mano y luego otra antes de soltarlas.

Mila, que estaba temblando de deseo y se había quedado sin habla, fue incapaz de hacer ninguna objeción cuando Thierry volvió a meter las manos en su jersey para abrocharle otra vez el sujetador. Cuando terminó, la atrajo de nuevo hacia sí, abrazándola con ternura.

Así, con la cabeza apoyada en su pecho, podía oír los rápidos latidos de su corazón y también su respiración, entrecortada como la suya. Thierry la besó en la cabeza y se apartó de ella.

Durante unos segundos que se le hicieron eternos, se quedaron mirándose el uno al otro. Mila no sabía qué esperaba que hiciese o dijese. Solo sabía que no había querido que aquello terminara tan pronto, y que el deseo que estaba consumiéndola no era nada comparado con el poder que Thierry ejercía sobre ella.

Aquel beso era una demostración de lo que su relación podría haber sido si hubiese permitido que se desarrollase de manera natural. Pero en vez de eso, por su descabellado plan, ahora Thierry creía que era otra persona, distinta de quien era en realidad. ¿Cómo podía esperar que confiara en ella cuando descubriera su identidad, después de lo que había estado haciendo?

Había creído que el fin justificaba los medios, pero ahora se daba cuenta de que había estado muy equivocada. Thierry le había dicho que la fidelidad en una pareja lo era todo para él. ¿Y no era la sinceridad complementaria a la fidelidad? Reprimió un sollozo y se recordó que en ese momento no era ella, la princesa Mila, sino una cortesana, una mujer experimentada en los placeres del sexo.

Buscó apresuradamente las palabras adecuadas, que disimularan lo agitada que estaba en ese momento. Esbozó una sonrisa trémula, inspiró, y le dijo:

–Si piensas besar así a tu prometida, estoy segura de que no tendrá ninguna queja. Ha sido…

–Peligroso –la interrumpió Thierry, dando un paso atrás y pasándose una mano por el corto cabello–. Cuando estoy cerca de ti soy incapaz de controlarme. No me esperaba esto. Sé que no debería desearte como te deseo, pero no puedo evitarlo.

Capítulo Trece

Thierry había estado dando vueltas por la cabaña como un tigre inquieto, incapaz de concentrarse en nada. Angel llevaba toda la tarde en la cocina, de donde no había salido para nada, aunque después de lo ocurrido en la biblioteca no podía culparla porque estuviera evitándolo.

De la cocina salían unos olores deliciosos, pero, a pesar de que sentía curiosidad por saber qué estaba preparando, había decidido que no sería buena idea ir allí. No, no era buena idea sentarse a mirar a Angel mientras cocinaba, porque sería una estampa demasiado hogareña, que le haría ansiar aún más algo que jamás podría tener.

Ya estaba anocheciendo, y estaba sentado en el salón, mirando el fuego e intentando controlar su mal humor, que había empeorado desde aquella mañana. Movió los hombros en círculos, gruñendo al notar lo tensos que tenía los músculos, y oyó entrar a Angel.

–Hawk, ¿quieres cenar? Ya tengo la mesa lista.

–Vaya, estás hecha toda un ama de casa, ¿eh? –comentó Thierry levantándose, y deseó no haber dicho eso al ver a Angel fruncir el ceño, ofendida–. Perdona, ha sonado un poco machista, ¿no? Gracias por ocuparte de la cena.

Angel se encogió de hombros.

–Tampoco he hecho nada especial; solo he calentado un estofado de carne que había en la nevera y he calentado unos bollos de pan en el horno.

Thierry la siguió a la cocina, donde habían estado haciendo todas las comidas, porque a los dos les parecía demasiado grande y frío el comedor. Y, aunque hicieran una comida sencilla, se había fijado en que Angel siempre ponía un jarroncito con flores frescas, el mantel y las servilletas de lino, y para cenar incluso velas.

Sin embargo, esa noche, a pesar del agradable ambiente que había creado, la conversación fue bastante forzada porque la tensión de aquella mañana seguía palpable entre los dos como una barrera invisible. Cuando terminaron de comer, Angel se levantó y empezó a recoger la mesa, pero él la detuvo.

–Deja eso –le pidió.

Ella, que estaba apilando los platos, lo miró contrariada.

–Solo iba a enjuagar los platos. ¿Vas a recoger tú?

Thierry se encontró devorándola con la mirada. El sensual vestido rojo de seda que llevaba le quedaba como un guante. La parte de delante era recatada, pero con cada movimiento la fina tela insinuaba de un modo delicioso las curvas de su cuerpo. Y, cuando se dio la vuelta para llevar los platos al fregadero, vio que el vestido dejaba parte de la espalda al descubierto, y se encontró fantaseando con recorrer beso a beso cada centímetro de su columna.

–¿Hawk? –lo llamó Angel girándose.

Thierry se dio cuenta de que estaba esperando una respuesta a su pregunta.

–Sí, ya lo haré mañana –contestó impaciente, levantándose–. Ven conmigo –le dijo tendiéndole la mano–. Hay algo que quiero enseñarte.

Angel parpadeó, pero tomó su mano, confiada, y le siguió.

–¿Adónde me llevas? –le preguntó mientras cruzaban el salón.

–A mi santuario –respondió él con una sonrisa enigmática, conduciéndola por el pasillo de la izquierda.

–Eso suena intrigante.

–Muy poca gente ha estado en el lugar al que te llevo, y jamás sin mi permiso. Es un sitio donde voy cuando quiero estar a solas.

Thierry se sacó un llavero del bolsillo, abrió el enorme portón de madera al final del pasillo y descendieron por una escalera de caracol.

–¿No me llevarás a las mazmorras, verdad? –bromeó Angel.

–No –contestó él riéndose–. Es más como… un tesoro escondido.

Accionó un interruptor en la pared y se encendieron unos discretos puntos de suave luz, colocados estratégicamente por la gruta. Bajaron los escalones de piedra, y sonrió al oír a Angel exclamar maravillada cuando vio la enorme piscina natural, cuyas aguas relucían en la penumbra. Sacó un mechero del bolsillo y fue encendiendo las velas que había aquí y allá.

Angel se acercó a la orilla y se agachó para meter la mano en las oscuras aguas.

–¡Está caliente! –exclamó–. No puedo creer que te hayas construido una piscina climatizada bajo tierra.

–No es una obra hecha por manos humanas, sino

de ese gran arquitecto que es la naturaleza –respondió Thierry–. El agua viene de un manantial de aguas termales y lleva siglos aquí.

Angel miró a su alrededor, inspiró profundamente y exhaló un largo suspiro.

–Es precioso; este sitio es mágico.

–Pensé que a lo mejor te apetecía darte un baño. Es una manera estupenda de relajarse. Sobre todo después de un mal día.

–Me encantaría. Voy a subir a por un bañador…

–No hace falta; te dejaré a solas para que disfrutes del agua el tiempo que quieras.

Angel ladeó la cabeza.

–¿Y tú no tienes ganas de darte un baño? Me parece que hoy tú tampoco has tenido muy buen día.

–¿Quieres que nos bañemos juntos?

Angel asintió.

–Creo que podría ser una lección interesante, ¿no?

Más bien un tormento, pensó él.

–¿Y qué aprenderé con esta lección?

–Pues… aumentará tu disfrute de los placeres sensoriales, de la combinación de la estimulación visual y la sensación del agua acariciando tu cuerpo. No tenemos por qué tocarnos, Hawk. Tú pones los límites, y yo los respetaré.

Decía que ella los respetaría, pero… ¿podría hacerlo él también? La observó mientras se llevaba las manos a la espalda para bajar la cremallera del vestido, que fue cayendo, dejando al descubierto un sujetador semitransparente de encaje.

El miembro de Thierry se puso duro al instante. No podía haber tenido una idea más estúpida. Debería haberse marchado, haberla dejado sola, pero era como si sus pies se hubieran quedado pegados al suelo, y se encontró allí plantado, observando cómo el vestido caía a sus pies.

Se le secó la boca al recorrerla con la mirada: sus pechos voluptuosos, la fina cintura, las sensuales caderas, los muslos... Tenía un cuerpo hecho para el pecado, para el placer.

Angel se desabrochó el sujetador y se lo quitó, liberando sus magníficos pechos. Los ojos de Thierry se posaron en los pezones sonrosados, y tragó saliva al ver que estaban erectos. Apretó los puños, haciendo un esfuerzo por contenerse, y notó cómo se le tensaban los músculos de los brazos.

Estaba ardiendo por dentro. Sabía que debería irse, pero era incapaz de moverse. Se moría por tocarla, por besarla... Angel enganchó los pulgares en la cinturilla de las braguitas y se las bajó.

–¿Vas a quedarte ahí plantado? –le preguntó.

Su voz sonaba aterciopelada, sensual, pero también algo trémula, y eso sorprendió a Thierry. Debía estar más que acostumbrada a las miradas lascivas de los hombres, y sin embargo, parecía nerviosa, y había un suave rubor en sus mejillas.

–Ahora voy –dijo él, con la garganta contraída por el deseo.

–Como quieras –contestó ella, esbozando una breve sonrisa.

Se dio la vuelta, y Thierry admiró cautivado su espalda y la forma de sus nalgas. La siguió con la mirada mientras descendía por la pequeña escalinata que se adentraba en la piscina, y cómo se iba sumergiendo.

Conocía muy bien la sensación de esas aguas calientes contra la piel desnuda, cómo acariciaba, de un modo tentador, esas partes del cuerpo que normalmente ocultaba la ropa.

–Esto es divino –comentó Angel, nadando de espaldas.

Desde su llegada, Thierry había estado luchando consigo mismo, pero en ese momento, por primera vez en su vida, fue incapaz de seguir reprimiéndose, y antes de que se diera cuenta se había quitado toda la ropa. Se metió en el agua y se deslizó hasta Angel, que se había sentado en el borde de la piscina con las piernas colgando dentro del agua.

Emergió entre sus muslos, le rodeó la cintura con los brazos y tomó sus labios casi con desesperación. Angel respondió al beso y gimió suavemente mientras le rodeaba el cuello con los brazos.

Thierry exploró con la lengua cada rincón de su boca con la sensación de que jamás quedaría saciado de su sed de ella. Tomó sus pechos en las manos y los masajeó suavemente, pellizcándole de cuando en cuando los pezones, mientras el cuerpo cálido y mojado de Angel se retorcía entre gemidos contra él.

Inclinó la cabeza para tomar un pezón en su boca. Dibujó círculos en torno a él con la lengua, y cuando lo mordisqueó suavemente, Angel se estremeció.

¿Cómo había podido negarse aquellos placeres durante tanto tiempo?, se preguntó. ¿Y cómo podría parar ahora que había dado rienda suelta a su deseo? Era como si se hubiesen abierto las compuertas de una presa y el agua estuviese saliendo a raudales.

Pero esas dudas abandonaron su mente en el momento en que Angel empezó a rastrillar su cabello con los dedos, sujetándole la cabeza contra su pecho mientras él le lamía los pezones y los succionaba.

Angel arqueaba las caderas contra las suyas, restregando sus pliegues, húmedos y ardientes, contra su miembro erecto. Y, aunque no lo hubiera creído posible, se le puso aún más grande.

Deslizó las manos lentamente por su cuerpo, la agarró por las nalgas y al atraerla más hacia sí gimió de placer.

–Eres un tormento, una seductora… –murmuró contra su garganta, antes de darle un pequeño mordisco.

–Y tú eres todo lo que siempre había deseado… –suspiró Angel.

Con las manos en sus nalgas, Thierry la hizo inclinarse un poco hacia delante hasta que la punta de su pene rozó su abertura. Angel movió un poco las caderas, y su miembro se deslizó parcialmente dentro de ella, haciendo que los dos jadearan extasiados.

Thierry no podía parar. Estaba tembloroso, y la respiración entrecortada de Angel y el increíble calor que se estaba generando en el lugar donde se unían sus cuerpos lo excitaba aún más. Empujó las caderas, pero en vez de hundirse por completo dentro de ella, se topó con algo que se lo impedía. Al principio no entendía qué pasaba, pero, al volver a intentarlo y fallar, de pronto comprendió: Angel era virgen…

Capítulo Catorce

–Por favor, no pares… –lo instó Mila.

Excitada por las increíbles sensaciones que estaba experimentando, se aferró a los hombros de Thierry, clavándole las uñas en la piel, pero de pronto notó que estaba apartándose.

–¿Qué ocurre? –le preguntó.

–Eres… eres virgen –dijo Thierry, como si no pudiese creer lo que estaba diciendo.

–Pues igual que tú, ¿no?

Lo miró a los ojos, esperando una respuesta, pero Thierry seguía aturdido.

–¿No te parece que así es más dulce? –le preguntó Mila, deslizando las manos por su cuerpo y rodeándole la cintura con los brazos, para atraerlo de nuevo hacia sí.

Notaba que los músculos de su vagina se estaban acomodando a la intrusión de su miembro, y le entraron ganas de arquear las caderas para que se hundiera más en ella. Besó a Thierry, simulando con la lengua lo que quería que siguiera haciendo y le susurró:

–Tócame… Ahí abajo, con los dedos… Tócame por dentro…

Thierry hizo lo que le pedía, y Mila vio cómo se le dilataron las pupilas cuando sus dedos tocaron la parte más íntima de su cuerpo. Cuando sus nudillos le rozaron el clítoris, se le escapó un gemido ahogado.

–Sí… Justo ahí…

–¿Así? –inquirió él, repitiendo aquella caricia.

–Sí… ah… sí…

Las oleadas de placer que habían comenzado a tomar posesión de ella se intensificaban con cada caricia, y se encontró moviendo las caderas en pequeños círculos, instándolo a seguir sus movimientos con la mano. Thierry aprendía rápido, y pronto los músculos de su vagina empezaron a contraerse y distenderse, en una muda invitación a hundirse más en ella, a romper la barrera que los separaba.

Y entonces, de repente, por fin aquella barrera desapareció, y Mila se encontró cabalgando una ola de placer tan intensa que se quedó sin aliento, extendiéndose por sus extremidades. Echó la cabeza hacia atrás y cuando gritó su nombre el eco lo repitió.

Thierry movía las caderas cada vez más deprisa, haciendo que el agua los salpicase, hasta que también él alcanzó el clímax, con los músculos de la espalda completamente tensos.

–¡Angel! –gimió contra su garganta, hundiéndose una última vez en ella–. ¡Te quiero!

Se derrumbó contra ella, y permanecieron un buen rato así, abrazados el uno al otro entre jadeos.

Cuando Mila sintió que estaba apartándose de ella, le rodeó la cintura con las manos y en un tono juguetón le preguntó:

–¿Tienes prisa por ir a alguna parte?

Pero él permaneció callado, y cuando la miró, con el rostro contraído, parecía, a juzgar por su expresión, que estaba empezando a arrepentirse.

–¿Hawk? –lo llamó ella–. ¿Estás bien?

–No –replicó él con fiereza, apartándose de ella–. No estoy bien. No deberíamos haber hecho esto. He sucumbido por culpa de mi debilidad a pesar de estar prometido a otra mujer. He destruido lo que para mí era más sagrado, lo que estaba esperando a compartir con ella.

Su voz destilaba tanto desprecio por sí mismo que Mila no podía soportarlo.

–Pero… –comenzó a decirle.

–No hay peros que valgan –la cortó él con firmeza–. ¿Es que no lo comprendes? Al hacerte el amor, me he convertido justo en lo que no quería ser. ¿Cómo voy a casarme ahora con la mujer con la que estoy prometido cuando es a ti a quien amo? Si hiciera eso convertiría todo en lo que creo, todo lo que soy, en una mentira.

Mila se quedó donde estaba, aturdida y muda mientras sus palabras, cargadas de dolor, atormentadas, resonaban en el eco de la cueva. Thierry cruzó la piscina y salió del agua.

–¡Hawk! ¡Espera, por favor! –le suplicó, yendo tras él–. Yo también te quiero…

Thierry se volvió hacia ella y sacudió la cabeza.

–Eso solo empeora las cosas. Soy rey. No puedo amarte ni aceptar tu amor. Toda esta situación es imposible, y sabiendo lo que sentía por ti debería haberte dicho que te marcharas el mismo día en que llegaste aquí, pero no lo hice.

Con un gruñido de irritación, sacó un par de toallas de un armario discretamente escondido en el muro de roca. Le lanzó una a ella, y se lio la otra alrededor de la cintura.

–Mañana te irás –le dijo–. Y yo no iré a despedirte.

La mente de Mila era un hervidero de pensamientos. Era como si de repente todo estuviera yendo cuesta abajo. Había conseguido lo que se había propuesto en un principio, que Thierry la amara, pero aun así todo se estaba desmoronando. Salvo que... Salvo que Thierry no sabía quién era en realidad.

–Tenemos que hablar –le imploró, desesperada por conseguir que la escuchara.

–No. Ya hemos hablado bastante y no hay nada más que decir. La culpa de lo que ha pasado es solo mía.

–Pero es que yo...

–¡Basta! –casi rugió Thierry–. He traicionado todo aquello en lo que creía, y ahora tendré que vivir con lo que he hecho. He tomado una decisión y no voy a volverme atrás: mañana a primera hora habrá un coche esperándote.

Y antes de que Mila pudiera decir nada más, se marchó. ¿Qué había querido decir con eso de que tendría que vivir con lo que había hecho? ¿Es que pensaba cancelar la boda? ¿Lo había echado todo a perder?

Thierry andaba paseándose arriba y abajo por la biblioteca. Había sido incapaz de conciliar el sueño porque no podía dejar de imaginarse a Angel desnuda junto a él, en la cama. Su cuerpo le decía que era un idiota, que en vez de haber abandonado la gruta, dejándola allí, debería habérsela llevado allí, al dormitorio, y haber aprovechado lo que ella le había ofrecido sin reservas. Podrían haber hecho el amor hasta que se hubiesen quedado dormidos de puro cansancio. Total, si no podía recuperar su virginidad, ¿por qué perder el tiempo lamentándose, cuando podría haber estado disfrutando de su libertad antes de convertirse en un hombre casado?

Y, si hubiera sido otra clase de hombre lo habría hecho, pero no lo era. El reloj dio la media. Pronto empezaría a salir el sol, comenzaría un nuevo día… y él aún no había tomado una decisión sobre qué hacer.

Ante todo estaba su compromiso con la princesa Mila. No le faltaría al respeto ni le sería infiel como su padre había hecho con su madre, pero sabía que jamás podría amarla como merecía. No cuando su corazón pertenecía a otra mujer.

Una media hora después empezó a oír movimiento. Se había puesto en contacto con Pasquale y, aunque no ansiaba en lo más mínimo tener compañía, le había dado instrucciones de que volvieran algunos miembros del servicio. Por la ventana vio llegar un coche y detenerse frente a la casa: el coche que se llevaría a Angel lejos de allí, lejos de él, para siempre. La sola idea le desgarraba el corazón. Tener que apartarla de él era lo más difícil que había tenido que hacer jamás, pero tenía que hacerlo.

Un ruido detrás de él lo hizo volverse. Era Angel, y parecía que había dormido tan poco como él. Estaba ojerosa, y tenía la mirada sombría.

—Ya está aquí tu coche –le dijo.

—Hawk, necesito hablar contigo. Hay algo importante que debo decirte antes de irme.

Hasta su voz sonaba apagada, cansada. Deseó poder aliviar su pena; tal vez debería darle la oportunidad de hablar, dejarle decir lo que quisiera.

—Adelante; habla.

Angel inspiró.

–Sé que estás debatiéndote contigo mismo por lo que hicimos anoche –comenzó a decirle–, pero quiero que sepas que todo irá bien.

–¿Que todo irá bien? –repitió él con una risotada de incredulidad–. ¿Cómo puedes decir eso? He traicionado todo en lo que creía.

–Sé que ahora te cuesta entenderlo, pero yo te quiero, Hawk. Tienes que creerlo.

Thierry sintió que la emoción lo embargaba, pero se negó a dejar que esa emoción ahogara la racionalidad que tan desesperadamente necesitaba en ese momento.

–Eso no cambia nada –dijo con aspereza–. Eres una cortesana, y yo un rey. Peor: soy un hombre comprometido con otra mujer.

–Lo sé, y no debes dejar que lo que hemos hecho impida tu matrimonio con la princesa. Debes seguir adelante con la boda.

–¿Que debo seguir adelante? ¿Quién te crees que eres para decirme lo que tengo que hacer? –le espetó él, refugiándose en la creciente ira que se estaba apoderando de él.

Estaba furioso consigo mismo, por una situación a la que había dado pie con su debilidad.

Por un segundo le pareció ver dolor en los ojos de Angel, pero luego su expresión cambió. Se tornó menos vulnerable, como si hubiese colocado una máscara sobre su bello rostro. Irguió los hombros, levantó la barbilla, y le dijo:

–Soy la princesa Mila Angelina de Erminia.

Thierry se sintió como si le hubiese caído encima una avalancha.

–Cuidado con lo que dices, Angel –le advirtió frunciendo el ceño–. Hay leyes muy severas contra quienes tratan de suplantar a otra persona.

–No te estoy mintiendo. Ya no.

Thierry apretó los labios.

–Será mejor que te expliques.

–Estaba en la universidad, en Boston, cuando vi en las noticias que hablaban de tu visita oficial a Nueva York. Habían pasado siete años desde el día en que nos conocimos, y solo faltaban unas semanas para nuestra boda, así que no pude resistirme a intentar ponerme en contacto contigo. Cuando nos encontramos en Nueva York, no fue por casualidad... bueno, no exactamente. Había ido a tu hotel con la esperanza de poder aunque fuera charlar un rato contigo, conocernos un poco mejor antes de la boda, pero me faltó valor. Estaba a punto de irme cuando te chocaste conmigo.

–Pero no te pareces en nada a...

Thierry no se atrevió a terminar la frase. ¿Cómo le decía uno a una mujer que de adolescente no había sido nada atractiva?

–¿A cuando tenía dieciocho años? No; he crecido. Cuando nos chocamos en la calle y no me reconociste me dolió, pero luego pensé que podía ser una buena oportunidad para conocer al verdadero Thierry.

–¿Y cuando te dejé en tu hotel?, ¿por qué no me dijiste entonces quién eras?

–Yo... no lo sé –admitió ella, bajando la vista–. El día que nos conocimos, hace años, pusiste tal cara de espanto al verme, que me quedé bastante acomplejada. En cambio, en Nueva York, haciéndome pasar por una chica cualquiera, me mirabas de un modo completamente distinto, y supongo que me daba miedo que dejaras de mirarme así cuando supieses que era yo.

Thierry se sonrojó, avergonzado. No podía negar que se había quedado espantado al conocer a su prometida, pero desde ese momento, se había comprometido con ella al cien por cien con su relación… bueno, hasta la noche anterior, cuando había acabado sucumbiendo al deseo. De pronto pensó en algo que todavía no le había quedado claro.

–¿Y qué hay de Ottavia Romolo, la mujer a la que contraté? –le preguntó–. ¿También formaba parte de todo esto? ¿No irá a chantajearme con…?

–¡No! –lo interrumpió ella–. No, nada de eso.

–¿Y entonces? –insistió él.

–Ella… está… está retenida en Erminia.

–¿Retenida? –Thierry apretó los puños y frunció el ceño–. ¿Qué significa eso? ¿La tienes retenida en algún sitio contra su voluntad?

Mila dejó caer la cabeza y, aunque no contestó, era evidente que no se equivocaba.

–¿Por qué? ¿Por qué has puesto en riesgo tu reputación… y la mía de esta forma? ¿Qué te hizo llegar hasta estos extremos, hasta el punto de mentirme? ¿No te das cuenta de lo que puede pasar si esto llega a saberse?

–Sentí que no me quedaba otra salida… –replicó ella– cuando me enteré de que mi prometido había contratado los servicios de una cortesana a solo unas semanas de nuestra boda –le espetó Mila, con una chispa de ira en la mirada–. Todos estos años me he esforzado para intentar convertirme en alguien a quien pudieras desear, a quien pudieras considerar digna de ti… Y voy y me entero de que has pagado los servicios de una mujer para meterla en tu cama… –miró hacia otro lado y bajó la vista–. No podía soportarlo. Por eso ocupé su lugar y me hice pasar por ella –cuando levantó la cabeza para mirarlo, había lágrimas en sus ojos–. Yo solo quería que me amaras…

El dolor en su voz, en su rostro, en sus ojos, hizo que se le encogiera el estómago. ¿Amor? ¿Había hecho todo aquello por amor? Cerró los ojos un momento e inspiró, en un intento por calmarse. Sabía que el amor no era algo que durase, sobre todo no en el caso de personas como él. Exhaló un suspiro y le dijo:

–No… no sé qué pensar. Me siento muy confundido.

–¿Por qué? ¿No soluciona esto las cosas? Tú me quieres, tú mismo lo dijiste, y yo también te quiero a ti. Puedes dejar a un lado tu sentimiento de culpa. Soy tu prometida; no me has traicionado. Podemos dejar esto atrás –le imploró.

–¿Eso crees?

Una parte de él querría que sus vidas pudiesen ser así de simples, pero sabía que era imposible. No eran como los demás, y su vida no era normal, sino una mezcla de lo que se esperaba de ellos, de innumerables normas de protocolo y situaciones sobre las que no tenían ningún control. Y aún estaba la cuestión del rocambolesco engaño al que lo había sometido.

–¿Sabes?, no puedo evitar preguntarme, después de lo que has hecho, por qué habría de creer una sola de tus palabras. Si hasta ahora me has mentido, ¿quién sabe qué otras mentiras puede que estés intentando hacerme tragar? Tal vez mientes cuando dices que me amas. Tal vez mientas en nuestra boda, cuando prometas amarme y respetarme. No puedo evitar preguntarme cómo voy a confiar en ti –se armó de valor, y añadió–: Y me respondo a mí mismo que no puedo; no puedo confiar en ti.

Mila dejó caer los hombros, y vio en sus ojos cómo se resquebrajaba y se desvanecía la esperanza, antes de que empezaran a rodar por sus mejillas las lágrimas que había estado conteniendo. Habría querido dar un paso hacia ella, abrazarla y asegurarle que todo se arreglaría, pero era imposible. Le había dicho lo que sentía por ella, más de una vez, y le había dicho lo importante que era la sinceridad para él. Y, aun así, había seguido mintiéndole.

–Márchate –le dijo.

–¡No! ¡Hawk…!

Mila dio un paso adelante, extendiendo sus manos hacia él, implorándole con aquel gesto y con la expresión de su rostro que no la apartara de él.

Aquello fue lo más difícil y doloroso que había hecho jamás, pero le dio la espalda, y no se movió cuando la oyó salir de la biblioteca con pasos pesarosos, ni cuando oyó cerrarse la puerta tras ella. A los pocos minutos la vio a través de la ventana, saliendo de la cabaña. Vaciló un momento cuando el chófer le sostuvo la puerta del coche para que subiera, y la observó con los labios apretados, diciéndose que había hecho lo correcto, aunque por dentro se sentía como si se le estuviese desgarrando el corazón.

A lo largo del día siguiente Thierry tuvo que luchar con su conciencia, contra el impulso de ir tras Mila y llevarla de vuelta a su lado, donde sentía que debía estar.

Había tomado la decisión de que llamaría a su hermano, el rey Rocco, y pediría reunirse con él para comunicarle que quería que se pospusiera la boda, pero aún no lo había hecho.

A la mañana del segundo día tras la marcha de Mila, estaba leyendo el periódico durante el desayuno cuando vio un titular en el interior que decía que él, el heredero al trono de Sylvain, había estado con otra mujer semanas antes de su boda. Párrafo tras párrafo especulaban acerca de la identidad de la desconocida, y de como él se había deshonrado a ojos de sus súbditos, faltando a su compromiso con la princesa de Erminia.

El estómago se le revolvió al leer todo aquello. A pesar de todas las precauciones que había tomado, de algún modo los medios lo habían descubierto. Aquella era la peor de sus pesadillas, un escándalo de proporciones monumentales. El artículo incluía varias fotografías tomadas con teleobjetivo desde algún punto del bosque en las que se los veía a Mila y a él paseando juntos a caballos, de picnic y besándose. Se levantó de la mesa, enfadado, y fue a hacer la maleta para abandonar la cabaña, que había dejado de ser su santuario. Cuando su equipo de seguridad averiguara quién había avisado a los medios, lo pagaría muy caro.

Justo cuando iba subirse al coche que lo llevaría de regreso a la dura realidad de su mundo, en medio, sin duda, de las críticas de su pueblo, apareció Pasquale con otro periódico que acababa de llegar. A Thierry se le erizó la piel al leer el titular de la página que estaba mostrándole: «¡Se desvela que la princesa Mila era la cortesana del rey!».

¿Habría orquestado ella esa noticia, en un intento

por obligarlo a seguir adelante con la boda? ¿Acaso pensaba que su temor a ser desprestigiado públicamente haría que dejase a un lado su enfado porque lo hubiese engañado?

Si era eso lo que pensaba, estaba muy equivocada. Dio media vuelta, entró de nuevo en la cabaña y fue a su estudio donde, por una línea segura, hizo una llamada.

–Rey Rocco –dijo cuando este se puso al aparto–. Lamento informaros de que no puedo seguir adelante con los planes de matrimonio con vuestra hermana. La boda queda cancelada.

Capítulo Quince

Mila se paseaba arriba y abajo por su dormitorio, llena de frustración. En el instante en que había cruzado la frontera, y había visto aparecer al general Andrej Novak, el mando supremo de las Fuerzas Armadas de Erminia, seguido de un guardia de palacio, había sabido que había sido descubierta su estratagema.

La habían llevado de vuelta a palacio, y desde ese momento había estado confinada en sus aposentos. No se le permitía hacer ni recibir llamadas, le habían confiscado el portátil, se habían llevado el televisor…

Empezaba a ver de un modo diferente cómo debía haberse sentido Ottavia Romolo durante su secuestro. Aunque según había sabido su cautiverio solo había durado unos días, porque parecía que había conseguido escapar y había informado a su hermano de lo que había planeado. Por eso se había encontrado con aquel «comité de bienvenida» en la frontera.

Mila detestaba esperar, y detestaba no saber qué pasaría cuando la llevasen ante su hermano, pero sobre todo tenía miedo de haber destruido cualquier posibilidad que pudiera tener de ser feliz junto a Thierry. Había sido una idiota.

Debería haber esperado a que estuviesen casados, haber dejado que su relación se desarrollase como lo habría hecho en circunstancias normales. Debería haber confiado en Thierry, aun cuando se había enterado de que había contratado a una cortesana. Debería haber confiado en él, haber creído que jamás haría nada que deshonrara su compromiso con ella.

Y ahí estaba el problema: no había confiado en él y, dejándose llevar por su inseguridad, había organizado aquel plan descabellado, mintiéndole deliberadamente. Por eso, ocurriera lo que ocurriera, sabía que se lo merecía.

Llamaron a la puerta y entró el general Novak.

—Alteza, acompañadme, por favor.

Sin decir nada, y llena de inquietud, lo siguió. Cuando llegaron al despacho de su hermano, el general llamó a la puerta y se la abrió para que pasara.

Mila entró y se inclinó, haciendo una marcada reverencia, y se quedó esperando, como indicaba el protocolo de la corte, a que Rocco le diera permiso para erguirse de nuevo.

—Qué bien que hayas vuelto a casa… —dijo su hermano, sentado tras su escritorio, en un tono gélido—. Levántate, Mila; es tarde para muestras de respeto después de cómo me has abochornado.

Mila se irguió y lo miró, buscando en su rostro algo de compasión, pero no la encontró. Sus ojos relampagueaban de ira, y tenía los labios apretados.

—¿Tienes la menor idea de lo que has hecho? —la increpó. Al ver que permanecía callada, añadió—: Tu impulsividad ha destruido cualquier posibilidad de una unión entre Erminia y Sylvain. El rey Thierry ha cancelado la boda.

Mila sintió una punzada en el pecho.

—¡No! —exclamó aturdida.

Le temblaban las piernas de tal modo que tuvo que agarrarse al respaldo de la silla que tenía a su lado.

–Ahora es imposible que nuestras naciones alcancen una paz estable –sentenció Rocco, levantándose y volviéndose hacia el ventanal.

–Pero… estamos en el siglo XXI –replicó ella–. Tiene que haber algo que podamos hacer.

–¿Hacer? –repitió su hermano, volviéndose hacia ella. Sacudió la cabeza y añadió–: Ya has hecho bastante: has abierto una brecha en nuestra seguridad. Había esperado que tu matrimonio nos diera la suficiente estabilidad como para que el problema se volviese irrelevante y no tuvieses que saberlo, pero…

–¿Saber el qué? –inquirió ella, frunciendo el ceño–. ¿Qué has estado ocultándome, y por qué?

–Antes de tu compromiso me informaron de ciertos rumores acerca de una amenaza contra mí que también podría repercutir en ti. Hemos tomado las medidas necesarias para erradicar ese riesgo, y creíamos que lo teníamos bajo control, pero antes de que regresaras esa amenaza se ha convertido en un peligro real.

El miedo hizo que a Mila se le secase la garganta.

–¿A qué te refieres?, ¿qué clase de amenaza?

–Al principio pensamos que podría tratarse de un ataque directo contra mí, pero parece que el auténtico objetivo es poner en cuestión mi derecho a ocupar el trono.

–¿Cómo? Pero si eres el primogénito, y el único hijo varón de nuestro padre.

–Soy el primogénito, y el único hijo varón legítimo de nuestro padre –la corrigió Rocco.

Mila se quedó paralizada.

–¿Tuvo… otro hijo?

Estaba tan agitada que ya no podía mantenerse en pie, y se dejó caer en la silla.

–Eso parece.

–¿Quién?

–Ese es el problema, que aún no lo sé. Pero lo averiguaré –dijo Rocco con decisión.

–Pero, aunque sea así y nuestro padre tuviera otro hijo, si es un hijo ilegítimo no puede reclamar el trono.

Rocco soltó una risa amarga.

–Eso creía yo también. Pero según parece hay una antigua ley, que aún está en vigencia, según la cual, a menos que haya contraído matrimonio antes de los treinta y cinco años y tenga un heredero legítimo, no podré seguir siendo rey.

–Bueno, eso tiene fácil solución, ¿no? No tienes más que casarte y tener un hijo. O conseguir que se revoque esa ley.

–Ya están preparándome una lista de posibles candidatas a convertirse en mi consorte –le explicó su hermano–, pero es esencial que actuemos con rapidez, así que, entretanto, estamos intentando que el parlamento revoque la ley. Sin embargo, esto ha generado toda una serie de nuevos problemas: ese otro aspirante al trono tiene sus partidarios, y parece que han estado avivando calladamente las llamas de la subversión.

–Dios mío… –murmuró Mila–. ¿Y qué vas a hacer?

–Seguir intentando desenmascarar a quien está detrás de esto antes de que sea demasiado tarde y acabe desatándose una guerra civil. Entretanto, necesitamos a todos los aliados que podamos conseguir, y por eso contaba con que tu boda con el rey de Sylvain, ahora cancelada, pudiera ayudarnos.

–Yo… Yo… –Mila estaba temblando y no sabía qué decir. De nada serviría una disculpa en ese momento–. ¿Hay algo que yo pueda hacer?

Su hermano rodeó la mesa, se acuclilló frente a ella y tomó sus manos.

–Necesito que vuelvas a Sylvain y hagas que el rey Thierry cambie de opinión. Puede que tu enlace con él sea lo único que podría salvar a Erminia.

A través de la ventanilla del helicóptero Mila observaba el paisaje nocturno mientras dejaban atrás la frontera iluminada de Erminia. Más allá se extendía Sylvain, donde le esperaba la que sería sin duda la tarea más difícil de su vida. ¿Cómo se convencía a un hombre, cuya confianza habías traicionado, de que te diera otra oportunidad?

–Aterrizaremos dentro unos minutos, alteza –oyó anunciar al piloto por los auriculares.

Esas palabras aliviaron a Mila, a quien siempre le había dado miedo volar.

–Gracias.

Cuando poco después empezaron a descender, el estómago le dio un vuelco.

–¿Estáis bien, alteza? –le preguntó el general Novak, que iba sentado a su lado.

Mila, que se había aferrado al reposabrazos de su asiento, giró la cabeza hacia él y asintió.

El general era un hombre joven, que aún no había cumplido los cuarenta, pero a ella siempre le había parecido muy serio, y su expresión severa la incomodaba.

No entendía por qué su hermano había insistido en

que la acompañara. Sobre todo teniendo en cuenta que era una reunión que pretendían que se llevase a cabo con la mayor discreción posible. Esperaba que al menos la dejase a solas con Thierry para que pudieran hablar.

Cuando por fin aterrizaron en el helipuerto del palacio de Sylvain, había un coche esperando. El general salió del aparato y la ayudó a bajar. Un hombre salió del vehículo y fue hacia ellos. Le hizo una reverencia a Mila y se presentó:

–Soy Pasquale de Luca, alteza, el secretario de su majestad el rey Thierry. Por favor, acompañadme.

–Gracias, señor De Luca.

Cuando el general Novak hizo ademán de ir con ellos, el secretario se detuvo abruptamente.

–Lo siento, general, pero su majestad me ha dado instrucciones precisas: solo la princesa puede subir al coche.

–Y las instrucciones que me dio a mí nuestro rey también fueron muy precisas –respondió Novak–: soy responsable de la princesa.

–Lo siento, pero su majestad solo verá a la princesa –insistió Pasquale.

–No pasa nada, general –dijo Mila, poniéndole una mano en el hombro a Novak–. Estaré bien.

El militar se quedó mirándola con el ceño fruncido antes de asentir brevemente y dar un paso atrás.

–Como deseéis, alteza.

Era evidente que no le hacía mucha gracia dejarla ir sola, pero Mila se sintió aliviada de que hubiese claudicado.

–Lléveme con su rey, señor De Luca –le pidió a Pasquale.

Cuando llegaron al coche, el secretario abrió la puerta trasera y la sostuvo para que entrara. Mila le dio las gracias con una sonrisa y subió al coche, pero como el interior del vehículo estaba en penumbra, no fue hasta que la puerta se cerró tras ella y se pusieron en marcha cuando se dio cuenta de que no estaba sola.

–¡Thierry! –exclamó sobresaltada al verlo.

–Querías verme –le dijo él–. Y aquí estoy.

No había la menor calidez en su voz, y su mirada era fría como el acero.

–Esperaba que tuviéramos esta reunión en palacio –respondió ella, alisando nerviosa la falda del vestido.

–No tienes derecho a esperar nada de mí.

–Lo sé –murmuró ella–. Lo siento; siento muchísimo lo que hice. ¿Podrás perdonarme? ¿Querrás darme… darnos otra oportunidad?

Thierry fijó la mirada en el cristal tintado que los separaba del chófer para darles más privacidad.

–¿Otra oportunidad, dices? No, yo no creo en las segundas oportunidades.

–Pero yo te quiero, y sé que tú me quieres a mí. Me dijiste que me querías. ¿Acaso me mentiste?

–No, no te mentí, pero solo con el amor no basta. Sabes, por las confidencias que te hice, qué es lo más importante para mí. ¿Lo recuerdas?

Mila tragó saliva.

–La sinceridad y la confianza –murmuró.

–Sí, la sinceridad y la confianza. Yo confiaba en ti, pero tu no fuiste sincera conmigo, a pesar de que tuviste sobradas ocasiones para contarme la verdad –le dijo Thierry, volviéndose hacia ella.

Mila no sabía cómo contestar a eso.

–Por nuestra posición, ninguno de los dos tuvimos una infancia ni una adolescencia fáciles. Y no hemos tenido en nuestros padres un ejemplo de lo que es el amor, pero es algo que los dos valoramos por encima de todo lo demás. Yo haría cualquier cosa por amor, y lo hice. Desde el día en que nos conocimos supe que me había enamorado de ti, pero me veía fea, torpe, no sabía nada del mundo… Creía que jamás podrías amar a alguien como yo, y por eso me pasé siete años intentando mejorar, convertirme en alguien de quien tú también pudieras llegar a enamorarte. Y cuando me enteré de que habías contratado a esa mujer se me partió el corazón. Yo… me había esforzado tanto… y pensé que tú habías decidido buscar en otra mujer lo que creías que yo no podría darte. Sé que lo que hice no estuvo bien, que fue estúpido, y hasta imprudente, pero volvería a hacerlo –alargó el brazo y puso su mano sobre la de él–. Quería llegar a tu corazón y comprenderte, no quería que nuestra unión fuese solo algo de cara a la galería. Quería un marido que me amara y que quisiera estar junto a mí. Me siento fatal por haberte engañado, pero mentiría si dijera que lamento esos días que pasamos juntos. Lo eres todo para mí. Por favor… créeme.

Por un momento creyó que podría haber resquebrajado la coraza de fría indiferencia de Thierry, pero cuando él apartó su mano, comprendió que no.

–No te creo. ¿Sabes qué lamento yo? Lamento haber confiado en alguien capaz de hacer lo que sea para conseguir lo que quiere, alguien a quien no le importan las consecuencias. Eres igual que mi madre.

Mila sintió cada palabra como un hachazo.

–Durante los últimos siete años solo ha habido una

mujer en mi vida: tú –continuó Thierry–. No sabía nada de ti, pero estaba dispuesto a esforzarme por conocerte cuando nos casáramos. Quería descubrir qué cosas te hacían feliz y cuáles te ponían triste. Qué cosas te daban esperanzas y qué cosas te enfadaban. Qué cosas te divertían y cuáles te aburrían. Quería compartir mi vida contigo, pero no me imagino cómo podría hacerlo ahora que has destruido con tus mentiras cualquier futuro que hubiéramos podido tener juntos. Sencillamente no puedo casarme con una mujer en la que no confío.

Thierry se inclinó hacia delante y pulsó el botón del intercomunicador.

–Llévenos de vuelta al helipuerto –le dijo al chófer–. La princesa está lista para volver a Erminia.

–No, por favor… –le pidió Mila con voz trémula–. Te lo ruego, reconsidera tu decisión. Podemos retrasar la boda. Tómate todo el tiempo que necesites hasta que sientas que puedes volver a confiar en mí. Dame otra oportunidad, por favor.

–No voy a cambiar de opinión –contestó él con aspereza, cuando el coche se detuvo en el helipuerto.

Mila se quedó mirándolo con el corazón en un puño.

–¿Tanto te cuesta perdonarme?

Se abrió la puerta del coche y Pasquale le ofreció la mano para ayudarla a bajar. Mila estaba esperando una respuesta de Thierry, pero este permaneció callado y con la vista al frente. Mila contuvo a duras penas las lágrimas. Tendría que ir a ver a su hermano y decirle que les había fallado a él y a su pueblo.

Volar de noche era preferible a hacerlo de día, pensó Mila cuando volvieron a subir al helicóptero y se elevaron. En la oscuridad no podía apreciarse la altitud.

Cuando solo unos minutos después notó que estaban descendiendo, giró la cabeza, extrañada, hacia el general Novak y le dijo:

–Da la impresión de que estuviéramos aproximándonos al suelo, pero es imposible que estemos ya en Erminia. ¿Ocurrirá algo?

–Tal vez por algún motivo el piloto haya decidido volar más bajo –contestó Novak, despreocupado.

Mila miró por la ventanilla. No, estaban descendiendo a tierra. Pero… ¿dónde estaban? En la oscuridad era imposible distinguir ningún punto de referencia en el paisaje. En cuanto aterrizaron, el piloto se bajó y el general hizo otro tanto. Mila se quedó en su asiento, preguntándose qué estaba pasando. Por la ventanilla observó a los dos hombres hablando, y luego, para su espanto, vio que el piloto sacaba una pistola y apuntaba al general. A continuación se oyó un disparo, y Mila gritó al ver a Novak caer al suelo.

El piloto fue hasta el helicóptero y abrió la puerta.

–Venga conmigo –le ordenó, apuntándola con la pistola.

Horrorizada, Mila obedeció.

–¿A qué viene todo esto? –le preguntó temblorosa.

–¡Silencio! –le gritó el hombre. Y, agarrándola por el hombro, la empujó delante de él–. ¡Camine! Y no haga ninguna estupidez, alteza –le dijo burlón–, porque no dudaré en despacharla como al general.

Se oyó el rugido de un motor, y de la oscuridad salió un todoterreno negro, del que saltaron varios hombres antes de que se detuviera por completo. Todos iban armados. ¿Qué iban a hacerle?, se preguntó Mila aterrorizada.

Capítulo Dieciséis

–¿Cómo que la princesa no regresó a Erminia? –exclamó Thierry frunciendo el ceño–. Vimos el helicóptero despegar con nuestros propios ojos.

–Lo sé, majestad –contestó Pasquale–, pero parece que se desviaron antes de llegar a su destino. La princesa ha sido secuestrada y nadie sabe dónde la han llevado.

–¿Y el piloto y su escolta?, ¿qué ha sido de ellos?

–Su escolta era el general Novak. Le dispararon, pero parece que logró escapar. Las informaciones que nos han llegado dicen que cuando recobró el conocimiento vio que se habían llevado a la princesa y habían dejado abandonado el helicóptero. Regresó al palacio pilotándolo él mismo.

Thierry se pasó una mano por el cabello y se puso a andar arriba y abajo. Aquello era culpa suya; no tenía que haberla echado de allí de malos modos, como había hecho. Si se hubiera mostrado más dispuesto a escucharla, a darle la segunda oportunidad que le había suplicado… nada de aquello habría pasado.

–¿Y qué se está haciendo por encontrarla? –le preguntó a Pasquale.

–El rey Rocco ha enviado a hombres de su ejército en su busca. El general no fue capaz de darles una descripción precisa del lugar donde la habían secuestrado.

Durante el vuelo de regreso estaba luchando por mantenerse consciente y parece que no recuerda demasiado.

–Pero consiguió llegar a palacio.

–Eso parece, majestad.

Allí había algo que no le cuadraba, pero no sabría decir qué era.

–¿Y en qué estado se encuentra el general Novak? –inquirió.

–Recibió un disparo a bocajarro, majestad –le informó Pasquale–. Había perdido mucha sangre y tuvieron que hacerle una transfusión y extraerle quirúrgicamente la bala.

Entonces no podía haber tomado parte en el secuestro, pensó Thierry. Estaba seguro de que el hermano de Mila se aseguraría de que lo interrogaran a fondo cuando se le pasaran los efectos de la anestesia, pero él no podía quedarse de brazos cruzados.

Cuando Mila le había pedido que la recibiera había accedido, pero, consumido como había estado por la ira, no había mostrado auténtica voluntad de escucharla.

Se había enfadado cuando le había revelado su identidad porque a ningún hombre le gustaba que lo tomaran por tonto, pero la verdad era que, poniéndose la mano en el corazón, tampoco había sido para tanto. Sí, le había abierto su corazón y había compartido con ella sus más profundos temores y sus secretos, pero… ¿y si en vez de ser ella hubiese sido de verdad la cortesana a la que había contratado? ¿No se habría arrepentido mucho más de compartir detalles tan íntimos, cuando solo debería haberlos compartido con su prometida?

En vez de eso, gracias a la estratagema de Mila había sido con ella, con la mujer con la que iba a casarse y de quien se había enamorado, con quien los había compartido.

Se había comportado como un idiota. No se merecía su amor. Mila había hecho lo que había hecho por los dos, por amor, y él lo había tirado todo por la borda. Tenía que recuperarla…

–Debo encontrarla, Pasquale. Trae al líder táctico de nuestras fuerzas especiales; inmediatamente.

–En realidad, majestad, el capitán ya viene hacia aquí.

Thierry lo miró sorprendido.

–¿Ya?

–Sabiendo lo que sentís por la princesa, pensé que querríais verle para trazar un plan, majestad.

–¿Cómo me conoces tan bien, Pasquale?

Su secretario esbozó una breve sonrisa.

–Es mi trabajo, majestad.

–Gracias, amigo.

Mila llevaba allí cinco días, y aquella reclusión la estaba volviendo loca. La habitación en la que la habían encerrado no tenía más que un camastro con un colchón viejo y una manta de lana y una silla de madera. Y aun así, pensó, debería agradecer aquellas pequeñas muestras de compasión que sus captores habían tenido con ella. Peor habría sido tener que dormir en el frío suelo de piedra.

Por la aspillera, la larga y estrecha abertura vertical en el muro, del tipo de las que en la Edad Media se usaban para lanzar flechas a los atacantes, había deducido que se encontraba en una vieja fortaleza abandonada, probablemente en algún punto de la frontera de Erminia. La frontera estaba salpicada de aquellas fortalezas medievales. La mayor parte de ellas se hallaban en ruinas, pero a juzgar por las bisagras y los cerrojos de la puerta de aquella habitación, parecía que aquella había sido al menos parcialmente rehabilitada.

En su celda, porque no podía llamarse de otra manera, ni siquiera tenía un lavabo o un inodoro, y la obligaban a hacer sus necesidades en un orinal que tenía que entregar, al terminar, a un guardia taciturno que también le llevaba la comida, cada vez más escasa.

La noche que la habían llevado allí, uno de sus captores le había explicado por qué la habían secuestrado, y la había dejado completamente aturdida. Le había dicho que era miembro de un movimiento cuyo propósito era aumentar las tensiones entre Erminia y Sylvain.

Parecía que la amenaza de una guerra potencial entre ambas naciones era un gran negocio, y había varias partes implicadas en aquel complot, incluido el supuesto hijo ilegítimo de su padre, que pretendía arrebatarle el trono a su hermano, y que había puesto sus condiciones: debían retenerla allí hasta que Rocco abdicara voluntariamente a su favor. Si se negaba ya no les sería de ninguna utilidad, lo que le había dejado muy claro que su vida pendía de un hilo.

No quería que su hermano abdicara. A pesar de sus diferencias, Rocco era un buen rey y un gran hombre. Se sentía fatal de solo pensar que estaba causándole aún más estrés y preocupaciones con todo lo que ya tenía sobre sus hombros, pero tampoco quería morir.

Era de noche, y el aire frío y húmedo que se colaba por la aspillera traía olor a tormenta inminente. Pensó en Thierry, en su último encuentro. No quería morir allí sin volver a verlo. Volvió al estrecho camastro y se acurrucó bajo la fina manta.

Cerró los ojos y se puso a rememorar la semana idílica que había pasado con él en las montañas. Pronto sintió que estaba quedándose dormida. Se sentía tan débil, tan cansada… El ruido de la puerta al abrirse, seguida de un murmullo de voces masculinas, la arrancó del sueño.

–¡Está aquí! –siseó uno de los hombres.

–¡Mila!, ¿estás bien? Despierta… –le susurró una voz familiar al oído.

¿Thierry? No, era imposible, se dijo, haciéndose un ovillo bajo la manta. Tenía que ser un sueño. O quizá la sed y el hambre que arrastraba por las míseras raciones de comida y agua estaban provocándole alucinaciones.

–¡Mila!, ¡despierta! –siseó la voz, un poco más fuerte.

Una mano fuerte se cerró sobre su hombro y la zarandeó. Abrió los ojos, pero en la penumbra era casi imposible ver quién era. Solo podía distinguir la silueta de un hombre, todo vestido de negro y con un pasamontañas, cerniéndose sobre ella. ¿Es que iban a matarla?

Iba a chillar, pero el hombre le tapó la boca con la mano y se quitó el pasamontañas. ¡Thierry! ¡Era Thierry! Thierry estaba allí… No, no podía ser real…

–¿Te han hecho daño? ¿Estás herida? –le preguntó en voz baja.

Ella sacudió la cabeza, y la aparición le quitó la mano de la boca y se inclinó para besarla en los labios. Aquel beso disipó sus dudas: era él.

–¿Puedes andar? –inquirió Thierry en un siseo.

Ella asintió, ya despierta del todo.

–Esa es mi chica –murmuró él con una sonrisa–. Venga, vamos a sacarte de aquí.

Lo que ocurrió a continuación se sucedió tan deprisa que después solo recordaría que iba flanqueada por un grupo de hombres armados y vestidos de negro, y el fuerte brazo de Thierry en torno a su cintura mientras la conducían a través de un pasadizo hasta que llegaron al exterior.

La operación completa, desde la fortaleza hasta el bosque que la rodeaba, no debió llevar más de diez minutos, pero Mila estaba temblando de miedo y alivio cuando dejaron de correr al llegar a lo más profundo de la espesura.

No alcanzaba a entender cómo podía ser que nadie hubiera intentado detenerlos en su escapada en ningún momento. No había habido disparos ni explosiones. Todo se había hecho con el mayor sigilo, y quizá precisamente por eso la experiencia había sido aún más surrealista.

–Toma –dijo Thierry, quitándose la chaqueta de forro polar que llevaba y ayudándola a ponérsela–. Está helada.

–¿Y ahora qué? –le preguntó Mila, a quien le castañeteaban los dientes.

–Ahora te llevaremos a casa.

De pronto se oyó un ulular, como de un ave nocturna.

–Esa es nuestra señal –le dijo Thierry–. Nuestro vehículo nos espera a un kilómetro de aquí. ¿Crees que podrás recorrer esa distancia?

–¿Tú vendrás conmigo?

–Por supuesto.

–Entonces sí. Contigo a mi lado puedo hacer cualquier cosa –contestó ella con sencillez.

Él se quedó mirándola, como si quisiera decirle algo más, pero uno de sus hombres le indicó con un gesto que tenían que irse ya.

–Hay cosas de las que quiero que hablemos –le dijo Thierry–, pero eso tendrá que esperar. Primero te pondremos a salvo –añadió muy serio, rodeándola de nuevo con el brazo.

A Mila se le hizo eterno ese último trecho, pero finalmente salieron del bosque y subieron a dos vehículos blindados que estaban esperándolos.

Estaba tan agotada que no podía ni hablar cuando Thierry la levantó en volandas y la metió en el coche.

–Avisad a palacio por radio –le dijo a uno de sus hombres–. Aseguraos de que tienen preparado un equipo médico para examinar a la princesa, e informad al rey Rocco de que la tenemos y la llevamos a casa.

–No, Thierry… –intentó protestar Mila, pero apenas tenía fuerzas para articular las palabras.

No quería irse a casa; quería estar con él.

Thierry se subió al coche con ella, y cuando la hizo recostarse sobre su regazo, el cansancio la venció, y pronto se quedó dormida.

Capítulo Diecisiete

Thierry observaba a Mila, que dormitaba en la enfermería del castillo. Su cautiverio la había dejado muy débil y se la veía agotada, pero el médico que la había examinado había dicho que tenía buena salud, teniendo en cuenta por lo que había pasado.

–¿Aún está dormida? –le preguntó Rocco, que acababa de entrar en ese momento.

Thierry, sin quitarle los ojos de encima a Mila, asintió con la cabeza.

–¿Pero no le quedarán secuelas?

–El médico ha dicho que no –respondió Thierry.

Rocco se sentó en una silla al otro lado de la cama.

–No sé cómo darte las gracias por…

–Entonces no lo hagas –lo cortó Thierry–. Hice lo que había que hacer. Lo que tú habrías hecho si la hubieseis encontrado antes que nosotros.

Había habido varios equipos buscando en distintas localizaciones posibles. El de Thierry simplemente había tenido la suerte de haber buscado en el lugar correcto.

Rocco asintió.

–Me han dicho que la fortaleza estaba vacía cuando mis soldados entraron. Sus raptores debieron marcharse cuando se dieron cuenta de que os la habíais llevado. Parece que había un túnel bajo la fortaleza que no figuraba en los planos. Suponemos que escaparían por allí.

–¿Decepcionado porque mis hombres no pudieran detener a los secuestradores?

–No, claro que no –le aseguró Rocco–. Si lo hubieran intentado Mila podría haber resultado herida… o muerta. Hiciste lo correcto al insistir en que la operación se llevase a cabo con sigilo para no alertar a los secuestradores. Pero acabaremos atrapándolos, y serán juzgados por lo que han hecho.

Thierry asintió, y se quedaron en silencio, observando a la joven a la que ambos tanto querían. Cuando finalmente Rocco se levantó para marcharse, se detuvo un momento al pasar junto a Thierry y le puso una mano en el hombro.

–Su corazón te pertenece, amigo mío –le dijo–. Cuida bien de ella.

–Es lo que pretendo hacer durante el resto de mi vida, si ella me deja –contestó Thierry.

Rocco asintió y se marchó, cerrando la puerta tras de sí sin hacer ruido, y al poco rato Mila comenzó a despertarse y abrió lentamente los ojos.

–Estás despierta –dijo Thierry. Le sirvió un vaso de agua fresca–. Toma, bébetelo. Órdenes del médico.

Mila se incorporó trabajosamente y lo tomó. Un sentimiento protector invadió a Thierry cuando vio cómo le temblaba la mano mientras bebía. Cuando hubo apurado el vaso se lo devolvió, y él lo dejó en la mesilla.

Mila miró a su alrededor, visiblemente confundida.

–¿Estoy en casa? –inquirió con voz algo ronca, rehuyendo su mirada.

Thierry asintió.

–Sí. Tu hermano pensó que lo mejor sería traerte de vuelta a Erminia.

Mila levantó la vista hacia él.

–No fue un sueño, ¿verdad? Estabas allí… en la fortaleza.

Thierry asintió de nuevo.

–Con un equipo de élite de las fuerzas especiales de mi país.

La explicación de cómo sus hombres habían recurrido a todas las fuentes legales –y otras no tan legales– para averiguar dónde había aterrizado el helicóptero y dónde la habían tenido retenida podía esperar a otro momento, se dijo.

Mila volvió a recostarse contra los almohadones y cerró los ojos.

–Gracias… por rescatarme –murmuró en un hilo de voz.

–No tienes que darme las gracias –le dijo Thierry–. Me siento responsable de lo que te ha ocurrido. Si me hubiera comportado como un adulto, en vez de como un niño malcriado con una pataleta que no atiende a razones, jamás habría pasado lo que ha pasado.

Mila, aún con los ojos cerrados, sacudió la cabeza y replicó:

–No debes culparte. No podrías haber hecho nada para detener a esos hombres.

–Si no te hubiese dejado marchar…

Mila volvió a abrir los ojos.

–Thierry, ¿a qué has venido? –le preguntó en un tono cansado.

–A pedirte que me perdones.

–¿Que te perdone? ¿Por qué?

–Por haberte tratado de un modo tan despreciable. Por no haberte escuchado. Por no haber aceptado tu amor cuando me lo ofreciste libremente con un corazón tan puro. Por compararte con mi madre y creer que eras igual que ella.

–Vaya, es una lista muy larga –murmuró Mila–. Pero sigo creyendo que por mi parte no hay nada que perdonar. Fui yo quien te mintió, quien te engañó… Incluso orquesté el secuestro de una mujer inocente para conseguir lo que pretendía. No soy precisamente un dechado de virtudes.

–Pero lo que hiciste lo hiciste por amor, porque estabas decidida a darnos a los dos la posibilidad de conocernos y aprender a querernos –respondió él calmadamente. Mila lo miraba sorprendida, como si no pudiera creer lo que estaba oyendo–. Cuando me enteré de que te habían secuestrado me di cuenta de que me había comportado contigo como un estúpido orgulloso, y de lo vacía que se quedaría mi vida sin ti –tomó sus manos, se las llevó a los labios y le besó los nudillos–. Te quiero, ángel mío, y espero que puedas darme otra oportunidad. Te prometo que me esforzaré por hacerte feliz.

Los ojos de Mila se habían llenado de lágrimas, que comenzaron a rodar por sus mejillas.

–¿Todavía me quieres?

–Jamás he dejado de quererte. Y precisamente eso hacía que mi enfado se me hiciera aún más difícil de soportar. Detestaba cada segundo que pasaba lejos de ti, pero me sentía herido en mi orgullo, y eso me impedía confiar en ti. Te quiero, Mila, y quiero que seas mi esposa, mi consorte, y que reines en Sylvain a mi lado. ¿Te casarás conmigo, Angel?

–Imaginar un futuro sin ti era una auténtica tortura, como un agujero negro sin fondo de soledad y desesperanza –le confesó Mila–. Sí, Hawk, me casaré contigo. Nada me haría más feliz.

Mila se levantó del asiento, y permitió que su hermano la ayudara a bajarse del carruaje, ricamente adornado, y le dirigió una sonrisa que le salió del corazón.

–Estás preciosa, hermanita –le dijo Rocco.

–Me siento preciosa –dijo ella–. ¿Cómo podría no sentirme así cuando soy la mujer más feliz del mundo?

–Te mereces toda esa felicidad –murmuró su hermano.

Mila se agarró a su brazo, y comenzaron a subir juntos la escalinata de la enorme catedral de Sylvain, decorada con una alfombra roja. A su alrededor se oían los vítores de las miles de personas que se agolpaban en las calles a ambos lados del templo y que portaban pequeñas banderas tanto de Erminia como de Sylvain.

–Tu también te mereces ser feliz, hermano –le dijo Mila, mirándolo preocupada, cuando se detuvieron a las puertas de la catedral.

–Tal vez llegaré a serlo algún día.

Mila deseó con todo corazón que así fuera, que un día llegara a experimentar el mismo amor que Thierry y ella sentían el uno por el otro. Rocco necesitaba encontrar a una mujer con la que pudiese contar, que lo respaldase y estuviese siempre a su lado.

Desde el instante en el que cruzaron las puertas de la catedral sus ojos se encontraron con los de Thierry y ya no se separaron. Y en el momento en que lo vio, tan guapo y tan alto con su uniforme militar de gala, sintió que el corazón le iba a estallar de orgullo.

La música del órgano inundó la catedral, ascendiendo hasta el techo, mientras su hermano y ella avanzaban por la alfombra roja. A su alrededor los asistentes se volvían para mirarla y murmuraban entre ellos comentarios de admiración.

Cuando Rocco la dejó junto a Thierry y fue a sentarse para que la ceremonia diera comienzo, Mila miró a su prometido y sonrió, como él, rebosante de felicidad.

Su amiga Sally, que estaba sentada también en el primer banco, se levantó para tomar su ramo y le siseó:

–¡Te lo dije!, ¡como un cuento de hadas!

Mila sonrió y le respondió:

–Tengo la sensación de que lo será toda mi vida.

Y comenzó la ceremonia, en la que Thierry y ella pronunciaron los votos que los ligaban el uno al otro hasta que la muerte los separase.

El resto del día pasó en un abrir y cerrar de ojos, en medio de la pompa y la ceremonia propia de una boda real, y Mila, a pesar de que estaba disfrutando celebrando con todos su felicidad, estaba impaciente por volver a tener a Thierry para ella sola.

Por eso, después del suntuoso banquete y del baile, se sintió inmensamente agradecida a Sally cuando se la llevó para que pudiera cambiarse para partir en su viaje de luna de miel. En los aposentos de palacio donde la habían alojado, se apresuró a cambiarse de ropa.

–Más despacio. Si no tienes cuidado acabarás haciéndole un jirón al vestido. Tampoco le pasará nada a Thierry porque le hagas esperar un poco.

–A él puede que no, ¡pero yo no puedo esperar más! –exclamó Mila riéndose mientras se quitaba la última enagua que llevaba debajo del vestido de novia.

–Me alegro tanto por ti… –murmuró Sally mientras la ayudaba con el elegante vestido que iba a llevar en el viaje–. Te merecías este «felices por siempre jamás».

–Gracias. Ojalá todo el mundo pudiera ser tan feliz como lo soy yo ahora mismo.

Y así era, se sentía feliz, increíblemente feliz. La única nube negra en el horizonte era la amenaza que aún pesaba sobre el derecho de Rocco al trono, pero no había nada que ella pudiera hacer al respecto, así que se obligó a apartar aquello de su mente.

Cuando llamaron a la puerta, Sally corrió a buscar los zapatos y el bolso de Mila.

–¡Un momento! –exclamó su amiga–. Te desearía todo lo mejor, pero creo que ya lo tienes –dijo antes de darle un cálido abrazo.

–Sí que lo tengo. Soy muy afortunada. Nunca sabrás cuánto agradezco que me sugirieras hacer ese viaje a Nueva York. Si no te hubiera hecho caso, ahora no estaría aquí, a punto de embarcarme en mi luna de miel con el hombre más maravilloso del mundo.

Sally dio un paso atrás y le sonrió.

–Bueno, no sé, quiero creer que el destino juega su baza en las cosas importantes de la vida.

–El destino, el tenerte como amiga… fuera lo que fuera, te estoy muy agradecida. Cuídate, Sally; nos vemos a la vuelta.

–Mándame una postal –le dijo su amiga con un guiño.

Mila abrió la puerta y se encontró con Thierry, que le ofreció su brazo.

–¿Lista, ángel mío?

–Más que lista –respondió ella.

HQÑ™

Arwen Grey

MI PARAÍSO ERES TÚ

*A veces el paraíso solo lo puedes encontrar
entre los brazos de la persona que amas*

Un novio guapísimo que apenas se sabe su nombre…
Un apartamento en un edificio histórico, en un barrio rodeado de
ruinas…
Un negocio que funciona de maravilla, que la tiene "un poco" es-
clavizada…
¿Una vida perfecta en la calle Paraíso?
Lo último que le faltaba a Ariadna era el interés repentino que
siente por ella el Lúgubre, el vecino más extraño de todo el
edificio.
¡Lo que las croquetas y la electricidad han unido, que no lo separen
ni las caseras maquinadoras, ni los novios perfectos, ni esas cosas
mundanas que nos empeñamos en creer que nos hacen felices!

No. 22

LORRAINE MURRAY

Despierta a mi lado

¿El destino de las personas está realmente escrito?

Fiona es una mujer libre e independiente, con una carrera de éxito como comisaria de arte en la National Gallery de Edimburgo y sin ataduras emocionales con ningún hombre. Le gusta ser así. Disfruta de la libertad que le produce cabalgar a lomos de su moto a gran velocidad. Hasta que una noche conoce a un guapo italiano en la taberna de siempre y pasan la noche juntos.

Las diferencias entre Fabrizzio y el resto de los hombres surgen cuando no huye en mitad de la noche como el resto de sus ligues y ¡hasta se queda a prepararle el desayuno! Descolocada, se refugia en la exposición que está preparando para el museo y se prepara para conocer al director de la Galería Uffizi de Florencia, amigo desde la universidad de su jefe, que se ha prestado a facilitar la colaboración entre ambos centros de arte… pero a veces la vida nos tiene preparadas muchas sorpresas.

No. 23

Los Medici
Leanne Banks

Hijo inesperado

Cuando el millonario Rafe Medici descubrió que tenía un heredero, quiso que el niño viviera bajo su techo. Solo la tutora legal del niño, Nicole Livingstone, se interponía entre su deseo y él. Pero nadie le llevaba la contraria a un Medici y, si tenía que recurrir a la seducción para ganarse a Nicole, Rafe estaba dispuesto a intentarlo. Solo tenía que asegurarse de que ella no le hiciera cambiar su regla de "todo menos amor".

Un trato muy especial

Cuando Michael Medici vio a la atractiva camarera del cóctel bar, movió ficha. Una extraordinaria noche después, supo que quería más de Bella St. Clair. Por desgracia, acababa de comprar la empresa de su familia, y ella lo despreciaba.

Michael le hizo a Bella una oferta: si era su amante, recuperaría la empresa. Ella accedió, pero se negó a rendirse a la norma de que no habría sentimientos de por medio. ¿Sucumbiría el atractivo millonario al deseo oculto de su corazón?

Nº 38

Los secretos de la novia

Durante toda su vida, Leonardo Grant había deseado ser más de lo que sus duros orígenes le habían permitido. Tras hacerse millonario, pensó que la solución estaba en casarse con la mujer adecuada para ganarse el respeto que el dinero no podía darle.

Cuando vio a Calista French, supo que ella era su complemento ideal, pero su encuentro había sido preparado meticulosamente… y no por él. ¿Qué tenía planeado aquella mujer tan "perfecta"?

HQÑ

el sello digital para los escritores
de novela romántica de habla hispana
te está esperando.
¿Tienes un manuscrito? ¿Has pensado en
escribir una novela? Esta es una
gran oportunidad para enviarnos tu historia.

Requisitos de tu novela:
- Una extensión mínima de <u>100 páginas</u>
(Times 12, interlineado doble)
- Que sea <u>romántica</u>, no importa la categoría:
contemporánea, histórica, erótica,
suspense, paranormal…

Si tu manuscrito resulta elegido, te ofrecemos:
- <u>Publicación internacional</u> en
formato digital en español.
- Posible publicación en formato papel.
- Realización de una <u>portada exclusiva</u>
para tu manuscrito.
- Apoyo de marketing para
el lanzamiento y difusión de tu libro.

¿A qué estás esperando?
No lo pienses más y envía tu manuscrito a
hqndigital@harpercollinsiberica.com